APPLIED OPERATIONS RESEARCH/SYSTEMS ANALYSIS IN HIERARCHICAL DECISION-MAKING

Studies in Management Science and Systems

Editor

Burton V. Dean

Department of Operations Research
Case Western Reserve University
Cleveland, Ohio

VOLUME 3

NORTH-HOLLAND PUBLISHING COMPANY – AMSTERDAM • OXFORD
AMERICAN ELSEVIER PUBLISHING COMPANY, INC. – NEW YORK

Applied Operations Research / Systems Analysis in Hierarchical Decision-Making

Volume I   *Systems Approach to*
            Public and Private Sector Problems

GEORGE K. CHACKO
The Systems Management Center
University of Southern California

1976

NORTH-HOLLAND PUBLISHING COMPANY – AMSTERDAM • OXFORD
AMERICAN ELSEVIER PUBLISHING COMPANY, INC. – NEW YORK

Library of Congress Catalog Card Number: 74-83723

North-Holland ISBN for the series: 0 7204 8700 5

North-Holland ISBN for this volume: 0 7204 8702 1

American Elsevier ISBN: 0 444 10767 3

Published by:

North-Holland Publishing Company – Amsterdam

North-Holland Publishing Company, Ltd. – Oxford

Sole distributors for the U.S.A. and Canada:

American Elsevier Publishing Company, Inc.

52 Vanderbilt Avenue, New York, N.Y. 10017

Printed in The Netherlands

78 018326

Dedicated in grateful esteem to
Doctors DAVID B. HERTZ *and* C. RADHAKRISHNA RAO
Respectively of Columbia University, New York and
Indian Statistical Institute, Calcutta
who, through their individual contributions,
inter-disciplinary, inter-national, and inter-religious,
to the improvement of my inadequate understanding,
made my academic pilgrimage a personal privilege

BOOKS BY THE AUTHOR

The Mar Thoma Syrian Liturgy, A Translation into English, 1956.
The Mar Thoma Syrian Church Order of Holy Matrimony, A Translation into English, 1957.
India — Toward an Understanding, 1959.
International Trade Aspects of Indian Burlap — An Econometric Study, 1961.
Today's Information for Tomorrow's Products — An Operations Research Approach, 1966.
Studies for Public Men, 1969.
Applied Statistics in Decision-Making, 1971.
Computer-Aided Decision-Making, 1972.
Technological Forecontrol — Prospects, Problems, and Policy, 1975.
Applied Operations Research/Systems Analysis in Hierarchical Decision-Making, 1976.
    Vol. I — Systems Approach to Public and Private Sector Problems.
    Vol. II — Operations Research Approach to Problem Formulation and Solution
Incomplete Information System (IIS) for Effective Management, 1976.

Long-range Forecasting Methodology, (contributor), 1968.
Reducing the Cost of Space Transportation, (editor), 1969.
The Recognition of Systems in Health Services, (editor/contributor), 1969.
Systems Technology Applied to Social and Community Problems, (contributor), 1969.
Planning Challenges of the '70s in the Public Domain, (co-editor), 1970.
Congressional Recognition of Goddard Rocket and Space Museum, (contributor), 1970.

Systems Approach to Environmental Pollution, (editor and contributor), 1971.
Hope for the Cities — A Systems Approach to Human Needs, (contributor), 1971.
The Use of Modern Management Methods in the Public Administration of Developing Countries, (contributor), 1972.
Alternative Approaches to the National Delivery of Health Care, (editor), 1972.

PREFACE TO VOLUMES I AND II

Volume I: *Systems Approach to Public and Private Sector Problems*
Volume II: *Operations Research Approach to Problem Formulation and Solution*

This work presents a unified treatment of Operations Research/Systems Analysis in terms of its two basic characteristics: one, conceptualization of the problem as a whole, or *diagnosis*; and two, development of prescriptive solutions, or *prescription*. As the title suggests, the accent is on the practical application, the elegance of theory being governed by the relevance to decisions.

Hierarchical Decision-Making: Decisions are recognized as a triad — those affecting the operation, activity, or relationship as a whole (organismic); those affecting the operation, activity, or relationship of significant parts of the whole (strategic); and those affecting the operation, activity, or relationship of components of significant parts of the whole (tactical) — the organismic, the strategic and the tactical comprising the decision hierarchy.

51 Applications: Real-life data are used wherever possible as the motivation for the decisions, so that the need for decisions dictates the choice of analytical methods to decipher the processes underlying the operation, activity, or relationship; and the insights into the processes offered by analysis are then related to the decisions — instead of unleashing an assortment of mathematical techniques for which applications have to be invented, like a solution looking for a problem.

The treatment of the important problems of the day in the public and private sectors suggest a classification into two: (1) unstructured problems, and (2) structured problems. The unstructured problems are those for which there is no applicable experience to describe the performance characteristics. On the contrary, in the structured problems, prior applicable experience is available. The discovery of the structure of the problem becomes the most

ix

important issue in the case of the unstructured problem, while the discovery of the number(s) which exactly satisfy the problem requirements and restrictions become the most important issue in the case of the structured problem.

These two types of problems — the unstructured and the structured — are treated respectively in Volume I and Volume II. In both volumes, the problems from both the public sector and the private sector are treated. Of the 29 applications of OR/SA to real-to-life problems in Volume I, 9 are historical and military; 7 are public sector and non-military; and 13 are private sector and non-military problems. In Volume II, of the 22 applications of OR/SA to near-real life problems, 5 are historical and military; 5 are public sector and non-military; and 12 are private sector problems (non-military).

In Part I, the three decades of progress of operations research is highlighted from the earliest, August, 1940 days of operatio*nal* research problems in *specific details*, reconstructing them in readable form in terms of variables, data, modeling factors, solution, and implementation of the solution to the *tactical problems* of war: through the developments of systems analysis, and program budgeting to the concerns with *policy problems*.

OR/SA Protocol: The three chapters (3, 4 and 5) of Part II deal with the substance and sequence of Operations Research/Systems Analysis (OR/SA) effort. The four major elements of context, cost, effectiveness—absolute, and effectiveness—relative, and the three major steps are combined into an OR/SA protocol which is a formal sequence of problem solving operations. The OR/SA protocol comprise four sequences: (1) initial structure of the problem, (2) sensitivity of system objective to subsystem performance, (3) considerations of cost-effectiveness, and (4) allocation of resources to subsystem activities.

What OR/SA prescribes needs to be implemented: and to implement, resources must be committed by appropriate authority. Therefore, the perspective of the decision-maker who has to implement the prescription is studied in Chapter 5.

Application to Public Sector Problems: The three chapters (6, 7 and 8) of Part III deal with the application of OR/SA Protocol to large, unstructured problems in the Public Sector. The problems studied are: (1) Ecological Investment, (2) Health Care Allocation, and (3) Air Pollution Reduction.

Application to Private Sector Problems: The four chapters (9, 10, 11 and 12) of Part IV deal with the application of OR/SA Protocol to large, unstructured problems in the Private Sector. The two major problems vital to any manufacturing and sales operation are: (1) sales, and (2) production. The problems studied are: (1) National Data Input to Company Potentials, (2) Predictive Mechanisms for Company Bookings, (3) Measurement of "Salesmanship", and (4) Resource Allocation for Production and Inventory.

From the unstructured and statistical problems in Volume I, we turn to the structured and mathematical problems in Volume II.

Many unstructured problems can be reasonably approximated by structured problems; therefore, we discuss structured problems in Parts V–VIII.

Structured Problems and Simplex Iterative Decision Processes: The four chapters (13, 14, 15 and 16) of Part V develop and apply linear programming methodology and its variants, the key to which is the repetitive process of improving the solution (Iterative), once the basic constraints are fulfilled. The guarantee of success for the iterative calculations, i.e., to arrive at the optimum solution comes from the simplex, the geometrical figure whose vertices house the optimum values. In the computer solution of the linear programming problems, a more efficient method than the historical Simplex Method is employed: Pivotal Condensation Method (PCM). Both PCM and Simplex are carried out in only three steps, compared with currently available steps numbering a dozen or more. The Transportation and Assignment Problems are shown to be subsets of the linear programming problem.

Structured Problems and Iterative Decision Processes: The three chapters (17, 18 and 19) of Part VI deal with problems of inventory, queuing and replacement, in which the emphasis is *not* iteration as in Part V, but upon *anticipation*. Demand for *goods* is anticipated; to meet which, appropriate decision rules of inventory control are worked out. The inventory decision rules, in turn, impinge upon warehousing considerations. Similarly, *services* are anticipated; to meet which, appropriate decision rules of service control are worked out. The service decision rules, in turn, impinge upon queuing considerations. Again, operational requirements are anticipated; to meet which, appropriate decision rules of maintenance control are worked out. The maintenance control rules, in turn, impinge upon replacement considerations. In Part VI, the solution is found by iteration, and the demand is assumed to be known.

Unstructured Anticipatory Problems and Interactive Decision Processes: From situations of known demand, where the solutions are found by iteration, we turn to *un*known moves made by opposing interests in the two chapters (20 and 21) of Part VII. A move is a selection among alternatives.

Each move of each participant depends upon not only his, but also the *other's* moves — the past moves, the present moves, and the future moves; the element of anticipation relating to the future moves. No one participant achieves the maximum that he desires, because he controls only some of the variables governing the outcome; and his moves are modified by those of his opponent (Interactive) who, as well as himself, anticipates each other's moves and the outcome.

Large, Unstructured Problems and Adaptive Structural Decision Processes: The assumption of opposing interests, which is central to Game Theory, is not required in the unstructured problems discussed in the three chapters (22, 23 and 24) of Part VIII. This concluding part introduces decision problems of great complexity which, like the lunar landing mission, literally take a leap into the unknown phase of the problem, on the basis of insights obtained prior to that phase, as in the case of attempting the 1968 lunar orbital flight on the basis only of *earth* orbital flight experience theretofore. The key to the decision problems of such great complexity is not the particular set of values of any one solution, but rather the *structure* of the decision processes that is employed in one phase which can be repeated with respect to the next phase, incorporating improvements. The mathematical foundations of this type of problem are provided by dynamic programming which is systematically developed, weaving theory and practice, as in the discussion of the implications of the Principle of Optimality for a diamond cutting problem, and of the Functional Equations to the reentry problem of the spacecraft.

The application of dynamic programming to the formulation of complex problems involving quantum jumps of *technology* from one stage to the next, is introduced by discussing the application of PERT network to the sequencing of events involving *time*. The Minimal Spanning Tree Method of Graph Theory is found to yield not only the slack time in a PERT network, but also the optimal minimax trajectories of a special case of minimax control processes, such as the reentry problem, formulated using functional equations of dynamic programming. The emphasis upon the application to real-life problems there yields thematic similarity between the two methods not generally associated with each other. In addition, the Graph Theoretical Method applicable to both sets the stage for the discussion of Pólya's theorem which places the powerful capabilities of combinatorial mathematics at the disposal of dynamic programming and PERT in Part VIII, as well as those of linear programming and transportation network problems already discussed in Part V.

The Audience: This work is written primarily for present and potential members of management, who will be involved in executive-type decision making as performers or advisors. A college algebra background is the only mathematical prerequisite. The persistent orientation to application to real-life problems should make the principles of mathematical methods clear to the practitioner. The mathematician will find the treatment of the mathematical methods not sufficiently rigorous to suit his taste. His forebearance is solicited in the interest of making available to as wide an audience of decision-makers today and tomorrow as possible, the offerings of Operations Research/Systems Analysis (OR/SA) which are intensely relevant to the *diagnosis* of complex problems in industrial, commercial, military and/or institutional environments, and the development of their *prescriptive solutions*.

George K. Chacko

CONTENTS OF VOLUME I

CONTENTS OF VOLUME II

Contents

PART I

**FROM SUCCESS IN STRUCTURED PROBLEMS
TO CHALLENGES IN UNSTRUCTURED PROBLEMS**

CHAPTER 1

RATIONAL PROFILE OF A TRANS-RATIONAL PROCESS

TECHNICAL OVERVIEW

American management is an object of admiration abroad. Europe would like to reproduce the American art of organization, which is associated with "rationalism". But management is not a matter of mere rationalism; it is a trans-rational process, and any rational analysis is bound to be limited in its usefulness for a trans-rational process.

The accent is on the unified treatment of diagnosis and prescription, which is the contribution of Operations Research/Systems Analysis (OR/SA) to decision-making. The decision-making hierarchy comprises a triad of three interrelated elements: (1) organismic, (2) strategic, and (3) tactical levels of decisions, ranging from the long term to the short term, and from the policy-maker to the procedure-supervisor.

Since each decision-maker is simultaneously playing all the three different roles in varying degree, there is concurrent conflict in the perception required of him. Within this context of decision-making, analysis to assist decision-making is applied to two kinds of problems: (1) unstructured; and (2) structured problems. The performance characteristics cannot be specified by any known probability distribution in the case of the former, while probability distributions are known (or assumed to be known) in the case of the latter. The former are the subject matter of Volume I: Systems Approach to Public and Private Sector Problems; the latter are the subject matter of Volume II: Operations Research Approach to Problem Formulation and Solution.

Some 50 real-life, or real-to-life, problems in both the public and the private sectors provide the challenge to policy analysis for decision-making in both the volumes. The problem-oriented exposition of OR/SA reasoning developed is applied to problems ranging from the allocation of resources to national health care, and the identification of

3

essential learning stages in the future space missions to the specification of the performance characteristics of the then-unknown Federal Time-Sharing System and the "price war" strategy selection by two competing service station operators.

EXECUTIVE SUMMARY

"Virtuosity in management" has been hailed as the secret of the success of American enterprise. The Europeanization of the American Virtuosity in management is seen as a test of "rationalism".

However, management is not a matter of merely "rationalism". Management, like marriage, is existential; it involves the very existence of the participants. Management, like the human anatomy, is organismic: a living system, the whole being greater than, or less than the sum of the parts. Again, management is an art, the final outcome of physically similar inputs often being quite dissimilar outputs. In short, management is a trans-rational process.

Operations Research/Systems Analysis (OR/SA) offers a rational approach to problem analysis for policy decisions. Being only rational, the most skillful application of OR/SA is bound to remain at best an aid to decision-making, which is a trans-rational process.

In real life, few problems fit into neat types, so that they can be conveniently solved in the same way. Instead, the problems of any consequence tend to be those in which the desirable performance characteristics themselves are far from known. For instance, how will we know if we have got a national health maintenance program working most efficiently? It is easier to recognize the landing of a man on the moon, some 250 000 miles away, and his return to earth, because the performance characteristics of the system, viz., the safety of the returned astronauts, is specifiable within limits, and could be measured in terms of measurable characteristics.

Can OR/SA assist in helping the management decision-maker to distinguish between inherently untractable problems, such as maintaining the nation's health, and the inherently tractable problems, such as finding the best route to transport products and services? The answer is yes. It is demonstrated with respect to 51 real-to-life problems in two volumes: 14 historical and military applications (9 + 5); 12 public sector and non-military applications (7 + 5); and 25 private sector applications (13 + 12), making a total of 51 applications, 29 of which are in the first and 22 in the second volume.

The 30-year old Tocqueville, in his assessment of the 60-year old democracy in the United States, comments upon the national dynamism which seeks restlessly to conquer new horizons:

> America is a land of wonders, in which everything is in *constant motion* and every change seems an improvement. The *idea of novelty* is there indissolubly connected with the idea of amelioration. No natural boundary seems to be set to the efforts of man; and in his eyes what is not yet done is only what he has not yet attempted to do.[1] (italics supplied)

1. "Virtuosity in Management"

Tocqueville's "constant motion", and "idea of novelty" appear to be perceived as the predominant characteristics of the Republic 130 years later by another Frenchman, 44-year old Servan-Schreiber. His volume, *The American Challenge,* traces the success of the United States to the dynamism of the American society; and identifies "virtuosity in management" as the key factor:

> Behind the success story of American industry lies the talent for accepting and mastering *change*. Technological advance depends on *virtuosity in management*. Both are rooted in the dynamic vigor of American education ... . This war – and it is a war – is being fought not with dollars, or oil, or steel, or even with modern machines. It is being fought with creative imagination and organizational talent.[2] (italics supplied)

If Tocqueville identifies the American *desire* for change, Servan-Schreiber identifies the *design* for change. His thesis is that to meet the American

---

[1] Alexis DeTocqueville (1805–1859), *Democracy in America*, Part I, 1835, Chapter 18.
[2] J.-J. Servan-Schreiber, *The American Challenge*, Atheneum, New York, 1968, pp. 67, xiii.

challenge in the "art of organization", Europe should build a technological community, which will require successful Europeanization of the American art of organization. He quotes approvingly *The Guardian* which contrasts Rationalism with Nationalism:

> A European technological community is the real Europe of the future. To build it will be a test of *nationalism* versus *rationalism* ... . It will demand far-reaching psychological changes. But the only alternative is economic decline, and probably complete domination by the United States.[3] (italics supplied)

The Europeanization of the American virtuosity in management is seen as a test of "rationalism". However, management is not a matter merely of "rationalism". If management could be reduced to rational principles and practices, that would make for direct transplanting of management from the small to the large, from one industry to another, from the military to the non-military, from outer space into inner space, and so on. But such transplanting is neither common nor easy.

The reason why such transplanting is not common or easy is because management is an art. The paradox in the practice of an art is that its individual imprint is what makes it a success; and individual imprint is what can never be successfully imitated. Since imitation is the best form of flattery, Servan-Schreiber's prescription to Europe that she imitates the United States is a pleasurable accolade which, like women's perfume, can be stimulating in small doses; but poisonous in large doses.

2. Operations Research/Systems Analysis (OR/SA) in Management: Diagnosis and Prescription

The major premise of this work is that the practice of management is an art; therefore, like the art of painting pictures, it has to be Caught rather than Taught. Nevertheless, the innate capabilities to manage can be aided by systematic study: of principles and practice which must, of necessity, relate to segments of the process. To use a medical analogy, diagnosis is an art; but the knowledge of the human anatomy can aid the diagnosis considerably. Of course, the teaching of the human anatomy would not be seriously mistaken

---

[3] *Ibid.*, p. 105.

for the successful practice of medical diagnosis. The anatomy lessons are a necessary condition, but not a sufficient condition for the practice of medicine.

This work presents a unified treatment of OR/SA* in management in terms of its two basic characteristics: one, conceptualization of the problem as a whole, or *diagnosis*; and two, development of prescriptive solutions, or *prescription*.

It should be remembered that the practice of medicine was not put off until the human anatomy was known in full detail; instead, the practice of medicine has proceeded with *in*complete knowledge of the anatomy. In the context of incomplete knowledge, the structure of the anatomy itself was partly understood from the results of the prescriptions. The results would confirm or contradict the then-known structure; in the light of which the structure could be re-formulated.

In the present *in*complete knowledge of the art of management, the structure of management becomes known in part from the results of the prescriptions. The "prescriptions" are decision-making by management; and to the extent that it is possible to relate effects with decisions, to that extent the knowledge of the anatomy of management is also furthered.

3. Operations Research in Hierarchical Decision-Making

This is the first of a two-volume work with the title: *Applied Operations Research/Systems Analysis in Hierarchical Decision-Making* which makes specific reference to management when it explicitly identifies "hierarchical decision-making". The accent is on the practical application, the elegance of theory being governed by the relevance to decisions.

The unified treatment of diagnosis and prescription is applied to a triad of decisions: (1) organismic, (2) strategic, and (3) tactical. Decisions affecting the operation, activity, and/or relationship *as a whole* are referred to as organismic, a term which suggests that the parts of the whole interact with each other, making the outcome either greater than or smaller than the sum of its parts. Decisions affecting the operation, activity, and/or relationship of significant *parts* of the whole are referred to as *strategic*. Decisions affecting

---

* Definition of the terms is developed in Chapter 2, Section 13.

the operation, activity, and/or relationship of *components* of a significant
part of the whole are referred to as *tactical*.

The record of the contribution of OR/SA is by no means uniform with
respect to the triad of decision-making. Beginning with the historical developments in 1940, there has been considerable success in prescribing
decision-making at the tactical level. As the nature of its location in the triad
suggests, the tactical level of decisions is the lowest; but not necessarily the
least. Consider, for instance, the devising of a decision rule with respect to a
sizeable inventory of hundreds of units of a large corporation. The assurance
to meet the demands for the various items will return handsome profits to the
corporation; and the contribution to repeatable decision-making in this instance, although at the technical level, is certainly significant.

However, the relative success at the tactical level is not matched by comparable success in the strategic level of decision-making; for instance, in
choosing a market strategy of developing new products. The batting average is
even less when it comes to the organismic level of decision-making; take, for
instance, the corporate policy in the next five years.

4. Management, A Trans-Rational Process

This work recognizes both the limitations and the possibilities of developing a
rational profile of management decision-making which is, to say the least, a
trans-rational process. As such, the most skillful delineation of the profile of
decision-making is bound to remain at best like a treatise on how to mix
colors which can, by no means, assure the creation of masterpieces.

Management, like marriage, is *existential*: it involves the very existence of
the participants. Management, like the human anatomy, is *organismic*: a living
system, the whole being greater than, or less than, the sum of its parts. Again,
management is an *art*, the final outcome of physically similar inputs often
being quite *dis*similar outputs.

These three characteristics — existential, organismic and being an art —
make management and its practice a perennial subject of controversy. It is
controversial because being *existential*, the success or failure will involve the
very existence of the participants who would maintain that the prescriptions
for its practice are clearly inadequate insofar as the existential involvement is
highly individualized. It is controversial because being *organismic*, the most

careful descriptions of the functioning of each of the parts would result in a sum which is rarely equal to the sum of its parts, facilitating the blame to be laid upon the manipulation of the individual parts. Again, it is controversial because *being an art*, the individual successes depend very much upon the ingenuity of the manager which transcends the elements that go into it, even as the performance of the music transcends the individual notes under the skillful direction of an imaginative conductor.

Circumscribed by these basic limitations, any discussion of the theory and practice of management is open to criticism from the protagonists of one or more of its characteristics. If the existential aspect is emphasized, the criticism would run in terms of organismic aspects, or in terms of the characteristic of being an art. If the careful delineation of the individual elements is undertaken, that is open to criticism as implying the portrayal of the system as a whole. If the fact of management being an art is emphasized, it is open to criticism from those who want some prescriptive measures as to how the art may be pursued.

5. Outline of This Work

The treatment of the important problems of the day in the public and private sectors suggest a classification into two: (1) unstructured problems, and (2) structured problems.* The unstructured problems are those in which no known probability distributions can specify the performance characteristics. The reason is that the phenomenon is so new that there is no experience which permits the characterization of the relevant performance characteristics in terms of identifiable frequencies of occurrence. For instance, what is the probability distribution applicable to the performance of a national program of health maintenance? We do not even know what constitutes health maintenance for an individual, much less for a community, not to speak of the nation. Yet, health has become a personal right, as much as life, liberty, and pursuit of happiness, and the assurance of health to individuals must be somehow calibrated.

In the case of national health maintenance, the performance characteristics are hard to define. It is easier to define the performance characteristics in the case of the lunar landing mission to which the nation was committed in 1961. It is possible to identify the phenomenon known as lunar landing because it

* For definition, see Section 6.2.

is possible to state: (1) the starting point — Cape Kennedy; (2) the destination — the Moon; (3) the route — Earth orbit to lunar orbit; and (4) the principal means — rocket propulsion. It is readily apparent that with respect to the question of National Health Maintenance, there are no comparable statements that can be made about these four essential elements.

The questions that are faced by decision-makers in both the public and private sectors have a large amount of unstructuredness about them. It stems from the fact that as variables increase arithmetically, their interactions increase at least geometrically, making it necessary to consider one interaction, x_1x_2, when only two variables, x_1 and x_2, are considered; but four interactions need to be considered when there are three variables, x_1, x_2 and x_3; and 49 interactions as the variables increase to only 5. Imagine what happens when a spacecraft which has 20 000 different parts (variables) is considered, giving rise to much more than 20 000 interactions! The performance of the spacecraft depends upon the *simultaneous* functioning of not only the 20 000 variables, but also their interactions. The unstructuredness resides in these intractable interactions.

If a decision has to be postponed until every interaction is identified and calibrated, it would make any problem of reasonable magnitude to be an unreasonable proposition. When we talk admiringly about the decisions that great men of industry or of government make, and have made, we are in fact paying tribute to their capabilities to *ignore* a large number of these interactions as irrelevant and immaterial to the performance of the given mission, whether it is the acquiring of a market for a product or the achievement of a feat in aerospace, or the influencing of a relationship in international relations. The quality of the decision made by the decision-maker in an unstructured situation depends upon the success with which he has ignored the *un*important interactions.

The best analysis can only highlight the important (and the unimportant) interactions. The decision to ignore some interactions must still be ultimately made by the decision-maker himself. It is this choice that makes management a trans-rational process. In making a large number of interactions explicit through analysis, there is no presumption whatsoever that such explication bids to supplant the management process of deciding which of those interactions to ignore and which to accept.

While most of the problems in both the public and private sectors are unstructured, a reasonable approximation can be made by treating them *as though* they were structured. The structured problems are those in which the performance characteristics can be represented by probability distributions. The probability distributions themselves may not be known, but they could be assumed with a reasonable degree of accuracy. Even when the probability distributions are known, the parameters of the probability distributions themselves may be unknown, and have to be determined for the particular problem on hand.

If we further simplify the nature of the structured problems, it becomes possible to handle such simplified problems through methods which are analytically powerful, and computationally feasible. Suppose there are 15 products which are produced by combining 3 resources in different combinations. The resources could be wood, pigskin, and plastics. The number of sporting goods items that can be made with varying combinations of the three resources is given by the combinations of 15 things taken 3 at a time which is 15_{C_3}. It works out to 455 products. This number is based on the assumption that *all* the 3 resources are used in *every* product. But we know that any one of the resources could be used to produce a product. The total number of products that can be made out of 15 resources taking one at a time is 15! or $15 \times 14 \times ... \times 1$, or 1 376 470 000 000. Which of these products should we manufacture in order to maximize profit? Even if a large number of possibilities are investigated, there is no guarantee that an important product made up of some combination of the resources has not been ignored; and, therefore, potential profits given up or even potential losses incurred.

Extensive enumeration of 15! alternatives would not be advisable as a method of selection because it would take too much energy and time. Therefore, even in simplified problems, there must be offered some mathematical properties which ensure that the computations themselves are held to a necessary minimum. Further, there must be the assurance that the result that has been found is in fact as good as the one that would have resulted from 1 376 470 000 000 enumerations.

These two types of problems — the unstructured and the structured — are treated respectively in Volume I and Volume II. In both volumes, the problems in both the public sector and the private sector are treated. Of the 29 applications of OR/SA to real-to-life problems in Volume I, 9 are historical and military; 7 are public sector and non-military; and 13 are private sector problems. In Volume II, of the 22 applications of OR/SA to near-real life problems, 5 are historical and military; 5 are public sector and non-military; and 12 are private sector problems.

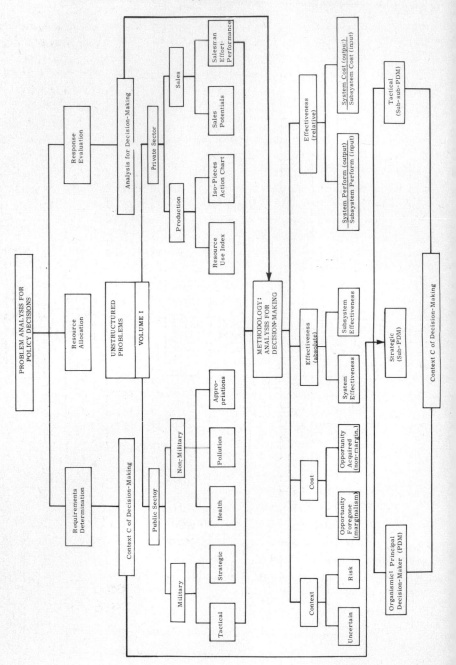

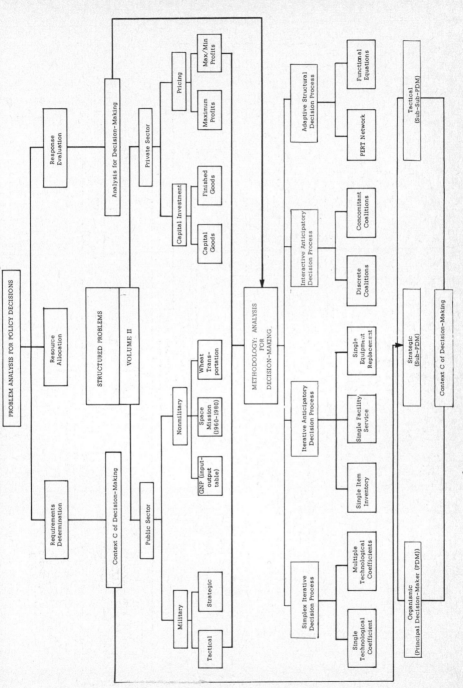

Fig. 1.1. Outline of Volumes I and II (continued).

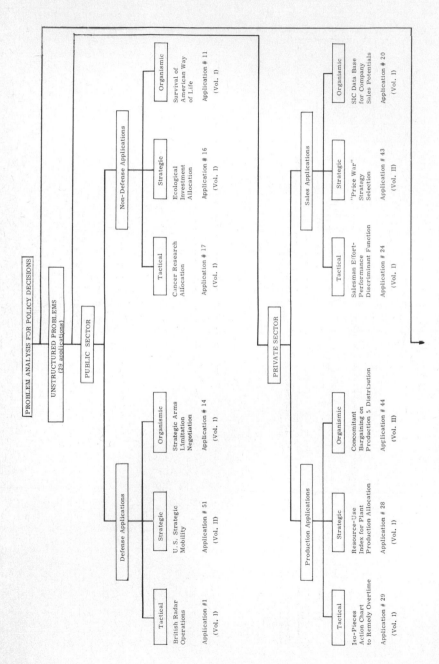

Fig. 1.2. Applications by sector in Volumes I and II.

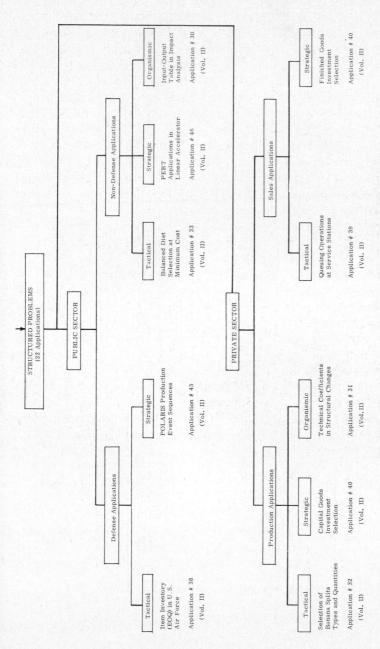

Fig. 1.2. Applications by sector in Volumes I and II (continued).

There are three major elements in the Problem Analysis for Policy Dec-isions pursued in the two volumes: (1) requirements determination, (2) re-source allocation, and (3) response evaluation. These three may be combined into two: (1) context C of decision-making, and (2) analysis for decision-making. The context comprises the perspective of the decision-maker, who may be at the highest level of policy-making with respect to the organism (organismic), the next highest level (strategic), and the next highest level (tactical). While these categories are relatively fixed in the *administrative* hierarchy, they are flexible from the point of view of the *objectives* hierar-chy. Because of the flexibility of the objectives hierarchy, every decision-maker has to play more than one role: With respect to those below him, he is at the organismic level; with respect to those above him, he is at the strategic level; and with respect to those two steps above him, he is at the tactical level. This simultaneous multiplicity of roles inherently leads to *concurrent conflict* in the perspective of the decision-maker; which conflict is underscored with reference to Context C (for Conflict) of decision-making in Fig. 1.1.

There is a difference in the methodology applied to the analysis for dec-ision-making between the unstructured and structured problems. In the un-structured, the objective is to identify the important *interactions* while in the structured, the objective is to identify the important *variables*. Therefore, the proportionate change in the system performance corresponding to the pro-portionate change in a small part of the system, i.e. a subsystem, is the most important single consideration for decision-making in the unstructured prob-lem. On the other hand, the system itself is identified in terms of variables in the case of structured problems, and the interactions are ignored, leaving the emphasis to be upon the values of the *variables* and their effect upon the system performance. While there are differences in methodology, their object-ives remain the same, viz., to perform problem analysis for policy decisions as shown in Fig. 1.1.

6. What This Work Offers and to Whom

This two-volume work presents a unified treatment of OR/SA in terms of its two basic characteristics: (1) conceptualization of the problem as a whole or *diagnosis,* and (2) development of the prescriptive solutions or *prescription.*

6.1. Problem-Oriented Exposition of OR/SA Reasoning

In Fig. 1.1, the accent is on real-life or real-to-life problems. Unstructured problems are the subject matter of Volume I, Parts I through IV, as well as in Volume II, Parts VII through VIII. Structured problems are the subject matter in Volume II, Parts V and VI.

In Fig. 1.2, the problem orientation is set forth in greater detail. The problems themselves are classified into two groups: Unstructured and Structured. The Unstructured Problems are further divided into those in the Public Sector, and those in the Private Sector; so also the Structured Problems are divided into those in the Public Sector, and those in the Private Sector.

The Public and Private Sectors are each divided into two in terms of the type of applications: (1) Defense Applications, and (2) Nondefense Applications in the Public Sector; and (1) Production Applications, and (2) Sales Applications in the Private Sector.

The problem orientation also accents the decision hierarchy in the form of the triad, comprising: (1) tactical, (2) strategic, and (3) organismic levels of decision-making. The triad itself is a relative hierarchy which can be applied to the President of the United States and his immediate subordinates, or a plant manager and his immediate subordinates, the only requirement being that the three decision levels be properly related to each other as part of the whole. However, in the choice of the problems for discussion, the decision triad has been made to correspond to the administrative hierarchy, it being easy to recognize the objective of the President of the United States as being at the organismic level.

Problems are thus the prime mover in the exposition of the methodology of Operations Research/Systems Analysis (OR/SA). How can the important problems of the day in both the public and private sector be addressed is the question; *not* how the available methodology can be applied to some problems. By making the problems the central focus, the elegance of solutions is subjected to the relevance to the problems.

6.2. Thematic Unity of Methodological Discussion

Based on the conviction that the value of OR/SA methodology derives from its wide applicability, a special effort has been made as to arrange the discussion of the problems which utilize a methodological sequence. Thus a sequence of four primary characteristics is developed to handle unstructured problems. These four characteristics give rise to an OR/SA protocol, which is applied successively to large problems in the public sector.

The thematic unity in the structured problems is brought out by the discussion, first, of the Input-Output Table, the forerunner of linear programming. The linear programming problem itself is shown as a subset of indirect methods of optimization, other members being the Gradient Method and the Lagrange Multipliers Method.

The linear programming problem itself is a generalization of the Transportation Problem and the Assignment Problem. The different computational algorithms applicable to the solution of these special problems of the linear programming class of problems are discussed with respect to both their analytical and computational considerations.

Similarly, kinship between the inventory problem and the queuing problem is brought out in real-life examples. The explicit recognition of demand over time which characterizes the queuing problem facilitates an appreciation of the changes in the analytical approach between inventory and queuing problems. Questions of replacement and maintenance of machinery are shown to be of a piece with the queuing and inventory problems; the U.S. investment in the inventory of capital goods provides the point of reference in arriving at the analytical approach toward replacement and maintenance models.

Turning from the maximization problems encountered in the linear programming and associated problems to the mixture of maximization problems handled by game theory, no participant achieves the maximum, but instead, each settles for less than the maximum. The new concept of *concomitant* coalitions in which each party plays with *and* against other party(ies) at the same time, is presented as an extension of the Von Neumann–Morgenstern concept of *discrete* coalitions in which one party plays with *or* against other party(ies).

The decisions involved in linear programming situations are aided by solutions obtained by *iterative* processes, in which the increments of each value are obtained in a prespecified manner. In the case of the replication of queues at a gas station, or other service facility, the relation between the first unit and the second unit may *not* be a simple numerical increment as in the case of an iterative process. Nevertheless, we may treat the repetitive choice of arrivals in the queue as being an iterative process insofar as the choice of the second member is performed by repeating the same process which yields the first member.

From the *iterative*, we turn to the *interactive* in the game-theoretic considerations. The reason why no individual can maximize his outcome is because the participants *interact* with each other; or, rather, the moves of each is governed by what he knows or assumes about the moves of the other.

From the iterative and the interactive, we turn to the *adaptive* in discussing multistage decision processes, in which the experience gained from one stage is applied to the *subsequent* stage. The event-sequencing of PERT Networks is used to set the stage for the discussion of dynamic programming approach to large, unstructured problems such as lunar landing and strategic mobility, which are adaptive decision processes.

A definition may now be attempted of the structured problems. Mention has been made in Section 5 that interactions increase geometrically as variables increase arithmetically, and that the contribution of OR/SA effort is in *selectively ignoring* the interactions in finding an approach to problem-solving. In this section, we find that the particular type of decision can be used to identify the structured or unstructured nature of the problem. For instance, a structured problem is one in which the solution can be found by a repetitive process, a special case of which is the iterative process. However, in an unstructured problem, the decision process is interactive and/or adaptive. There is no learning process in the decision-making in structured problems, while the learning proces is essential in the decision-making in unstructured problems.

A *structured problem* is one in which the solution can be found by a repetitive process, including an iterative process, ignoring the interactions among the variables of the problem, and denying any learning curve in the performance characteristics of the problem, as well as in the exercise of the decision-making process.

6.3. Intended Audience

This two-volume work, with its central emphasis upon problem solving, and its maintenance of thematic unity and integrity of OR/SA methodology, should be of interest to the present and potential members of management, in both the public and private sectors.

It lends itself to use in a one-semester graduate, or advanced undergraduate, course each in Systems Analysis and Operations Research, or a two-semester course in the OR/SA approach to problem formulation and solution. The treatment is self-contained, and the development is built up from fundamentals. Therefore, those with no more than high school algebra background will be able to instruct themselves in the reasoning and application of the methodology of OR/SA.

This two-volume work should be of interest to the decision-makers in the public and private sectors. The 51 applications in the two volumes are real life, or near-real life problems. Several of these applications are designed to provide an opportunity for the decision-maker to get a feel for how one goes about formulating the problems and finding their solutions.

In addition to present and potential members of management, the two-volume work offers a readable reference to the increasing number of concerned citizens who seek an active awareness of how to appreciate, understand, and go about solving the large problems of personal and professional interest in the community, nation, and the world.

PROBLEMS

This introductory chapter presents the perspective of the 2 Volumes of the book: which is one of relevance, instead of elegance; practical application, instead of theoretical construction. The purpose of the following questions is to develop an appreciation for the thematic unity and integrity of Operations Research/Systems Analysis Methodology which combines theory and practice.

A. *The Discipline*
   1. J. Bronowski wrote in 1951 in his review of the first book in Operations Research (Philip M. Morse and George E. Kimball, *Methods of Operations Research*, Wiley, New York, 1951):

> What was new and speculative on the battle field turns out, in the practical affairs of industry, to become only a painstaking combination of cost accounting, job analysis, time and motion study and the general integration of plant flow. There is an extension of this to the larger economics of whole industries and nations, but it is hardly likely to be rewarding to first-rate-scientists and calls at bottom for the

immense educational task of interesting economists and administrators in the mathematics of differentials and of prediction.[4]

Discuss Bronowski's prognostication.

    2. Distinguish between Operations Research and Systems Analysis.

B. *The Types of Problems*

    3. What are "structured" and "unstructured" problems?

    4. Outline a hierarchy of decisions which is common to industry, military, government, and institutions.

C. *Types of Solutions*

    5. What is the difference between solutions to structure-oriented problems and solution-oriented problems?

    6. How would you know that a study is an Operations Research/Systems Analysis study?

[4] J. Bronowski, Review of Philip M. Morse and George E. Kimball, *Methods of Operations Research*, Wiley, New York, 1951, in *Scientific American*, October 1951, p. 75.

CHAPTER 2

FROM SELECTING TACTICS TO FORMULATING POLICY

TECHNICAL OVERVIEW

The birth of operational research in August, 1940, in war-time England, and its growth into operations research in the United States during the last two decades, is traced in terms of the types of decisions to which the new profession has contributed: from choosing tactics to formulating policy.

The two "first" documents of operations research are drawn upon to reconstruct the earliest problems and decisions – not theoretical, but immensely and immediately practical problems, such as how to preserve Great Britain from enemy attacks by the brand new capability of radar, and how to arrive at the proper size of the convoys so that losses could be minimized. The variables, the data, the probabilities, the "variational method" and the solution obtained through the comparison of derivatives are reconstructed; as well as the convoy escort formula traditionally employed, and the change made in it after the operational research study was implemented, and the resulting reduction in convoy losses.

Why was operational research successful? The right auspices is one factor: the convoy escort study rose from "discussions that took place at the Prime Minister's fortnightly U-boat meetings." The "intimate collaboration between operational service staffs and operational research workers" was another factor. A third factor was the inter-disciplinary nature of the group, as distinguished from the merely multi-disciplinary: there was communication between people trained in different backgrounds: "a lively, paradoxical, exchange of ideas between amateur and professional war-makers." From these factors are derived desired conditions for success in operations research efforts: (1) understand more than one discipline, (2) look at the forest, not at the trees, (3)

22

"Homely" communications. The success of operations research in tactical *decisions, as well as the failure of operations research in* strategic *decisions can be traced to the success or failure of "homely" communication. The communication is not merely one of content; but as much, if not more, one of context: to whom, when, and how.*

The importance of communication notwithstanding, there would have been no profession called operations research if it had not been sustained by the development of mathematical foundations. Three developments of importance are: (1) Linear Programming *by George B. Dantzig in 1947, (2)* Dynamic Programming *by Richard Bellman in 1953, and (3)* Theory of Games *by John von Neumann and Oskar Morgenstern in 1944. Dantzig, in his presentations to the First Conference on Linear Programming held in June, 1949, referred to an earlier model developed by von Neumann in 1933, and to the input-output model developed by Wassily W. Leontief in 1936. Unlike the linear programming problem of maximizing (minimizing) the linear objective function subject to linear constraints, dynamic programming breaks up a complex, N-dimensional problem into N one-dimensional problems in such a way that the optimum solutions to the latter ensure the optimum solution to the former. Both Dantzig and Bellman acknowledge their indebtedness to, or the antecedence of their research to von Neumann whose proof of the Minimax theorem, which he developed at the age of 23, provides a way of playing the game in such a way that, no matter what one's opponent does, player A can be sure to minimize his loss, and player B can be sure to maximize his gains.*

Continuing with the growth of operations research, we come to "systems analysis" which came into being in the early 1950's, RAND Corporation's first efforts having been "concerned with the selection and evaluation of weapons systems for development". Two examples are considered to highlight the accent on the qualitative *in systems analysis: one, Polaris; two, Strategic Aircraft Bomber bases.*

The substantial costs, associated with the development of new weapons systems in the postwar period, were to be spread over increasingly longer periods from development to deployment as the weapons grew in complexity. A very important policymaker at the national level, the Chairman of the House Committee on Appropriations, wrote to the

Secretary of Defense in September 1960, on the subject of relating costs to mission: "for more useful information and for a practical means of relating costs to missions." Charles J. Hitch, who became Assistant Secretary of Defense (Comptroller) in 1961, introduced nine major programs, each of which contained program elements which, for decision purposes, because of either their supportive role or substitutional capabilities, could be considered as a group. The Department of Defense Directive issued on July 1, 1965, recognized "cost-effectiveness" as an essential element in planning and executing large systems.

The difficulties of cost-effectiveness analysis are illustrated with respect to three major decisions: (1) the March 1961 decision to reduce the size of the Titan II force, (2) the December 1962 decision to cancel Skybolt, and (3) the April 1965 decision to ask for authority to build four Ro-Ro ships to be used as floating depots.

The need for an interdisciplinary approach to policy-making began to be recognized as newer methods and procedures were applied to larger and complex problems, neither the components of which nor the interactions among their multitudinous components were obvious to the decision-makers in the public and private sectors. It is significant that mathematician E.S. Quade of the RAND Corporation, who has edited two books on systems analysis, was the first editor of the new International Journal, Policy Sciences. In his first editorial in January, 1970, Quade defined the interdisciplinary nature of policy sciences resulting from the need "to bring the knowledge and procedures imbedded in the "soft" or behavioral sciences into systems engineering and aerospace technology" and "to introduce the quantitative methods of systems analysis and operations research into the normal approaches by social and political scientists."

The development of the professional activities of operations research, in the form of the Operations Research Society of America which started with 10 people in January, 1952, and has grown to a total of 7445 members as of March, 1970, is traced; so are the symposia and short courses which have contributed particularly to the growth of the profession.

The change in emphasis, from tactics to strategy, is reflected in a 1961 definition of operations research as "the heuristic art of prescriptive application of the scientific method to executive-type problems,

whose solutions are not immediately obvious, and which arise in behav-
ioral aspects of entities, more or less with respect to decision-making, in
industrial, commercial, military, and/or institutional environments."

EXECUTIVE SUMMARY

The "Virtuosity in Management" for which American Private Enter-
prise is hailed today in Europe owes much to the beginnings in August,
1940, in wartime England, when operational *solutions had to be found*
for the most pressing problem in the public sector: survival of England
in the Second World War.

Given the air superiority of Germany, how should England defend
itself from air raids? The approaching enemy aircraft had to be identi-
fied early enough to let the population seek shelter. A new technology
for detecting objects in the air was expected to provide aid to defense
and buy valuable time to prepare retaliatory capabilities. However,
when the new technology, radar, was finally put into operation, it was
found that the warning that could be obtained was worse than what the
innumerable Britishers peering into the sky with their binoculars were
able to provide until then.

Prime Minister Churchill wanted an answer in a week or two. A
group of people was "hurriedly collected" whose training was in dif-
ferent fields ranging from mathematics to mensuration. The exchanges
among people with different backgrounds upon the same subjectmatter
led to a fresh understanding of the problem, and in devising an ap-
proach to solve the problem. Radar was not the only problem that was
studied and solved successfully by a group of people with backgrounds
in different disciplines. Of these, a total of 9 applications of the new
methodology is discussed, not only in wartime England, but also in
post-war United States.

Why has this activity been successful? Four elements of success are
identified on the basis of the past successes. The initial success in the
'40s were largely in military tactics. In the '50s, with the advent of
missiles as a major weapon, it was found necessary to talk not only
about a single weapon, as in the case of a rifle, but of a weapon
"system", the success of the weapon system being dependent upon all

the component parts of the system working in concert with each other toward the accomplishment of the single goal. By the '60s the emphasis changed from the sum of the fire-power of missiles to their accuracy; and, a newer emphasis upon credibility *of one's* capability *to the would-be adversary. In the '70s, public attention increasingly turned to matters of home and hearth: health, education, pollution, and so on.*

These problems are more complex than the initial military tactics; but the activity known as Operations Research/Systems Analysis (OR/SA) appears to have something to offer to the understanding and solution of the larger problems. Part of the success of OR/SA lies in the mathematical foundations of the method. The mathematical methods do not *claim to provide answers to problems. They merely state that if the problems can be put into certain mathematical forms, then the answers are those provided by the method. The caveat "if" is sometimes overlooked, leading the enthusiasts to claim that their solutions are what the decision-maker should rely upon, while the method may not at all be applicable to the problem.*

The development of OR/SA reflects the response of the profession to the demands of real-life problems. The formulation of the problem is given more emphasis; the factors of cost have been given increasing recognition, the Department of Defense Directive issued on July 1, 1965, recognizing "cost-effectiveness" as an essential element in planning and in configuring large systems. Further, it has been found desirable to bring the methods of behavioral sciences to OR/SA, one of the efforts being embodied in a new international journal, Policy Sciences.

Two prime characteristics of OR/SA are: (1) diagnosis, and (2) prescription. Even as in the medical context, collection of X-rays from the top of one's head to the tip of one's toe does not perform diagnosis, so also computational and analytical aids, by their weight of numbers, do not diagnose the OR/SA problem. Its contribution is in insisting upon looking at the problem as a whole, and resisting the temptation to be side-tracked by the different symptoms. Unlike in the medical situation, there is no definitive diagnosis, only a *diagnosis. Given a diagnosis, appropriate prescriptions can be found; however, there is no guarantee that the patient will take his medicine. If he does not, the best doctor in the world cannot help him. OR/SA offers some help to understand, as well as to handle practical problems encountered at different levels*

> *of management; and the profession seeks to anticipate, and to respond*
> *to, new challenges of larger dimensions and broader implications.*

---

1. "Operational Efficiency Rather Than Novelty of Equipment"[1]

Operations research, as it is known in the United States, traces its origin to *Operational Research** associated with the work of Professor P.M.S. Blackett of the University of Manchester, who was a Fellow of the Royal Society, a Nobel Laureate, and a former Naval Officer; who assembled in August 1940, during the early phase of the decisive Battle of Britain, what must have appeared to be certainly an unorthodox group including "three physiologists, two mathematical physicists, one astrophysicist, one Army officer, one surveyor, one general physicist, and two mathematicians", [a group which was known as] "Blackett's circus".[3] The only American member of "Blackett's circus" was Professor Philip M. Morse who became, in May 1952, the first President of the Operations Research Society of America. He recalls having rechristened the then emerging activity as *Operations Research*, with an "s" instead of "al", in the title of the first American book on the subject[4] reflecting "maybe a rebellion against the niceties of English grammar".[5]

Professor Blackett wrote two documents, one in December 1941, and another in May 1943 as operations research was emerging. In reprinting these articles, with minor modifications, he says:

---

[1] Winston S. Churchill, *The Gathering Storm*, Houghton Mifflin, Boston, 1948, p. 156.
* At the "conversazione" held on December 4, 1967, at the Royal Society, London, with Professor P.M.S. Blackett in the chair, to commemorate, not the founding of Operational Research, but the naming of it, Dr. E.C. Williams said: "For the life of me I can't recall which man invented the name, A.P. Roe or Sir Robert Watson-Watts," quoted in footnote 2.
[2] William H. Sutherland, "UK: Thirtieth Anniversary of 'Operational Research' ", *Washington Operations Research Council Newsletter*, Vol. 7, February, 1968, pp. 13–14.
[3] Florence N. Trefethen, "A History of Operations Research", in Joseph M. McCloskey and Florence N. Trefethen (eds.), *Operations Research for Management I*, Johns Hopkins, Baltimore, 1954, p. 6.
[4] Philip M. Morse and George E. Kimball, *Methods of Operations Research*, Wiley, New York, 1951.
[5] William H. Sutherland, *op. cit.*, p. 14.

The first of these, entitled "Scientists at the Operational Level", was written in December 1941, in order to inform the Admiralty of some of the developments which had occurred in the Operational Research Sections already established at Fighter, Anti-Aircraft and Coastal Commands. It so happened that this hurriedly and somewhat flippantly written document received subsequently a rather wide circulation in Service Departments both in this country and also in the United States, where it seems to have had some influence on the setting up of similar organisations.

The second document, under the title "A Note on Certain Aspects of the Methodology of Operational Research", originated in 1941 as an attempt to set out, for the benefit of new scientific recruits to the operational research sections, some of the principles that had been found to underlie the work of the first two years of the war. The text as reproduced here dates from May 1943. A few notes have been added to the original documents. As the nearest existing approach to a "text book" of operational research, it also received a fairly wide circulation, and has, along with the former document, been fairly extensively quoted in various official and semi-official documents. It must be emphasised that these two papers cover only a small part of the great field of operational research as developed in Great Britain and the United States during the war and that very many important achievements are not mentioned at all. For instance, the examples given were chosen rather haphazardly and mainly with a view to illustrating points of methodology.[6]

1.1. Two "First" Documents of Operations Research

We shall draw upon these two *"first" documents of operations research,*[7,8] as well as subsequent writings of Professor Blackett, to identify what constituted operations research at its beginnings. Clearly, the accent was on the military aspects. He identifies weapons, tactics, and strategy as the three main fields of operations research:

> The main fields of operational research can be classified under the following headings, the study of weapons, the study of tactics, and the study of strategy. The first consists mainly in analysing how and why existing weapons perform as they do, with the object of finding out how they could be improved. The second

[6]P.M.S. Blackett, *Studies of War*, Hill and Wang, New York, 1962, pp. 169–170.
[7]P.M.S. Blackett, "Scientists at the Operational Level", British Admiralty, 1941 (*Document I*).
[8]P.M.S. Blackett, "A Note On Certain Aspects of the Methodology of Operational Research", British Admiralty, 1943, (*Document II*).

consists of analysing the various tactical methods in use, with the same object of finding methods of improving them. The third consists in studying the results achieved by various types of operation, and the cost in the resources of war of achieving them. The actual form of the method of variational analysis lends itself immediately to the calculation of "marginal" profits and costs – which is in general what is required.[9]

2. APPLICATION 1: Operational Problems of Radar

Among the important problems which stand out in the mind of Professor Blackett in his "Recollections of Problems Studied, 1940–45", are those relating to (1) radar, and (2) convoys.

To appreciate the role of operations research in radar problems, it is important to recognize what radar meant to British defenses. In his memoirs of the Second World War, Churchill gives unqualified praise to the role of radar: "Unless British science had proved superior to German, and unless its strange sinister resources had effectively been brought to bear on the struggle for survival, *we might well have been defeated*, and being defeated, destroyed.... My four years' work upon the Air Defence Research Committee had made me familiar with the outlines of *radar problems*. I therefore immersed myself so far as my faculties allowed in this Wizard War, and strove to make sure that *all that counted came without obstruction or neglect* at least through the threshold of action."[10] (italics supplied)

To Great Britain, radar was not just another tool in the waging of war; it was the very essence of self preservation. The extent of extreme dependence upon radar of British policy is disclosed in Churchill's words: "The plans for the air defence of Great Britain had, as early as the autumn of 1937, been rewritten around the assumption that the promises made by our scientists for the still unproven radar would be kept." [11] Considering the fact that a really adequate radar anti-aircraft system was achieved only by 1944, the significance of trusting virtually the entire defense of Great Britain to "the promises made by our scientists for the still unproven radar" emerges with startling criticality. What if the promises were *not* kept!

[9] P.M.S. Blackett, *Document II, op. cit.*, pp. 2–3.
[10] Winston S. Churchill, *Their Finest Hour*, Houghton Mifflin, Boston, 1949, pp. 381–382.
[11] Winston S. Churchill, *The Grand Alliance*, Houghton Mifflin, Boston, 1951, p. 45.

The first problem that "Blackett's circus" was called upon to handle was the *operational use* of radar sets, guns, and predictors. Blackett points out that in August 1940, gun-laying radar sets (GL. 1 and later GL. 2) were then being delivered to the anti-aircraft batteries around London. The radar data came from the operators giving range and bearing (and subsequently height) of approaching aircraft. The data were far too crude, in the sense of being subject to much too large errors, so that they could not be fed directly into mechanical predictors; instead, manual plotting of the position of the enemy aircraft, as determined from the radar set, was employed. Since the usefulness of the anti-aircraft guns depended upon the predicted future positions of the enemy aircraft, the large errors of the radar data on approaching aircraft actually rendered them of limited value; and instead of aiding, they impeded the efficiency of operations. To quote Blackett: "Thus the first months of the A.A. Battle against the night bomber were fought with highly developed radar sets and guns, but with the crudest and most improvised links between them, belonging technically to the First rather than the Second World War."[12]

So here was the new instrument upon which Great Britain was betting its very survival, which proved to be far less effective in its use under *actual conditions of war*, than its performance in the laboratory suggested. The question therefore was: How best to make use of the radar data to direct the guns? Churchill notes: "The Germans would not have been surprised to hear our radar pulses, for they had developed a technically efficient radar system which was in some respects ahead of our own. What would have surprised them, however, was the extent to which we had turned our discoveries to *practical effect*, and woven all into our general air defence system. In this we led the world, and it was *operational efficiency rather than novelty of equipment* that was the British achievement."[13] (italics supplied)

The role of operations research in making the new instrument operational is identified by Blackett in terms of four tasks:

> 1. Help to work out in a week or two the best method of plotting the GL data and of predicting the future enemy position for the use of the guns, on the basis only of pencil and paper, range and fuse tables.

[12] P.M.S. Blackett, *Studies of War, op. cit.,* p. 208.
[13] Winston S. Churchill, *The Gathering Storm*, Houghton Mifflin, Boston, 1948, p. 156.

2. Assist in the design of simple forms of plotting machines which could be manufactured in a few weeks.

3. Find means of bringing the existing predictors into use in conjunction with the radar sets. This was found to be possible if, by intensive training of the predictor crews the inaccurate data could be *smoothed* manually. A special school was set up by A.A. Command to work out the best methods of doing this and to give the necessary training.

4. Modify the predictors to make them handle the rough GL data more effectively. This proved possible with the Sperry predictor.[14]

3. APPLICATION 2: Operational Problems of Convoy Escort

As a maritime power, Great Britain's strength lay in her shipping. In what Churchill describes as *"one of the most important* [letters] I ever wrote,"[15] (italics supplied), he told President Roosevelt on December 4, 1940:

> The decision for 1941 lies upon the seas ... . Our *shipping losses*, the figures for which in recent months are appended, have been on a scale almost *comparable* to that of the *worst year of the last war*. In the five weeks ending November 3, losses reached a total of 420 300 tons. Our estimate of annual tonnage which ought to be imported in order to maintain our effort at full strength is *forty-three million tons*; the tonnage entering in September was only at the rate of *thirty-seven million tons*, and in October, of thirty-eight million tons. Were *this diminution to continue* at this rate; it would be *fatal*, unless indeed immensely greater replenishment than anything at present in sight could be achieved in time.[16] (italics supplied)

The loss of the British shipping was thus a two-edged sword; it depleted the military defenses of Great Britain; and additionally, it strangled her vital life line across the oceans. The critical losses at sea became a problem for operations research as a result of discussions at no less than the highest level, viz., with the Prime Minister. In Blackett's words:

> In the autumn of 1942 the U-boat war on our shipping was exceedingly menacing; the huge toll of shipping losses, up to 800 000 tons a month, unless rapidly checked, might make the invasion of Europe in 1943 or even 1944 impossible through lack of shipping ... .

[14] P.M.S. Blackett, *Studies of War, op. cit.,* p. 208.
[15] Winston S. Churchill, *Their Finest Hour*, Houghton Mifflin, Boston, 1949, p. 558.
[16] *Ibid*, p. 560–561.

Looking back, I think we operational research workers at the Admiralty made a bad mistake in not realising as soon as the group was formed in the spring of 1942 the vital importance of working out a theory of the best size for a convoy. However, it was not until the late autumn that the problem became focused in our minds, largely through *discussions that took place at the Prime Minister's fortnightly U-boat meetings*. The problem arose as to what was the *best division of our limited shipbuilding resources between merchant ships and the anti-U-boat escort vessels.* Every merchant vessel completed brought into the United Kingdom additional much needed goods; every escort vessel completed added to the protection of the convoys and so reduced their losses by U-boat attacks and so *saved* more ships and cargoes.[17] (italics supplied)

Professor Blackett points out that the first step in the analysis was to break down the statistics of loss in such a way as to relate the changes in the shipping losses to the main variables of immediate interest.

3.1. Operations Research Model: (1) The Variables

The *variables* were:
  Number of escorts,
  Size of convoy,
  Speed of convoy,
  Amount of air cover.

3.2. Operations Research Model: (2) The Data

The two main sources of *data* were: (1) the statistical data available on the shipping losses, and (2) the tactics pursued by the U-boats in their "wolf-pack" in carrying out attacks on the British convoys, as described by the prisoners of war from the sunken U-boats.

3.3. Operations Research Model: (3) The Probabilistic Factors

The *probabilistic factors* postulated the conditions under which a given merchant ship would be sunk in any voyage:

(a) the chance that the convoy in which it sailed would be sighted; (b) the chance that, having sighted the convoy, a U-boat would penetrate the screen of escort vessels around it; and (c) the chance that, when a U-boat had penetrated the

[17]P.M.S. Blackett, *Studies of War, op. cit.,* pp. 227, 228.

screen, the merchant ship would be sunk. It was found: (a) that the chance of a convoy being sighted was nearly the same for large and small convoys; (b) that the chance that a U-boat would penetrate the screen depended only on the linear density of escorts, that is, on the number of escort vessels for each mile of perimeter to be defended; and (c) that when a U-boat did penetrate the screen, the number of merchant ships sunk was the same for both large and small convoys – simply because there were always more than enough targets. These facts taken together indicated that one would expect the same *absolute number* of ships to be sunk whatever the size of convoy, given the same linear escort strength, and thus, the *percentage* of ships sunk to be inversely proportional to the size of the convoys. Hence the objective should be to reduce the number of convoys sighted by reducing the number of convoys run, the size of the convoys being increased so as to sail the same total number of ships.[18]

3.4. Operations Research Model: (4) The Variational Method

What should be the size of the convoys? We saw in Section 3.1, that the variables of immediate interest were four. Blackett applied what he calls the "variational method" to assess the relative importance of each of these variables to the shipping losses. The heart of the method is observing the result of relatively small changes in some of the variables upon the tactics under consideration. He points out that numerical estimation of *all* the variables in question is *not* essential. In his words:

> The first attack on any operational problem is often to estimate as many of the derivatives as possible: first the *tactical* derivatives to judge what changes of *tactics* would lead to improved yields; then the material derivatives to estimate the effect of improved *weapons* ... . A desired derivative dY/dX_1 may often be obtained from another operational derivative $(dY/dX_2)_{obs}$ by using (a) a theoretical or (b) an experimental relationship between the assumed causally related increments δX_1, and δX_2.
>
> Formally one can express the above method by the relation
>
> $$\frac{dY}{dX_1} = \left(\frac{dY}{dX_2}\right)_{obs} \times \frac{\partial X_2}{\partial X_1} ,$$
>
> where $\partial X_2/\partial X_1$ is determined either theoretically or by special experiment.[19]

3.5. Operations Research Model: (5) The Admiralty Rule

The results yielded by the analysis of shipping losses data by the variational

[18] P.M.S. Blackett, *Studies of War, op. cit.*, p. 232.
[19] P.M.S. Blackett, *Document II, op. cit.*, p. 6–7.

method ran counter to the established policy. The longstanding Admiralty Rule was 3+N/10, which laid down a minimum of 3 escort vessels for a very small convoy, and one additional escort vessel for every 10 ships in the convoy. This rule was supposed to make the convoys of different sizes equally safe, resulting in the *same average percentage losses* for all types of convoy.

However, the operations research calculations showed that "an increase of number of escort vessels from 6 to 9 led to a reduction of losses by about 25 percent."[20] Further, contrary to the Admiralty view, large convoys were *not* relatively more dangerous. "Dividing convoys into those smaller and larger than 40 ships, it was found that the smaller convoys, with an average size of 32 ships, had suffered an average loss of 2.5 percent, whereas the large convoys with an average size of 54 ships, had suffered only a loss of 1.1 percent. Thus *large convoys* appeared to be in fact over *twice as safe* as small convoys."[21] (italics supplied)

3.6. Operations Research Model: (6) Solution through Comparison of Derivatives

Having found a result which directly contradicted the British Admiralty in two respects: (1) the size of the convoy, and (2) the number of escorts, the operations research group proceeded to determine the optimum size of the convoy by considering the variation of shipping losses with respect to the size of the convoy. Drawing upon the results derived in the previous paragraph, they could state than an increase in size from an average 32 to 54 was associated with a decrease in fractional losses (i.e., ships sunk : ships sailed) from 2.5 percent to 1.1 percent, i.e., a *reduction of losses by 56 percent.*

Each of the four main variables: (1) number of escorts, (2) size of convoy, (3) speed of convoy, and (4) amount of air cover, was investigated with respect to its contribution to shipping losses. The application of the variational method by comparing the derivatives was as follows:

> Since in each of these derivations it was verified that the average value of the other variables was about constant, the four results represent in effect four partial derivatives.
>
> Making the reasonable assumption that these derivatives are causally signifi-

[20] P.M.S. Blackett, *Document II, op. cit.,* Appendix B, p. 1.
[21] P.M.S. Blackett, *Studies of War, op. cit.,* p. 231.

cant, one can use them to calculate the relative value in saving shipping in 1941–1942 of the four factors, numbers of escorts, size of convoy, speed, and air cover.

Thus it follows immediately that the number of escorts would have to be increased from 6 to 14 to make a convoy without the above amount of air cover as safe as one with air cover. Such an extrapolation, from 6 to 14 escorts, must be considered a rather large extrapolation, and so be subject to a large probable error. The same consideration applies to the following comparisons.

Similarly the number of escorts would have to be increased from 6 to 10 to make the average slow convoy as safe as the average fast convoy.

Again the *number of escorts* would have to *be increased from 6 to 11* to reduce the percentage loss of ships in small *convoys* of average size 32 to the losses in *larger convoys of average size 54.* [22] (italics supplied)

3.7. Operations Research Model: (7) Implementation of Solution

Professor Blackett recalls:

This analysis convinced us that the Admiralty orders about the size of convoys should be altered. After some weeks of earnest argument the alterations to this order were made in the spring of 1943 and the average size of the Atlantic convoys gradually grew ... . During the summer of 1944, the Admiralty [which had previously considered a convoy of 40 merchant vessels as about the best size and which had *prohibited* convoys of more than 60 ships] gave publicity to the successful arrival of a convoy of 187 ships![23]

Reflecting upon the problem ten years later, Professor Blackett was convinced that without the theory of the greater safety of large convoys, the considerable economy in escort vessels could not have been achieved. Because of the reduction in number in escort vessels, a number of anti-submarine escort vessels could be moved from the Atlantic to support the invasion of Normandy in June 1944.

4. "Decipher the Signals ... and Explain to me in Lucid, Homely Terms ..."[24]

The contribution of operations research to World War II suggests several important precepts for the successful practice of operations research.

[22] P.M.S. Blackett, *Document II, op. cit.,* Appendix B, p. 2.
[23] P.M.S. Blackett, *Studies of War, op. cit.,* pp. 233, 231.
[24] Winston S. Churchill, *Their Finest Hour, op. cit.,* p. 382.

4.1. Operations Research Desiderata *: (1) The Right Auspices – Of the Decision-Maker

The fact that the operations research study of convoy escorts stemmed from "discussions that took place at the Prime Minister's fortnightly U-boat meetings" is of utmost significance. For, without the interest on the part of the decision-maker, the Admiralty could well have stuck to their longstanding $3+N/10$ rule for escort vessels, and the number 40 as the best number for a convoy of merchant vessels.

The need for the active interest in operations research on the part of the decision-maker was recognized by Professor Blackett who wrote in 1941: "An Operational Research Section should be an integral part of a Command and should work in the closest collaboration with the various departments at the Command."[25]

4.2. Operations Research Desiderata: (2) The Intimate Working Relationships – With the Operational Levels

Professor Blackett followed his own advice:

> When, in March 1941, I was posted to Coastal Command, ... on one organizational point I was most insistent. The operational research group must be an integral part of the Commander-in-Chief's staff and all the reports or recommendations must be to the C.-in-C. of the Command and not to the Air Ministry direct. The importance of this lies in the fact that a considerable part of the work of an operational research group at a Command must inevitably involve criticisms of the work of the Command coupled with suggestions for improvement. For any part of the Command's work in which no improvement seems possible is not likely to be subject of a report by the group. When, however, the group finds, say, that some tactics in use are faulty and could be improved, their report would necessarily have a critical character. If these reports were sent (as at one time was the suggestion) direct to the Air Ministry, then the staffs at Command would rightly feel aggrieved and the *intimate collaboration between operational Service staffs and operational research workers*, which is the essential basis of fertile operational research, would become impossible. If, however, the report went to the C.-in-C., and if the recommendations were adopted successfully, the Air Ministry would hear of it first as a successful achievement of the Command itself.[26] (italics supplied)

* Plural of desideratum – something needed or desirable.

[25] P.M.S. Blackett, *Document I, op. cit.,* p. 5.
[26] P.M.S. Blackett, *Studies of War, op. cit.,* p. 213–214.

This lesson is vital for successful operations research activity. The right auspices of decision-making authority as the sponsor of the operations research activity must be combined with "intimate collaboration between operational Service Staffs and operational research workers, which is the essential basis of fertile operational research." The end product of operations research is *implementation*. Thus, the changes in the decision-making process, attributable to the activities of operations research are the measure of effectiveness of operations research, *not* reams of paper, or scores of formulae, generated in the process of understanding the problem.

4.3. Operations Research Desiderata: (3) The Interdisciplinary, Not Multidisciplinary Approach

The unorthodox group which constituted "Blackett's circus" represented different backgrounds: mathematics, mathematical physics, astrophysics, general physics, military science, and mensuration. It was a group with Professor Blackett had "hurriedly collected" to work with him. Clearly, the choice was dictated by the exigencies of the circumstances, and the availability of the personnel. Nor was Blackett's the only circus in town. During the course of World War II, Newman lists unorthodox collaborators with the professional military from thirteen disciplines from astronomy to zoology, physics to paleontology, and mathematics to psychology:

> *Mathematicians* discussed gunnery problems with British soldiers in Burma; *chemists* did bomb damage assessment with *economist* colleagues at Princes Risborough, a "secure" headquarters outside London; generals conferred about tank strategy in the Italian campaign with *biochemists* and *lawyers*; a famous British *zoologist* was key man in planning the bombardment of Pantellaria; naval officers took *statisticians* and *entomologists* into their confidence regarding submarine losses in the Pacific; the high command of the R.A.F. and American Air Force shared its headaches over Rumanian oil fields, French marshaling yards, German ball-bearing and propeller factories and mysterious ski sites in the Pas-de-Calais with *psychologists, architects, paleontologists, astronomers*, and *physicists*. It was a *lively, informal, paradoxical exchange of ideas between amateur and professional warmakers and it produced some brilliant successes.* It led to the solution of important gunnery and bombardment problems; improved the efficiency of our antisubmarine air patrol in the Bay of Biscay and elsewhere; shed light on convoying methods in the North Atlantic [See Section 3]; helped our submarines to catch enemy ships and also to avoid getting caught; supplied a quantitative basis for weapons evaluation; altered basic concepts of air to air and

naval combat; simplified difficult recurring problems of supply and transport. There were of course many more failures than successes but the over-all record is impressive.[27] (italics supplied)

What made the "lively, informal, paradoxical exchange of ideas between amateur and professional warmakers [produce] some brilliant successes"? The British mathematician J. Bronowski highlights the persistent scientific outlook that the members of the team drawn from different disciplines, brought to bear upon operational problems: "A war or a battle, a mission or a sortie, none is repeatable and none is an experiment. Yet the young scientists brought to them the conviction that in them and nowhere else must be found the empirical evidence for the rightness or wrongness of the assumptions and underlying strategy by which war is made. The passion of these men was to trace in operations involving life and death the tough skeleton of experimental truth."[28]

No matter how intense the conviction that the experimental method was the sure guide to operational inquiries, the collection of specialists from different disciplines would have created nothing but a Babel of scientific dialects if they brought *only* their separate disciplines with them. In fact, a sure recipe for instant failure is to assemble a powerful *multidisciplinary group*, and expect it to produce, on short order, miraculous solutions. A collection of multidisciplinary specialists will no more produce meaningful solutions than the assemblage of different nationalities, each speaking only his own language, could produce a conversation.

4.3.1. Operations research desiderata: (3a) understand more than one discipline
Before a meaningful syllable can be uttered in communication across languages, there must be either a common language which *all* the parties to the conversation can adequately handle; or there must be the capability to handle one other language, in addition to one's own, which at least *two* can communicate in.

Militating against communication across disciplines is the increasing tendency towards specialization. The requirement to know so much about so

[27] James R. Newman, *The World of Mathematics*, Simon and Schuster, New York, 1966, p. 2158.
[28] J. Bronowski, Review of Philip M. Morse and George E. Kimball, *Methods of Operations Research*, Wiley, New York, 1951, in *Scientific American*, October, 1951, p. 75.

little, puts such a premium on depth, that professional breadth has to be acquired at some cost to the depth in one's primary field of specialization. Despairing of such a development in an earlier day, G.M. Young wrote:

> ... The common residual intelligence is becoming impoverished for the benefit of the specialist, the technician, and the aesthete: we leave behind us the world of historical ironmasters and banker historians, geological divines and scholar tobacconists, with its genial watchword: to know something of everything and everything of something: and through the gateway of the Competitive Examination we go out into the Waste Land of Experts, each knowing so much about so little that he can neither be contradicted nor is worth contradicting.[29]

If the specialists can only talk to other specialists in their own disciplines, they *cannot* ever hope to emerge as an operations research group. If, on the other hand, while being specialists in their respective disciplines, each member of the group can claim informal knowledge of at least one other field, then interdisciplinary conversation in *pairs* can be initiated. Once the conversation in interdisciplinary pairs gets started, conversation *between pairs* will hopefully emerge. But none of this will even get started with a multidisciplinary group in which each as in Victorian England, knows "so much about so little" that he cannot be contradicted, and so little about everything else that he is not worth contradicting.

4.3.2. Operations research desiderata: (3b) look at the forest, not the trees

The initiation of interdisciplinary communication is a *necessary* condition; but not a *sufficient* condition for success. If "Blackett's circus" had not looked at the *overall definition* of the problem, they could still be arguing about statistically significant methods of establishing the validity of the Admiralty rule of $3+N/10$, or the magical number, 40, hallowed by Naval tradition.

It is this overall point of view that Professor Blackett referred to as the "imaginative insight into operational realities"[30] which paid handsome dividends in the case of the new instrument — radar — converting it into an operational tool, instead of a mechanical novelty. The concern was not with the bits and pieces of data that radar was able to provide, nor with the

---

[29]G.M. Young, *Victorian England*, Oxford University Press, London, 1937, p. 160.
[30]P.M.S. Blackett, *Studies of War, op. cit.,* p. 208.

accuracy of data obtained from the human radar — the Observer Corps. But instead, the concern was in arriving at a forecast of approaching enemy aircraft so that defensive tactics could be appropriately worked out and executed.

5. APPLICATION 3: Discontinuance of a New Weapons Effort

Again, in another instance, work on an entirely *new weapon* — the proximity depth charge pistol — *was discontinued* as a result of the overall point of view brought to bear upon the fragmentary reports from air crews about their attacks upon German U-boats. The Admiralty ordered that depth charges be set to explode at 100 feet depth, on the theory that the U-boat could dive down to 100 feet in two minutes after sighting the British aircraft. What the analysis of E.J. Williams, Director of Operational Research at Coastal Command, showed was that *on the average* the 100-feet depth was probably accurate. However, if the aircraft had not sighted the U-boat for any length of time, the aircrew would not know where to drop the depth charges; and consequently, the bombing accuracy would be very low. On the other hand, if the aircrew had just sighted the U-boats, the boats would be too close to the surface and the depth charges would still be ineffective, the radius of lethal damage of the depth charges being only 25 feet.

The 100-foot setting was thus shown to be ineffective in both cases: (1) when the U-boats were visible at the time of attack; and (2) when they were not visible. Williams' solution was to change the setting of the depth charges from 100 feet to 25 feet. The shallow depth setting was introduced into Coastal Command in early 1942 with spectacular results.

The contribution that operations research made to the problem was the attention focused upon the *combined outcome* of the air attack and U-boat operations *taken as a unit*. If Williams had studied any one segment of the problem in isolation, he could not have arrived at the solution of the problem as a whole. Thus, if he had concentrated upon the efficiency of the aircrew operations, he could conceivably have suggested better methods of sighting the U-boats. If he had concentrated upon the elusive movements of the U-boats, he could have deluged the aircrew with involved calculations of the probability of the U-boat movements. Or, if he had concentrated upon the desirable dimensions of the new weapon — the proximity depth charge pistol — (which would explode whenever it got close to the U-boat, setting off the proximity fuse as the depth charge fell through the water past the U-boat, he could have recommended several elements which would probably have complicated the untried new weapon out of existence. Instead of these fragmentary views of the problem, Williams looked at the given tactical problem *as a whole*. Six years later Professor Blackett wrote:

> This work of Williams constitutes perhaps *one of the most striking major achievements of the methods of operational analysis*. This method is simply that of the scientific study of the actual operations of war, using all the statistical material that can be collected combined with a detailed knowledge of the physical properties of the weapons used and of the actual tactical situation. Such work can only be achieved by the closest collaboration between scientists of great analytical ability and the Service operational staffs.[31] (italics supplied)

5.1. Operations Research Desiderata: (4) The "Homely" Communication

While the exigencies of the War and the rapidity of the new weapons development, tended to make the traditional military departments to be receptive to the idea of amateurs nosing around matters of professional warmaking, the *communication of the findings* was quite another matter. Referring to the operations research study of the convoy escort problem discussed in Section 3, Professor Blackett observed: "The difficulty was to get the figures believed. But believed they eventually were — something of the Whitehall battle has already been described — and more long-range aircraft were made available to Coastal Command, with the already mentioned startling results."[32]

If hard battles had to be fought and won at the *tactical* level, even higher confrontations had to be made at higher levels of government to affect the problems of strategy. In his volume *Science and Government*, Sir C.P. Snow analyzes in detail two major decisions of British war policy: (1) the decision made in 1935 and 1937 to give the development of radar the highest possible priority; and (2) the decision in 1942 to make the bombing of German cities a major part of the British war effort. Churchill, who made the decision to give the development of radar the highest priority, specifies two qualifications of his adviser Professor Frederick Lindemann in influencing the decision. They emphasize the imperative need for communication of complicated results in "homely terms" to decision-makers. Churchill wrote:

[31] P.M.S. Blackett, *Obituary Notices of Fellows of the Royal Society*, Vol. V, March, 1947, p. 1.
[32] P.M.S. Blackett, *Studies of War, op. cit.*, p. 230.

> There were no doubt greater scientists than Frederick Lindemann, though his
> credentials and genius command respect. But he had two qualifications of vital
> consequence to me. First, as these pages have shown, he was my trusted friend
> and confidant of twenty years. Together we had watched the advance and onset
> of world disaster. Together we had done our best to sound the alarm. And now
> we were in it, and I had the power to guide and arm our effort. How could I have
> the knowledge?
>
> Here came the second of his qualities. Lindemann could *decipher the signals
> from the experts on the far horizons and explain to me in lucid, homely terms*
> what the issues were. There are only twenty-four hours in the day, of which at
> least seven must be spent in sleep and three in eating and relaxation. Anyone in
> my position would have been ruined if he had attempted to dive into depths
> which not even a lifetime of study could plumb. What I had to grasp were the
> practical results, and just as Lindemann gave me his view for all it was worth in
> this field, so I made sure by turning on my power-relay that some at least of these
> terrible and incomprehensible truths emerged in executive decisions.[33] (italics
> supplied)

Churchill's trust in Lindemann, coupled with the latter's ability to communicate in "homely terms", exerted a decisive influence upon the course of the
Second World War. Snow upholds the role of Sir Henry Tizard, and regrets
that instead of Tizard's counsel, it was Lindemann's that prevailed. Nevertheless, for our present purposes, the interest is in the emphasis upon the
effectiveness of communication from the adviser to the decision-maker. In
this respect, even according to Snow, Lindemann was an unqualified success.
In his words:

> Judged by the simple criterion of getting what he wanted, Lindemann was the
> most successful court politician of the age. One has to go back a long way, at least
> as far as Pere Joseph, to find a gray eminence half as effective ... . Throughout his
> partnership with Churchill, Lindemann remained his own man. A remarkable
> number of ideas came from him. It was a two-sided friendship ... . It is ironical
> that such a friendship, which had much nobility and in private showed both men
> at their human best, should in public have led them into *bad judgments*.[34] (italics
> supplied)

6. APPLICATION 4: Bad Judgment in a Strategic Decision

The "bad judgments" that Snow refers to include the 1942 decision to aban-

[33]Winston S. Churchill, *Their Finest Hour, op. cit.,* pp. 382–383.
[34]C.P. Snow, *Science and Government*, Harvard University Press, Cambridge, 1961.

don traditional military doctrine of waging war against the enemy's armed forces in favor of the planned attack on civilian life.

Since we have looked at the success of one of the two major decisions analyzed by Snow, viz., the highest priority accorded to the development of radar, and briefly discussed the role of operations research in making the radar operational in Section 2, we should also look at what Snow and Blackett consider the major policy disaster in the Second World War. Professor Blackett, writing 20 years later, deeply regrets that he was unable to persuade the decision-makers of the fallacy of that decision in time. In his words:

> As I was deeply involved in this, ... I will also say something of the historic background and of the aftermath of the decision to concentrate a major part of the British war effort on the destruction of German housing ... . The origin of the Allied bombing offensive ... was [in] the rise of the air forces of the world and of their determination to evolve a strategic role for air power that would have made them independent of the two older services, the army and the navy. Since this requirement excluded cooperation with either of these two services as its major role, the air force sought the strategic role of attacking the sources of economic and military power in the enemy country ... .
>
> From my talks with Lindemann at this time I became aware of that trait of character which Snow so well emphasized; this was his *almost fanatical belief in some particular operation or gadget* to the *almost total exclusion of wider considerations*. Bombing to him then seemed the one and only useful operation of the war ... .
>
> If the Allied air effort had been used more intelligently, if more aircraft had been supplied for the Battle of the Atlantic and to support the land fighting in Africa and later in France, if the bombing of Germany had been carried out with the attrition of the enemy defences in mind rather than the razing of cities to the ground, I believe the war could have been won half a year or even a year earlier. The only major campaign in modern history in which the traditional military doctrine of waging war against the enemy's armed forces was abandoned for a planned attack on its civilian life was a disastrous flop. I confess to *a haunting sense of personal failure*, and I am sure that Tizard felt the same way. *If we had only been more persuasive* and had forced people to believe our simple arithmetic, *if we had fought officialdom more cleverly and lobbied* ministers more vigorously, might we not have changed this decision?[35] (italics supplied)

The key to Professor Blackett's regret, and to the consequent "haunting

---

[35] P.M.S. Blackett, "Science and Government", *Scientific American*, April, 1961.

sense of personal failure", is the lack of "homely" communication with the decision-maker. It is this lack of communication which denied the decision-makers the wisdom of his counsel. It should be recognized that by lack of communication, we do not imply that Professor Blackett did not put forth his ideas in intelligible language; on the contrary, on a matter of such vital importance as that of changing the entire history: of "waging war against the enemy's armed forces" being "abandoned for a planned attack on its civilian life", Professor Blackett, indeed, would have tried hard to communicate. But the results of this effort were far from satisfactory. He wistfully wonders: "If we had only been more persuasive and had forced people to believe our simple arithmetic."

The opposition was far too strong. As a matter of fact, it shows the imperative necessity of having the ear of the right people. In this matter, Professor Blackett simply did not have the ear of the right people. He was successful when he did, as in the case of the convoy escort discussed in Section 3. It will be recalled that the very problem was brought to surface at the "Prime Minister's fortnightly U-boat meetings". However, with respect to the larger question of strategic bombing of Germany, it was Professor Lindemann who had the Prime Minister's ear. It is striking to note that in his talks with Lindemann, Blackett found him to be obsessed with a *"particular operation or gadget"*, to the almost total exclusion of "wider considerations". In other words, Lindemann was so bent on seeing the trees that he would not see the forest. And Blackett did not have access to Churchill so that he could effectively counter the narrow and gadgetry point of view that was being espoused by the "most successful court politician of the age".

Communication is thus not merely a matter of content; but as much, if not more, one of context: to whom, when, and how. The "simple arithmetic" of Sir Henry Tizard and Professor Blackett did not get through to Churchill, as the simple calculations of E.J. Williams got through to the Admiralty. The success of Professor Blackett with respect to *tactical problems* was due to the *content* and the *context* of the communication. His administrative position directly reporting to the decision-maker at the various commands, provided the right context for the content that he had to communicate in the case of *tactical questions*. In the case of the wider *strategic question*, he had the content but not the context. The content of communication is a necessary condition, but not a sufficient condition for successful decision-making. The content and the context of the communication together are what constitute the necessary and sufficient conditions for successful decision-making.

7. "The Heroic Age is Over; ... Extension of [Operations Research] Hardly Likely to be Rewarding to First-Rate Scientists"[36]

With the unquestionable success in several tactical questions and the clear failure with respect to some strategic questions, the question arises as to whether there is any future to the activity known as Operations Research. Six years after the War, reviewing the first book on Operations Research published in the United States, the British mathematician, Bronowski decidedly felt that there was nothing more worth doing. He felt that the extension of Operations Research "to the larger economics of whole industries and nations" was "hardly likely to be rewarding to first-rate scientists". In his words:

> The heroic age is over; and dropping with a sigh the glamour and the heady sense of power, we have to face the recognition that the field of opportunity will never again be quite so blank, so simple, and so lavish. What was new and speculative on the battlefield turns out, in the practical affairs of industry, to become only a painstaking combination of cost accounting, job analysis, time and motion study and the general integration of plant flow. There is an extension of this to the larger economics of whole industries and nations, but it is hardly likely to be rewarding to first-rate scientists and calls at bottom for the immense educational task of interesting economists and administrators in the mathematics of differentials and of prediction.[37]

Five years later, James R. Newman in his commentary on Operations Research in Volume 4 of *The World of Mathematics*, concurred with Bronowski's view when he said:

> The examples are confined to military problems but I should point out that, having got a start in the war, operations research is now being extended to engineering, to communication, to coal mining, to business, to manufacture, and to other branches of industry. The new problems are not as easy or as enticing as were many of the military services (even the art of war, now that the simple

[36] J. Bronowski, Review of *Methods of Operations Research, op. cit.*, p. 77.
[37] J. Bronowski, *Ibid.*, p. 77.

mistakes have been put right, offers a less "creamy surface to skim") and opinions differ as to whether first-class men will find satisfaction in such work. I incline to Bronowski's view ... .[38]

Perhaps Bronowski's dour prediction of the decline and fall of operations research is more readily understandable than that of James Newman. For one thing, Newman saw five years of post-war activity in operations research; and he lists the several areas wherein operations research was applied. For another, Newman must have had available to him several titles in operations research which had made their appearance during 1951—56. It could well be that even if he perused them, the importance of some of the fundamental findings, which are obvious today in the light of experience, may well have been hidden from the reader at the time these fundamental documents originated.

Since this volume develops the mathematical and analytical framework which constitute the basis of applied operations research, we shall now take a quick historical glance at the development of ideas and algorithms, for which we are heavily indebted to a group of innovators whom Bronowski and Newman foreswore as ever likely to be induced to take an interest — "first rate scientists", and "first-class men". It is quite possible that even the brief historic glimpses will enable us to echo the sentiments of Mark Twain who lived to be 75, well beyond the Biblical "days of our years [which are] three-score years and ten."[39] Prior to his death, in fact 13 years ahead, a whole host of obituaries appeared in the press; whereupon, he cabled the Associated Press from London: "The reports of my death are greatly exaggerated."[40]

8. Development of Operations Research: (1) Mathematical Foundations — Linear Programming

The stimulus for the development of the mathematical foundations of opera-

[38] James R. Newman, *The World of Mathematics*, Simon and Schuster, New York, 1956, p. 2159.
[39] *Holy Bible*, King James version, Psalms 90 : 10.
[40] Mark Twain, Cable from London to the Associated Press, 1897, quoted in John Bartlett, *Bartlett's Familiar Quotations*, Fourteenth Edition, Little, Brown and Company, Boston, 1968, p. 763.

tions research in the United States came from the postwar demands of the U.S. Air Force. The optimum relationship between the goals and activities of a given U.S. Air Force plan defied solution by the then available tools of analysis, in particular, Wassily W. Leontief's input-output analysis which was first published in 1936,[41] with a fuller exposition five years later.[42] To meet the problem, George B. Dantzig developed in 1947 a technique for planning the diversified activities of the U.S. Air Force.[43] In a volume published 11 years later, the contribution of Dantzig's method is recalled:

> The novelty in Dantzig's problem arises from the fact that in Leontief's scheme there is only a *single set of sector output* levels that is consistent with a specified pattern of final products, while in Air Force planning, or in planning for any similar organization, there are generally found to be *several different plans* that fulfill the goals. Thus a criterion is needed for deciding which of these satisfactory plans is best, and a procedure is needed for actually finding the best plan ... . It is necessary to consider a number (perhaps large) of *interconnected partial production functions*, one for each type of activity in the organization. The technique of *linear programming* is designed to handle this type of problem. The solution of the linear-programming problem for the Air Force stimulated two lines of development. First was the application of the technique to *managerial planning* in other contexts.[44] A group at the Carnegie Institute of Technology took the lead in this direction.[45] Second, a number of economists, with T.C. Koopmans[46] perhaps in the forefront, began exploring the implications of the new approach for economic theory generally.[47] (italics supplied)

[41] Wassily W. Leontief, "Quantitative Input and Output Relations in the Economic System of the United States", *Review of Economic Statistics,* August 1936, pp. 105–125.
[42] Wassily W. Leontief, *The Structure of American Economy, 1919–1929,* Harvard University Press, Cambridge, 1941.
[43] George B. Dantzig, "Maximization of a Linear Function of Variables Subject to Linear Inequalities", Circularized privately since 1947, and published in Tjalling C. Koopmans (ed.), *Activity Analysis of Production and Allocation*, Wiley, New York, 1951, pp. 339–347.
[44] Abraham Charnes and W.W. Cooper, *Management Models and Industrial Applications of Linear Programming*, Volumes I, II, Wiley, New York, 1961.
[45] Abraham Charnes, W.W. Cooper and B. Mellon, "Blending Aviation Gasolines: A Study in Programming Interdependent Activities in an Integrated Oil Company", *Econometrica*, April, 1952, pp. 135–139.
[46] Tjalling C. Koopmans (ed.), *Activity Analysis of Production and Allocation*, Wiley, New York, 1951.
[47] Robert Dorfman, Paul A. Samuelson and Robert M. Solow, *Linear Programming and Economic Analysis*, McGraw-Hill, New York, 1958, pp. 3–4.

The first conference on "linear programming" was held in Chicago at the Cowles Commission for Research in Economics, June 20–24, 1949. The interdisciplinary nature of the interest in the new tool was reflected in the composition of the conference – mathematicians, statisticians, economists, and administrators. The origin of the term "linear programming" is explained by Tjalling C. Koopmans who edited the conference volume:

> The name of the conference topic, "linear programming", requires explanation. In earlier phases of the work reported on in this volume, contacts and exchanges of ideas among its authors were stimulated by a common interest in the formal *problem of maximization of a linear function of variables subject to linear inequalities*. The term "linear programming" became a convenient designation for the class of allocation or programming problems which give rise to that maximization problem.[48] (italics supplied)

In presenting one of his papers to the conference, Dantzig refers to an earlier model developed by John von Neumann. Von Neumann's paper was developed as a contribution to the mathematical seminar conducted in Vienna in 1933 by Karl Menger, where Karl Schlesinger[49] "formulated a suggestion, made also by Zeuthen[50] that economic theory should explain not only nonnegative prices and quantities produced of scarce goods but also which goods are scarce and which are free (i.e., have a zero price)."[51] This question of nonnegative prices was raised earlier by Neisser[52] and von Stackelberg.[53] According to Koopmans:

[48]Tjalling C. Koopmans (ed.), *op. cit.*, p. 5.
[49]Karl Schlesinger, "Über die Produktionsgleichungen der ökonomischen Wertehre", *Ergebnisse eines mathematischen Kolloquiums,* No. 6, Franz Deuticke, Leipzig, 1935, pp. 10–11.
[50]F. Zeuthen, "Das Prinzip der Knappheit, technische Kombination und ökonomische Qualität", *Zeitschrift für Nationalökonomie*, Vol. 7, No. 1, 1933, pp. 1–24.
[51]Tjalling C. Koopmans (ed.), *op. cit.*, p. 1.
[52] Hans Neiser, "Lohnhohe und Beschaftigungsgrad im Marktgleichgewicht", *Weltwirtschaftliches Archiv*, Vol. 36, 1932, pp. 413–455.
[53]Heinrich von Stackelberg, "Zwei kritische Bemerkungen zur Preistheorie Gustav Cassels", *Zeitschrift für Nationalökonomie*, Vol. 4, No. 4, 1933, pp. 456–472.

Wald[54],[55],[56] proved the existence and uniqueness of a solution to an equation system expressing this problem. His discussion concerned a static model of production in which each commodity in demand can be produced in one way (a given amount of production requiring the input of proportional amounts of primary factors of production). He assumed that the total availabilities of primary factors are given by nature and that there is a given static structure of demand (demand functions satisfying a monotonicity condition).

In a later contribution to the same seminar [Karl Menger's mathematical seminar in 1933], von Neumann[57],[58] generalized this model of production in several directions. He introduced alternative methods of producing given commodities singly or jointly, each method again involving fixed technological coefficients (ratios between inputs and outputs). Thus he derived not only *which goods are free* but also which productive activities (methods) go *unused*. Also, a commodity could appear *simultaneously as input* of one activity *and* as *output* of another. This circularity idea was extended even to goods demanded by consumers, through the somewhat forced concept of an activity producing labor by the absorption of consumption goods in fixed proportions. The model thus became a closed one, with no inflow of primary factors from outside or outflow of final products out of the system considered ... . Like Wald, von Neumann treated prices (including an interest rate) as determined in competitive markets so as to satisfy a *zero profit condition* on all activities engaged in.[59]

The "programming of interdependent activities", which Dantzig presented to the conference on linear programming opens with the reference to the von Neumann model and to the Leontief model:

[54] Abraham Wald, "Über die eindeutige positive Lösbarkeit der neuen Produktionsgleichungen", *Ergebnisse eines mathematischen Kolloquiums*, No. 6, Franz Deuticke, Leipzig, 1935, pp. 12–20.

[55] Abraham Wald, "Über die Produktionsgleichungen der ökonomischen Wertlehre", *Ergebnisse eines mathematischen Kolloquiums*, No. 7, Franz Deuticke, Leipzig, 1936, pp. 1–6.

[56] Abraham Wald, "Über einige Gleichungsysteme der mathematischen Ökonomie", *Zeitschrift für Nationalökonomie*, Vol. 7, No. 5, 1936, pp. 637–670.

[57] John von Neumann, Über ein ökonomisches Gleichungsystem und eine Verallgemeinerung des Brouwerschen Fixpunktsatzes", *Ergebnisse eines mathematischen Kolloquiums*, No. 8, Franz Deuticke, Leipzig, 1935–36, pp. 73–83.

[58] John von Neumann, "A Model of General Economic Equilibrium", *Review of Economic Studies*, Vol. 13, No. 1, 1945–46, pp. 1–9.

[59] Tjalling C. Koopmans (ed.), *op. cit.*, pp. 1–2.

The mathematical model discussed here and in Chapter 11[60] is a generalization of the Leontief interindustry model. *It is closely related to the one formulated by von Neumann*. Its chief points of difference lie in its emphasis on dynamic rather than equilibrium or steady states. Its *purpose is close control* of an organization – hence it must be quite detailed; it is designed to handle highly dynamic problems – hence it puts greater emphasis on time lags and capital equipment; it takes into consideration the many different ways of doing things – hence it explicitly introduces alternative activities; and it recognizes that any particular choice of a dynamic program depends on the *"objectives" of the "economy"* – hence the selection and types of activities are made to depend on the *maximization of an objective function.*[61] (italics supplied)

A mathematical development of profound consequence arose from Dantzig's maximization of this objective function. His original paper on the subject (referred to in footnote 43) establishes the history of the development of the Simplex Method of linear programming:

> The author wishes to acknowledge that his work on this subject stemmed from discussions in the spring of 1947 with Marshall K. Wood, in connection with Air Force programming methods. The general nature of the *"simplex"* approach (as the method discussed here is known) was stimulated by discussions with Leonid Hurwicz.
> The author is indebted to T.C. Koopmans, whose constructive observations regarding properties of the *simplex* led directly to a proof of the method in the early fall of 1947 .... The purpose of this chapter is to discuss the so-called *"simplex"* techniques, which consist in constructing first a feasible, and then a maximum feasible, solution.[62] (italics supplied)

Following the publication in 1951 of Dantzig's paper, a number of practical applications of the simplex method were reported. Developments in the theory of linear programming and computational methods kept up with the pace of applications, and, in turn, contributed to further applications. In the second symposium on linear programming, the progress in the field was re-

[60]George B. Dantzig, "The Programming of Interdependent Activities: Mathematical Model", in Tjalling C. Koopmans (ed.), *op. cit.,* p. 19–32.
[61]Marshall K. Wood and George B. Dantzig, "The Programming of Interdependent Activities: General Discussion", in Tjalling C. Koopmans (ed.), *op. cit.,* p. 15.
[62]George B. Dantzig, "Maximization of a Linear Function of Variables Subject to Linear Inequalities", in Tjalling C. Koopmans (ed.), *op. cit.,* p. 339, 340.

viewed, *inter alia*, by R. Bellman, A. Charnes, W.W. Cooper, G.B. Dantzig, J. Marschak, L.W. McKenzie, A. Orden, G. Tintner, and A.W. Tucker.[63]

9. Development of Operations Research: (2) Mathematical Foundations – Dynamic Programming

One of the contributors to the second symposium on linear programming, as pointed out above, was Richard Bellman of the RAND Corporation. RAND originated in late 1948 growing out of Project Research and Development of Douglas Aircraft Corporation. RAND's mission was well expressed by the first Chairman of the Board, Rowen Gaither, in one of his last public statements, made to the Board of the RAND Corporation on the occasion of its tenth anniversary in 1958:

> The war in which we will be engaged for years to come places burdens unprecedented in their *complexity and consequence* upon our government ... . I am sure that I do not have to prove to this Board that political as well as physical survival may well turn on the speed and efficiency with which technology is converted into weapons and weapon systems ... . Not only must these [our intellectual, our scientific and our economic] resources be readily available, but they must be competent, they must be responsible. We must find the *organizational instrumentalities for bringing our resources to bear on the task of survival* by assuring their responsible availability to government.[64] (italics supplied)

RAND's response to the challenge to bring "our resources to bear on the task of survival" in the form of systems analysis, is discussed in Section 11. Our present discussion focuses upon the mathematical developments at RAND which provided an operational means to cope with the "complexity and consequence" of technological developments which, as Chairman Gaither pointed out, "places burdens unprecedented". The question of complexity and consequence are by no means confined to weapons and weapons systems. Exploration of space is clearly an example.

[63] H.A. Antosiewicz, (ed.), *Proceedings of the Second Symposium in Linear Programming*, Volumes I, II, National Bureau of Standards, Washington, D.C., 1955.
[64] Rowen A. Gaither, *Report to 10th Anniversary Session*, RAND Corporation, Santa Monica, Calif., November 21, 1958, unpublished; quoted in Charles J. Hitch, *Decision-Making for Defense*, University of California, Berkeley, 1967, p. 4.

One of the consequences of a highly complex problem like space mission, is that its solution is plagued with "the curse of dimensionality".[65] Direct enumeration of *all* the alternative values that could be assumed by each variable becomes virtually an unattainable goal; not that even if direct enumeration were possible, it would provide aids to decision-making. Can some means be found by which the enumeration could be *reduced* to practical dimensions, so that a decision can be made on the space mission, which has *never* been attempted *before*, and which comprises some 20 000 elements in the *spacecraft* component of the mission *alone*? For this, the classical techniques of calculus and calculus of variations "were clearly limited in range and versatility, and were definitely lacking as far as furnishing numerical answers was concerned."[66]

The original continuous variational problem, such as the trajectory of the spacecraft, has to be first replaced by a discrete variational problem, for which an objective function has to be maximized. Bellman points out the technical infeasibility of total enumeration, even for a small problem:

> To begin, consider a simple situation where each of the independent variables x_i can run over ten different values. The N-variables maximization process will then involve 10^N different sets of choices ... .
>
> For a ten-stage process, we will then have 10^{10} cases to examine. This may not seem to be a very large quantity, but a small amount of calculation gives some idea of its true magnitude. At the rate of examination of one set of x_i-values per millisecond, 10^7 seconds would be required. This is something more than 10^5 hours, and thus of the order of magnitude of ten years. This is an unreasonable amount of time to spend on the numerical solution of a problem which represents reality as crudely as the one we have posed.
>
> Suppose that we wish to consider a slightly more complex problem in which there are twenty different activities. Arguing loosely, as above, assume that this involves 10^{20} different possibilities. Since this quantity is 10^{10} times as large as 10^{10}, we see that no matter how much we reduce the time of the search process, this exponential growth in the number of possibilities as the dimension of the process increases renders enumeration of cases impossible ... .
>
> How is it, nonetheless, that the technique of dynamic programming enables one to easily and quickly resolve problems of far more complex nature than the type described above? ... .

[65] Richard Bellman, *Dynamic Programming*, Princeton University Press, Princeton, 1957, p. ix.
[66] Richard E. Bellman and Stuart E. Dreyfus, *Applied Dynamic Programming*, Princeton University Press, Princeton, 1962, p. vii.

It is the *principle of optimality* that furnishes the key. This principle tells us that having chosen some initial x_N, we do not then examine *all* policies involving that particular choice of x_N, but rather only those policies which are optimal for an N-1 stage process with resources $x - x_N$. In this magical way, we keep operations essentially additive rather than multiplicative. The time required for a twenty-stage process is now almost precisely twice the time required for a ten-stage process.[67]

Dynamic Programming contributes more to *formulating the problem*, than to solving it. Without dynamic programming, problems of great complexity, such as that of the space mission, would defy solution. However, once the *structure* of the problem is understood, several computational methods can be employed to find solutions. According to Bellman, *"The problem is not to be considered solved in the mathematical sense until the structure of the optimal policy is understood."*[68]

The basic ideas of dynamic programming were developed during 1949–52. The "principle of optimality" is a particular application of what Bellman called "principle of invariant imbedding". The *functional equation* governing the multi-stage allocation process under study is obtained by an application of the principle of optimality, and is related to the "Point of Regeneration" method used in the study of branching processes.[69] The basic ideas of dynamic programming were elaborated in a monograph in 1953, which is the first publication of the original paper on dynamic programming.[70]

10. Development of Operations Research: (3) Mathematical Foundations – Theory of Games

The originators of linear programming and dynamic programming, both acknowledge their indebtedness to, or the antecedence of their research to John von Neumann. Thus, George Dantzig says:

[67]Richard E. Bellman and Stuart E. Dreyfus, *op. cit.,* pp. 19, 20.
[68]Richard E. Bellman, *Dynamic Programming*, Princeton University Press, Princeton, 1957; p. ix.
[69]R. Bellman and T. Harris, "On Age-Dependent Binary Branching Processing", *Annals of Mathematics*, Vol. 55, 1952, pp. 280–295.
[70]Richard Bellman, "An Introduction to the Theory of Dynamic Programming", RAND Corporation, Santa Monica, Calif., 1953.

J. von Neumann first pointed out [1947] that a game problem can be reduced to a program problem. He was also the first to point out that a problem concerning the maximizing of a linear form whose variables are subject to a system of linear inequalities could be replaced by a solution to an extended system of linear inequalities. This result depends on the use of an important lemma on inequalities stated in the last section of this chapter.[71]

Richard Bellman acknowledges his indebtedness to von Neumann and to Wald:

> Finally, before ending this prologue, it is a pleasure to acknowledge my indebtedness to a number of sources: First, to the von Neumann theory of games as developed by J. von Neumann, O. Morgenstern, and others, a theory which shows how to treat by mathematical analysis vast classes of problems formerly far out of the reach of the mathematician — and relegated, therefore, to the limbo of imponderables — and, simultaneously, to the Wald theory of sequential analysis, as developed by A. Wald, D. Blackwell, A. Girshick, J. Wolfowitz, and others, a theory which shows the vast economy of effort that may be effected by the proper consideration of multi-stage testing processes; second, to a number of colleagues and friends who have discussed various aspects of the theory with me and contributed to its clarification and growth.[72]

Further, Bellman (with co-author Dreyfus) dedicates the second book on dynamic programming published five years after the first, "To the Memory of John von Neumann — Inspiration and Friend."[73]

When he was 23, John von Neumann presented his first paper on game theory to the Mathematical Society of Gottingen, in which he had worked out a rational strategy for matching pennies. The main theorem of theory of games, known as the Minimax Theorem, proves the existence of a way of playing the game in such a way that, *no matter what one's opponent does*, player A will not get any less than a specified outcome (MaxMin), and player B will not have to pay any more than a specified outcome (MinMax)[74]

---

[71]George B. Dantzig, "A Proof of the Equivalence of the Programming Problem and the Game Problem", in Tjalling Koopmans (ed.), *op. cit.*, p. 330.

[72]Richard Bellman, *Dynamic Programming*, Princeton University Press, Princeton, 1957, p. xvii.

[73]*Ibid.*, p. 5.

[74]J. von Neumann, "Zur Theorie der Gesellschaftsspiele", *Math. Annalen*, Vol. 100, 1928, pp. 295–320.

Sixteen years later, von Neumann and Oskar Morgenstern published the basic work on theory of games.[75] The latter part of the title, "economic behavior", discloses the economic context of the mathematical development, even as in the case of linear programming, where George Dantzig emphasizes the *dynamic* aspects of interdependent activities, as distinguished from the *static* aspects of the von Neumann formulation in 1945 (see footnote 58).

We noted that dynamic programming makes manageable for the first time, problems which are *multi-dimensional*, with decisions which are *multi-stage*. Theory of games makes manageable for the first time, *not* problems of maximization (as handled by linear programming, and formulated by dynamic programming), but problems with a *mixture of maximum problems*.

There are two basic contributions of theory of games. The first is the notion of the *mixture of maximum* problems which arises from the *parallelism of interests* of the two players, A and B. The authors say: "The *aim* of all participants in the social economy, consumers as well as entrepreneurs, is assumed to be money or a single monetary commodity; and further this is supposed to be identical with utility."[76] Both A and B want to maximize the gains from the game that they play; hence the parallelism of interests. What the Minimax Theorem assures is that irrespective of his opponent's actions, A can be assured of minimizing his losses, and B of maximizing his gains, provided they employ the Minimax *strategy* (which is nothing more than a sequence of moves employed at each occasion of play).

The second major contribution of the theory of games is the *formation of coalitions* when there are more than two players. Players A and B will form a coalition against player C, only if the coalition can obtain *more* than what individual members of the coalition could obtain. Since this additional gain has to come from none other than player C (the algebraic sum of the gains of each player being zero: hence zero-sum), player C could induce player A or B to join with him in a coalition against player B or A. Which of the possible coalitions (A and B against C; A and C against B; and B and C against A) will be formed will depend upon, *not* the certainty of outcome, but the *probability of outcome* at each stage of the play. Nor does the coalition have to be permanent. In one play, A and B could be a coalition against C; in another play, A and C could be against B, and so on.

[75] J. von Neumann and Oskar Morgenstern, *Theory of Games and Economic Behavior*, Princeton University Press, Princeton, 1944.

[76] J. von Neumann and Oskar Morgenstern, *op. cit.*, p. 8.

In terms of application, theory of games lags well behind linear programming and dynamic programming. However, in terms of its presentation of alternative views of questions of national strategy, theory of games thinking has served to clarify issues, and crystallize alternatives. As J.D. Williams put it: "The concept of a strategy, the distinctions among players, the role of chance events, the notion of matrix representation of the payoffs, the concepts of pure and mixed strategies, and so on give valuable orientation to persons who must think about complicated conflict situations."[77] Ten years later, Clayton J. Thomas referred to the "no soft spots" principle according to which "each defended target yields the same payoff to the attacker and the undefended targets yield less" [78] as having had much application:

> The principle of "no soft spots" has been of tremendous value in the allocation of defenses. This derives in part from its appeal as a simple unifying concept. Also of importance, however, has been the recognition of the principle by key personnel and their ingenious applications of it in defense planning over a period of several years. This has given a mathematical framework within which to fit otherwise unrelated observations. It has aided in the evaluation of different weapon systems and different defense systems. The principle has served as the point of departure for other interesting investigations also, like the search for a method of dividing a budget between strategic offense forces and continental defense forces.[79]

11. Development of Operations Research: (4) "Prologues"[80] to Policy – Systems Analysis

In Section 9 we referred to the response of RAND Corporation to its mission

[77] J.D. Williams, *The Compleat Strategyst*, McGraw-Hill, New York, 1954, p. 217.
[78] Melvin Dresher, "Mathematical Models of Conflict", in E.S. Quade and W.I. Boucher (eds.), *Systems Analysis and Policy Planning*, American Elsevier, New York, 1968, p. 239.
[79] C.J. Thomas, "Some Past Applications of Game Theory in the United States Air Force", Paper presented at the NATO Conference on the Theory of Games and Its Military Applications, June 29–July 3, 1964, Toulon, France.
[80] Macbeth: [Aside] "Two truths are told,
　　　　　　As happy prologues to the swelling act
　　　　　　Of the imperial theme – I thank you, gentlemen."
William Shakespeare, *Macbeth*, Gosset and Dunlap, New York, 1911, Act I, Scene III, 1. 128.

to "find the organizational instrumentalities for bringing our resources to bear on the task of survival" in the form of *systems analysis*. The new terminology came with new responsibilities in the '50s, in some sense paralleling the broadening of scope of operations research studies from tactics to strategy attempted in Great Britain.

We saw in Section 1.1 that, according to Professor Blackett, the main fields of operations research were: "The study of weapons, the study of tactics, and the study of strategy." The most successful efforts of "Blackett's Circus" would be properly regarded as *tactical*, the major failure of operations research in influencing *strategy* being related to the British decision to bomb German housing.

Reflecting on the change in RAND's own efforts from the tactical to the strategic questions, and from the purely quantitative to the qualitative and the analytical methods, Edward S. Quade says:

> In the early phases of systems analysis, the studies were highly preoccupied with the analytic techniques of operations research – linear programming and game theory, for example. Complicated mathematical models, featuring an astronomically large number of machine computations designed to pick out the optimum system, were popular. We soon realized, however, that real-world defense planning was *too complicated for* such a *purely quantitative approach* ... . We now realize that the impact of subjective considerations – such as the system's flexibility, its compatibility with other systems (some yet unborn), its contributions to national prestige abroad, and its effect on domestic political constraints – can play as important a role in the choice of alternatives as any calculation of war outcomes. In addition, we realize that such *intangibles* as the extent to which superiority in residual forces can be effectively used to coerce the enemy to discontinue the conflict, or the perception each side has of its own or its enemy's strengths, must be taken into account. Thus, it should be no surprise that many of the component studies, and even a major part of the over-all analysis, are *verbal rather than quantitative* in nature ... .
>
> Thus, RAND's *first defense study* focused its attention on the *tactics* for shooting down enemy bombers. Today, the corresponding study would look for the less obvious values of defense, relate active defense to other military missions, consider the use of warning systems for surveillance and related "nonspasm" uses, investigate the different kinds of contingencies in which defense might be useful, and so on ... .
>
> The term "systems analysis" came into use because the first postwar efforts were concerned with the selection and evaluation of *weapon systems* for development ... . (italics supplied)
>
> Systems analysis ... can be characterized as *a systematic approach to helping a*

decisionmaker choose a course of action by investigating his full problem, searching out objectives and alternatives, and comparing them in the light of their consequences, using an appropriate framework — in so far as possible analytic — to bring expert judgment and intuition to bear on the problem. [81]

The selection of weapons systems (several of which are yet unborn) necessarily becomes a question of weighing not only the capability of the predicted systems, but also their potential use. The former could be expressed quantitatively; but not the latter, at least in the initial go-around. Nor is the role of the *qualitative* confined to the weapon systems as a whole; it can play a crucial role even in projecting the technological feasibility from the past and the present into the future.

We shall consider two examples, one in which technical feasibility considerations, which made a critical difference in the very creation of the system, were initiated in *qualitative* terms; and another in which the broadening of the purely deployment question was initiated in *qualitative* terms, again making a critical difference in the design for the effective use of the weapons system.

12. APPLICATION 5: Technological Anticipation — Polaris

The first example relates to *Polaris*. According to Whitmore:

> In the summer of 1957, a Navy study group known as Project NOBSKA developed reasons for recommending the use of ballistic missiles from submarines, but was somewhat appalled by the actual embodiment of the system built about the solid propellant version of JUPITER, utilizing a payload basically intended for ICBM ranges. Edward Teller was a consultant to NOBSKA, and made the simple observation "why use a 1958 warhead in a 1965 weapons system?" He went on to indicate that radically smaller and lighter warheads should be available on a compatible time scale to the submarine development. He could not spell these out in detail, but produced historical evidence of the trends in warhead dimensions which was convincing enough to set the pace of design for what became *Polaris*. Here again, there was much painful and analytical work to be done, including an intensive three months' study of all the weapons systems parameters by govern-

---

[81] E.S. Quade and W.I. Boucher, *Systems Analysis and Policy Planning — Applications in Defense*, American Elsevier, New York, 1968, pp. 14, 15, 3, 2.

ment agencies and contractors. But the germ of the whole idea – the thing which turned the FBM from a monster into a weapon (as one eminent consultant remarked) – was in Teller's remark.[82]

The "historical evidence of the trends in warhead dimensions" which Teller recounted to give credence to the possibility that smaller and lighter warheads should be available for a future weapons system, eight years thence, could not have been primarily quantitative. Quantities were definitely involved in the measurements of successive dimensions. However, what is important was the *qualititative* judgments which Teller made on the basis of the "hunch" that it should be possible to develop radically smaller and lighter warheads out of miniature electronic equipments, only prototypes of which were available at the time of prognostication. The remark "Why use a 1958 warhead in a 1965 weapons system?" is the key to Teller's foresight, which made the critical difference in the very design for what became *Polaris*.

Teller's contribution was in viewing the weapons system *as a whole*. It was this view which enabled him to postulate a technologically feasible system. The primary contribution was a *qualitative insight* – which was followed by intensive *quantitative studies* before the decision was made.

13. APPLICATION 6: Overseas Base Construction for U.S. Air Force

The second example relates to the positioning of Strategic Air Command (SAC) bombers. According to Quade:

> For fiscal year 1952, Congress authorized approximately $3.5 billion for air base construction, about half to be spent overseas. RAND was asked to suggest ways to acquire, construct, and maintain air bases in foreign countries at minimum cost. The analyst who reluctantly took on this problem regarded it at first as essentially one of logistics. He spent a long time – several months, in fact – thinking about it before he organized a study team. Although he had little of the information needed to make recommendations, he was able to see the *problem in relation to the Air Force as a whole.* He came to the conclusion that the real problem was *not* one of the logistics of foreign air bases, but the much *broader* one of where and how to base the nation's strategic air forces and how to operate them in

---

[82]William F. Whitmore, "Military Operations Research – A Personal Retrospect", *Operations Research*, March–April, 1961, p. 263.

conjunction with the base system chosen. He argued that base choice would critically affect the composition, destructive power, and cost of the *entire strategic force* and thus that it was not wise to rest a decision about base structure and location merely on economy in base cost alone. His views prevailed and he led the broader study, the results of which contributed to an Air Force decision to base SAC bombers in the continental United States and use overseas installations only for refueling and restaging.[83] An Air Force committee later estimated that the study recommendations *saved over $1 billion in construction costs alone.* In addition, it sparked a tremendous improvement in strategic capability, particularly with regard to survival, and stimulated, a good deal of additional research on related questions.[84] (italics supplied)

The $1 billion *savings* resulted from the broadening of considerations initiated in *qualitative* terms. These qualitative considerations overrode the several quantitative considerations given in the terms of reference. The reason why the analyst overrode them was because he considered the "problem in relation to the *Air Force as a whole*". It is this point of view which transformed the purely *tactical* question of selecting foreign air bases into the *strategic question* of selecting and *using* SAC air bases.

It is precisely in this area of providing assurance that the model is meaningful that systems analysis has no adequate theory to offer guidance. Once the problems are modeled, then their manipulation becomes possible, and quite often successful. According to Quade:

... systems analysis is a fairly new discipline, and history teaches us that good theory usually comes late in the development of any field and after many false starts. Where the attention of systems analysis has turned to methods, it has focused mainly on the development of mathematical techniques for handling certain specialized problems, common in the practice of operations research — rather than on building a basic theory for the treatment of the broad questions typical in defense planning. This attention to technique *has* met with great success. Models have become easier to manipulate, even with many more variables represented, and the computational obstacles in systems analysis now cause comparatively little difficulty. The more important philosophical problems, however,

[83] A.J. Wohlstetter, F.S. Hoffman, R.J. Lutz and H.S. Rowen, *Selection and Use of Strategic Air Bases*, The RAND Corporation, R–266, April, 1954.
[84] E.S. Quade, "Principles and Procedures of Systems Analysis", in E.S. Quade and W.I. Boucher (eds.), *Systems Analysis and Policy Planning – Applications in Defense*, American Elsevier, New York, 1968, pp. 36–37.

such as occur in providing assurance that the model is meaningful, in devising schemes to compensate for uncertainty, or in choosing appropriate measures of effectiveness, still remain troublesome.[85]

14. Development of Operations Research: (5) Prologues to Policy — Program Budgeting*

The substantial costs, associated with the development of new weapons systems in the postwar period, were to be spread over increasingly longer periods from development to deployment as the weapons grew in complexity. With longer intervals between development and deployment, the true costs associated with any new weapon system became quite intractable in the once-a-year defense budgetary reviews. The Secretary of Defense had to pass on requests for *small segments* of weapon systems in various stages of research and development, with virtually no knowledge of when the systems in the early phases of development would, if ever, become operational; and if so at how much total cost.

The Honorable George H. Mahon, Chairman of the House Committee on Appropriations, addressed two letters to the Secretary of Defense on the subject of relating costs to mission. Charles J. Hitch, who became Assistant Secretary of Defense (Comptroller) in 1961, recalls these letters, as well as the parallel concern which he and his associates shared at RAND:

> In his first letter he stressed the importance of looking at the defense program and budget in terms of major military missions, by grouping programs and their cost by mission.[86] In his second letter, he called "for more useful information and for a practical means of relating costs to missions."[87]

[85]E.S. Quade, "Introduction", in E.S. Quade and W.I. Boucher (eds.), *op. cit.*, p. 18.
* Short for Planning-Programming-Budgeting System (PPBS).
[86]Letter from Representative George H. Mahon, Chairman of the House Subcommittee on Defense Appropriations, to Secretary of Defense Neil McElroy, August 18, 1959 (unpublished), quoted in Charles J. Hitch, *Decision-making for Defense*, University of California, Berkeley, 1967.
[87]Letter from Representative George H. Mahon, Chairman of the House Subcommittee on Defense Appropriations, to Secretary of Defense Thomas Gates, September 6, 1960 (unpublished), quoted in Charles J. Hitch, *Decision-Making for Defense*, University of California, Berkeley, 1967.

Many other students of the defense management problem had reached the same conclusion, including the group with which I had the honor to be associated at the RAND Corporation. Many of these conclusions found their way into a book, *The Economics of Defense in the Nuclear Age,* [88] which was published for the RAND Corporation in March 1960, some ten months before I was called upon as Assistant Secretary of Defense (Comptroller) to help introduce them into the Defense Department.[89]

Hitch presents the format of a program budget on page 56 of *The Economics of Defense in the Nuclear Age*, in which planning and budget structures are recast in terms of major programs related to mission. During his term as Assistant Secretary, Hitch introduced nine major programs, each of which contained program elements which, for decision purposes, because of either their supportive role or substitutional capabilities, could be considered as a group.

Once having introduced the programming function, Hitch proceeded to follow it up by associating the missions with their corresponding costs. The imprint of this innovation is seen in the DOD Directive issued on July 1, 1965, which recognizes three phases in the development of a weapons system: (1) concept formulation, (2) contract definition, and (3) full development. According to the Directive, the initial stage of concept formulation must demonstrate that the following have been accomplished:

1. Primarily engineering rather than experimental effort is required, and the technology needed is sufficiently in hand.
2. The mission and performance envelopes are defined.
3. The best technical approach has been selected.
4. A thorough trade-off analysis has been made.
5. The *cost-effectiveness* of the proposed item has been determined to be favorable in relationship to the *cost-effectiveness* of competing items on a DOD-wide basis. (italics supplied)
6. Cost and schedule estimates are credible and acceptable.[90]

[88]Charles J. Hitch and Roland N. McKean, *The Economics of Defense in the Nuclear Age*, Harvard University Press, Cambridge, 1960.
[89]Charles J. Hitch, *Decision-Making for Defense*, University of California Press, Berkeley, 1965, pp. 26–27.
[90]Office of the Secretary of Defense, *Initiation of Engineering and Operational Systems Development*, DOD Directive 3200.0, July 1, 1965.

The fifth prerequisite to progress from concept formulation to contract definition is the *cost-effectiveness* analysis. It should be noticed that two types of cost-effectiveness analyses have to be performed: (1) of the proposed item, (2) of competing item across the board.

The comparison of new proposed items with all other alternative ways of accomplishing the same mission was a logical sequel to the programming function which Hitch introduced into the Department of Defense. The new item would be a part of: (1) Strategic Retaliatory Forces, (2) Continental Defense Forces, (3) General Purpose Forces, (4) Airlift and Sealift, (5) Reserve and Guard, (6) Research and Development, (7) General Support, (8) Retired Pay, and (9) Military Assistance. Does the proposed item perform the mission, or contribute to performing one of the nine missions, more effectively than available alternatives?

The Strategic Retaliatory Forces and the Continental Defense Forces Program are two major programs in the context of a general nuclear war, while the General Purpose Forces are designed to fight local or limited conflicts. In each of the major programs, their component parts are organized along service lines. One of the functions of cost-effectiveness analysis is to determine that developments proposed by different Services are compared with each other, and against the mission of the major program element so that "competing items on a DOD-wide basis" are taken into account systematically in arriving at a final choice.

The sheer dimensions of DOD operations suggest the need for cost considerations on a massive scale — salaries and wages amounting to 40 percent of a \$50 billion budget, the remaining 60 percent being used for procurement every year. The value of the 1965 DOD inventory of equipment, weapons and supply was, according to Hitch, about \$135 billion. Says Hitch:

> Our principal installations and facilities number in the thousands, and we control nearly 15 000 square miles of land. Our military operations extend around the world, and we spend almost \$3 billion a year in other countries. [Therefore it is a small wonder that] I alluded, in connection with the first phase of the planning-programming-budgeting process, to the need for military-economic studies which compare alternative ways of accomplishing national security objectives and which try to determine the way that *contributes the most for a given cost* or *achieves a given objective for the least cost*. The extensive and comprehensive use of these *"cost-effectiveness"* studies or systems analyses was the *second major innovation*

introduced into the decision-making process of the Defense Department.[91]
(italics supplied)

The cost-effectiveness analysis must clearly have two components: (1) cost, and (2) effectiveness. When the costs are known, or knowable, there are no problems, except that of computation. Effectiveness, on the other hand, is less tractable. A given weapon system has not only to perform its mission (such as, successfully firing a weapon and hitting the target), but also establish its contribution to the larger mission of national security. On an elementary level, the number of "bulls-eyes" scored with a rifle can give a direct measure of its effectiveness. But if the targets are no longer specified (which are instead drawn from a probability distribution); if we are not allowed to fire the weapons at any of the targets (but merely have to project the performance under controlled and friendly conditions to uncontrolled and hostile encounters); and if we are asked to provide a measure of effectiveness in terms of the success of the yet unborn weapon, by itself and in consort with all other present and potential weapons, in *not* hitting any given number of enemy targets, but in *deterring* the potential enemy from launching the attack — we get a rough idea of the difficulties in developing satisfactory measures of effectiveness to which cost can be associated.

15.APPLICATION 7: Reduction of Titan II Force

These difficulties of cost-effectiveness analysis may be illustrated with respect to three major decisions: (1) the March 1961 decision to reduce the size of the Titan II force, (2) the December 1962 decision to cancel Skybolt, and (3) the April 1965 decision to ask for authority to build four Ro-Ro ships to be used as floating depots.

James R. Schlesinger*, Director of Strategic Studies and Senior Staff Member of RAND's Economics Department (which Hitch headed up before joining DOD) points out that the new Administration took a "quick and dirty look" at the force-structure program inherited from the Eisenhower administration. It should be recalled that the "missile gap" was a major premise of

[91]Charles J. Hitch, *Decision-Making for Defense*, University of California, Berkeley, 1967, pp. 22, 43.
* U.S. Secretary of Defense since 1973.

the decision. The emphasis was on a second-strike capability. In March 1961 the decisions were made to expand the Minuteman and Polaris force and to reduce both the size of and the emphasis upon the Titan II force. According to Schlesinger:

> The upshot was that, as a result of calculations based mainly on cost, decisions were made, in effect, against large payload missiles and for small payload missiles ... . It now is clear that major difficulties existed in formulating the early-on *cost-effectiveness studies which served as their basis*. On the one hand, there were major uncertainties regarding the size and character of prospective Soviet forces and also regarding the strategic concept that we would adopt. In addition, major technical uncertainties regarding both Minuteman and Titan II remained unresolved. As a consequence of these deficiencies in information, it was inevitable that only the *crudest observations* could be made regarding the *effectiveness component* of the decisionmaking schema. *Cost considerations, therefore, became dominant*. Yet, even here, because of the unresolved technical problems, not much confidence could be placed in the cost calculations. As it turned out, these calculations were strongly biased against Titan II because of the drastic underestimation of missile operations and maintenance costs. This favored the missile with the lower initial capital cost, that is, Minuteman.[92] (italics supplied)

16. APPLICATION 8: Cancellation of Skybolt

The second example relates to Skybolt. In 1960, President Eisenhower had agreed with Prime Minister MacMillan that the United States would provide Great Britain Skybolt air-to-ground missiles, which would be launched from a bomber in two stages. In the fall of 1961, McNamara decided to let the project proceed, based on what Hitch points out as "a gross underestimate of costs". In his words:

> ... we must recognize that if the objectives or the costs or the measurements of military effectiveness are wrong, the answers will also be wrong. The SKYBOLT air-to-ground missile is a case in point. A gross underestimate of costs in 1961 led to a decision to carry that project into the production stage. When the full dimensions of the ultimate cost later became apparent, the decision was made to drop the project since it was not worth the increased cost in the light of the other

---

[92] James R. Schlesinger, "The Changing Environment for Systems Analysis", in E.S. Quade and W.I. Boucher (eds.), *Systems Analysis and Policy Planning*, American Elsevier, New York, p. 381.

alternatives available, namely, expanding the MINUTEMAN force and retaining more of the HOUND DOG air-to-ground missiles which were already in the inventory. You may recall that this decision led to some very painful moments with our British colleagues as the United Kingdom had also planned to use the SKYBOLT missile with its bombers. Our decision to drop the project created some very difficult problems for the British Government at the time and led to a meeting at Nassau between President Kennedy and Prime Minister MacMillan.[93] Yet, no responsible military or civilian official in our Defense Department or, I believe, in the British Defense Ministry, would argue in favor of the SKYBOLT today [1965].[94]

17. APPLICATION 9: Cost Effective Sealift: Ro-Ro Ships

The third example relates to Ro-Ro ships. In Hitch's *The Economics of Defense in the Nuclear Age*, airlift was discussed, almost to the exclusion of sealift, which was regarded as too slow to be a competitor. However, five years later, Hitch reported that sealift could indeed be cost-effective. The development of this new view of sealift indicates the merit of cost-effectiveness, which emerges from Hitch's narrative:

> A great problem with prepositioning is the difficulty of acquiring real estate for the purpose in foreign countries and the likelihood that the real estate, if acquired, and the prepositioned stocks will turn out to be in the wrong country (or even the wrong continent) when hostilities actually threaten or break out. So this analyst thought: why not pre-position on ships? A pregnant thought. We now have many "forward floating depots" – Victory ships stocked with Army equipment – in the Western Pacific, ready to steam to any threatened area and substantially augmenting our airlift rapid deployment capability.
>
> At about the same time a more straightforward decision development or "invention" produced the Roll-on/Roll-off, or "Ro-Ro", ship which can rapidly load and unload Army vehicular equipment at even primitive ports.
>
> Then a third invention was made by an ingenious systems analyst who simply combined the characteristics of the forward floating depot and the Ro-Ro ship and developed an appropriate operational concept for the combination. This defi-

[93] See text of joint communique and "Statement on nuclear defense systems" issued by President Kennedy and Prime Minister MacMillan, December 21, 1962 at Nassau, the Bahamas, *New York Times*, December 22, 1962, p. 3.
[94] Charles J. Hitch, *Decision-Making for Defense*, University of California Press, Berkeley, 1967, pp. 55–56.

nitely made sealift competitive with airlift for rapid deployment in many situations, and we have asked Congress in the 1966 budget for four specially designed Ro-Ro's to be used as forward floating depots.[95]

18. Development of Operations Research: (6) Prologues to Policy — Policy Sciences

We said in Section 4.3 that a collection of specialists from different disciplines would have created nothing but a Babel of scientific dialects if they brought *only* their separate disciplines with them.

The need for an *interdisciplinary* approach to policy-making began to be recognized as newer methods and procedures were applied to larger and complex problems, of which neither the components nor the interaction among their multitudinous components being obvious to the decision-makers in the public and private sectors. As early as 1951, Professor Harold D. Lasswell[96] proposed a new term: *Policy Sciences* to identify the synthesis of skills from different disciplines to develop and communicate insight into interrelationships designed to improve decision making.

The concept of "policy sciences" is visualized as having application, not only to the domestic political scene, but also to development scenes abroad. For the latter purpose, Lasswell uses the term "policy sciences of development".[97]

It is significant that mathematician E.S. Quade of the RAND Corporation, who has edited two books on systems analysis, was the first editor of the new International Journal, *Policy Sciences*. In his first editorial, Quade defined the interdisciplinary nature of policy sciences resulting from the need "to bring the knowledge and procedures imbedded in the 'soft' or behavioral sciences into systems engineering and aerospace technology" and "to introduce the quantitative methods of systems analysis and operations research into the normal approaches by social and political scientists".[98]

[95]*Ibid.,* pp. 54–55.
[96]Harold D. Lasswell, "The Policy Orientation", in Daniel Lerner and Harold D. Lasswell (eds.), *The Policy Sciences: Recent Developments in Scope and Method*, Stanford University Press, Stanford, 1951, p. 3.
[97]Harold D. Lasswell, "The Policy Sciences of Development", *World Politics*, January, 1965, pp. 286–309.
[98]E.S. Quade, "Why Policy Sciences?", *Policy Sciences*, Vol. 1, No. 1, 1970, p. 1.

Professor Yehezkel Dror of the Hebrew University of Jerusalem has been an active proponent of policy sciences. During his 1968–70 visit to the United States as a Senior Professional Staff Member of the RAND Corporation, he identified more than 10 graduate university programs devoted to policy sciences:

> The graduate university programs about which I happen to know include, in no particular order: The program in public policy at the John F. Kennedy School at Harvard University; the Doctoral Program in Policy Sciences at the State University of New York at Buffalo; the Graduate School of Public Affairs at the University of California, Berkeley; the Doctorate Program in Social Policy Planning, also at the University of California, Berkeley; the Graduate Program in Planning at the University of Puerto Rico; the Institute for Public Policy Studies at the University of Michigan; the School of Urban and Public Affairs at Carnegie-Mellon University; the Doctorate Program in Public Policy Analysis at the Fels Institute of Local and State Government at the University of Pennsylvania; the Program in Planning and Policy Sciences, also at the University of Pennsylvania. Also moving in the same direction seem to be the Lyndon B. Johnson School of Public Affairs at the University of Texas, a proposed Center for the Policy Sciences at Brown University, and a proposed new school at the University of Hawaii.[99]

At the 136th Annual Meeting of the American Association for the Advancement of Science held in Boston in December 1969, Dror presented a paper in which he said: "Policy sciences hardly exist." He offered eight essential features which he would require of policy sciences:

> Establishment of policy sciences as a new supradiscipline involves a scientific revolution, requiring fargoing innovations in basic paradigms. Particularly essential are: (1) Integration between various disciplines, and especially of social sciences with analytical decision approaches; (2) bridging of the "pure" vs "applied" dichotomy; (3) acceptance of tacit knowledge as a scientific resource; (4) changes in interface between science and values; (5) broad time perspectives; (6) focus on metapolicies; (7) commitment to policymaking improvement; and (8) concern with extrarational and irrational processes, such as creativity.[100]

[99] Yehezkel Dror, *From Management Sciences to Policy Sciences*, The RAND Corporation, Santa Monica, P–4375, May 1970, p. 45.
[100] Yehezkel Dror, "Prolegomena to Policy Sciences", *Policy Sciences,* Vol. 1, No. 1, 1970, p. 135.

19. Development of Operations Research: (7) Professional Activities – ORSA

In January, 1952, ten interested people met in Cambridge, Massachusetts. This meeting was the genesis of the Operations Research Society of America (ORSA)*, established in May 1952. Eighteen years later, as of 31 March 1970, there were 2 356 Members, 4 508 Associate Members, and 781 Student Associate Members, for a total membership of 7 645.[101]

The Society hosts diverse professionals interested in the application of operations research to a wide variety of problems as reflected in the roster of National Technical Sections:

Cost-Effectiveness Section,
Health Applications Section,
Military Applications Section,
Space Sciences Section,
Transportation Science Section,
Educational Sciences Section,
Urban Sciences Section.

The Society has a vigorous program of publications which began with the November 1952 issue of Volume 1, Number 1 of the *Journal of the Operations Research Society of America*. A new series of books made their initial appearance in 1958, "designed to provide comprehensive and authoritative studies of some of the basic theories, new concepts, and practical applications likely to be of general use in operations research".[102] In addition to the Society, some of the Technical Sections also undertake publications of volumes which represent developments of particular interest to the Section membership. [103]

---

* Business Office: 428 East Preston Street, Baltimore, Md. 21202.

[101] Minutes of the 1970 Annual Business Meeting, *Bulletin of the Operations Research Society of America,* Vol. 18, Suppl. 2, Fall, 1970, B–198.

[102] Philip M. Morse, *Queues, Inventories and Maintenance,* Wiley, New York, 1958, Dust Jacket.

[103] George K. Chacko (ed.), *The Recognition of Systems in Health Services*, ORSA Health Applications Section, Arlington, 1969.

20. Development of Operations Research: (8) Professional Activities – Symposia and Short Courses

We saw in Section 8 that the mathematical foundations of operations research owed much to the first conference on "linear programming" that was held in Chicago at the Cowles Commission for Research in Economics, June 20–24, 1949, which led to the publication of the Koopmans volume including, inter alia, Dantzig's original paper on the Simplex Method.

The Case Institute of Technology (now Case Western Reserve University) started a "short course in Operations Research" in Cleveland in the summer of 1952. Out of these annual courses emerged the first widely used textbook which was published five years later.[104]

Similarly, the short courses on systems analysis offered by RAND for twelve years beginning in 1953 to Senior Military Officers and civilians associated with the Armed Forces, led to the publication of the Quade volume on systems analysis, based in particular on the 1965 courses.[105]

During the same year, 1965, the first symposium on cost-effectiveness was held in Washington, D.C., by the Washington Operations Research Council. It resulted in the publication of the Goldman Volume on cost-effectiveness.[106]

As we saw in Section 18, the first symposium on policy sciences was held at the Annual Meeting of the American Association for the Advancement of Science in Boston, December 28, 1969. Professor Yehezkel Dror arranged the symposium and several of the papers presented were published in the first issue of *Policy Sciences.*

21. Development of Operations Research: (9) Professional Activities – Degree Programs

The Case Institute of Technology (now Case Western Reserve University) was the first institution of higher learning to offer a curriculum in operations

---

[104]C. West Churchman, Russel L. Ackoff and E. Leonard Arnoff, *Introduction to Operations Research*, Wiley, New York, 1957.
[105]E.S. Quade and W.I. Boucher (eds.), *Systems Analysis and Policy Planning*, American Elsevier, New York, 1968.
[106]Thomas A. Goldman (ed.), *Cost-Effectiveness Analysis,* Praeger, New York, 1967.

research leading to the degree of Master of Science, the first M.S. degree being awarded in 1957. Ten years later, the Education Committee of ORSA reported the basic elements of 27 programs concerned with operations research offered at the following Institutions: [107]

American University,
Arizona State University,
Carnegie Institute of Technology,
Case Institute of Technology,
Columbia University,
Cornell University,
Georgia Institute of Technology,
Johns Hopkins University,
Massachusetts Institute of Technology,
New York University,
Northwestern University,
Ohio State University,
Oklahoma State University,
Purdue University,
Stanford University,
United States Air Force Academy,
United States Military Academy,
United States Naval Academy,
United States Naval Postgraduate School,
University of Arizona,
University of California,
  Berkeley - School of Business Administration,
  Berkeley - College of Engineering,
  Los Angeles - Graduate School of Business Administration,
University of Florida
University of Michigan,
University of Pennsylvania,
University of Southern California.

[107]ORSA Education Committee, "Special Report on Educational Programs in OR", *Bulletin of the Operations Research Society of America*, Vol. 15, Supplement 2, Summer, 1967, pp. B−113/B−114.

22. OR/SA

Operations research has come a long way since its World War II beginnings in 1941, when the accent was on the military; and the aspects of decision-making were tactical. The beginnings, in the 1950's, of the discipline of systems analysis, have marked a change from the tactical concerns to those of strategy; and subsequently, from the strategic to the organismic. From the purely quantitative, the methodology has increasingly incorporated qualitative considerations. This change in emphasis in methodology somewhat paralleled the increase in the scope of the problems: from the merely tactical to the nearly policy-oriented.

There has also been a shift in the areas of concern. The military dominated the concerns in the 1940's and '50s; in the '60s, space became a prime concern; and by the '70s social concerns, including urban problems, pollution, health and education, have increasingly vied for the attention of the analytical methodology.

Having briefly reviewed the highlights of the changes in the concerns and in the methodology during the three decades since its beginnings in the 1940's, the question may well be raised whether what started out as operational research in England in the 1940's still survives.

Understandably, this question is aired at the meetings of the professional society which bears the name of operations research, viz., Operations Research Society of America. Perhaps the fusion, as it were, of the quantitative and the qualitative in the methodology that has come to be applied to problems at the different levels — ranging from the tactical military level to the social policy level — over the three decades, is reflected in the title of the newsletter of the Society which reads: OR/SA, lending itself to be recognized as Operations Research/Systems Analysis, or as the abbreviation of the name of the society itself: ORSA.

To the author, the terms Operations Research and Systems Analysis are reasonably interchangeable; and contemporary practice recognizes the equivalence of the two terms. It is customary that the professional discussion in the early days of a profession would focus upon identifying that which is specific to the profession. During that era of operations research, one offered the following definition in the ORSA Journal:

> Operations research is the heuristic art of prescriptive application of the scientific method to executive-type problems, whose solutions are not immediately ob-

vious, and which arise in behavioral aspects of entities, more or less with respect to decision-making, in industrial, commercial, military and/or institutional environments.[108]

This definition of operations research is discussed at some length in a subsequent publication.[109]

One would today offer the same definition to cover both Operations Research and Systems Analysis.

The characteristic of being an art has been touched upon in Chapter 1 and will be further discussed in Chapter 3, Section 1. The qualifying term, "heuristic" means "serving to discover". The word was used by George Polya:

> Heuristic, or heuretic, or "ars inveniendi" was the name of a certain branch of study not very clearly circumscribed, belonging to logic, or to philosophy, or to psychology, often outlined, seldom presented in detail, and as good as forgotten today. The aim of heuristic is to study the methods and rules of discovery and invention, ... heuristic, as an adjective, means "serving to discover."[110]

The need for prescriptive answers to the problems will be discussed further in Chapter 3. The essential fact is that the "scientific method" with which every self-respecting study would identify itself be invoked to arrive at practical answers to real-life questions. The essentials of the scientific method are: (1) an abiding faith in the rationality of nature, (2) the idea of statistical control, and (3) experimentation as the method of gathering evidence.

It was pointed out in Chapter 1 that OR/SA is confined to the rational approach to problems, while the decision processes are trans-rational. Therefore, when the scientific method is employed, it unequivocally states that any answers provided are based on the fundamental assumption that phenomena have causes; and that these causes can be discovered through observation and construction. Even the statement that the stone broke the glass window is a theoretical statement which posits a connection between the phenomenon of the broken glass window and its "cause" of stone-throwing. As additional

---

[108] George K. Chacko, review article, *Operations Research*, September-October, 1961, p. 760.

[109] George K. Chacko, *Today's Information for Tomorrow's Products — An Operations Research Approach*, Thompson, Washington, D.C., 1966, pp. 15–26.

[110] George A. Polya, *How to Solve It*, Princeton University Press, Princeton, 1947, pp. 112–113.

observations are made which suggest the relationship between phenomena and causes, the theory may be confirmed, modified, or denied. If denied, another theory is postulated, and further observations are compared with the consequences of the theory.

The idea of statistical control again presupposes that the variations in the observed phenomena can be traced to "assignable causes" and "unassignable causes". Only when the "assignable causes" are identified and removed will the phenomenon be considered to be in a state of statistical control. The advantage of the notion of statistical control is that it is not essential to know the nature of the underlying causes itself, all that matters is the controlling of all assignable causes. Thus, when one twiddles the knob of a radio set, and selects a particular program, very little knowledge of the propagation of sound waves and the electromagnetic theory is required for the proper operation. The operator has merely to know what is "noise" and what is "signal". By noise is meant anything from atmospheric disturbances to unwanted transmissions. To receive the signal, or the desired program, all that the operator has to do is to remove the "assignable cause" of noise so that the desired program may be received.

Not every problem is an operations research problem. To qualify as the subject for OR/SA, the problem must be one which involves the allocation of resources which have multiple uses; and consequently, the commitment to one particular use makes the resource scarce with respect to all the other potential uses to which it could have been put. This concept is further discussed in Chapter 3, Section 5.

OR/SA is concerned with problem-solving where executive-type decisions are involved, where conflicting demands on limited resources with alternative uses need to be resolved at the managerial level. This allocation process must be observable. The observation can be direct, as when certain resources are utilized; or indirect, as when the results of the investment of resources "before" and "after" are compared. The behavioral aspects provide the observable effects of decision-making, as well as the observable means to effect the status of the entities.

The decision-making aspect is slightly modified when the executive-type problems are designated as those which arise "more or less with respect to decision-making". While the decision to make no decision is itself included in decision-making, it is conceivable that the most important contribution of an OR/SA effort is to provide a better understanding of the structure of the problem itself. This understanding may not readily be recognized as decision-making; hence, the caveat that the executive-type problems would be "more or less" with respect to decision-making.

23. Operations Research Contributions to Hierarchical Decision-Making

In Chapter 1, the contribution of operations research was characterized as a rational profile. The profile can at best be a limited representation because the process it represents and/or seeks to assist is more than rational; it is trans-rational. However, instead of cursing the darkness of trans-rational nature of the process, what operations research hopes to do is to light a candle of rationality. The candlelight can only conquer the darkness in a limited area, and should the light drawn by the candle throw into relief undesirable characteristics and/or relationships; and if an effort is made to avert, ameliorate, and/or avoid the characteristics disclosed as undesirable, it will probably further the achievement of the objectives of trans-rational process itself. However, no claim whatsoever can be made about the extent of darkness that is dispelled by the candlelight; and much less about the effectiveness of the indicated line of action, especially if it is ignored. No one would think of blaming the physician if the patient does not follow the prescription; but many more would be ready to condemn the inefficiency of the rational analysis after having blithely ignored its prescriptions.

In Chapter 2, the claim to success at the tactical military level and acknowledged failure at the strategic military level have both been identified. The origin of the interest in the tactical and strategic problems at the *organismic* level, contributing to their successes, has also been highlighted.

The historical examples of the application of OR/SA have also brought out the fact that the operations research methodology and the hierarchy of decision-making interact with, and influence, each other. Thus, a problem perceived as a tactical level problem, may indeed, have to be raised to the organismic level; and a problem, attention to which is called at the organismic level, may find an appropriate solution at the tactical level. Again, it is the rule rather than the exception that the decision-making level at which the solution is implemented is *not* the same as the decision-making level at which the problem is perceived.

For instance, the operational problems of convoy escort surfaced in the

letter from Churchill to Roosevelt — "one of the most important (letters) I
ever wrote" — which is clearly at the *organismic level*. Blackett refers to the
discussions "that took place at the Prime Minister's fortnightly U-boat meetings", again, at the organismic level.

The solution to the problem that operations researcher Blackett found ran
in terms of a revised rule which replaced the long-standing Admiralty Rule on
the size of the convoy. The analytical methods were variational and probabilistic, and the solution clearly tactical.

Similarly, in the case of the operational problem of radar, the concern
originated at the organismic level, Churchill having caused the re-writing of
the entire defense of Great Britain "around the assumption that the promises
made by our scientists for the still unproven radar would be kept". The
solution, again, was clearly tactical: employ predictive mechanism of the
future enemy positions by using data that were smoothed manually.

An example to the contrary, viz., the perception of the problem being at
the tactical level, while its solution was at the organismic level, is found in the
case of the RAND study of the location of the worldwide bomber bases for
the U.S. Strategic Command. The assignment that was given ran in terms of
allocating construction budgets between the bases at home and abroad. The
location of the bases themselves is essentially tactical, once the decision has
been made that the bases be constructed; and that they should be divided
between domestic and overseas locations.

The study director "came to the conclusion that the real problem was not
one of the logistics of foreign air bases, but the much broader one of where
and how to base the nation's strategic air forces and how to operate them in
conjunction with the base system chosen". Thus the problem which was
perceived as the tactical problem was lifted up to the next higher level of
strategic decision-making. Instead of discussing the logistics of foreign air base
locations, it became a question of the strategic positioning of aircraft around
the world in such a way that they can be *utilized*, when necessary.

The transformation of a problem perceived at the tactical level which
essentially entered a dead-end street; and which did not move out of that
impasse until the problem was lifted up not just to the next higher level of
strategic operations, but to the highest level of the decision-making hierarchy,
viz., the organismic level, is illustrated by the deliberations on Project
NOBSKA.

Essentially, to meet the problem of submarine launchings of missiles, the project group conceptually tried combining the off-the-shelf products of technology. It was found that the platform simply would not be able to sustain the weapon system, let alone fire it. It was not until Edward Teller made the pregnant observation: "Why use a 1958 warhead in a 1965 weapons system?" that the problem became manageable. With that comment, Teller changed the perception of the problem from a tactical one of combining off-the-shelf technology to an organismic one of perceiving the parallel developments in technological breakthroughs in both the weapon system and the platform construction. To test out the feasibility of Teller's remark, it took much painstaking and analytic work. However, what turned an impossible monster into a workable weapon was the transformation of the perception of the problem from the tactical to the organismic.

The upshot of the review of the relationship between the analytical aids offered by OR/SA and the hierarchy of decision-making levels is that more often than not, the level at which the problem is perceived and the analysis initiated is not the level at which the solution is found and the recommendations implemented. The role of OR/SA is to supplement the trans-rational process of management; not to supplant it.

PROBLEMS

The discipline of Operations Research/Systems Analysis (OR/SA) which was called upon in the '40s to tackle tactical military problems has been called upon in the '70s to tackle strategic non-military problems. However, if there were no development of analytical methodology applicable to these problems, the discipline would not have survived. The purpose of the following questions is to identify the highlights of the historic developments in relation to the changing types of problems.

A. *Tactical Problems*

1. "Who" asks the question indicates who would be interested in the decisions based on the results. Identify the source of interest in the tactical problems handled by "Blackett's Circus".

2. What guidance can be derived from the performance of Blackett's group about the desirable organizational position of OR/SA effort?

3. What type of collaboration is desirable between the OR/SA analysis

group and the operational group?

4. Reconstruct the analytic approach to one tactical military problem of the '40s.

B. *Strategic Problems*

5. What was the strategic problem with respect to which Blackett had a "haunting sense of personal failure"? Could the failure have been avoided?

6. Discuss the March, 1961, decision to reduce the size and emphasis upon Titan II force, indicating the limitations of cost estimates.

C. *Mathematical Foundations*

7. What are the principal mathematical foundations of OR/SA? Indicate the type of problems that each is particularly suited to handle.

8. What are the contributions to the OVERVIEW of problems that each of these foundational methods make?

D. *Professional Profile*

9. What are the essential elements of an OR/SA activity?
10. What is the status of OR/SA as a profession?

PART II

SYSTEMS APPROACH TO UNSTRUCTURED PROBLEMS

CHAPTER 3

SUBSTANCE OF OR/SA EFFORT

TECHNICAL OVERVIEW

*The substance of OR/SA effort is identified after defining what consti-
tutes management.*

*Departing from the traditional definition of management in terms of
what the manager* does *(such as planning, coordinating, and organizing),
attention is focused upon what the manager* accomplishes. *The analogy
of orchestra conductor as manager is developed. It is seen that the
manager contributes not a single note to the music, yet he is the highest
paid member of the group because without him there would be a babel
of beautiful noises, but no music. However, he himself produces* no
thing, *and is paid the most for producing* no thing. *The cynic may
suggest that the manager produces* nothing.

*To assist the manager in his assignment to produce no thing, OR/SA
offers assistance in four essential areas: (1) context; (2) cost; (3) effectiveness–absolute; and (4) effectiveness–relative. Context is the perception of the boundaries – external (of the problem) and internal (of the
capabilities) – by the decision-maker. The context could be risky or
uncertain. If it is uncertain in the sense that the probability distribution
of the performance characteristics is unknown, then one contribution
of the OR/SA effort is to reduce uncertainty to risk, in the sense that
the probability distribution of the performance characteristics is
known.*

There are two types of costs*: (1) cost of opportunity foregone, and
(2) cost of opportunity acquired. In the familiar use of the term cost,
the marginal principle is implicit. The contribution of an* additional *unit
of the* same kind *to the total utility (total* potential satisfaction*) is
marginal utility. The allocation of resources among different activities
must be in accordance with the marginal principle – that $1 invested in*

any one activity must yield the same satisfaction as $1 invested in any other available activities.

What happens when the $1 is to be invested in an activity, the like of which is not available? Recalling that the basic requirement for the marginal principle is that the additional unit be "of the same kind", the inadequacy of marginalism emerges when a drastically new activity is envisaged. Thus, to guide the allocation of resources for the lunar landing mission, there was nothing "of the same kind" to guide the marginal allocation of resources so that $1 in aerospace could be considered say, as an additional $1 in aircraft. Similarly, the decision to marry cannot be based on the marginal principle, because the addition of one extra person is not "of the same kind". As a matter of fact, a new entity emerges which never existed before. Therefore, the retort to the question "How is married life" in the phrase "Compared to what?" does have an element of truth in it − "before" marriage, there were two people with two names; "after" the marriage, "the twain shall become one", the "twain" being a de novo entity altogether, unlike the two that existed separately.

Operational systems, whether new or old, should be costed for the entire life-cycle from birth to death. The specific elements of total life-cycle costs are: (1) research and development; (2) acquisition; and (3) operation and maintenance costs.

Costs are incurred for one reason: the system should perform. The performance can be identified in terms of, or separate from, the physical characteristics. Effectiveness−absolute is the ratio of actual performance to desired performance. Efficiency is a similar ratio, with the exception that the denominator is the maximum, instead of the desired, performance. The OR/SA effort should make it possible to calibrate system sensitivity, i.e., expected change in the system performance when either the subsystem performance or the total system life-cycle costs are varied.

More than the absolute measure of performance of the subsystem (or the system), the proportionate change *in the system performance corresponding to the proportionate change in the subsystem performance is of greater interest to the decision-maker. These proportionate changes indicate to him the combined effect of the interactions, some of which he may be able to ignore without consequence.*

The contribution of the OR/SA effort is in assisting the decision-maker to allocate resources on the basis of the sensitivity of the system objective to the policy activity chosen, identifying the cost of the policy and at least one alternative, cost being not only opportunity foregone, but also opportunity acquired.

EXECUTIVE SUMMARY

OR/SA is only rational, while management is trans-rational.

To recognize the role of OR/SA in decision-making, it is necessary to define management. Instead of defining management in terms of what a manager does, *a definition is developed in terms of what he* achieves. *The orchestra conductor, as a manager, may be described in terms of what he does: shake his head, wave his baton, plead, get mad, etc. But none of these identifies what he does to earn his salary. He is paid for making music. He is not simply coordinating the work of several experts in the symphony orchestra, who can both perform on their respective instruments, and read correctly the musical directions pertaining to their individual parts in the symphony. What he does is to convert what would otherwise be a babel of beautiful noises into a piece of music.*

The decision-maker in the public and private sectors can derive considerable assistance from OR/SA effort which can explicate the expected changes in overall system performance corresponding to changes in performance and/or cost of small segments of the system. To do this, the OR/SA effort must identify the nature of the boundaries of the problem as perceived by the decision-maker, the context. *It should identify the nature and magnitude of the costs, not only as opportunity foregone in the sense that 15¢ spent on an ice cream cone means that all other ways of spending the 15¢ are foregone to make the purchase of the ice cream possible. In addition, cost must also be recognized as opportunity acquired, in the sense that the activity creates something which has never been available before, e.g., the capability to detect missile launching created by the Ballistic Missile Early Warning System.*

In addition to explicating the context and cost, the OR/SA effort will also define effectiveness in absolute terms: the chosen level of performance characteristics with which can be compared the actual level, giving effectiveness as the ratio of actual performance to desired performance. Further, what happens when the input is changed? Corresponding to a small change in either the performance or the cost of the subsystems, by how much does the system performance itself change? The intent of OR/SA identified in these four elements of context, cost, effectiveness—absolute, and effectiveness—relative, is to provide the decision-maker with an insight into the interactions which he may want to selectively ignore.

The user of OR/SA is much less concerned with the elegance of the solution offered, and much more with its relevance to the decisions. The test of the solution is in its implementation.

1. Toward a Definition of Management

Since management is trans-rational, and OR/SA is only rational, it is inevitable that the use by the decision-makers would necessarily entail modification of the rational solution. Should the solution (assumed to be a competent solution) be rejected, that by itself does not invalidate the contribution offered by OR/SA. It only means that the particular form of solution may have been overruled by issues which were not lighted up by the candle of rationality.

1.1. The Capability to Cope with Change of Management

To recognize the role of OR/SA in hierarchical decision-making, it is necessary to arrive at a working definition of the trans-rational process of management itself. The accolades accorded American management by the French refers to its capability to cope with change. How this capability becomes increasingly important in the context of technological advances is reflected in the Presidential greetings to the Society for the Advancement of Management on the occasion of its Diamond Jubilee:

> Mankind's achievements have been due in large part to an ability to cope with change. Expanding populations, social and political upheavals, and a scientific

revolution have made it imperative for our society to find solutions to growing
and increasingly complex problems with as little delay as possible... .

It is to Managers who grow with the needs and resources of their times that we
must continue to look for the new ideas and their implementation to meet the
challenges of the future.[1]

What constitutes management?

It has been defined in many different ways. Varying emphasis has been
placed upon the producing of results from a combination of men, machines,
material, money, and market. The reason for defining the term in the present
context is to identify features which may distinguish the practice of management from other activities, so that the role of rational analysis in furthering
the practice may be identified.

1.2. Avoidance of Loss as Well as Acquisition of Gains

It is as important to identify what management does as it is to identify what
it does not. Distinction has to be made between important, but intangible,
contributions and important and tangible contributions. For instance, a decision not to enter into a particular business venture may save the corporation
substantial sums of resources which would otherwise have been wasted. However, the success of that particular decision would not be as readily appreciated as, say, the increase in the sales revenue by launching a new product or
a promotional activity at a particular time. From the point of view of the
furthering of the goal of the organism, the avoidance of loss of capital is
probably more important than the accrual of additional profits. This is not to
say that deliberate decisions to invest resources in the hope of future revenue,
which would mean that in terms of the present accounting, the investment
does not have any tangible returns, but only presumably losses, is not consistent with the organismic objectives of the corporation. In evaluating the
contribution of the practice of management, avoidance of losses as well as
acquisition of gains are more or less equally important.

[1]John F. Kennedy, Diamond Jubilee Greetings to the Society for Advancement of
Management, August 19, 1963.

1.3. Results of Management Decision-Making Displaced in Time

The results of management decision-making are generally removed in time from the point at which the decisions are made. Therefore, the criteria to appraise the worth of the management function must include elements which are independent of the eventual results; it is desirable to appraise the decision-making in terms of its own frame of reference.

1.4. Orchestra Conductor as a Manager

To answer the question: what does management do, an analogy is in order. Consider an orchestra. Each of the members of the orchestra is a musician in his own right; and he knows his part of the music well. If each of the members of the orchestra knows what he should perform, then why does an orchestra need a conductor?

Without the conductor, the best of orchestras would only produce a collection of *individual* sounds, each perfect in its own production. What the conductor does is to provide feedback to the individual members and/or to the different parts of the orchestra. To do this: (1) the conductor must know the *whole* piece; (2) the conductor must know not only the notes but also the *intent* of the composer; (3) the conductor must evaluate the actual performance in the light of his concept of the ideal performance; and (4) the conductor must unambiguously communicate to each part of the orchestra what it must do in its production of individual sound, so that the end-result would be the realization of the musical intent of the composer as modified by the conductor.

Notice that the conductor himself *does not* necessarily play a single note (although he may well participate as a performer in addition to being a conductor). With*out* physically contributing to the output, the conductor transforms notes and sounds into music.

What distinguishes one conductor from another? Different performances of well-known pieces such as Handel's *Messiah* are clearly different, depending upon the conductor and the choral group. Handel himself made few dynamics markings in several passages of the *Messiah*. This leaves considerable room for the virtuosity of the individual conductor. In other words, the conductor has ample room for imaginative interpretation of the intent of the composer, which, by the way, far transcends the faithful reproduction of the individual notes. Virtuosity of the conductor is vividly reflected in the recordings of Arturo Toscanini, under whose baton the well-known and the well-trodden pieces of music leap to life as never before.

1.5. Two Unusual Features of Management

Two unusual features of management emerge from this musical analogy. One, that the manager does not necessarily contribute physically to the output, like the conductor who does not need to play a single musical note. Two, the manager must have a concept of the task at hand as a whole, and how each part fits into it. He must be able to adapt the available resources to the ideal goals on hand by means of skillful feedback. This flexible reinterpretation of the original goal in the light of contemporary realities is what makes or breaks the management function; and which clearly transcends the nice confines of any rational analysis.

1.6. Utilization of Scarce Resources

To accomplish the organismic objective, management utilizes resources. These resources, whether they be men, materials, money, or machines have multiple uses. Therefore, once committed to a particular use, it becomes unavailable for simultaneous use elsewhere. In other words, with respect to the possible uses, each resource is *scarce*. Money commands multiple uses. When 15 cents is used to purchase an ice cream cone it may appear that at that moment the 15 cents was not scarce because there was only one objective which was satisfied by the employment of the resource. However, the scarcity comes from the fact of *potential* uses to which the resource could be put. For instance, the 15 cents could be used to purchase an ice cream sandwich, or a cold drink, or a newspaper, or a cup of coffee.

By having devoted the particular 15 cents to the purchase of the specific ice cream cone, all the other alternative ways in which it could have been utilized are foreclosed. In this sense, virtually every resource is scarce. A universal resource which is not scarce is air. Not being a scarce resource, it does not come under the utilization of scarce resources. However, the cleaning up of the air does require the commitment of resources which have alternative uses; therefore, air pollution is a potential subject for the management function.

1.7. Tunnel Vision Imposed on Subsystem Managers

In the case of the orchestra conductor, it was tacitly assumed that he knew the whole piece; and furthermore, that he knew the intent of the composer with respect to the whole composition. Those who manage scarce resources to achieve organismic objectives are not necessarily always in the happy position of knowing the whole score. When Jonathan Strauss came to Boston in 1872, he was astonished to find that the orchestra numbered some 10 000 compared with the 70 or 80 that he had been accustomed to on the Continent. His musical sensitivities were considerably upset by the potential degradation of his musical concept into a babel of noises. He was installed in a lighthouse-like structure where he could be seen by a host of conductors who, in turn, would conduct segments of the mammoth orchestra. Strauss reconciled himself to the situation, and settled for the mass music spectacle.

The individual conductors, who were managing the segments of the orchestra under Strauss, had two advantages over the contemporary manager in a corporation. The first advantage was that each saw the superconductor Strauss at every crucial point, although he was not physically proximate to the supermanager. The second advantage was that the manager had a written piece of music which said in print what the composer had in mind.

These two advantages are rarely available to the large number of managers at different levels of the corporate hierarchy of decision-making. The same holds true of the hierarchy of decision-making in any large decision-making process — whether government, military, space, institutional, commercial, and/or corporate. As a matter of fact, given any level of decision-making, one higher and one lower hierarchy which will impinge upon the given level of decision-making can be identified. In other words, every manager has to reckon with somebody above him and somebody below him. He is both the manager, and the managed. The former is more readily apparent than the latter; in the musical analogy, the conductor is seen to be directing his group. However, how the choral and/or orchestral group itself directs the conductor is hard to perceive directly. Nevertheless, they do direct him by the level of their responses to his direction, which reflects both their capabilities and their temperament. The success of the conductor depends equally, if not more, on his *human* skill in precisely assessing the temperament of his group as his *technical* skills in calibrating the capabilities of his musicians.

1.8. Definition of Management

Management may be defined as follows:

> The process of creative utilization of scarce resources to satisfy departmental goals consistent with organizational objectives, without necessarily contributing materially to the output.*

2. Four Major Elements of OR/SA

By and large, the repeatable contributions of OR/SA methodology are confined to the rational realm of the utilization of scarce resources. In other words, the assistance that can be offered is primarily in the *technical skills* area. But the touchstone of management is in the *human skills* part of decision-making.

What can the OR/SA practitioner offer?

There are four major elements that any competent OR/SA should display. They are:

(1) context,
(2) cost,
(3) effectiveness (absolute),
(4) effectiveness (relative) – i.e., sensitivity.

3. Element 1: Context – "Get a Bigger Map"

During the war with Napoleon, the Duke of Wellington received a report from a Lieutenant who said: "Sir, Napoleon's forces are advancing; the battle is lost." He called him aside and said: "Get a bigger map, and you will see that *we* have won the battle."

What appeared to be defeat from the Lieutenant's point of view was

---

* I am happy to acknowledge the impetus to this eventual definition given by our then 8-year old son, Rajah Yee Chacko, who, catching the word "management" in a conversation as we were driving through traffic, asked, "What is management?" – which immediately brought out the extemporaneous analogy of the orchestra conductor. Thank heaven for little boys, to paraphrase Maurice Chevalier, with big questions!

victory from the point of view of the Commander of the Forces. It is not known if that particular battle itself was critical to the whole campaign; but what is known is that even if that single battle were lost, that loss was overshadowed by the context of the campaign as a whole which was known to the Commander, and not to the Lieutenant.

It should be counted a cardinal sin of omission if an OR/SA analysis does not specify the context − the frame of reference − within which alone its concepts and solutions can have validity.

3.1. Description of the Context

The description of context is the characterization of the situation as it appears *in* the study, and *to* the study. The situation may at best be partially known; but for the purposes of the analysis, the study may *assume* that the situation is in fact fully known. Unless this drastically simplifying assumption is made explicit, the precise conclusions that are drawn from the data which were treated as if they exhibited the assumed characteristic, would emerge as irrelevant, arbitrary and highly misleading. The conclusions of the study must incorporate the caveats, including the simplifying assumptions that are made in order to make the rational analysis quantitative, or quantifiable.

3.2. The Nature of the Context − Risky and Uncertain

If the data are only partially known, it should be stated why the data are only partially known. In the case of a decision with respect to the investment in a new oil well in Saudi Arabia, the data on that new well are simply unavailable. If the experience of others who have attempted to dig oil wells in the neighborhood of the proposed location were to be utilized, the justification for such use must be clearly stated. It should include reasons for the choice of, say, a 5-mile radius of the proposed site, and not, say, a 10-mile radius of the proposed site. It should also include reasons for considering only, say, three years of data, and not, say, ten years of data to arrive at the estimate of the likelihood of striking oil at the new site.

If applicable data can be established, as in this case, the situation may be referred to as being *risky*.

Based on the applicable history of oil drilling, the number of times the effort has met with success, as well as the frequency of occurrence of different yields, can be considered as indicative of the respective probability distributions. In other words, *risky situations are those in which applicable probability distributions are known*, or can be assumed to be known: the parameters of which have to be determined with respect to each individual situation of decision-making.

There are situations in which *no* probability distributions could be assumed to exist, which may be referred to as being *uncertain*. For instance, unlike the applicable experience from prior instances of oil drilling, there exist no data on the use of nuclear weapons in a hostile encounter. Since no data exist, the probability of occurrence of the event cannot be assigned any probability distributions on the basis of analogous reasoning. It becomes clearly an instance in which any estimate of the likelihood of occurrence of the event would have to be based within the context of unknown probability distributions, as well as of course unknown values of their parameters. In other words, this is a situation where one's guess may be argued to be as good as anyone else's.

The careful stipulation of the origins of the context of the study has two advantages. One, it does make it unambiguous to the decision-maker that the mathematically precise relationships depend for their validity upon quite *imprecise* realities. Two, it makes it possible for additional studies to be made in which the reality is better approximated, and the imprecision further reduced. It may also indicate whether the potential improvement in the decision-making would have any justification for the incurring of additional costs to improve the accuracy of the portrayal of the real-life situation.

Quite often, an uncertain situation may be treated as a risky situation. Even more often, the unknown parameters of a risky situation are treated as known. The enormity of the implication of the former is no comparison to that of the latter. Yet, the failure to signal the distinction between the two can lead to disastrous consequences.

3.3. Identification of the Operational Context

While the origins of the context — whether risky or uncertain — are beyond the control of the study, the selection of the particular problem, or particular aspect of the problem is at least partially within control of OR/SA analysis.

It behooves the study to make clear that the *operational* context of its scope is circumscribed by its particular location within the organismic hierarchy of decision-making. The study is, say, at the tactical level: which means that the actions and/or attitudes at the strategic level can make or break the careful conclusions and recommendations. Such an explication protects both the advisor (recommendor) and the actor (decision-maker). It protects the advisor because it forces him to identify at least one level above the area of decision-making to which the analysis is addressed; and therefore, provides a healthy measure of circumspection. It protects the decision-maker because it portrays the inherent *functional* limitations of his own courses of action (e.g., the section is inherently subordinate to the Department) quite apart from the formal and informal lines of organization.

Nor must the identification of the operational context stop with the strategic level; the organismic level, of which the strategic is a part, must also be identified. OR/SA should specify a "before" and "after" profile of the situation under study. The proper result of an OR/SA study is *prescription*; therefore, an elaborate report which says that much can be said about one course of action, does not fulfill the *implementation imperative* of an OR/SA effort. The study should "bite the bullet", as it were, and based on all the limitations inherent in the situation and inherent in the study, still prescribe a course(s) of action: the results of which must be judged within the operational context of the recommendations.

4. APPLICATION 10: Defining Performance Characteristics in an Uncertain Context — Federal Time-Sharing System

The context of decision-making is the perception of the problem boundaries by the decision-maker. By boundaries we mean the coming together of what can be with what is. This coming together depends upon the balancing of the opportunities on the one hand, and the limitations of resources on the other.

In an uncertain context — which is more often the context of OR/SA efforts incorporating technological changes — how can we specify what the output should be?

In April 1972, the Government Supply Agency awarded the contract for a Federal Time-Sharing System to Computer Sciences Corporation. The decision-making context was one of *uncertainty*. Why? Because the entity called "time-sharing" was of terminals successfully sharing the same computer. However, a "federal time-sharing system" was unknown in 1971 when bids were invited from the different hardware manufacturers and providers of software services.

What makes the federal time-sharing system uncertain is the very fact that there was nothing like it before. If the entity itself is unknown, then any performance characteristic pertaining to that entity would be hard to define meaningfully. Nevertheless, a decision had to be made in 1972 with respect to an unknown entity called the federal time-sharing system. If the experience with time-sharing were confined to 5, 10 or 100 terminals, the new federal time-sharing system would include say, 5 000 terminals. There is no knowing whether that which worked with 5, 10, or 100 terminals would work when the size increases 500 ... 1000 times.

To arrive at a decision in the uncertain context, the uncertainty has somehow to be reduced to risk. In other words, some specific probability distributions would have to be demonstrated as reasonably relevant to the behavior of the unknown system. How would one discuss the capability of a vendor who claims that he can in fact provide such a federal time-sharing system? The test is straightforward, while not simple. It consists of the vendor's perception of what the unknown system would perform. How does he characterize the success, or lack of it, of his venture to build the new system? In other words, what are the *performance characteristics* that he deems vital to the unknown entity, so that its success can be measured in those terms?

If the vendor were to say that his federal time-sharing system would have a large capability to store data, that would probably be important; but that certainly would not be the primary distinguishing characteristic of the federal time-sharing system. If he were to suggest that the federal time-sharing system would work say, 600 hours out of 720 hours in a month, that too could be an important requirement in providing the mechanical services necessary. However, that is not the most important characteristic of the federal time-sharing system either.

The raison d'etre of the time-sharing system at the federal level is the availability of the computing facilities to all the federal agencies who could use them. The key, then, is the *use* by the various decision-makers. What are the uses envisaged by the many different customers of time-sharing throughout the vast number of federal agencies? There would certainly be no single, common use, nor would the nature of use necessarily remain constant with respect to the same individual agency. Some would want an update of their data; some others would want certain manipulations of their data; and yet

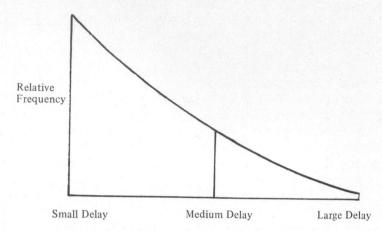

Fig. 3.1. Probability Distribution of Turn-around Time – More Expensive.

some others would want to use mathematical models to analyze the data. No matter what particular use is envisaged by the individual users, from their point of view the most important performance characteristic of the federal time-sharing system is that the turn-around time for most of the operations (e.g., data update, data manipulation, mathematical modeling) would be acceptably small. In other words, given the demand for *any* job at *any* time, the federal time-sharing system should provide the user with a satisfactory answer with only a small delay time.

Having defined a performance characteristic of the unknown federal time-sharing system, the nature of the probability distribution apropos the performance characteristic can be investigated. The turn-around time can be broken down into: small, medium, and large, which criteria are universally applicable. The desired performance characteristic would be to have the highest frequency for the smallest delay, and the lowest frequency for the highest delay. Therefore, a probability distribution can be constructed as in Fig. 3.1. It may well be that such a distribution would be frightfully expensive. If moderate delays could be tolerated without degrading the decision-making, then an alternative criterion would be to have the maximum frequency for the medium delays, instead of the small delays. Additionally, the very large delays, and the very small delays may be kept to a minimum. The probability distribution would then appear something like Fig. 3.2.

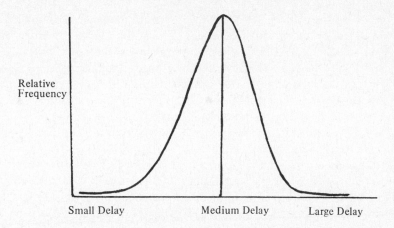

Fig. 3.2. Probability Distribution of Turn-around Time — Less Expensive.

We see that the problem of uncertain context has now been reduced to one of a risk context. The process of reduction derives its validity from the appropriateness of the performance characteristics and the specification of the respective frequencies. Our choice of turn-around time has claims of being universally applicable to any conceivable performance of the unknown entity called federal time-sharing system; it is also flexible to accommodate a whole variety of calibrations that are possible of the turn-around times themselves.

5. Element 2: Cost

The second element which is indispensable to any OR/SA effort is the specification of the cost.

5.1. Cost of Opportunities Foregone

Consistent with the definition of management as "creative utilization of scarce resources", the "cost" of the ice cream cone in Section 1.6 is comprised of all the alternative uses of the 15 cents which were foregone by the investment in the particular ice cream cone — ice cream sandwich, cold drink, newspaper, cup of coffee, etc. To evaluate the cost of investment of any resource, its alternative uses have to be identified in a reasonable manner. The comparisons have to be *potential*; and they run in terms of consideration such as: "if the group of technical experts were to be assigned to Project X, instead of Project Y, the likelihood of acquiring each of which is unknown, what shall have been lost?" Assuming that the particular group of technical experts is equally suited to both Project X and Project Y, the decision to bid on Project X, and not Project Y, carries with it the cost of *foregoing* Project Y. Compounding the situation is the possibility of *not* being awarded the project for which the commitment was made.

This underscores the importance of explicating the basis for estimating the cost, as well as the significant alternative(s) for the utilization of the resources, that have been considered. Project Y may *not* be the only likely candidate; Projects Z, M, and Q also may be equally effective candidates. If this were so, the cost of foregoing opportunities considered in terms only of Project Y would be an inadequate cost computation; the costs of all foregone opportunities must be considered even if only one of them is computed.

5.2. Cost of Opportunities Acquired

Projects X and Y in Section 5.1 could be similar in nature; or they could be *dis*similar.

If Project Y is dissimilar from Project X, the successful bidding on Project Y brings a new element in its costs. It is the cost of the opportunity acquired. For instance, Project X could be the manufacture of aircraft, while Project Y could be the manufacture of missiles. Or, Project X could be an aerospace activity while Project Y could be an urban development activity. Bidding successfully on Project Y would mean more than simply the opportunity to utilize the technical group in a productive activity; it represents a new *way* of utilizing the capabilities of the technical group. The very capabilities of the group are enhanced, increasing their inherent capability for subsequent assignments.

This new capability acquired is one of *process*; it could equally be one of *product*. In other words, it could be psychic or physical.

Considering only the physical product aspects of alternative projects, the cost of opportunities acquired is a recurring phenonemon whenever new technologies are involved. The capability acquired by successful lunar landing definitely presents an opportunity acquired. This opportunity represents not only the *direct* ability to achieve escape velocities and to utilize the gravitational pull of the earth's satellite, the Moon, but also the *indirect* ability to develop heat-resistant material, to recycle materials, etc. Similarly, the investment in "over-the-horizon-radar" is to be compared with the inability theretofore to detect enemy missile launchings, making it impossible to respond within a very short period. The investment in the first early warning system should therefore be weighed against the entirely new opportunity acquired by the new capability; which is a quantum jump over its nearest alternative, even as lunar landing is a quantum jump over trans-Atlantic flight.

6. Cost Considerations in Defense and Nondefense Problems

In Section 5, cost has been discussed as the second element in the OR/SA protocol. Two types of costs were identified: (1) cost of opportunities foregone, and (2) cost of opportunities acquired. This distinction has a particular bearing upon the decisions with respect to defense or nondefense systems which are drastically different from existing systems, or which are entirely new.

6.1. The Inadequacy of Marginalism

Underlying the notion of the cost of opportunity foregone is the notion of marginalism. The marginal cost is simply the cost of the last unit. If the total cost for producing (purchasing) 73 units of an item is $730, and if the total cost of producing (purchasing) 74 units of the same item under the same circumstances is $745, then the marginal cost being the increase in the total cost due to the addition of the last unit (the 74th unit in this case), is obtained by subtracting the total cost for the 73 units from the total cost of the 74 units, i.e., $745 minus $730 equals $15.

Since the acquisition of the 74 units is not for its own sake, but to satisfy some need, the cost of acquisition must be weighed against the worth of acquisition. It is this worth that decides whether the 74th unit is "worth" the $15.

The important question to be raised about the "worth" is when is it effective? For instance, if the 74th unit happens to be somehow "worthless", does it mean that the purchaser made the wrong decision? If we further stipulate that the money is nonrefundable, he has now lost both the money and the item.

Economists have called the significance of goods and services their "utility". Utility is the "worth" of goods and services to the individual who acquires them. This worth is *potential worth* or *potential satisfaction*. The commitment of the resources has to be made *before* the goods and services change hands. Whether or not the actual billing takes place at the time of the exchange, or after it, or before it, is of no consequence. What matters is that the utility is always the potential utility, based upon which the decision is made to commit or not commit the resources.

Returning to the question of $15 for the 74th unit, the two physical items are $15 and the 74th unit. In order for the purchaser to part with the $15, the utility of the 74th unit must be equal to the utility of $15. Since the $15 is not retained for its own sake, but for the command over goods and services that it represents, the decision-maker must determine that the potential satisfaction he would get out of the 74th unit must be equal to the potential satisfaction that he could get from any other goods and/or services purchasable for the $15 at that time.

If, instead of the decision to acquire or not acquire the 74th unit of item 1, the purchaser has also to decide whether or not to buy the 29th unit of item 2, the 924th unit of item 3, etc., the marginal principle would require that the marginal utility, i.e., the unit incremental potential satisfaction of each of those marginal units, must be equal. In other words, the potential satisfaction from an additional monetary unit ($) must be equal. If the unit incremental potential satisfaction is, on the other hand, greater for item 2 than item 1, he will do well to buy more of item 2 and less of item 1. The implicit assumption is that he is trying to maximize the total potential satisfaction. The principle applies equally if he chooses to withhold the spending of money at the present time, which would imply that to him the potential satisfaction from spending the resources, viz., $15 today is less than the potential satisfaction from spending the money at some time in the future.

There is one catch to the marginal principle: it cannot be verified. By definition, the homo economicus, the economic man, is one who practices the marginal principle, equating the marginal price to the marginal utility. However, utility is subjective, therefore, the utility of the same goods and/or services would change for the same individual, depending upon his mood, his taste, and his environment. If the utility of one individual for one item itself is subject to wide fluctuations, how can any comparison be made between the utility of the same commodity for two persons at different times, not to speak of interpersonal comparisons of utility over time for different goods and services?

In OR/SA efforts dealing with large systems in defense or nondefense problems, the notion of cost as opportunities foregone raises an enormous number of problems. What does it mean to say that $1 spent for defense has more utility than $1 spent for education? As a matter of fact, the statement is more often of the form: an *additional* $1 spent for defense has more utility than an *additional* $1 spent for education. To whom does the expenditure have more utility? To the one who is defended, or to the one who is educated? Or, is it to the Chairman of the Appropriations Subcommittee? More often than not, the same Subcommittee Chairman would *not* compare the incremental dollar for defense and education. If any comparisons are made, that is at the level of total budget for education versus the total budget for defense. And the winner is usually the more persuasive Chairman, his success having very little indeed to do with the utility of education or defense.

6.2. *Nonmarginal Considerations in Penalty for Nonfulfillment*

In discussing the allocation of resources to national cancer research and an auxiliary wing of a county hospital in Chapter 7, Section 6, the starting point is the ordering of organismic objectives. The objective of good health is stated as achievable by pursuing eight major elements, which are the strategic objectives. The cancer research and the auxiliary wing are related to one or more of these strategic objectives in the form of tactical objectives.

Of the two, the former is riddled with technological uncertainty, but the latter is not, being only one of a group of events which are qualitatively and quantitatively similar to it; therefore, the contribution that the new hospital wing could make to the care and cure of patients can be reasonably postulated. This can be done by adapting the probability distribution of the behavior of equivalent hospital wings in the same hospital, or in other hospitals, and by making the assumption that the new hospital wing would perhaps function more or less along similar lines.

However, the outcome of the investment in research on cancer offers little precedence which can be applied with minor or major modifications. The process leading to the discovery of the vaccine for the cure of polio may be invoked as a plausible precedent. However, the cancer researchers will be quick to point out the many dissimilarities. Further, claims have been repeatedly made that the cancer virus in the human has been successfully isolated, only to find that on closer inspection the claim has been disproved.

If the solution to the problem as a whole defies direct understanding, then it may be necessary to break the problem into segments which are both realistic and logical so that the solutions to the segments are *most likely* to lead to the solution of the problem as a whole. The test of logical consistency, and the test of realistic representation, are vital safeguards in trying to reduce the uncertainty of the problem to one of risk. Here the triad of organismic objectives, strategic objectives, and tactical objectives developed in Chapter 7, Section 6, can be quite helpful. Notice that no claim is made to the uniqueness of the triad, only to its realistic representation and logical consistency. *Alternative* triads are not only possible, but, to some extent, mandatory.

The burden of the alternate triads is decision-making, much more than the prognostication of the future. Thus, with respect to cancer research the top of the triads, viz., organismic objective, is an *operational* statement of an objective to be accomplished. The action considered at the tactical level is the specific means to accomplish the organismic objective. Of course, the intermediate levels of successive triads can each be looked upon as a means to achieve the organismic objective also.

The focus thus becomes decision-making with a purpose, succinctly represented by the DO statement discussed in Chapter 4, Section 1. The DO statement is a policy statement. It says: Take a particular course of action in order to achieve a specific objective. For the purpose of decision-making, what is essentially required is the plausibility that the action taken has a specifiable relationshp with the outcome desired. Applying this consideration to the allocation of $3.5 million between cancer research and a county hospital wing, the primary question is *not* the specification of the research outcome itself, but rather, what to do about it and/or with it. In discussing the competing actions, viz., cancer research and hospital wing in Chapter 7, Section 6, the penalties for nonfulfillment are associated with the competing lines of action. The two actions are placed within the context of eight major elements of health for individualized care and cure. The rationale for assigning penalties for nonfulfillment is discussed in Chapter 4.

These penalties are employed in trying to arbitrate between two worthy lines of action, viz., cancer research and auxiliary wing, because it is less difficult to get agreement on what constitutes a disaster than what constitutes a desirable goal. After ordering the two competing action items within their respective major elements of health care and cure, they are weighted by the different levels of administrative hierarchy with which they are associated. Five administrative levels are utilized: Federal, Regional, State, County, and Township/City. The penalties for nonfulfillment of the two competing actions are weighted by the administrative hierarchy with which they are associated, and a weighted score is obtained for each action, making it comparable within the context of the organismic objective of achieving effective individualized health care and cure.

Notice that the *uncertainty* associated with the outcome of research on cancer cure is subsumed under the preferences of the decision-making organism. The onus is put upon the decision-maker who is forced to make explicit his hopes and fears for the outcome of each competing action. In assigning his penalties for nonfulfillment, he is in fact implicitly utilizing a probability distribution, or rather, extracting a single point from that distribution to represent a single event. What the technique of penalties for nonfulfillment provides is the representation of a whole complex of forces; and this representation is a *relative* representation, comparing the estimate of the consequences of one course of action with another.

We may consider this method of reducing the uncertain situation into one of risk utilizing the penalties for nonfulfillment as an *implicit reduction*. The method has been illustrated in detail in Chapters 4, 5, and 6. The important point is that *any* ordering can be associated with these three objectives, or for that matter, any other set of objectives. The possibility of altering the scheme of preference at any one time, or from time to time, has built into it the safeguard of explication, as contrasted with the implicit indices of utility which are, by definition, subjective, changing, and noncomparable. In arguing for funds to be allocated to education at the expense of defense, or vice versa, the explication of the preferences of the individual makes it possible to follow the logic of allocation in terms of the fulfillment of the objectives. As the member of the Appropriations Committee, The Honorable John O. Marsh, points out in Chapter 6, Section 2:

> I was impressed by the fact, that, once the technique has been mastered, it seems particularly adaptable to the assistance of computers. The human judgments are preserved at every stage of the process, but the adjustments, reflecting the interac-

tion of these judgments on other elements of the budget, can be worked out speedily by the computer, and the effect of an increase or decrease in an appropriation item shown promptly in terms of the overall budgetary objective which has been selected at the start.

6.3. Total System Life-Cycle Costs

One of the contributions of the McNamara–Hitch system of cost effectiveness basis for the allocation of defense resources, referred to in Chapter 2, Section 8, has been to insist that at the time of the request for $1 for research into a new weapons system, the cost of not only research and development but also the initial acquisition, and the operation and maintenance costs of the yet-to-be-developed weapons system has to be identified. Under each of these three categories, a number of component elements can be identified.

Gene Fisher, Head of Rand Corporation's Resource Analysis Department, presents a number of characteristics associated with a new strategic manned bomber aircraft, reproduced as Table 3.1. We could simplify the notation and generalize the total system cost of not only a weapons system, but also a nonweapons system by making the three components of life-cycle costs the rows of a matrix, and the subelements of each of the component costs, the columns. For instance, Row 1 would identify Research and Development Costs. All the elements of research and development can be identified as columns, so that the entry in cell $(1,1)$, called c_{11} would be the dollar cost of the first component of the research and development category. Based on Table 3.1, the first component of Research and Development is Design and Development; therefore, the entry in the cell c_{11} would be the cost in dollars for design and development of the new weapons system (or a new nonweapons system). Similarly, the entry in the cell c_{12} would be the dollar cost of System Test. The entry in cell (24) would be the dollar cost of Aerospace Ground Equipment, and so on.

The sum of the entries in all the cells in the first row would yield the total cost of research and development. The addition of all the entries in the cells in Row 2 would yield the total cost for investment costs (acquisition costs) and the addition of all the cells in Row 3 would yield the total for the operating (and maintenance) costs.

To get the total system life-cycle cost, the entries in the cells represented by c_{ij} have to be added over all the columns. It does not make much sense to

Table 3.1.
Cost Categories of Hypothetical Strategic Bomber B-x

RDT&E Costs	Initial Investment Costs	Annual Operation Costs
Design and Development	Facilities	Facilities Replacement and Maintenance
Airframe	Primary Mission Equipment (PME)	PME Replacement
Initial Engineering	Airframe	Airframe
Development Support	Manufacturing Labor	Manufacturing Labor
Initial Tooling	Manufacturing Materials	Manufacturing Materials
Engines	Sustaining and Rate Tooling	Sustaining and Rate Tooling
Avionics	Sustaining Engineering	Sustaining Engineering
System Test	Other	Other
Flight Test Vehicle Production	Engines	Engines
Airframe	Avionics	Avionics
Manufacturing Labor	Unit Support Aircraft	PME Maintenance
Manufacturing Materials	Aerospace Ground Equipment (AGE)	PME POL
Sustaining and Rate Tooling	Miscellaneous Equipment	Unit Support Aircraft POL and Maintenance
Sustaining Engineering	Stocks	AGE Replacement and Maintenance
Other	Spares	Personnel Pay and Allowances
Engines	Personnel Training	Personnel Replacement Training
Avionics	Initial Travel	Annual Travel
Flight Test Operations	Initial Transportation	Annual Transportation
Flight Test Support		Annual Services

Source: W.E. Mooz, "The B-x: A Hypothetical Bomber Cost Study," in E.S. Quade and W.I. Boucher (eds.), *Systems Analysis and Policy Planning: Applications in Defense*, American Elsevier, New York, 1968, p. 166.

add them over the rows, because there is not much logical connection between the first component of research and development, the first component of acquisition costs, and the first component of operating and maintenance costs, which are represented by the entries respectively in cell c_{11}, c_{21}, and c_{31}. Therefore, the total system costs for the new system can be represented as $\Sigma_j c_{ij}$.

In Table 3.1, there are further breakdowns below the component levels. The design and development component is broken down into airframe, initial engineering, airframe development support, and airframe initial tooling. It would be well to develop matrices for subcost elements, so that the sum of the entries in the cells in the row called airframe would yield the total cost of airframe design and development; the sum of the entries in the cells in Row 2 would give the total cost of engines design and development; and the sum of the entries in the cells in Row 3 would give the total cost of avionics design and development. The sum of the three rows would then be the entry in cell c_{11}: design and development costs in research and development.

6.4. System Performance and Subsystem Performance

For the successful performance of the system as a whole, its components must perform successfully. However, considering the fact that the profile of the system performance is a thing of the future, it will be possible to identify major subsystem performances. As a matter of fact, major components such as the propulsion unit, the guidance unit, the control unit, etc., can be meaningfully identified ahead of time as contributing significant elements of the total system performance. The significance to the cost calculations of the functional subsystem categories is in raising the question: Would additional effort in improving the performance of subsystem i contribute significantly to the performance of the total system? If the system under consideration is an educational innovation which has not been tried before, and if we adopt the monetary measure of effectiveness in the form of lifetime earnings, we could ask the question: Will the educational innovation contribute more to the increase in lifetime earnings if introduced at the college level? If the innovative system were to be introduced at the secondary and high school levels, the question can be raised: By how much will the system effectiveness (i.e., increased lifetime earnings) be improved if additional efforts were spent to adapt the innovation at the college level?

6.5. Operational Environmental Costs

A weapons system operates within an institutional context. Therefore, the cost of operation must include the cost of *all* the relevant elements which make the functioning of the weapons system possible. Similar considerations also apply to any nondefense systems as well.

The contribution of McNamara–Hitch PPBS (Planning, Programming, and Budgeting System) is the explicit recognition of the fact that a single mission requires the concerted use of several resources. Thus, the aircraft that is required for a mission may be under the jurisdiction of the Air Force or of the Navy, but the fact is that the mission requires different types of aircraft irrespective of their administrative auspices. Pursuing the thought further, there are certain minimums that have to be observed for meaningful consideration of a mission or submission. In his discussions of a hypothetical "new strategic manned bomber aircraft called the B-x", Fisher specifies the organizational unit as "similar to the present B-52 System – a wing-type organization with 15 aircraft per wing, with an additional 10 percent in command support (maintenance pipeline)." In other words, the cost considerations should take into account the institutional requirement that there must be 15 aircraft per wing. Further, he talks about the alert concept, which specifies that 7 B-x aircraft in each wing are to be on continuous ground alert.

In the case of a new weapons system, the training that is essential before the weapons system can be operational must be taken into account. The training costs are not merely the investment in time and money of both the instructors and those instructed, but also the particular learning curve experience of the group. If they have had transferable learning, and if they were highly motivated, it is likely that the errors in operation will be a miminum; therefore, the cost would be less than if there were no applicable experience and poor motivation. Without explicitly taking into account the learning curve of the new personnel, only part of the environment in which the new system operates will be taken into account, thereby *under*estimating the total operational environmental cost.

The size of the operational unit thus becomes an important element in preparing realistic cost estimates. In nondefense problems, the same considerations apply. Consider the innovation of new water recycle usage methods which can be installed in homes. The cost of the equipment itself when available is a recognizable cost. However, the operational environment re-

quires that the recycle equipment be available, but more important, it should
be utilized. The acceptance on the part of the home owners is far more
critical than the operational capability of the new equipment itself. The
"cost" of nonacceptance would be prohibitive, making the investment leading
up to the availability of the equipment itself to be almost totally wasted.
Therefore, in considering the cost-effectiveness of the new recycle equipment,
definite provision must be included to mediate the public acceptance of the
product. The operational environmental cost should include publicity and
educational campaign costs, as well as any discounting practices which would
stimulate the use of the new equipment.

6.6. Estimated Costs

Most systems, both defense and nondefense, will have incorporated into
them some element of novelty compared with the immediately preceding
products of the older system. This element of novelty makes it impractical to
apply the same cost characteristics of the previous system to the present
system. How should the modifications be incorporated in the estimated
costs?

In order for cost characteristics of the old system to be applicable to the
new system, there must be similarities in *performance characteristics*. The
focus of attention upon the performance characteristics makes it possible to
relate cost to effectiveness, which is the index of performance.

Given the similarity between the old and the new system, it would often
be advisable to find relationships between the performance characteristics and
physical characteristics of both the systems. Generally speaking, for the same
physical characteristics, the performance characteristics of the new system
will be higher, larger, or better. The cost should therefore be expressed as a
function of (performance characteristics/physical characteristics).

The determination of this ratio is hard. For one thing, a single performance measure may depend upon a number of physical characteristics, and
vice versa. For another, the very nature of the relationship between the
physical and performance characteristics would be different for the new system from that of the old. Nevertheless, in estimating costs of a new system,
the performance characteristics must be given prime consideration. This emphasis is likely to help explicate hidden assumptions about the capabilities of
the new system vis-à-vis the old. However crude such an explication may be,

the effort to first establish the nature of the relationships, and second, the magnitude of the relationships, would be invaluable in considering the responsiveness of system performance to subsystem performance discussed in Section 6.4.

6.7. Discounted Costs

Since the decisions are made today to commit resources for a system, product, or process which cannot be operational before tomorrow, the cost of using the money between today and tomorrow must be calculated as part of the total system costs study.

Why should payment be made to someone who lends you his money? *Interest is the price for liquidity*. In other words, you are able to use the money today because you have the cash on hand. In borrowing, the lender has to give up cash on hand so that the borrower can use it. For the convenience of today's use, the borrower pays a price — the interest.

When the borrower uses $100 today and returns it tomorrow, say a year later, the borrower has to return to the lender the additional price of $6 or $7 or $8, making the liability a year from now of $100 made available by the lender today to be $106 or $107 or $108.

The precise rate of interest which is applicable varies with the particular type of requirement and the availability of funds. In any event, based on the principle that today's liquidity is preferable to tomorrow's, the borrower agrees to pay $108 for every $100 a year hence, or $116.64 two years hence, or conversely, $116.64 two years hence is worth $100 today, or $108 a year from now is worth $100 today.

The Department of Defense tends to use 10 percent for the rate of interest calculations. The particular figure varies from time to time, but the fact that money should be discounted remains the same.

6.8. Relating Cost to Effectiveness in Defense and Nondefense Problems

The value of a cost model lies in identifying the *relative* change in the performance characteristics corresponding to a small change in the total systems cost, much more than in providing an absolute figure for the cost.

The total system costs of a new system are at best estimates. In planning a new system, choosing it over an alternative system(s), the question really is the rate of change in the performance of the system, rather than the absolute measure of performance.

The total system costs must therefore be converted into elements that can be related directly or indirectly with the performance characteristics of the system. There are three categories which comprise the inputs represented by the total system costs: (1) performance characteristics; (2) physical characteristics; and (3) the number of units of the system.

Costs can thus be considered as yielding a larger, smaller system; red colored, blue colored system; heavier, lighter system. These physical characteristics can be related to the performance characteristics, such as the smaller the system, the faster the flight; the lighter, the faster the flight; the bluer, the faster the flight, and so on.

The reason for considering the number of units is to take into account the economies of scale. It can take the form of lower average cost of production beyond a certain minimum number of units of systems. The shape of the learning curve should also be considered in arriving at the applicable costs of the system; the average cost per new trainee declining after a certain level of information and skill acquisition.

The upshot of all systems analysis is to roughly calibrate the expected change in the system performance when the total system life-cycle costs are varied. The variation can be in terms of performance characteristics, physical characteristics, or number of units of the system(s) under consideration. Much more important than the numbers representing costs or effectiveness is the care with which the major elements are identified, and the applicable relationships are established, or the *concepts* are more important than the *constants*.

Effectiveness should be considered within the concept of the overall objective as the context of evaluation of a given system. The inadequacies of the marginal concept, representing costs as opportunity foregone should be recognized in the context of the newness of the systems — defense or nondefense — under consideration. These safeguards of *concept* would help mitigate undue emphasis upon computations and misplaced emphasis upon accuracy in calculations based upon data pertaining to uncertain situations, and help the really significant contribution of OR/SA effort emerge in the form of implicit reduction of an uncertain situation into a risky context where the future systems are chosen with better awareness of the limitations of context, cost, and sensitivity as they relate to the overriding consideration of improving the chances, in the long run, of fulfilling the organismic objectives by pursuing policies at the tactical level.

7. Element 3: Measure of Effectiveness — Absolute

A third element which is indispensable to any OR/SA effort is the explicit specification of a measure of effectiveness. With this third element, we turn from the *nature* of context and cost to the *magnitude* of context and cost. The uncertain and risky *nature* of the context discussed in Section 3 is reflected in the *magnitude* of logical relationship between subsystems and between subsystems and the system discussed in Section 7.2.4. Similarly, the nature of cost of opportunity foregone and opportunity acquired discussed in Section 3 is reflected in the *magnitude* of dollars and cents and of loss of capital and loss of potential profits discussed in Sections 7.2.4. and 7.2.5.

The measure of effectiveness will naturally have to be a systems measure, not a subsystems measure. While the impetus for the study itself may have come from a subsystem, its value has to be judged in relation to the system as a whole. Thus, a headache may have instituted a diagnostic and prescriptive effort; but the value of the prescription lies in not what happens to the headache, but to the well-being of the whole organism. It would not be acceptable if the symptom of uneasiness, viz. headache, is transferred from one location to another, say from the head to the stomach, trading a headache for a stomach upset. That is why the removal of headache would *not* be a proper measure of effectiveness for the organism as a whole. In fact, if the objective of the treatment is merely to remove the headache, that would be a proper statement with respect to the immediate and the visible state of the subsystem; but it would be *im*proper with respect to the organism as a whole; and the interim and long-term effects of the system as a whole.

7.1. Systems Objective as a Prerequisite for Subsystem Effectiveness Measure

To avoid the myopic mistake of defining the effectiveness of the subsystem to the exclusion of the recognition of the hierarchical relationships between the tactical, strategic, and organismic hierarchy of objectives, it becomes mandatory to order the objectives of the system as a whole, to which the accomplishment of the subsystem objectives is contributory in a subordinate way.

In any large system, the relationship between the subsystems and the system is by no means easily or directly established. Nor is it necessary that an unbroken chain of succession from the system to the subsystems, and from the subsystems to all their sub-subsystems be established for an equitable ordering of subsystem objectives. As a matter of fact, the operational relationship between the various subsystems and the system as a whole will necessarily be affected as a result of the implementation of the prescriptive solution. Change being the order of the day, it would be counter-productive to freeze forever the subsystems-system relationships at any given point, in time or space.

Instead of a frozen administrative hierarchy, a dynamic functional relationship is what should be reflected in ordering the objectives of the system in terms of the hierarchy of decision-making. The dynamic relationship between subsystems requires a *logical* ordering of their functions. Such an ordering must be in relation to the long-term objectives of the organism as a whole.

7.2. Elements of Subsystem Effectiveness

There are five basic elements to any consistent measure of effectiveness of a subsystem. They are:

(1) measure of output (O),
(2) measure of input (I),
(3) measure of criterion (C),
(4) measure of contingency (K),
(5) measure of cost (D).

7.2.1. Measure of output (O)

The measure of output must relate subsystem performance directly to system objective accomplishment. It could vary from direct and physical measures to indirect and abstract measures: from nuts and bolts for a product to the "satisficing" of the need for well-being in a pluralistic society. If not a quantity, the measure must be *quantifiable*. More often than not, a quantitative measure of output is rarely available. In assessing the value of SALT negotiations, the measure of output could *not* be the number of operable weapon systems on either side, because the annihilating capability is by no means reckoned in the number of missiles that can be fired in anger. Recognizing

that SALT agreement when reached itself is a *subsystem* of avoidance of
nuclear confrontation, the objective of the system itself would be to minimize the chances of nuclear confrontation, if not to eliminate it altogether.
But how can the avoidance of nuclear confrontation be assessed as the fulfillment of the subsystem objective in the light of the system objective itself;
i.e., how much do the SALT negotiations contribute to the avoidance of the
nuclear confrontation itself?

Since the event of nuclear confrontation can have only one of two outcomes, viz, yes, or no, and nothing in between, the subsystem measure of
effectiveness of SALT negotiations has to settle for something other than a
yes or no proposition with respect to nuclear confrontation. An alternative
would be the proximity to the nuclear confrontation. The idea of proximity
implies that there is some kind of a scale which can indicate "greater than" or
"less than" relationship with respect to nuclear confrontation possibility.
While it would be foolish to associate a specific value to the occurrence of the
event (what does it mean to say that the nuclear confrontation would occur
with a 0.6 probability, when the event has never occurred before) it would be
less taxing the imagination to suggest that the susceptibility to a confrontation may be greater than on a previous occasion.

Thus, it is reasonable to state that the possibility of nuclear confrontation
was much greater at the time of the 1962 Cuban Missile Crisis than say, the
1961 Berlin Wall Crisis. Since the "greater than" relationship only requires
that one event be displaced from another, but does not indicate by how
much, the 1962 Cuban Missile Crisis could rank as high as say, 135 on a scale
of 0 to 150, and the 1961 Berlin Wall Crisis could be ranked as high as 134,
or as low as 0.1 on the same scale. Since the ranking merely requires that the
ranking of the 1962 crisis be higher than that of the 1961 crisis, it allows for
the accommodation of a wide variety of characterizations of the gravity of
the two crises, none of which would contradict the *diagnosis* of the decision
situation. Whatever differences there be would arise in the *prescription*, it
being understandable why the measures recommended by those who rank the
1961 crisis at 134 would feel differently from those who rank it as 0.1 when
compared with the rank of 135 for the 1962 crisis.

The development of the appropriate measure of effectiveness is thus by no
means direct or simple. In fact, the success or failure of the OR/SA effort
depends, to a large measure, upon the devising of the appropriate measure of
effectiveness which will reflect both what the system is to accomplish in the

long run, and how the contribution to the system objective by the subsystem elements can be consistently ordered within the hierarchical structure of decision-making.

7.2.2. Measure of input (I)
The measure of input is more easily tractable than the measure of output. It generally runs in terms of the physical and the visible; the number of man-hours, the competing alternatives which have been foregone, etc. Since the adverse outcome of a sustained effort can well mean an adverse impact upon the morale of the technical and administrative resources that have been devoted to the particular effort, the measures of input must also include the potential degradation of the resources as an added factor.

7.2.3. Measure of criterion (C)
The measure of criterion and the measure of contingency are both related to the measure of output. The measure of criterion should identify the terms in which the accomplishment of the objectives of the system would be measured: how do you know it when you have reached where you wanted to go to? The choice of the number of products, "utils", units of "satisficing" yielded etc., are associated with the criterion. Naturally, the selection of a unit of measurement presupposes the selection of the identification and ordering of objectives.

7.2.4. Measure of contingency (K)
The measure of contingency is the specification of the perceived logical relationship between the subsystems themselves and between the subsystems and the system. The validity of the answer depends upon the specification of the contingencies which are taken into account. In war-time movies, the disappearance of the specified contingencies and the emergence of new contingencies is a recurring theme. Thus, the red brick store in the plaza which would have signalled the accomplishment of your mission is no longer there when you get there, forcing you to respecify the contingencies within the broader framework of the goal of your mission, viz. to pass on or receive a message.

A soap manufacturer does not have to label his product with the warning: "Not to be used for breakfast or taken internally". However, imagine that the soap is introduced into a region of the world where it is an absolute novelty.

It is quite possible that, consistent with the universal learning mechanism of the infant which puts everything it can touch into its mouth, the cakes of soap would also be so subjected to the learning process of oral contact, and even ingestion. Should ailments occur as a result of the ingestion of cake(s) of soap, it does not reflect in any way upon either the purity of the product or its appropriateness for intended use, even as the disappearance of the red brick store in the plaza does not reflect in any way upon either the authenticity of the mission or its design for fulfillment. What should be pointed out is that the soap manufacturer did not explicate the context in which his product could be utilized, even as the originator of the mission did not suggest that the red brick store may no longer be there. He may be held accountable for not recognizing the lack of orientation of the potential users of his product, the soap; or the lack of imagination or the extent of inexperience of the messenger to handle himself in unforeseen contingencies. In other words, he should have explicated the contingency for which his product/mission was designed.

Unfortunately, in many OR/SA studies, the contingency for which the effort was prepared, and which alone gives validity to the conclusions and prescriptive solutions, is *in*adequately explicated. Unlike in the case of the cake of soap, the user of the OR/SA results does not see an unusual object in the form of a cake of soap; he only sees words and numbers. He would not want to admit that the words and the numbers were not readable in a physical sense. He would be less prone to admit that the words and the numbers were probably not readable in an abstract sense. Therefore, he is more likely to be like the emperor who, trying on the "new clothes" made to order and not seeing or feeling a single stitch of material on him, would be rather naked than be embarrassed. Not only would he not admit to himself that he had been had, but also would he not have his courtiers admit to themselves or to him that in fact they did not understand the contingency for which the "invisible" clothes were designed.

7.2.5. *Measure of cost* (D)

The measure of cost is related to the measure of output. Measure of output is the end product in terms of the results of the application of resources to specific tasks, while the cost would be the administrative accounting of the employment of those resources. Thus, the measures of input could be the recommendations that were made, the conferences that were held, the votes that were taken; the measures of cost would be the number of manhours spent, the volume of raw materials used, the depreciation of the fixed plant and equipment. Whether the costs were for opportunities foregone or acquired, the measure of cost should aggregate the tangible as well as the intangible outlays which give rise to the output(s).

These five elements, with understandable interdependence, together provide an absolute measure of performance of the subsystem. If there were numerical measures for each of the five elements, they could *not* be added up to provide a meaningful measure of subsystem performance. A certain amount of custom-tailoring would be essential to utilize the various elements of effectiveness. More important than the single quantity, or quantifiable measure, is the *process* of perceiving the performance itself. The final outcome could well be a statement that the performance measure of subsystem X is greater than the performance measure of subsystem Y, both being component elements of System S.

8. Element 4: Measure of Effectiveness — Relative

A fourth element which is indispensable to any OR/SA study is the explicit specification of a measure(s) of effectiveness of the system in relation to the subsystem activity. Like Element 3, this also deals with *magnitude*: the magnitude of change, or more specifically, the rate of change of system effectiveness with changes in subsystem activity.

The job is only half done if two absolute measures of effectiveness of systems performance are compared with each other. The absolute measures relate to *one* set of values of the five elements of effectiveness. Even when the statement is made that the effectiveness measure of subsystem X is greater than that of subsystem Y, it only refers to a *single* value of input, output, cost, criterion, and contingency. What would happen if the values of the criterion and the contingency were to change? The values of input, output, and cost would be different. Will the difference in the output be significantly different with the second set of values than with the first? If so, the additional effort incurred in changing the set of values from the first to the second may well be worthwhile.

These changes are at the *sub*system level. Corresponding to the changes in the subsystem activity, the *rate of achievement* of the system objectives can also change. Will the change in the rates be significantly different for the system objectives fulfillment?

For instance, consider Strategy I for SALT negotiations. Change the parameters in Strategy I, and derive Strategy II. Let us say that Strategy II provides different sets of recommendations and clauses for negotiations, but the second set costs more than the first.

Before adopting Strategy II for the subsystem, it is necessary to know if the changed recommendations resulting from Strategy II will have any appreciable change in the effect of the SALT negotiations as a whole. It could well be that the final outcome would be rather *in*sensitive to the changes in the subsystem. Clearly, the potential changes in the final SALT negotiations are at best hypothetical: the outcome is not exclusively in the hands of one group or the other. Therefore, whether or not the extra effort in pinpointing clauses of the agreement would in fact have any perceptible influence upon the final terms would be an educated guess at best. Nevertheless, that guess has to be made; and it has to be made with reference to not only Strategy I and Strategy II of subsystem X but also with respect to Strategy I and Strategy II of subsystem Y, and other series of subsystems which may be judged to be consequential in the accomplishment of the organismic objective.

8.1. *Operational Measure of Performance – "Rate of Change"*

The relative measures of performance have to be compared over time. In other words, it is not only the single *change* in the system performance corresponding to the change in the subsystem performances that matters; instead of the one-time change in the system objectives fulfillment compared to the change(s) in the elements of the subsystem, the *rate of change* of the systems objective fulfillment over *time* as the subsystem activity changes, must be studied.

The *sensitivity* measure is the rate of change in the system objective accomplishment corresponding to the rate of change in the subsystem activity and/or accomplishment, when all other subsystems are held constant. Thus, if the SALT agreement is the system, the rate of change in the accomplishment of the SALT system objective corresponding to the rate of change in the subsystem X when subsystems Y, Z, A, ..., N are held constant is what needs to be measured.

Table 3.2
Number of variables and order of interactions

Sequence	Total interactions	Variables	First-order interaction	Second-order interaction	Third-order interaction	Fourth-order interaction	Fifth-order interaction
1	1	A, B	AB 1				
2	4	A, B, C	AB, BC, CA 3	ABC 1			
3	11	A, B, C, D	AB, BC, CD, DA, DB, AC 6	ABC, BCD, CDA, DAB 4	ABCD 1		
4	27	A, B, C, D, E	AB, BC, CD, DE, EA, EB, EC, DA, DB, CA 10	ABC, BCD, CDE, BDE, EAB, EBC, EDA, DAB, CDB, ECD, DAC 11	ABCD, BCDE, CDEA, DEAB, EABC 5	ABCDE 1	
5	49	A, B, C, D, E, F	AB, AC, AD, AE, AF, BC, BD, BE, BF, CD, CE, CF, DE, DF, EF 15	ABC, ACD, AEF, BCD, BEF, CBE, CEF, DEF, DFA, DFC, EAB, FAB, FBC, CAE, BDF 15	ABCD, BCDE, CDEF, DEFA, EFAB, FABC, FBCD, FBDA, ECBA, FCBE, BEDF 11	ABCDE, BCDEF, CDEFA, DEFAB, EFABC, FABCD, FBCDE 7	ABCDEF 1

8.2. Ignoring Interactions Unimportant to Rate of Change

To determine which of the subsystems should be held constant to assess the rate of change in the system objective accomplishment, it is necessary to identify the more important and less important subsystems. In fact, one of the essential contributions of an OR/SA study lies precisely in identifying the interactions in terms of their importance to the organism as a whole. Merely to state that an event is dependent upon a number of factors and their interactions contributes little to the understanding or the management of the problem. Again, to state that action taken at any one point in the system will probably affect a number of other parts of the system is to state nothing more than the obvious.

However, if one were to be able to say that out of all the possible subsystems and their interactions, *a small number* would probably make the difference in the accomplishment of the system objective; and identify the small number of significant subsystems, that would indeed be a major contribution.

To appreciate the magnitude of interactions involved in any problem, consider the rapidity with which the interactions increase with the number of variables. With two variables, A and B, there is one interaction, AB. When there are three variables, A, B, and C, there are three first-order interactions (AB, BC, CA), and one second-order interaction (ABC). As the number of variables increases to four, and then to five, both the number and complexity of the interactions increase as shown in Table 3.2.

The increase in complexity when the number of variables increases from 5 to 10 and from 10 to 20 is considerable. Any problem that is a subject of an OR/SA study will have more than 5, and quite often, more than 10 major variables. The contribution of the sensitivity measures lies precisely in *reducing* the number of interactions of subsystems, as well as the number of subsystems themselves, that need to be considered for effective decision-making purposes.

9. Relevance to Decision-Making of Subsystems Studies

The four major elements considered indispensable to any OR/SA study are designed to enhance the usefulness of the rational analysis that OR/SA offers to the trans-rational process of management decision-making. The reason why rational analysis is essential to the exercise of management is that, unaided, the human mind can conceive of three or four subsystems; even then, it is unlikely to recognize in detail the 11 interactions of the three subsystems in as full a detail as is desirable. When the subsystems increase to four, the grasp on the 27 interactions of the subsystems becomes formidable; and when the number of subsystems increase to five, the 49 interactions of the subsystems tax the most imaginative decision-maker.

Should the larger number of variables in the form of subsystems, and their interactions be considered in detail by OR/SA, and if recommendations are made as to which among the subsystems and the interactions of the sub-systems can be, prima facie, ignored without serious repercussions, the decision-maker can accept the analysis, modify it, or reject it altogether, with the advantage that the necessary considerations to facilitate his decision-making have been employed, so that his course of action has a reasonable chance of accomplishing the long-term objectives of the organism.

PROBLEMS

The three chapters, 3, 4 and 5, of Part II deal with the substance and se-quence of OR/SA effort. The present chapter deals with the substance *of OR/SA effort. The purpose of the following questions is to highlight the four principal elements that constitute the substance of OR/SA.*

A. *System Context*

1. What is meant by the Context of decision-making?
2. What are the three types of Context into which the different systems under study can be classified?
3. If the principal contribution of OR/SA effort is the OVERVIEW, and if not everyone has access to the highest level decision maker of the organism, how can the value of the OR/SA effort be identified?

B. *System Cost*

4. Distinguish between two types of System Cost.
5. Why is Marginalism inadequate as a System Cost concept?
6. How would you relate Cost to Effectiveness in a defense problem?
7. How would you relate Cost to Effectiveness in a non-defense problem?

C. *System Effectiveness – Absolute*

8. Why is the System Objective a pre-requisite to determining measures of effectiveness for the subsystems?

9. Outline the Concept of Penalty for Non-fulfillment.

10. Illustrate the need for qualitative measures of effectiveness with respect to significant questions of national security.

D. *System Effectiveness – Relative*

11. What is the "rate of change" of the System Performance corresponding to the subsystem performance?

12. How do you choose between two alternative action courses at the subsystem level, when they are both part of the same system?

CHAPTER 4

SEQUENCE OR OR/SA EFFORT: AN OR/SA PROTOCOL

TECHNICAL OVERVIEW

The substance of OR/SA effort identified in Chapter 3 is translated into a sequence in Chapter 4.

To crystallize the four major elements of OR/SA effort into an action sequence, three major steps are identified: (1) DO Statement, (2) Data Sources, (3) Analytic Approach. The DO Statement is a mechanism to precipitate a decision as the outcome of the OR/SA effort with a justification. The policy action comes at the end of policy analysis when the decision is taken. However, precipitating a prior statement on what one would do with the result makes it possible to concentrate upon the detail considerations which are most relevant, as in the adversary system in which the commitment to defend or to prosecute puts the onus upon the defending and prosecuting attorneys to find all that can substantiate their respective decisions. This does not prejudge the issue — that is done by the jury (the decision-maker) who weighs the evidence on both sides.

The four major elements of context, cost, effectiveness–absolute, and effectiveness–relative, and the three major steps are combined into an OR/SA protocol which is a formal sequence of problem-solving operations. The OR/SA protocol comprises four sequences: (1) initial structure of the problem, (2) sensitivity of system objective to subsystem performance, (3) considerations of cost-effectiveness, and (4) allocation of resources to subsystem activities.

To enable the decision-maker to choose between alternatives, the concept of penalty for nonfulfillment *is introduced. The penalty is the adverse effect of* not *doing an activity: What will happen if an activity is* not *performed? The penalties are assigned to activities at the same level (horizontal) which compete for the approval and/or re-*

120

sources from the same source (vertical). The initial DO Statement would thus reflect the gravity of nonfulfillment at the organismic level compared to corresponding to the nonfulfillment at the tactical level. Of course, several triads of organismic-strategic-tactical levels of decision-making may well be applicable to a problem.

The performance of the system can be studied in terms of the corresponding performances at the lower levels – strategic and tactical. The effectiveness–relative indicates the relative allocation of resources in terms of the system performance change due to subsystem performance.

EXECUTIVE SUMMARY

The proof of the pudding is in the eating; the proof of the OR/SA study is in its implementation.

The center of attention is the implementation imperative: DO. It is only too easy to loose sight of the management objective of exercising control through decision-making. To avoid this, we write into the basic approach itself the particular course of action that may be followed if the initial hunches are proven. In other words, it is a declaration at the beginning by the OR/SA effort that pursuing the policy and/or procedure expected to arise from the study will result in bringing about certain specified outcomes.

The second task of the DO statement is the phrase "in order to". Why should the organism accept the change recommended by the OR/SA study? To provide the motivation, the "in order to" phrase must stipulate preferably an improvement in the performance of the organism as a whole, or a component part of it. By so explicating the approximate quality and the approximate outcome, ahead of time, *the OR/SA study puts itself and others on notice that the end-product is an* operational policy and/or procedure of specific interest to the organism.

A formal sequence of problem-solving operations is developed as a guide to a systematic approach to problems in both the public and the private sector. A format for OR/SA effort presentation is also developed.

Four major elements of OR/SA have been identified in Chapter 3: (1) context, (2) cost, (3) effectiveness–absolute, and (4) effectiveness–relative.

Context is the perception of the boundaries by the decision-maker. Cost is opportunity foregone or acquired. Effectiveness—absolute is the actual performance as percent of *desired* performance, distinguishing it from efficiency which is the actual performance as percent of *maximum* performance. Effectiveness—relative is the proportionate change in systems objective achievement corresponding to subsystem performance.

The judgment of an OR/SA effort runs in terms of these four major elements. Having briefly identified the substance of OR/SA effort (what) we now turn to its sequence (how).

1. Three Major Steps in OR/SA Study

The proof of the pudding is in the eating; the proof of the OR/SA study is in the implementation.

1.1. Step 1: "DO" Statement

To focus attention upon the implementation, it would be helpful to devise a format which would accent the directive to perform an operation, as distinguished from the mere conduct of a study. As a result of the insights gained from the study, and the ignoring of less important interactions, the OR/SA study should be able to make a contribution to the transrational process of management decision-making. The results of the study would probably take the form of several alternatives to accomplish the given end(s); however, some of the alternatives would be more preferable than some of the others when only the rational considerations as they are known to the OR/SA study are considered.

It would be most helpful to the decision-maker to know precisely what those recommendations for action are. When he knows them within the context in which they are offered, it would be much easier to over-rule them in the light of additional considerations, which may be called extra-rational. The overruling of the rational recommendations on the basis of extra-rational considerations is no reflection upon the merit of the study or of the decision. It simply means that life is not only or always rational.

The recommendation to pursue a particular course of action comes naturally at the end of a study. The recommendation may well be to do nothing;

which, by itself, is as significant a contribution as a recommendation to do something.

There is a certain danger in letting the study take its course, leading to a logical conclusion. It is academically most appealing, because no assumptions have to be made ahead of time which would predispose the course or context or conclusions. However, it should be remembered that an OR/SA study is *not* an academic exercise in which the pursuit of truth is an avowed objective. The end-product is a recommendation; preferably to do something, or not to do something, which was not otherwise obvious. Therefore, it would be reasonable to start out with an initial DO statement, the purpose of which is to explicate the a priori disposition toward action of the OR/SA study. By forcing an initial DO statement, it will necessitate the recognition of the *operational* context of the management decision-making: what it is that the management is planning to do now; and what it is that the management would do differently if they were shown reasonable cause.

The focus upon the end-result in terms of the implementation imperative forces the OR/SA study to accent the relevance to the decision-making situation, instead of being captivated by the elegance of the solution. It would make it possible for the management to feel that the rational studies do have something to contribute which might make a difference to the management's point of view and course of action. It puts the OR/SA study participants on notice that the onus is upon them to communicate clearly and unambiguously to the management the findings of their exhaustive analytical pursuit. If instead, they feel that they will merely "study the problem", there is no urgency to be productive or relevant; on the other hand, if they select one or two specific alternative courses of action as emerging from the proposed study, then the course and character of the study itself would be distinctly oriented to the management decision-making process.

1.1.2. "Do ... in order to"

A decision to take a particular course of action is, by itself, *in*adequate. What would happen if a particular course of action were taken? By making the profile of the end-result directly related to the course of action, it becomes possible for the management to recognize the content of the DO Statement in the context of the operation of the organism. The DO Statement must have an "in order to" clause which relates the potential results with the planned course of action. The results have to be verifiable in their own terms of reference; therefore, they have to be both tangible and visible to management.

1.2. Step 2: Specification of Data Sources

One advantage in pre-specifying the change in the operations of the organism as a result of the study is the effective selection of indispensable data elements. Often, highly interesting relationships can be speculated upon by the OR/SA study, which can neither be confirmed nor denied on the basis of real data. If such speculations can neither be confirmed nor denied, the assertions based on them are at best reduced to one group's word against another's, between which the management may have little to choose.

The data that are used to confirm or deny the premises of the Do Statement need not be confined to real and present data, or real and past data; they can be hypothetical and future data, hypothetical and present data, or hypothetical and past data. Whatever type of data are used, their nature must be clearly stated, so that the validity of the conclusions that are based upon their manipulations may be clear to those who have to base their decisions upon them.

As soon as the *initial* Do statement is made, the types and sources of data should be specifically identified so that the OR/SA study itself may choose to modify its initial Do Statement in the light of the absence altogether, or partial unavailability, of the data sources which were envisaged at the start of the study. Should the data be unavailable, it may necessitate the re-structuring of the initial DO Statement; after all, one could not dive into where there is no water.

By basing the analysis upon accessible data the conclusions become far more credible than if there were no data base to support them. Data are notorious for their misbehavior in that they do not readily lend themselves to convenient mathematical manipulations or statistical constructs. They challenge the ingenuity of the analyst to work around them without abandoning them altogether, or selectively ignoring the misbehaving pieces of data. The struggle with the data, whether they be real-life or near-real-life, or whether they be hypothetical projections based on individual pieces of data on the performance of subsystems, forces the study to recognize interrelationships which may have otherwise been unapparent.

1.3. Step 3: Specification of the Analytic Approach

Given the DO Statement and the data sources, it is possible to indicate how one would utilize the data sources to verify, modify, or deny the initial assumptions with respect to decision-making that were made in the study. Clearly, if the data become unavailable, or unsuitable, the analytic methods may have to be changed; and new methods substituted for the ones originally intended.

The advantage in specifying the analytical approach(es) at the outset is that the study has to provide explicit recognition of the demands upon the data to make them suitable for processing by the proposed analytic methods. For instance, if the analytic methods required that the variables be random, and if it is known that by no stretch of the imagination the data could be considered random, then that particular method will have to be abandoned; or specific adjustments made to the results based on the assumption of randomness in the behavior of the variables considered.

The initial specification of the analytic approach also provides for explicit considerations of the use of computers. Should a computer program(s) be utilized, additional operations on the data would be necessary; and, consequently, additional cost. If there is a tendency to utilize the computer simply because it is there, the requirement to consider the analytic approach at the outset should make it possible to raise the question: Is this computer calculation really necessary? The computer calculation should provide insights otherwise unobtainable; or insights additional to the ones obtainable from the analytic approach(es). Since most computer calculations require some modelling, the analytic approach would be implicit in any study; the difference being in the nature and magnitude of the analytic approach. Therefore, by prespecifying the analytical approach(es) to be employed, alternative strategies in modeling the data could be considered, without necessarily excluding the analytical or the computational. The fact that as much was derived analytically as could be from the data would lend credibility to the additional calculations by the computer, both from the point of the OR/SA study and from the point of view of the decision-maker.

2. Four Protocol* Sequences in OR/SA

How can the four major elements of any competent OR/SA effort be accomplished in an orderly fashion while observing its three major steps?

It will be recalled that the four major elements identified in Chapter 3, Section 2 were:

Element 1:   context,
Element 2:   cost,
Element 3:   effectiveness (absolute),
Element 4:   effectiveness (relative) – sensitivity.

It will also be recalled that the three major steps discussed in Section 1 were:

Step 1: DO Statement,
Step 2: Data Sources,
Step 3: Analytic Approach.

The four major elements of Chapter 3, Section 2 and the three major steps of Section 1 can be combined into four major sequences of an OR/SA Protocol. They are:

Sequence 1: Initial Structure of the Problem,
Sequence 2: Sensitivity of System Objective to Subsystem Performance,
Sequence 3: Cost Effectiveness Considerations,
Sequence 4: Allocation of Resources to Subsystem Activities.

2.1. Sequence 1: Initial Structure of the Problem**

The DO Statement is an *initial* statement, which is intended to bring into the open what the OR/SA study hopes to accomplish by way of impacting upon the decision-making process. How can the statement be made specific to the problem?

---

* Used here in the sense familiar to behavioral science. Allen Newell and Herbert A. Simon write in *Human Problem Solving* (Prentice-Hall, Englewood Cliffs, 1972): "The data are a transcript of the subject's verbalizations during the course of problem solving – what is called a *protocol*. The protocol also includes additional data, about either the subject or the environment, that bears on total performance." (p. 163). The four sequences of problem solving in OR/SA comprise the OR/SA protocol.

** The OR/SA Protocol is applied step-by-step to large problems of policy in the public sector in Chapters 6, 7 and 8, and in the private sector in Chapters 9, 10, 11 and 12.

Recognizing that most often, *sub*systems are asked to be studied, and not systems, the DO Statement has to be made in terms of those subsystems. The level of decision-making is *tactical*. In other words, the subsystem seeks to accomplish goals which are its own. However, it would make as much sense to say that the subsystem must achieve its goals as to say that the head wants to get rid of the headache. The statement of goals in terms of the subsystem, viz., head, makes sense only within the context of the body as a whole.

2.1.1. Identify at least two subsystems

In the case of large, unstructured systems, the trouble is that the anatomy of which the head is a part cannot be directly perceived. It may be easier to recognize another subsystem which is on the same level. If the two subsystems are at the same level of decision-making, viz., the tactical level, then it is much easier to recognize them as two similar subsystems, competing for both support from and contribution to the same next-higher-order subsystem; e.g., two Sections within the same Department.

Once two subsystems are identified at the same level — and the identification has to be in terms of the tactical level of decision-making that each contributes to — then, the next higher level to which both subsystems owe allegiance can be identified. In other words, the start can be made with *any* level of activity; all that is required is to find another activity which is at the same level in the hierarchy of decision-making. These two are then to be related to the next higher level.

The advantage in this procedure from the management point of view lies in the identification of the specific location of the management decision-making at two alternative subsystems. From the point of view of the OR/SA study, the advantage lies in the recognition of at least another subsystem with which the recommendation for action for the subsystem under study will compete for the allocation of organismic resources.

2.1.2. Concept of penalty for nonfulfillment

How can the decision-maker choose between two subsystems?

The concept of fulfillment of the organismic objective, and the contribution of the tactical level activity toward the fulfillment, would appear to be a logical first step. However, it is rather difficult to specify the value of fulfilling an organismic objective. Consider, for instance, the organismic objective of the Department of the Interior. Can it be stated in terms of enhancing the environment? It would have a ready appeal, in that the various functions of the components of the Department of the Interior are presumably contributing to making the environment more liveable much longer than otherwise possible. How would one measure the enrichment of the environment? Would one count the number of trees, the number of blades of grass, the number of new streams? It raises the question of not only verifiable measures, but more importantly the question of viewpoints and value judgments which would make it extremely difficult to arrive at an operational consensus on when the organismic objective has been fulfilled.

On the other hand, consider a *negative* approach to defining the organismic objective. If the environment is enhanced, it would thereby reduce the erosion of the environment and its degradation. If one were to consider the purity of the air as an index of the enrichment of the environment, the question is: how clean is clean? On the other hand, agreement can be much more readily obtained if *un*cleanliness, instead of cleanliness, is in the terms of reference of the organismic objective.

There was an air pollution episode in the Eastern Unites States at Thanksgiving in 1966. There was an atmospheric inversion which effectively stagnated the air over the East, including New York City for several days. This meant that the impurities made a concentrated attack upon the population instead of being wafted away by the wind as would be normal. It is estimated that some 180 *additional* deaths could be attributed to the atmospheric inversion on that day:

> Occasionally a high-pressure system becomes almost motionless over some part of the United States and tends to interrupt the usual cycle of ventilation. As a consequence, the usual daily afternoon dispersion and dilution are diminished, and pollutants may accumulate to high concentrations over a period of several days ... .[1]

Such an occurrence is called an "episode". The effect of an episode is more directly visible, the 180 deaths making much more of a direct impact than tons of grass that may have silently grown during that day throughout the nation. In other words, "episodal avoidance", meaning thereby the pre-

[1] Jack C. Fensterstock and Robert K. Fankhauser, "Thanksgiving 1966 Air Pollution Episode in The Eastern United States", HEW, National Air Pollution Control Administration Publication No. AP-45, Raleigh, North Carolina, July 1968, p. 3.

vention of the recurrence of the episode like the one which occurred in New York City at Thanksgiving, 1966, becomes a much more readily agreeable organismic objective for the Department of Interior than the organismic objective of "environmental enrichment".

As in other documented air pollution episodes, the high levels of air pollution in the Eastern United States during the period from November 24 through 30, 1966, created adverse health effects. Researchers in New York City found an increase in death rate of approximately 24 deaths per day during the period.[2]

To determine the contribution that any particular tactical level decision can make to the achievement of the organismic objective, one would think in terms of the *penalty for nonfulfillment* of the organismic objective; i.e., the episode is a penalty for nonfulfillment of the organismic objective of environmental enrichment. Consistent with the penalty for nonfulfillment at the organismic level, there will be penalties for nonfulfillment at the strategic and at the tactical levels. Therefore, to arbitrate between two subsystems whose activity at the tactical level competes for resources of the organism, the respective penalties for nonfulfillment can be used as an operational measure.

To begin with, the penalty for nonfulfillment of the tactical objectives at subsystem I level could be stated as being greater than those at subsystem II. Conceivably, there will be several subsystems at the same tactical level. The relative penalty for nonfulfillment of each of these can be rated on a scale of 0 to 10.

If there are subsystems I, II, ..., n, all tactical level activities corresponding to the same strategic level, then the penalty for nonfulfillment at the strategic level has to be considered to be much greater than the sum of the penalties for nonfulfillment of the individual subsystem. Thus, if the penalties for nonfulfillment of the subsystems were, say, 7, 3, 5, 9 and 2, then at the strategic level, nonfulfillment would have a penalty which is much more than $(7 + 3 + 5 + 9 + 2 =) 26$. It may well be that there are other subsystems at the tactical level which are not included in the consideration. To allow for their subsequent incorporation as we learn more about the interrelationships of the system and its subsystems without reworking the whole scheme, we allow for a much greater penalty than the sum of the component subsystems.

[2]*Ibid.*, p. 35.

It may be preferrable to use 2-digits for the penalties of nonfulfillment at the *strategic* level. In this case, the corresponding penalty for nonfulfillment at the strategic level should be much more than 26. Since there will be other strategic level activities, they are also each assigned penalties for nonfulfillment in two digits. In other words, the range of the penalty for nonfulfillment at the strategic level will be 10−99. Which of these numbers in this range is chosen for the particular strategic level would depend upon the relative position of the particular strategic level with respect to other strategic level activities at the same level. We may, for instance, consider the particular strategic level as one of three. If it is the least important among the three at the strategic level, its score (which has to be greater than 26) would be something like 37, which will be exceeded by the other two; for instance, 57 and 82.

Similar to the construction of the two tactical level activities *horizontally* and one strategic level, *vertically*, the penalty for nonfulfillment at the organismic level can also be derived. The organismic level should be directly related to the corresponding strategic level. It does *not* necessarily have to relate to the organism as a whole. It may take several iterations to arrive at the highest level of the organism. It bears repetition that most of the OR/SA studies do not have the luxury of being conducted at the highest organismic level.

Since the digits 0−9 were allocated to the tactical level, and the digits 10−99 were allocated to the strategic level, it would seem natural to allocate the numbers 100−999 to the organismic level. The same rule that the penalty measures for nonfulfillment at the strategic level be much higher than the sum of the penalty measures for its component subsystems at the tactical level applies to the allocation of the penalty measures for the nonfulfillment at the organismic level with respect to the strategic level.

An OR/SA study must consider the minimum of a single-triad of organismic-strategic-tactical levels of decision-making. The initial DO Statement should reflect at least the organismic level of the first triad. It could be designed to reflect the penalty for nonfulfillment at the organismic level at the pinnacle of not just the first triad, but the second, third, ..., the *n*th triad which is derived successfully by repeated processing of logical identification of interrelated decision-making.

The steps in the initial structuring of the problem are identified in Table 4.1.

Table 4.1
Sequence 1: Initial structure of the problem

1. An initial decision: DO...in order to...
2. Triads from the initial decision at the tactical level to the organismic objective level (minimum 1 triad)
   2.1. Hierarchical ordering of objectives—a single triad[a]
        2.1.1. Organismic objectives
        2.1.2. Strategic objecrives
        2.1.3. Tactical objectives
3. Penalty scores relating the nonfulfillment at the tactical level with the nonfulfillment at the organismic level
   3.1. Establishing horizontal and vertical *functional ordering*
        3.1.1. Identify a tactical level decision of immediate interest to analyst
        3.1.2. Identify another tactical level decision similar in subsystem function fulfillment
        3.1.3. Identify an immediately higher order decision at the strategic level of which both 3.1.1 and 3.1.2 are logical consituents
   3.2. Ordering *penalty measures* for nonfulfillment
        3.2.1. Concept of penalty—most unacceptable outcome must be assigned the highest cost penalty
        3.2.2. Assign arbitrary penalty measures of nonfulfillment to 3.1.1
        3.2.3. Assign relatively consistent penalty measure of nonfulfillment to 3.1.2 to reflect the significance of 3.1.2 in relation to 3.1.1
        3.2.4. Assign relatively consistent penalty measure of nonfulfillment to 3.1.3 to reflect the significance of 3.1.3 in relation to 3.1.1, 3.1.2
        3.2.5. Continue the cycle of penalty measure assignment until the operational organismic objective for this OR/SA problem is fulfilled[b]

[a] George K. Chacko, *Today's Information for Tomorrow's Products – An Operations Research Approach*, Thompson, Washington, D.C., 1966, pp. 29–43.
[b] See Chacko, *Today's Information*, pp. 41–72, for U.S. National Defense Objectives with penalty for nonfulfillment measures ranging from 10 at lowest tactical level to 7 680 000 at highest organismic level.

2.2. Sequence 2: Sensitivity of System Objective to Subsystem Performance

The procedure of the other three steps is similar to that of the initial structuring of the problem. The system objective has to be identified as the one in terms of which the potential contribution of the subsystem at the tactical level has to be evaluated. For this, a measure of performance has necessarily to be identified. This was discussed at length in Chapter 3, Section 7.

The guideline for the second major sequence in the OR/SA protocol is that the proportionate increase in systems objective fulfillment corresponding to the subsystems performance change must be preferably much greater than one. In other words, by investing "X" worth of resources to carry out the tactical-level decision-making, the resultant fulfillment of the organismic objective must be considered to be much greater than X, say $10X$. When the objective of the system is nonrepresentable in terms of monetary equivalents, some measure of translation has to be found which would convert the units of investment of resources at the tactical level into units of return at the organismic level.

The steps in the evaluation of the sensitivity of system objective to subsystem performance are identified in Table 4.2.

2.3. Sequence 3: Cost-Effectiveness Considerations

In the case of the third sequence in the OR/SA protocol the primary consideration is that of cost which has been discussed at length in Chapter 3, Section 6. The comparison of the proportionate change in the output of the organism in the preceding sequence was with reference to the *input* at the tactical level. There was no discussion of the *cost of the input* at the tactical level; this has now to be explicitly introduced: not only, as cost of opportunity foregone, but also as cost of opportunity acquired. The implementation of the tactical level decision is going to incur costs which are different from those for non-implementation. There may well be a *reduction* in the cost in

Table 4.2
Sequence 2: Sensitivity of system objective to subsystem performance

(1)	Component elements of subsystem performance (at least two) reflecting the tactical level decision.
(2)	Measure of performance of (1).
(3)	Data on component performance at the aggregate level.
(4)	Evaluation of effect of (3) on system objective achievement.
(5)	The proportionate increase in system objective achievement corresponding to the subsystem performance preferably much greater than 1.
(6)	Revised structure of the problem in the light of (5).

implementing the new subsystem; against which has to be weighed the cost of the study itself.

The improvement in the accomplishment of the organismic objective does *not* necessarily have to be judged on the basis of returns on cost. It may well be that the cost of the subsystem would be much higher than the equivalent returns at the organismic level. The installation of the Ballistic Missile Early Warning System (BMEWS) would necessarily represent an increase in cost at the subsystem level, for which the returns at the system level would have to be postulated; e.g. futuristic improvement in the potential warning time made available by BMEWS for response to a nuclear confrontation. Even when the increase in the effectiveness of the system's objective fulfillment, due to the new subsystem at the tactical level is less than one, there may be additional reasons to assign a greater weight to the fact of increased effectiveness at the organismic level: an increase in the nature, if not in magnitude of the system objective fulfillment as shown in Table 4.3.

2.4. Sequence 4: Allocating Resources to Subsystem Activities

The fourth major sequence in the OR/SA protocol is the allocation of the organismic resources to the implementation of the tactical level decision-making. The allocation of resources to the subsystem must justify itself on the basis of its contribution to the fulfillment of the organismic objective. Since the organismic objective is not considered in terms of fulfillment, but in terms of *penalty for nonfulfillment*, the allocation of resources must be guided by the penalty measures for nonfulfillment at the *highest* organismic level considered. The penalty measures at each level represent the best judgment of the understanding of the processes at each level, as well as their relationship to the whole. Therefore, the allocation of resources to the par-

Table 4.3
Sequence 3: Cost-effectiveness considerations

(1)	Increase in cost due to the new subsystem for the tactical level decision.
(2)	Increased effectiveness of the system objective achievement due to the new subsystem for the tactical level decision.
(3)	The ratio of (2) over (1) preferably greater than 1, but even if it is less than 1, the increase in effectiveness should be given greater weight.

Table 4.4
Sequence 4: Allocating resources to subsystem activities

---

(1)   The total $ amount allotted to or required for fulfilling organismic objective is equated to the penalty measure for nonfulfillment.

(2)   Multiply the total $ amount by the fraction:

$$\frac{\text{penalty measure for any level nonfulfillment}}{\text{penalty measure for nonfulfillment of organismic objective}}$$

(3)   Repeating the (functional ordering—penalty measures) process in Table 4.1.

    3.1.   Every change in any element at any level affects every other element.

    3.2.   Change functional ordering of one element: specify changes in horizontal and vertical functional hierarchy elements.

    3.3.   Apply relative changes in functional ordering all the way back to organismic objectives, and reapply 2. in Table 4.1.

---

ticular subsystem activity would be proportional to its share in the penalty for nonfulfillment in relation to the penalty for nonfulfillment at the organismic level.

The process is repeated. The functional ordering-penalty measures process is reconstituted in the light of the initial allocation of resources based on the initial DO Statement as shown in Table 4.4.

2.5. Criteria and Format

The judgment of an OR/SA effort is based on the prime criteria of:
(1) choosing a problem with uncertain context,
(2) reducing it to a *risk* context, based on,
(3) as hard *data*, either direct or indirect as possible; and
(4) developing an operational measure(s) of effectiveness,
(5) examining the sensitivity of the system objective to the policy activity chosen,
(6) identifying the costs of the policy and at least one alternative, cost being not only opportunity foregone but also opportunity acquired, and
(7) discussing the *allocation* of resources to the policy activity, and its revision, carefully delineating institutional idiosyncracies affecting the implementation.

Table 4.5
A format for OR/SA effort presentation

---

(1)   Title (not more than 5 words)

A.   BACKGROUND
(2)   Introduction, Background
(3)   Initial DO Statement

B.   CONTEXT
(4)   Uncertainty element(s) in the decision-making
(5)   Applicable data to reduce uncertainty to probability

C.   EFFECTIVENESS
(6)   Performance characteristics of the system
(7)   Performance measure(s) of the system

D.   SENSITIVITY
(8)   Sensitivity of system performance to policy activity
(9)   Sensitivity of system performance to alternative activity(ies)

E.   COST
(10)   Cost of policy activity — opportunity foregone
(11)   Cost of policy activity — opportunity acquired
(12)   Effectiveness measure(s) of activity
(13)   Cost-effectiveness analysis

F.   IMPLEMENTATION
(14)   Initial allocation of resources to activity
(15)   Revised allocation
(16)   Institutional idiosyncranies in implementation
(17)   Conclusions
(18)   Recommendations
(19)   Limitations

A format for presentation incorporating the OR/SA Protocol developed above is given in Table 4.5.

PROBLEMS

The three chapters, 3, 4 and 5, of Part II deal with the substance and sequence of OR/SA effort. The present chapter deals with the sequence of OR/SA effort. The purposes of the following questions is to highlight the four principal elements of the OR/SA sequence.

A. *Initial Problem Structure*

1. Diagnosis, without prescription, is inadequate. Therefore, how can the prescription be incorporated into the OR/SA sequence?

2. How can you choose between two alternative courses of action at the subsystem level?

B. *System Objective Accomplishment*

3. What is the role of inter-relationships in relating subsystem performance to the System Objective Accomplishment?

4. What principal assumption is made when alternative subsystem investments are considered to improve System Performance?

C. *Cost-Effectiveness Considerations*

5. Indicate how inputs of costs can be estimated.

6. Illustrate the inherent error in future product cost estimates.

7. How would you relate opportunity acquired to effectiveness?

D. *Resource Allocation to Subsystems*

8. With*out* the allocation of resources, there is no tangible measure of support to a given activity. How would you allocate resources to a subsystem activity, reflecting its importance to the System Objective Accomplishment?

9. In altering the allocations to an activity, how can its impact upon the rest of the system be explicitly recognized?

CHAPTER 5

CONTEXT C: PERSPECTIVE OF THE
PRINCIPAL DECISION-MAKER (PDM) ROLES

TECHNICAL OVERVIEW

Context is the perception of the boundaries by the decision-maker. How he perceives the boundaries of his decision-making as uncertain (with no applicable experience) or as risky (with some applicable experience) has a good deal of influence upon his understanding of the problem, as well as his handling it.

In addition to the hierarchical level at which he operates, the decision-maker will find himself circumscribed by different decision roles that he has to play. A Principal Decision-Maker (PDM) is one who is at the top of the administrative hierarchy whose actions affect a given unit more potently than anyone else. In relation to him, the PDM, we can identify sub-PDM and sub-sub-PDM roles.

It is possible to draw a parallel between the organismic objective and the PDM role; the strategic objective and the sub-PDM role; and the tactical objective, and the sub-sub-PDM role. However, a decision-maker may have to play more than one role, and probably all three roles at the same time *which, because of the differences in perspective between the roles, gives rise to a built-in conflict.*

This conflict can be identified in terms of the different timeframes that are employed in the exercise of management functions at the three levels: long-term, intermediate-term, and short-term. The long-term is often the enemy of the short-term, because the long-term is not merely a stretching of the short-term into the future, but instead, a different orientation altogether. Because of this difference in orientation, the PDM ignores *the perspective of his sub-PDM. When the President of a corporation ignores the perspective of his Vice President, it is probably because the President sees the long-term prospects for the survival and growth of the company in newer products and/or services; while, the*

Vice President probably sees them in terms of the products and/or services that are under his immediate purview.

In three applications, the inherent conflict between the different PDM roles, both at the National and at the Corporate levels, are highlighted. The reorganization of the Office of Management and Budget (OMB) in April, 1973 to make the Federal Departments responsive to "Presidential Priority" goals is used to raise the question: What is the overall national objective? The physical survival of the 50 States is clearly included in the notion of survival. Equally, if not more, important is the survival of what is loosely described as The American Way of Life. If survival means existence, quality of life would mean enjoyment. Enjoyment itself comprises: (1) health, and (2) happiness. How can health and happiness be operationally measured? Arguments are presented for measurable outcomes which appear to reflect most closely the abstract notions of health and happiness.

The President's Priority goals must include the expected survival of the American Way of Life as reflected in the measures of: (1) the percent of U.S. population earning income under the poverty level, (2) the percent of U.S. population unable to pursue its own choices because of lack of health, and (3) the percent of U.S. population unable to pursue its choices for lack of opportunity. The input of data at the OMB level, the Department level, and the sub-Department levels, must be oriented toward answering the question of the President: at this rate, what will be the expected survival of the American Way of Life?

With respect to the President as PDM, the Secretary of Defense is at the sub-PDM level. Given the objective of national survival at the PDM level, what must be the corresponding strategic objective at the sub-PDM level?

To arrive at an operational measure of survival as perceived by the sub-PDM, three distinguishing characteristics of Department of Defense activity are identified: (1) DOD produces goods and services for non-use; (2) the adversary of the future is unknown both in terms of form and forte; and (3) the technological options that will be available tomorrow increase exponentially, and it is these potential increases that have to be specifically enumerated today in making the decisions.

Again, how can the expected potential performance of future technological options be operationally measured today? The measure has to take into account the known facts of the performance of "our" choices compared with "their" choices; and the comparisons have to be made on the basis of known performance characteristics on the one hand, and unknown characteristics on the other; after all, the USSR does not tell the USA their test results, much less their plans for new weapons, and vice versa.

The emphasis upon the objectives hierarchy gives clear direction to the OR/SA effort; the input of data at the Office of Secretary of Defense Level, the Joint Chiefs of Staff Level, the Services Level and the sub-Services Level must be oriented toward answering the question of the Secretary: at this rate, what will be the expected potential performance of technological options – ours and theirs; and the index of sufficiency of survival?

Turning from the public sector to the private sector, the roles of the price mechanism and the profit mechanism exercise significant difference.

The question of credibility is, however, common to both the national defense, and the private product operations. In the former the role of credibility is to ensure non-use; *in the latter, the role of credibility is in insuring* use.

Technological operations are important to the private sector. But technological performance is not *the deciding factor. Instead, it is technological* packaging. *The advertisement for Tang orange juice is not geared to its technological performance in providing Vitamin C, but instead, it is geared to the technological* packaging. *Because it was chosen for use in outer space, the glamor of space technology is sought to be rubbed off on Tang orange juice. To the corporate PDM, in weighing the credibility competition, the battle is waged in the arena of the technological packaging. At this rate, what will be the expected potential credibility of technological packaging – ours and theirs – and the index of the market acquisition in terms of sufficiency of survival?*

Whether in the public sector or the private sector, the PDM overrules the sub-PDM; and the sub-PDM overrules the sub-sub-PDM. Yet, the overruling takes place in the name of long-run survival and growth; which is precisely what the sub-PDM levels are not *paid to concentrate upon. At the national level, the President as PDM overrules the Secre-*

tary of Defense; the former wants the SALT negotiations to succeed, which are based on insufficiency *of nuclear capabilities of the super-powers, brought about by mutual agreement. However, as sub-PDM, the Secretary of Defense is dedicated to* sufficiency *of nuclear weapons for survival. As sub-sub-PDM, the Secretary of the Air Force, asks for funds to support the* absolute *technological capability of air and space weap-onry, in competition with the demands for land and water warfare. The demand for funds to support* absolute *technological capability are, of course, completely at variance with the PDM posture of renouncing, by mutual agreement, the* absolute *technological capabilities.*

At the same time, the strength of the PDM in the negotiations for the mutual reduction of strategic weapons does in fact stem from the absolute *capabilities which the sub-PDM and the sub-sub-PDM espouse. Therefore, the PDM overrules the sub-PDM and the sub-sub-PDM; but in overruling, he is really drawing upon the efficiency of the work done by his sub-PDM, and sub-sub-PDM. In other words, the better the work of the sub-PDM and the sub-sub-PDM, the better it is for the PDM to undermine the search for the very capability that his subordinates are building up. The better the performance at the sub-levels, the faster their demise.*

The context C (for concurrent conflict) is not necessarily so dra-matic in all its instances. Nevertheless, the essence of conflict itself is undeniable. While in this illustration, we have physically separated the three decision-makers, the three types of decisions could well be made by the same decision-maker. It is important, therefore, to specify the relative importance of each of the three roles, and the relative frequen-cy with which it is played. The frequency itself must be tempered by the gravity of the consequences. An index of importance of PDM roles should be developed; and an approach to this is suggested.

EXECUTIVE SUMMARY

In any decision-making hierarchy, most decision-makers can identify at least one level higher than himself, and another lower than himself. In an organization of any size, three such levels: the top level, the middle, and the lower level of management are identifiable.

Such an identification can be absolute, in the sense that there is only one President for the corporation. It can also be relative in terms of the relative *decision-making authority and responsibility. The notion of a Principal Decision-Maker (PDM) is in order. He is the one who is at the top of the administrative hierarchy and whose actions affect the given unit more potently than anyone else. He commands a unit of significant administrative responsibility with resources and authority, which is charged with an identifiable objective.*

A PDM can be the President of a corporation; he can also be a division manager; or a plant manager. While the plant manager is administratively several steps below the President of the corporation, he is the PDM with respect to the 200–300 employees of the plant.

When we recognize that every level of management is part of a threesome: one above, one below, and one in the middle, which, because of their connected nature may be called a triad, an interesting classification, as well as a conflict, *emerges.*

The Classification is parallel to the three levels: top, middle, and lower management; and can be called PDM, sub-PDM, and sub-sub-PDM. The plant manager is the sub-sub-PDM with respect to the company President. He is the sub-PDM with respect to the division manager; and he is the PDM with respect to the plant employees.

The conflict arises in the fact that the plant manager has to play all three roles simultaneously. *He may not be called into the office of the President very often; he may communicate with the division manager more often. Most of the time, it is with his employees that he is dealing. In other words, in terms of the allocation of time, the plant manager plays the PDM role most often, sub-PDM less often, and sub-sub-PDM most infrequently.*

However, the frequency is not the best measure of the importance. The one meeting he may have with the President in six months may be the most important as far as the operations of the plant itself are concerned. Therefore, frequency has to be weighted by criticality. An index can be devised which combines the frequency with the criticality.

The conflict between the three roles of a decision-maker has crucial implications for the Management Information Systems (MIS). The MIS has to provide the plant manager with information in the form of forecasting, not only in the immediate (for the PDM role), but also, simultaneously *in the intermediate (for his role as the sub-PDM), and for the indefinite period (for his role as sub-sub-PDM). No single raw data base can provide all the three forecasts with equal validity. Nevertheless, it is precisely in providing forecasts which he can use in the three roles that the value of an MIS lies.*

Context C (for Concurrent Conflict) of the PDM is developed in four applications, both in the public, and in the private, sectors. The President of the United States as PDM, the Secretary of Defense as PDM; and the President of a corporation as PDM − all require specific MIS inputs. These inputs are specific forecasts. The forecasts are meaningful only to the extent that they respond to the needs of the PDM.

Operational measures of the objectives that each PDM fulfills must be recognized to guide the MIS efforts. Such measures are developed for both the public sector and the private sector in the different applications. In the light of the operational measures, the conflicting demands upon the PDM roles are identified. An index has to be developed to reflect the relative importance of the different roles as a guide to the particular type of MIS required.

The first of the four substantive elements of OR/SA identified in Chapter 3, *Context*, is the perception of the boundaries by the decision-maker. The context could be risky or uncertain. If it is uncertain in the sense that the probability distribution of the performance characteristics is unknown, then one contribution of OR/SA effort is to reduce uncertainty to risk.

The purpose of the OR/SA effort is to aid decision-making. Therefore, it is important to identify the perspective of the decision-maker.

1. Notion of Principal Decision-Maker (PDM)

Given any level of management, a higher and a lower level can always be specified. Therefore, management has to be viewed in the hierarchical context. A minimum view of management hierarchy will thus have three related levels: the higher; the in-between; and the lower − which have been called organismic, strategic, and tactical.

To provide perspective on the triad, the notion of a *Principal Decision-Maker* (PDM) is in order. He is the one who is at the top of the administrative hierarchy and whose actions affect the given unit more potently than any one else. Thus, the PDM can be: The President of the United States; the President of a corporation; The Secretary of State; the Division Manager of a products division; the owner of a gas station, and so on. The identifying characteristics are that the PDM command a *unit of significant administrative responsibility with resources and authority, which is charged with an identifiable objective.*

2. Diverse PDM Roles — Simultaneous and Successive

If a higher and a lower level of management can always be specified, then the notion of PDM is not an absolute one, but a *relative* one. In the successive triads of decision levels developed in the different rounds in Chapter 6, Section 7, the tactical level of Round 1 is the organismic level of Round 2 when the objectives are defined top-down and the organismic level of Round 1 is the tactical level of Round 2 when the objectives are defined top-up. In other words, the decision-making roles at any level are *relative*.

The relative nature of PDM underscores the need to recognize the different hats worn by the same manager *simultaneously*. In Chapter 6, Section 5, recognition of these simultaneous demands is made when we identify the Congressional Decision-Maker as not only (1) a national law maker, but also (2) the member of a national political party, who nevertheless has been sent to Congress as (3) the protector of the interests of his own Congressional District. While to his district voters he may often appear to be at the organismic level, he is at the strategic level in piloting legislation of special interest to his district, through his party, and at the tactical level with respect to national legislative issues.

Since the decision-maker can *not* be all things to all people at all times, he has to choose, by design or by default, those roles which he shall emphasize at any given time to the de-emphasis, if not exclusion, of others. Thus, if the Congressional decision-maker leaves the appropriations hearings in progress to listen to the Police Chief of his Congressional District who asks him, over long distance telephone, to help find an entertainer for the forthcoming Policeman's Benefit, and if the congressional decision-maker finds on return to the hearings room that $10 000 have been appropriated while he was

away, it shows that the PDM role of protector of district interests was emphasized during that phone conversation to the exclusion of his role as national law maker. The $10 000 is not an exaggeration when it is considered
that the Appropriations Subcommittee appropriated $5 billion for NASA
in five days. On a 10-hour day, the hourly rate of appropriation was
$(10^9/10 =)$ 10^8; a 6-minute call, or 10^{-1} hour represented $(10^8 \times 10^{-1} =)$
10^7, or $10 000 000.

The reversion to the organismic role as national law maker on his return to
the appropriations hearings from his PDM role with respect to his district
which is at the tactical level (with respect to his national law maker role)
shows the *successive* nature of his roles: from tactical to organismic or from
organismic in Round 1 to organismic in Round 2 in a top-up defining of
objectives.

The PDM roles are: (1) simultaneous; and (2) successive. To fix ideas, let
us first consider PDM levels and how the same decision-maker becomes sub-
PDM, and sub-sub-PDM:

Organismic	PDM
Strategic	Sub-PDM
Tactical	Sub-sub-PDM

3. Primary Concerns of the PDM

The PDM is the one who has to define and redefine what the organism should
achieve. For any organism, there are two basic goals: (1) survival, and (2)
growth. If one goal is to be sacrificed, that will be growth, because without
survival there simply can be no growth. The first requirement for a systems
approach to decision-making at the PDM level is to define operationally what
survival means to the given organism. We shall do this by considering a number of different organisms which are bound to define survival differently.

3.1. Survival of Organismic Capabilities

Survival means the continuance of the capabilities to perform at the existing
level. Survival of the physical resources is clear enough to understand. For
instance, an automobile is said to survive as long as the performance of the
transportation function is acceptable to its operator. The "existing level" of

performance has both a physical characteristic and a psychic acceptance. The physical characteristics can be calibrated, but the psychic acceptance is clearly subjective, and, therefore, subject to change from time to time for the same person, and from person to person at the same time. Among the physical characteristics of the automobile are the time required for ignition, the time for warmup, the ease of operations, such as acceleration, deceleration, and braking, etc. Given identical physical characteristics of physical operation, the same car may be acceptable to one operator, but at the same time, not acceptable to another operator.

Survival, as applied to the nonphysical resources of the organism, is much harder to define. The primary component of the nonphysical characteristic is the human resource; and human skills and motivation are clearly much harder to define let alone measure than the survival of the physical resources.

There is a further complication to the dimension of human skills and performance. It arises from the fact that the PDM has to view the survival, not for its own sake, but in terms of the demand for the survival by some source(s) external to the organism. Whether it is in the production of goods or of services, the PDM has to deploy the human skills at his command in such a way that some external demand for the goods and services that can be produced are satisfied. Even with the best of human capabilities at his command, the PDM will be able to take little comfort in the survival of the organism in terms of its human capabilities, if there is no demand for the wares that the capabilities can fashion. Therefore, to interpret the survival as applied to the human capabilities of the organism, the PDM has to think in terms of the *transformation* of the supply of human capabilities to meet present and potential demand.

As applied to the *physical* resources of the organism, survival can be specified in terms of the continuing capability to perform *present* functions. However, as applied to the *human* resources of the organism, survival can be specified in terms of the continuing capability to perform *present and potential functions*. The reason why only the present can be applied to the physical resources is that a machine must be designed to be function-specific, and any alteration would require retooling. Should the retooling be extensive, it may be worthwhile to scrap the machine and start all over again. However, in the case of the human capabilities, the educational process is ideally designed to develop discipline of the mind which can be applied to diverse functions. Knowledge of the subject matter is indeed essential, but unlike the machine which has to be dedicated to a single function, the human capabilities can be dedicated to several functions at the same time. Therefore, from the point of view of the PDM, survival of the physical resources means *specificity* of functions, while the survival of the human resources means *versatility* in the functions that can be performed.

3.2. User Orientation of PDM

By definition, the PDM looks at the survival of the organism on the long term. Insofar as the survival of the organism depends upon the matching of the internal capabilities with external requirements he has to perceive the changes in the demands that will be made by the present users, as well as potential users. In the objectives hierarchy, the highest operational level is represented by the perspective of the PDM in his efforts to be responsive to his environment. These responses reflect a balancing of the two types of variables: (1) technological variables, and (2) environmental variables. Of the two, environmental variables, since they represent the profile of the user, are the initiating variables; and the technological variables as they pertain to the internal capabilities of the organisms, reflect the profile of the response that the organism can make via responding variables.

4. APPLICATION 11: Perspective of the Principal Decision-Maker — National Level

Even at the national level of decision-making, viz., that of the President of the United States, the PDM has to be user-oriented in carrying out the charge of the electorate.

4.1. User Orientation

The power of the user in this case is perhaps the least direct and the least effective in the balancing of the national requirements with the Federal capabilities. The reason is the absence of the *price mechanism* which is operative in the private sector. Price is the calibration by users of the worth of the goods and services offered by the organism.

While the private organism could survive for some time by taking advan-

tage of the wide variations in information on products and services and disposition towards them of the users, it will have to respond seriously to the
willingness of the market as expressed in its demand at different prices. No
such mechanism exists in the public sector; therefore, the influence of the
user is much more remote, and much less effective. The legislative or executive leadership can be made to feel the displeasure of the users with their
services mostly at stated intervals, and then en masse; unlike the provider of a
product and/or service from which the users can stay off in droves at any
time, thereby making the preferences of the users more directly felt.

4.2. OMB Reorganization for Better User Orientation

The Office of Management and Budget (OMB) was reorganized in April 1973
to reflect "Presidential Priority" goals. Earlier, the President in a letter to the
Heads of Federal Departments and Agencies directed each unit to give "particular attention to objectives which you consider to be of Presidential-level
importance."

The reorganization of the OMB as of April 1973 reflects the requirements
of the users, i.e., the American Public, as perceived by the national decision-
maker. There are four program areas headed by associate directors:

National Security and International Affairs,

Economics and Government,

Natural Resources, Energy, and Science, and

Human and Community Affairs.

In other words, the four program areas represent the areas of importance
to the public, the user, as perceived by the President who is the PDM at the
national level. Two of the four refer to the human resources and natural
resources, which is a classification already reflected in the earlier executive
reorganization in which super cabinet level coordinators were appointed for
human resources and natural resources development. So also, the direct involvement of the President in the context of diplomatic communications with
China and the Soviet Union, and the conclusion of the SALT treaty and the
Vietnam peace accord, and the role of the Presidential Advisor for National
Security Affairs, finds a natural sequel in the third program area in OMB of
National Security and International Affairs. The fourth program area could
be considered the monetary resources and fiscal resources areas of govern-
mental operations.

The highlighting of the four program areas: (1) human resources; (2) natural resources; (3) monetary and fiscal resources; and (4) security resources, makes it possible to articulate the system objectives. In other words, the national objectives can be expressed in terms of these four program areas, each of which has to contribute integrally to the achievement of the overall national objective.

4.3. National Objective of Survival

What is the overall national objective? It can be stated in a number of different ways, but from the point of view of developing the calibration of the progress towards achieving national objectives, some *operational* objectives have to be enunciated. The constitutional promise of "liberty, justice, and the pursuit of happiness" certainly provides an acceptable starting point for the national objectives statement. Each of the three components of the national organismic objective admits of wide latitude in interpretation. This is as it should be, because they are ideals which are never reached, but which, forever urge the nation to reach out for elements beyond its grasp.

Using the notion of survival introduced in Section 3.1, what does national survival mean? Certainly, the physical survival of the 50 states is included in the notion of survival. Not only does the survival refer to the existence in the same physical form, but also to a continuance of the capability to perform equivalent functions, i.e., yielding the means of food, shelter, and other necessities of life to the population of the 50 states.

Equally, if not more, important is the survival of what is loosely described as The American Way of Life. In other words, not only should the physical resources be capable of yielding food, shelter, and other necessities of life, but they should also be acquirable in a manner to which the American people have grown accustomed. Just like liberty, justice, and the pursuit of happiness, The American Way of Life is also subject to varying interpretation at various times. By specifying survival as the survival of The American Way of Life, the emphasis is placed upon *results* which may be calibrated, however inadequately, than terms such as liberty, justice, and the pursuit of happiness.

4.4. Probability as in Probability of Survival

There is no assurance that the organismic objective of national survival will ever be accomplished. All the efforts directed toward survival have to be couched in terms of the *probability* of survival. The objective of the organism must therefore be stated as: The expected survival of The American Way of Life. The merit of the four major program areas of OMB has to be assessed in terms of the improvement in the expectation of the survival of The American Way of Life.

The use of the term "expected" raises the question of *mathematical expectation* which is a precise quantity. The national survival, represented by variable X_i, can take different values with the different probabilities, represented by p_i. To fix ideas, the value of the throw of a die, represented by the variable X_i, can take the values 1, 2, 3, 4, 5, or 6. Any one of the 6 values can occur in any throw of the die, and every value is as likely as any other. In other words, the value of the throw could be 1 or 6; which means that in 100 throws, it could all be 1's or 6's, both of which would fulfill the requirement that each value be equally likely.

One concept of probability, that which is most often used, is that of relative frequency: The number of times the specified result occurs expressed as a percentage of the total number of occurrences. If, in 60 throws of a die, the number 4 occurred 20 times, the probability of X_i ($i = 4$) is 20/60 = 0.33; and if the number 5 occurred 10 times, the probability of X_i ($i = 5$) is 10/60 = 0.16. In any one throw, *either* 4 or 5 (or 1, 2, 3, 6) occurs. Therefore, the value of the throw is 4 or 5 (or 1, 2, 3, or 6). However, a *composite* of the different outcomes may be constructed by stating that the *expected* value of the throw is made up of the sum of the products of each value multiplied by its probability. In the case of the 60 throws, the number 4 occurs with the probability 0.33, giving rise to a product (4 × 0.33=) 1.32; the number 5 occurs with the probability 0.16, giving rise to a product (5 × 0.16=) 0.80.

We have so far only accounted for (20 + 10=) 30 throws out of the 60 throws. Let us say that the number 1 occurs 15 times, the probability of X_i ($i = 1$) is 15/60 = 0.25; and if the number 6 occurs the remaining 15 times, the probability of X_i ($i = 6$) is also 15/60 = 0.25. The corresponding products are (1 × 0.25=) 0.25, and (6 × 0.25=) 3.00.

Having accounted for the values of a throw, X_i, in all the 60 throws, we can now compute the *expected* value of a throw of the die by adding the products of each value and its probability. The number 4 yielded a product of 1.32; the number 5 a product of 0.80; the number 1 a product of 0.25; and the number 6 a product of 3.00 − the sum of the products being (1.32 +

0.80 + 0.25 + 3.00=) 5.47. In other words, based on this *particular expe-rience*, we say that the expected value of a throw of this die is 5.47. Since there is no such number on the die, it means either 5 or 6 may be expected to occur in a throw of the die in the *long run*.

This result is higher than what one would expect from a die in which each value is equally likely to occur in every throw. Notice that in the 60 throws we had no 2's or 3's. If each of the 6 numbers occurred exactly as often as the other, in 60 throws, there would be 10 1's, 10 2's, 10 3's, 10 4's, 10 5's, and 10 6's. The product of X_i ($i = 1$) and its probability, p_i (10/60=) 0.16 will be (1 × 0.16=) 0.16. Similarly, the other products would be obtained by multi-plying the numbers 2, 3, 4, 5, and 6 by the identical probability 0.16. The sum of the products of the $X_i p_i$ is (0.16 + 0.32 + 0.48 + 0.64 + 0.80 + 0.96=) 3.36. In other words, based on this *particular experience,* we say that the expected value of a throw of the die is 3.36. Since there is no such number on the die, it means that either 3 or 4 may be expected to occur in a throw of the die in the long run. The value 3.36 reflects the error in rounding 1/6 to 0.16. If the probability value is carried out to further decimal places, the expected value will come out as 3.50, instead of 3.36.

As stated earlier, any one of the numbers could occur at any time just as often as any other. Therefore, the expected value relates to a composite occurrence, where the composite is made up of not 1 or 2 or 3 throws, but a large number of throws, an infinite number of throws to be precise. Since infinity is beyond the realm of finite numbers, the expected value is a state-ment about a *tendency* which is ever approached, never realized. In other words, projecting the experience of the particular instances of throws, the expected value will be approached closer and closer as the number of trials approaches infinity.

The expected survival of The American Way of Life is thus a *composite* experience which can only be approached as the number of times the speci-fied outcome is calibrated an infinite number of times.

As Hamlet says, "There's the rub"; for, there can be no infinite number of trials to calibrate the values of the national organismic survival. Furthermore, the inflexible requirement — that any value, i.e., from total devastation to the maximum successful survival of the national organism in its preferred Way of Life, can occur with equal frequency in every trial — can in no way be fulfilled in practice. Therefore, the concept of probability has to be a differ-ent one from that of relative frequency.

Four kinds of probability have been discussed elsewhere.[1] Suffice it to say
here that the subjective concepts of *belief in events* and/or *belief in propositions* have to be employed as the measure of probability instead of the
relative frequency of events. In the former instance, one exercises one's own
judgment with respect to the specified events in spite of any evidence or
postulates to the contraray. Thus, when the weather forecaster announces
that the probability of rain is 65%, he is presenting the relative frequency
concept of probability, because he is drawing upon the extensive experience
of the weather bureau in the confluence of factors that produce precipitation,
such as humidity, wind changes, temperature, etc. Looking upon the experience over a long time of a number of instances, he is saying that if tomorrow is like all the yesterdays, in the long run, when the confluence of weather
factors was similar to what is likely to occur tomorrow, nearly two out of three
times it resulted in rain. Notice that he would be quite correct in the probabilistic sense if in fact there were no rain at all the next day, because his
statement only relates to the long run.

Listening to the weather forecaster's relative frequency concept of probability, the individual decides his *belief in events*, in this case the occurrence of
rain. Let us say, that he says the probability of rain is 0.1. It does *not* mean
that he has in fact performed extensive experimentation in the forecast of
rain and its occurrence to come to such a conclusion. It only means that is his
"belief", which may be based on no repeatable or verifiable basis, but simply
factors such as "my hunch", "my bunions", and so on. There needs to be no
repeatable, observable, and/or verifiable basis at all for the determination of
0.1 probability. The consequence of the probability is his decision not to take
an umbrella or raincoat. In daily life, this "belief" is in fact exercised time
and again. What should be pointed out is that while it is a valid basis for
decision-making, the expected value concept can *not* be applied as was done
earlier with respect to the throws of the die.

The belief in the propositions is similar to the belief in events, with one
exception. The exception is that while there needs to be no perceivable basis
for the probability in the case of the belief in events, two or more events,
activities, and/or relationships have to be explicitly identified with the particular event in question. Consider the statements:

[1] George K. Chacko, *Applied Statistics in Decision-Making*, American Elsevier, New
York, 1971, pp. 51–74.

The Sun shines only at night.
The Sun shines now.

Given these two propositions, the observation that

The Sun is shining now

can only result in the conclusion that it is now nighttime. Notice that the truth or otherwise of the first two propositions has no influence upon the conclusion. All that is required is that two such propositions be related in such a way that an unmistakable conclusion can be drawn on the basis of an observation, such as the fact of the shining of the Sun.

Even when such a propositional relationship is involved, the conclusion is inevitable only if *logical probability* is the concept employed. In the case of *subjective probability*, instead of the conclusion that it is nighttime now, the conclusion could be: it may be nighttime now. In other words, given the same body of evidence, i.e., the fact of the sun shining now, there is no unique determination as to the outcome, i.e., daytime or nighttime.

> Let our premises consist of any set of propositions *h* and our conclusions consist of any set of propositions *a*, then if a knowledge of *h* justifies a rational degree of belief in *a* of degree *A*, we may say that there is a probability-relation of degree *A* between *a* and *h*.
>
> Given a statement *S* and a body of evidence *E*, there is one and only one real number *p* such that it may correctly be said that the probability of *S* relative to *E* is *p*.
>
> The subjectivistic view of probability differs from the logical view. Kyburg points out:
>
> The subjectivistic view is to be distinguished from the logical view precisely by its denial of the latter assertion. On the subjectivistic view, probability represents a relation between a statement and a body of evidence, but it is not a purely logical relation. It is a quasilogical relation and the numerical value attached to it represents a degree of belief. On the subjectivistic view, this value is not uniquely determined: a given statement may have any probability between 0 and 1, on given evidence, according to the inclination of the person whose degree of belief that probability represents.[2]

In his eminently readable book, *Decision Analysis: Introductory Lectures*

---

[2] George K. Chacko, *op. cit.*, pp. 59–60.

on Choices Under Uncertainty, Howard Raiffa presents a *"constructive"* approach to "choosing an act that is consistent with [an individual's] basic judgments and preferences." He calls for consistent behavior on the part of the decision-maker, and the calculation of the implications of his actions:

> We have shown that if the decision-maker adopts two principles of consistent behavior, transitivity of preferences and substitutability of indifferent consequences in a lottery, then he's pretty well fenced in. He should scale his preferences for the consequences at the tips of the decision tree in terms of utility values and scale his judgments about uncertain events in terms of probability assignments at chance moves, and, finally he should select his best strategy for experimentation and action by the process of averaging out and folding back. ... He must consciously police the consistency of his subjective inputs and *calculate* their implications for action.[3]

In his procedure, Raiffa argues that subjective probabilities could be treated as if they were objective because *so far as action is concerned* one should not worry about "mixing some objective and some subjective or judgmental probabilities together in the same formula."

4.5. Operational Measures of Survival — Quantity

The expected survival of the American Way of Life has thus to be interpreted in terms of probability concepts other than that of relative frequency. Irrespective of the concept of probability employed, it is essential to provide *operational* measures. If survival is the continuance of the capabilities to perform the functions at the existing level, the operational measure should specify what fraction of the population would be able to enjoy what levels of food, shelter and other necessities of life. In the 1964 election, the question of what constituted the poverty level was raised, and it was set at $3 000 per capita. In other words, it could be interpreted as the statement that if someone did not earn $3 000 a year in 1964 dollars, then he would *not* be surviving, not having the accepted level of food, shelter and necessities of life. The number of people who were not surviving in 1964 was placed at between 12 and 15 million. With a population of 210 million, the percentage of those not surviving was between 5.7% and 7.1%. With the change in the purchasing power of the dollar, this level would naturally change. As an operational

---

[3] Howard Raiffa, *Decision Analysis: Introductory Lectures on Choices Under Uncertainty*, Addison-Wesley, Reading, Mass., 1968.

measure, one could state that survival of the American Way of Life means that not more than $X\%$ of the U.S. population should earn below poverty level income.

4.6. Operational Measures of Survival – Quality: (1) Health

The American Way of Life expresses something more than mere survival. It has to include in it the concept of "quality of life". If survival means *existence,* quality of life would mean *enjoyment.* Enjoyment itself comprises: (1) health, and (2) happiness. Both can be defined in a number of different ways. One operational way of defining health would be: *The physical and mental capability to pursue one's own choices.* Notice that the intensely personal elements of physical and mental health only are included in the definition of health. Notice also that only the ability to pursue one's choices is specified; nothing is said about the opportunity to do so. The phrase "one's own choices" requires that there be a number of choices available because the personal preferences of individuals tend to be different; also that there be no restriction in the selection of particular vocation, avocation, and/or leisure.

To measure the health of the U.S. population, the number of days in which the U.S. population was prevented due to physical and/or mental health from pursuing their choices could be counted. The number of mandays lost due to illness can be established on the basis of the work records of employed population. The same concept can be applied to those pursuing avocations, as well as those pursuing leisure. A floor could be established as to the percentage of the U.S. population *not* being able to pursue their choices *only* due to health matters.

4.7. Operational Measures of Survival – Quality: (2) Happiness

The calibration of happiness is perhaps more elusive. However, the concepts of individual freedom embodied in the words of the Constitution: life, liberty, and the pursuit of happiness, and the concept of health as developed in the preceding paragraphs, can be utilized to arrive at an operational measure of happiness. According to Maslow, the highest element in the hierarchy of human needs is: self-actualization. To realize self-actualization, we could say that there must be: (1) personal objectives; (2) personal capabilities, and (3) individual and/or institutional facilities to pursue the personal objectives employing the personal capabilities.

In other words, if health means the capability to pursue one's choices, *happiness is the opportunity to pursue one's choices.* The percentage of the U.S. population that is *un*able to pursue their own choices because of lack of opportunity, is harder to measure than the percentage of people unable to work because of poor health. For, the minimal standards of health can be specified and measured: "there is nothing wrong with you"; or "go home and rest in bed", etc. However, the lack of opportunity would be a function of the individual's own objectives which would and do change from time to time, and from person to person. The philosophy behind the free enterprise system is that the supply of one's capabilities is brought into balance with the demand for the products and/or services it can produce via the price mechanism. However, the government operates *outside* the price mechanism. The commitment to land a man on the Moon and to return him safely to the Earth was not based on the market value of the Moon rocks. Instead, it was based upon the national reach exceeding its grasp in the area of exploring the unknown. That decision created a $25 billion industry, and, by the same token, abolished that industry when space exploration was abandoned as a serious national effort. The demand for the capabilities of scientists and engineers that was created in the 1960's by the accelerated space effort, was withdrawn in the 1970's. The opportunities for self-realization of some very highly skilled people were almost irretrievably squashed by the reversal of the Federal emphasis on aerospace.

Nor is the individual scientist and engineer the only loser. The many years of training and the many years of experience represented in each individual scientist and engineer, when unused, become an irreplaceable waste of *national* resources. This national waste would be reflected in a measure of happiness as the percentage of the U.S. population unable to pursue its own choices due to the lack of opportunity. By investigating the second and third choices in the individual's objectives, the institutional facilities required to fulfill those objectives can be planned for at the national level.

4.8. Operational Measures of Resource Allocation: Value of Life

The choices pursued come from an education which is the source of developed skills — technical and human. The contribution of education to the quality of life can be intuitively appreciated. However, in discussing the allocation of resources for education, directly or indirectly, another concept emerges as the generic source. It is the concept of lifetime earnings.

The genesis of the lifetime earnings is better appreciated if the insurance industry practice of determining the economic value of human life is recognized. Despite the intitial abhorrence of the idea of anything so crass as placing a dollar sign on human life, there is some justification for the computational procedure. Any insurance is to rectify a loss should it occur. In the case of the human life, what can constitute the rectification? Clearly, none of the contributions that the individual makes to his family, community, and country could ever be replaced. Therefore, a negative approach in the sense of the minimum contributions that he would have made towards an immediate circle of obligations, has to be evolved. The minimum contributions are counted in terms of the monetary support that he would have provided had he continued with those pursuits in force at the time of his death.

Thus, the value of the human life, the loss of which is to be rectified, is counted in pure and simple dollar terms. How much would he have earned at the present rate? Here the averages are terribly misleading, because each individual can accomplish significantly differently from every other individual with similar backgrounds. Nevertheless, it is generally recognized that the average lifetime earnings of a college graduate are much higher than those of a high school graduate. This comparison provides the floor, as it were, of lifetime earnings. Precisely because the individual earnings can vary significantly, there is no limit placed upon the monetary value that an individual can contract for in his life insurance policies.

The lifetime earnings can be considered as a specific operational measure of the value of one's life. In discussing the appropriate allocation for college education, the cost of the education can be compared with the results of the education. The more important results of the college education are personal and individual; but only the monetary measure of earnings is usually considered in the allocation process.

4.8.1. Life table population

Underlying the notion of lifetime earnings is the concept of Life Table Population, familiar to demography which is the study of population. The Life Table Population is an abstraction. It is the composite experience of a large number of babies (100 000 or 1 million) born at the same instant. The experience of the 100 000 babies is a composite, because the experience of surviving from age 0 to age 1 should reflect the experience of the people throughout the United States (or any other country) under consideration. It means that the experience of an infant of surviving from age 0 to age 1 in the city, in the rural areas, in the slums, in the suburbs, in the north, in the south, in the east, and in the west, must all be reflected to yield any valid composite experience. Similarly, the experience of morbidity/illness should also be reflected in the Life Table Population. A third important element, in addition to mortality and morbidity is the reproductive experience of the Life Table Population. Does the population reproduce itself, leaving 100 000 babies to take the place of the original 100 000 who have lived and died? Or, does the Life Table Population leave more than 100 000 babies or less? Closely associated with the reproductive experience of the Life Table Population is the age distribution of the population. A "young" population is one which has a larger fraction of the younger ages, particularly in the reproductive period, and an "older" population is one which has a larger fraction of the older people, particularly beyond the reproductive period.

The lifetime earnings are closely related to the Life Table Population. It is the Life Table Population which specifies the probability of survival from one age to the next, and from one age group to the next group. Therefore, given the average earnings of a college graduate, the probability of his acquiring the lifetime earnings as a college graduate, depends upon the probability of his surviving beyond graduation. Implicit in any lifetime earnings calculation is the Life Table Population, which must therefore be explicitly ascertained before placing credence upon the lifetime earnings.

It should be emphasized that the lifetime earnings, as an admittedly crude measure of the value of life, is an *expected* earnings figure. As an expected figure, it is only the *population* comprising a large number of units such as the 100 000 babies born at the same instant which experiences the earnings. In other words, out of a very large number of babies, a fraction became high school graduates, and another fraction became college graduates. Some earned more and some earned less. Making a composite of the experiences of all the graduates and the nongraduates, the fraction of the total population earning more than or less than a specified lifetime earnings, say, $250 000 can be determined. With each earnings figure, such as $250 000, $275 000, $110 000, $192 000, $500 000, etc., a fraction of the total population which earns that amount can be determined on the basis of past experience. A composite of the various experiences, of both the earnings figure and the population fraction that earns that figure, is utilized in arriving at an individual's expectation of lifetime earnings. The national resources allocation for human resources development often uses the lifetime earnings concept.

4.9. Value of Life as a Measure of Happiness

The number of things in one's possession may be considered an index, but it would be a poor measure if we consider happiness to be an inward index. One's index of happiness would vary from time to time, and it certainly does vary from person to person. The search for a generic expression of happiness must therefore be related to a univeral experience. Birth is one; death is another. What is the measure of happiness at death, it being meaningless to ask the question at the time of birth? Since death is the cessation of the pursuit of one's chosen activities, the measure cannot be related to the continuance of the same activities. We are forced to settle for a negative measure. Instead of asking the question: what would make one the most happy, the question should be: what would make one least unhappy at the time of death?

Recalling that more significant elements of value in one's life had to be abandoned in favor of the basic minimum of a monetary index in the form of one's lifetime earnings to represent the value of life, we may pursue the implications of the same measure as an index of happiness at the time of death. What would one be most concerned about in terms of the monetary considerations? Not the size of his earnings per se, because they shall have stopped. As a social animal, the continuation of one's lifetime contributions takes the form of his immediate family, which is the basic minimum that is universally applicable. For the survival of that family unit without the deceased individual, there are monetary requirements of varying intensity and length. We can refer to these as the obligations of his estate. These obligations also vary with the individual. Therefore, the minimum requirement which can be universally applied for the avoidance of unhappiness at the time of death can be stated as the condition that the value of one's estate at the time of death should be equal to or greater than the obligations of that estate.

4.10. Presidential Priorities and Measures of Survival

The emphasis upon the Presidential Priorities was underscored by OMB Director Roy L. Ash:

> We have to set specific targets. Every agency has hundreds of goals and objectives. Some of them are of importance to the President; most are not. The President

may have a hundred things he wants to accomplish in the year. We're going to help the President do it by focusing the agency's attention on his priority goals.[4]

The President's priority goals must include the *expected survival of the American Way of Life as reflected in the measures of:* (1) the percent of U.S. population earning income under the poverty level; (2) the percent of U.S. population unable to pursue its own choices because of lack of health; and (3) the percent of U.S. population unable to pursue its choices for lack of opportunity.

Starting with operational measures which express the PDM's perspective at the national level, the individual Agencies and Departments of the Federal Government can identify objectives which they consider to be of Presidential level importance. The PDM's objectives are organismic objectives, and the Departments' and Agencies' objectives are strategic objectives which seek to carry out the organismic objectives of the PDM. The four program areas under the new organization of the OMB indicate the PDM's perspective on the strategic level objectives. Several Departments and Agencies would come under the purview of the same program area, and the same Department and Agency may come under the purview of several program areas of OMB. The emphasis upon the Presidential priorities cuts across the administrative hierarchy. The administrative hierarchies may come and go, but the objectives hierarchy remains. The emphasis upon the objectives hierarchy gives clear direction to the OR/SA effort: Provide forecasts to the PDM to enable him to exercise control. The input of data at the OMB level, the Department level, and the subDepartment levels must be oriented toward answering the question of the President: At this rate, what will be the expected survival of the American Way of Life?

5. APPLICATION 12: Perspective of the Principal Decision-Maker – Cabinet Level

The survival of the 50 states is a precondition to the opportunity for, and the capability to, pursue one's own choices. One of the four program areas of

[4] David S. Brader, "OMB Reorganized by Ash", *The Washington Post*, April 26, 1973, p. A4.

OMB, viz., national security and international affairs, is devoted to the satisfying of this precondition.

Given the organismic perspective of the PDM at the national level, how can
the Department (Defense Department), and the Agencies (Atomic Energy
Commission, Central Intelligence Agency, Defense Intelligence Agency, etc.)
state their *strategic* objective which will permit operational measurement?

5.1. Three Distinguishing Characteristics of DOD Activity

Unlike in the case of the other Departments, the Department of Defense
produces goods and services for *nonuse*. The value of the products and services of the Department of Health, Education, and Welfare is in the *use* of the
educational services, the health services, and the welfare services that are
provided by the Department. On the contrary, the value of the weapons
systems that are produced by the Department of Defense lies precisely in their
nonuse. In the words of President Kennedy: "Only when our arms are sufficient beyond doubt, can we be certain beyond doubt that they will never be
employed." [5]

In other words, if the U.S. arms are strong enough, their capability has to
persuade the would-be adversary of the credibility of its use. If the would-be
adversary believes that the U.S. arms are strong enough, then he would not
employ his weapons, and the U.S., dedicated to the doctrine of no-first-strike,
will not have to use its weapons. In other words, *credibility* is more important
than *capability*; a credibility which will ensure the nonuse of the weapons
systems.

Another distinguishing characteristic of the products and services of the
Department of Defense is that there is in fact a real, physical, ever-present,
adversary(ies). The weapons systems are intended to make credible the U.S.
capability to a would-be adversary. The capability, therefore, has to be
adversary-specific. However, the identity of the adversary as well as his forte
changes with time. The weapons systems are created today; rather, they are
designed today to be created tomorrow, the tomorrow being several years
away. Who the adversary will be *at that time*, and where the encounter will
take place if deterrence fails become critical questions in the development
of our capability for their credibility.

[5] John F. Kennedy, *Inaugural address*, January 20, 1961.

A third distinguishing characteristic which is unique to the Department of Defense is that *tomorrow's technology* is the arena in which the battle of credibility is fought. Technological options do enter into the choices of every Department and Agency, but, while the unavailability of appropriate technology may impair the effectiveness of the operation of the other Departments, such failure would imperil the very existence in the case of the Department of Defense. Based on the exponential growth of the number of choices made available through science and technology leaps, which results in say, 70 agricultural pesticides being available now compared to only three choices four years earlier, the decision to design a weapons system today using the illustrative three technological options available must survive against weapons system(s) based on a much higher number, e.g., 70, of technical choices tomorrow and the day after.

The three distinguishing characteristics which are unique to the Department of Defense, viz: (1) preferred nonuse of products and services; (2) unidentified form and forte of future adversary; and (3) today's options encountering tomorrow's technology, have to be reflected in the objective of the PDM in the Department of Defense.

5.2. Operational Measure of Defense Performance

To emphasize their nonuse characteristics and to recognize the fact that the assessment of capabilities is made under controlled conditions, we refer to *potential performance* of weapons systems. That would be appropriate insofar as the weapons systems which are in being, or even under construction, are concerned. However, simply to know that the Trident missile will perform with certain specified characteristics is *in*adequate. The real question is: How well will the Trident perform in its intended environment, against an adversary whose form may be known, but certainly not his forte, *in the future environment*? If the Trident's performance is judged to be inadequate in the future environment, then the replacement for Trident has to be designed. The design really means the selection from among technological options. Therefore, to take into account the escalatory nature of the technological options over time which are embodied in successive generations of weapons systems, we refer to *potential performance of technological options.*

We should not forget that we can only talk about *expected* values of the performance and the technological variables. We have to take into account the role of the adversary, to whom we are the adversary. Therefore, it is not only the expected *potential* performance of technological options that are open to us that matters, but also the expected potential performance of technological options open to *them*.

The key word is "potential" whether it be with reference to the performance of the weapons system marked "ours" or "theirs". Even if the testing were done openly, and the observers of both parties were present overtly (as distinguished from the current tracking of testing and other efforts covertly), there remains the necessity to overcome the attitude: "I see it, but I don't believe it." In the absence of visual confirmation, the persuasion has to remain a function of the estimate of the reported potential capability of the yet-to-be-developed weapons system of the adversary.

Nor are the comparisons confined to the present. Even if the testing of the current weapons systems were to be made available to both parties, they have to make estimates of the counterweapons systems of the future. Consider the following simplified version of potential performance of competitive choice of options:

Time	Our choice	Their choice	Present–present	Present–potential
t_0	W_{00}	W_{01}	W_{01}/W_{00}	W_{13}/W_{00}
t_1	W_{12}	W_{13}	W_{13}/W_{12}	W_{25}/W_{12}
t_2	W_{24}	W_{25}	W_{25}/W_{24}	W_{37}/W_{24}
t_3	W_{36}	W_{37}	W_{37}/W_{36}	W_{49}/W_{36}

The second subscript designates the chronological order of the operational decision with respect to each weapons system. Our choice is 0, theirs is 1; followed by our choice of 2, and theirs of 3. Similarly, we start with 4, they respond with 5; followed by our choice of 6 and theirs of 7, etc.

The first element of the suffix denotes the calendar period in which the operational decision has been made. Thus, our choice of weapons system 0 comes at time t_0, denoted by the double subscript W_{00}. Their choice of weapons system 1 is also in the time t_0, denoted by the double subscript W_{01}. Our choice of weapons system 2 is in time t_1, denoted by the double subscript W_{12}, followed by their choice of weapons system 3, also in time t_1, denoted by W_{13}, etc.

The potential performance of competitive choice of options must take into account not only the present-present comparison in Column 4, but also present-potential in Column 5. Only one set of comparisons is shown in Column 5, viz., comparing the present with the potential in the next time period. However, the comparisons may well run into subsequent periods in the future as well, such as W_{25}/W_{00}, W_{37}/W_{00}, and W_{49}/W_{00}, in addition to W_{13}/W_{00} indicated in Column 5.

It should again be emphasized that the effectiveness measure is probabilistic. It is not even the potential performance that is being compared really, but the *expected* potential performance. However, this strategic objective of sufficiency in performance capability is measurable. It can be measured in terms of the percentage of the sufficiency of our technological options to meet the expected environment in which they would operate. Clearly, there will be occasions on which some of the technological options in land, water, or air (including space) would *not* meet the threat environment. There would simply not be adequate resources to be sufficient in all environments at all times. What is needed is the balancing of the insufficiency in one area by the sufficiency in more than one alternate area, so that an overall strategic balance may be maintained. The emphasis upon the objectives hierarchy gives clear direction to the OR/SA effort: Provide forecasts to the PDM to enable him to exercise control. The input of data at the Office of the Secretary of Defense level, the Joint Chiefs of Staff level, the Services level and the subservices levels must be oriented towards answering the question of the Secretary: At this rate, what will be the expected potential performance of technological options — ours and theirs; and the index of sufficiency of survival?

6. APPLICATION 13: Perspective of the Principal Decision-Maker — Corporate Level

There is a fundamental difference between the *public sector* perspectives of the President at the national level and the Secretary at the Cabinet level, on the one hand, and the *private sector* perspective of the president of a manufacturing or nonmanufacturing corporation. It is the absence of the price mechanism in the former, and the presence of the price mechanism in the latter.

Equally, if not more, important is the absence in the former of the profit mechanism, and the presence of the profit mechanism in the latter. The price and the profit mechanisms are related to each other. Without the former, the latter is hard to identify, although in a barter economy the excess of the in-flow over the out-go can be reckoned as profit. In a "not-for-profit" activity, there is a parallel concept of excess of income over expenditure which, while not de jure profit, is de facto profit. The term, "profit motive", is applied to the private sector in general; the acquiring of higher intake than the out-go being basic to the survival and growth of the private sector activities.

The exercise of control by the PDM in the private sector at the corporate level can thus be identified in terms which are much more tangible than those of the PDM at the national and the cabinet level. The terms of reference are much less abstract than the expected survival of the American Way of Life, and the expected potential performance of technological options — ours and theirs. Instead, some concept of profit can be identified, and quite tangibly measured.

The PDM at the corporate level is also guided by the two primary goals of any organism, viz., survival and growth. If one of the two had to be sacrified, that would be growth, because without survival, there can be no growth. What constitutes survival in a corporate context of profit motive calibrated by price mechanism?

6.1. User Orientation

The concern of the corporate PDM can be identified in terms of the question: Are there new and/or related needs of customers which I can satisfy with my present resources and/or with added resources?

This user orientation of the corporate PDM is obviously for acquiring profits which permit the survival and the growth of the corporate organism. Therefore, to excercise control, the corporate PDM must be able to assess *operationally* the tendency toward profit as reflected in the nature and magnitude of the demands that are met by the products and services of the corporate organism.

Why do the customers make it profitable for the corporate organism to engage in the production of goods and services? It is because the customers have needs, real or imaginary, which the products and services are expected to satisfy. It is important to recognize that to the customer the satisfaction is *potential.* He has to pay for the potential satisfaction ahead of time. It is possible that the customer will not be satisfied, in which case, a refund of the money paid by the customer is offered in some cases as an inducement to the customer to try the products and services of the organism. The lack of satisfaction due to any physical defect is almost universally rectified by supplying the user with a replacement for the defective product. However, if the lack of satisfaction arises from the expectations of the consumer which the product was never designed to satisfy, the cause lies not in any physical defect, but in the psychic divergence — between what the customer thought that he was purchasing, and what the manufacturer advertised he was selling.

If the psychic divergence is not resolved, and if hundreds of customers purchase the product with expectations of potential satisfaction which are consistently at variance with the capabilities of the product, then that would result in a significant loss of both the present customers and potential customers. Therefore, to the corporate PDM, what his product(s) *promises* is equally, if not more, important than how the product *performs*. In other words, promises are coequal with performances. The intent of the promises is to induce credibility; the substratum of the credibility is the performance, which is based upon capability.

What emerges is the fact that *credibility* is equally, if not more, important than *capability*. Recall that in Application 12, credibility was found to be more important than capability. The reference was to the credibility of the would-be adversary in the capability of our weapons — their credibility about our capability.

6.2. Difference in Credibility Between Defense and Consumer Activities

There is a fundamental difference between the importance of credibility in Applications 12 and 13. In Application 12, the role of credibility was to ensure *nonuse*; in Application 13, the role of credibility is in ensuring *use*.

Under the free enterprise system, several products and services are offered by the same manufacturer and/or different manufacturers to satisfy the same need. Therefore, the promise of capability to satisfy made by each organism competes with a similar promise to satisfy the same need made by other organisms. If the same manufacturer offers two products to satisfy the same need, they should be considered to be in competition with each other as though they were offered by two distinct organisms. The overriding importance of credibility in consumption is underscored by the findings, from time to time, of Federal government regulatory agencies that the physical contents of a fast-selling, higher priced product are, in fact, not only not superior, but really inferior to, those of the a lower priced product which can satisfy the same need at much less cost. It means that the customers are really buying credibility rather than capability.

To ensure survival through effective control, the PDM at the corporate level may therefore be obligated to give more attention to the question of credibility of his products and services than the capability itself. The credibility is achieved through advertising, endorsements, "independent" test results, and so on. Advertising serves to induce credibility in the mind of the customer, even to induce the need in some instances. However, after the customer has physically been brought face to face with the product, he may be dissuaded from purchasing the product because of its packaging. One reason why the public purchases the product with ingredients which are even inferior to another product to satisfy the same need is that it is better packaged, or merchandised. True, advertising and merchandising do not add one iota to the inherent characteristics of the product and/or services. However, insofar as the purchase of the customer is the commitment of his resources to *potential* satisfaction, he is really buying credibility rather than capability, and credibility is certainly induced by advertising and merchandising.

Credibility is competitive. It is the credibility of the customer about our capability versus their capability. The product and/or service is seldom one of a kind. Even if it is one of a kind at the moment, it is quite likely that under the exercise of free enterprise, there will soon be someone on the horizon who will do his best to induce credibility in our customer about their capability. The corporate PDM, operating in the long run, has decidedly to take into account the competitive credibility question with respect to not only the present offerors of the same product (service) but future ones too. In other words, he has to assess on a continuing basis, the competitive credibility of "our" products and services with respect to "their" products and services.

In the case of Application 12, it could be said that money was no object, because national security was at stake. Therefore, the exponential growth in technological options could be realistically considered as the arena in which the battle for credibility is waged. Similar exponential growth in technological options also applies to the production of goods and services in the private sector. As a matter of fact, planned technological obsolescence is the way of life in Detroit. While the basic principles and practices of propulsion have remained virtually unchanged since the early days of the first automobile, with probably the exception of the legislative requirement that the combustion be pollution-free by 1976, the styles have changed every year, and what is really being sold is a different packaging of the combustion engine every year, rather than a significantly different capability for *performance*. The advertising is aimed at creating in the consumer a need for "This Year's Model" because of its packaging rather than its performance.

6.3. Primacy of Packaging Over Performance

The principal difference, therefore, between Applications 12 and 13 is that *performance* is the prime criterion in Application 12, while *packaging* is the prime criterion in Application 13. It takes time to introduce a customer to a need, and it takes longer to instill in him loyalty to a particular brand. Even though it will be technologically easier to produce another brand in the short run, it would be virtually impossible to create a need in the mind of the consumer for the new brand, and what is more, to wean him away from the familiar brand. Color photography, developed several years earlier, has been deliberately withheld from the market, because the customers were still in the process of getting used to the idea of taking pictures on their own with portable cameras in black and white. If the customers, to whom the idea of portable photography was drastically new, were to be suddenly told that not only did they not have to go to the studios to have their pictures taken in black and white, but also that they could do one better, and take *color* pictures on their own, that would have virtually ruined the market for portable photography in black and white which itself had to be carefully cultivated.

Technological options are important to the private sector. But technological performance is *not* the deciding factor. Instead, it is technological *packaging*. The advertisement for Tang orange juice is not geared to its technological performance in providing Vitamin C, but instead, it is geared to the technological *packaging*. Because it was chosen for use in outer space, the glamor of space technology is sought to be rubbed off on Tang orange juice. Again, the Teflon skillet is advertised to accent the technological glamor by packaging it as a "product of space age technology". The credibility is induced in the mind of the consumer by the association with "space age technology"; not in terms of what the kitchenware can do or endure.

6.4. Operational Measure of Private Sector Performance

To the corporate PDM, in weighing the credibility competition, the battle is waged in the arena of *technological packaging*. How will the credibility of "our" technological packaging of products and/or services compare with the credibility of "their" technological packaging of products and/or services is the deciding question. As in the case of Application 12, the form of today's adversary, or competitor, is probably known, but certainly not his forte tomorrow. Of course, tomorrow other competitors may arise, and today's competitor may acquire new capabilities by augmenting his internal resources, or by acquiring external resources, such as another company. Therefore, the *potential* technological packaging, which encompasses the future capabilities of the organism and its competitors, is the prime consideration.

The PDM's perspective is that of the long run. Therefore, he is waging his battle on the basis of expected credibilities — ours and theirs. Given the present performances and packaging, what is the *absolute* credibility in our products and services, and what is the *relative* credibility of our products and services in terms of theirs, not only today, but also tomorrow?

The expected potential credibility of technological packaging — ours and theirs — is measurable. It can be measured in terms of the present and potential share of the market for the PDM's products and/or services. As in the case of Application 12, there will be occasions in which some of the technological packagings *would not* compete successfully with alternative technological packagings. There would simply not be adequate resources to capture the entire market for all products and services at all times. What is needed is the balancing of the displacement of one's products in one area by the displacing of alternative products in some other area, so that an overall balance may be maintained by the corporate organism. The emphasis upon the objectives hierarchy gives clear direction to the OR/SA effort: It should provide forecasts to the PDM to enable him to exercise control. The input of data at the Corporate Staff Services level, the Corporate Vice-Presidential level, the Corporate Divisions and Subdivisions level must be oriented to answering the question of the Corporate President: At this rate, what will be the expected potential credibility of technological packagings — ours and theirs — and the index of market acquisition in terms of sufficiency of survival?

7. From the Perspective of PDM to that of SubPDM

In Applications 11, 12, and 13 discussed in Sections 4, 5, and 6, the perspective of the PDM has respectively been at the national level, the cabinet level, and the corporate level.

From the point of view of the PDM at the national level, the survival of the American Way of Life is of paramount importance. From the point of view of the PDM at the cabinet level, e.g., the Secretary of Defense, the insuring of the physical survival of the United States by insuring the technological options to be competitive with respect to would-be adversary is of paramount importance.

The Secretary of Defense is at the strategic level with respect to the national PDM. Therefore, the OR/SA effort in support of the Secretary of Defense has two purposes: (1) to enable the Secretary to exercise control over the activities of the Department of Defense, in which role he is the PDM; and (2) to enable the Secretary of Defense to act as the *subPDM* with respect to the President. These two functions are *simultaneous*. Therefore, there are two different requirements that are imposed upon the OR/SA effort which the Secretary draws upon.

8. APPLICATION 14: Perspective of the SubPDM – Subcabinet Level

The major difference in the perspective between the PDM and subPDM is reflected in the lengths of the respective planning horizons. At the organismic level, the interest is *long term*. The long term perspective of a PDM quite often deliberately ignores the intermediate-term point of view of the subPDM at the strategic level.

8.1. Secretary of Defense as SubPDM to the President

An instance where the President in his role as PDM, will *ignore* the point of view of his subPDM, the Secretary of Defense, will be with respect to the SALT negotiations. One of the basic premises of the Salt agreement is that by making the United States and the Soviet Union vulnerable to *attack*, there can be achieved the beginnings of the limitation of the number and kind of strategic weapons amassed by the superpowers. This point of view would certainly not be palatable to the Secretary of Defense as PDM, for, in that role, his principal criterion is that of the parity or superiority of U.S. weaponry — present and potential. To renounce the very capability that he requires to fulfill his function as PDM can make sense only when he considers that to the President he is only a subPDM. Therefore, the PDM *ignores* the perspective of the subPDM or in this case, in his role as the PDM, the President ignores the perspective of the Secretary of Defense.

8.2. The Secretary of the Air Force as SubPDM to the Secretary of Defense

Even as subPDM to the President, the Secretary of Defense has to reconcile himself to the ignoring of his objectives by his PDM, the President, so also the Secretaries of the Air Force, the Army, and the Navy have to swallow the bitter pill of being totally ignored by their PDM, the Secretary of Defense. In other words, the best technological options represented in the finest weaponry, say, self-detecting and guiding missiles which will act on their own to intercept and destroy any missiles launched from anywhere in the world toward the United States, which is the best decision that the Secretary of the Air Force can make as PDM, could be completely ignored by his PDM, the Secretary of Defense.

Here are the *conflicting* demands made upon the same decision-maker. On the one hand, the OR/SA effort should provide the Secretary of the Air Force with unsurpassed technological parity, or preferably superiority, in the options that he may choose in the foreseeable future. While that would adequately serve the function of the OR/SA effort in support of the PDM, it would probably be totally *in*adequate to serve the Secretary of the Air Force as the subPDM. In that role, what he needs to have is a different perspective, viz., that of the Secretary of Defense, who himself has been overruled by the President.

8.3. The Secretary of the Air Force as Sub-subPDM to the President

The inherent contradictions in the role that is demanded of the same decision-maker become apparent when the OR/SA effort for the Secretary of the Air Force is considered with respect not only to the Secretary of Defense but also with respect to the President. In addition to the roles of: (1) PDM, and (2) subPDM, the Secretary of the Air Force becomes (3) the sub-subPDM with respect to the President. But it is the self-same OR/SA effort that has to provide the Secretary of the Air Force with not only the information enabling him to succeed in achieving technological superiority, but also in reducing the competitive bid for technological superiority in weaponry, which are essentially *contradictory*. Superimposed on these two conflicting demands is the national strategy of *mutual* limitations upon the defense capability of superpowers. In other words, the OR/SA effort has to *simultaneously* forecast: (1) sufficient *absolute* technological capability in air and in space; (2) sufficient *relative* technological capability in land and water warfare, so that the Secretary of the Air Force can establish his case for funds in competition with the Secretary of the Army and the Secretary of the Navy; and (3) *in*sufficient relative technological capability with respect to would-be adversaries.

The selection of the data, their decoding, and the forecasting based on the data would naturally vary with the utilization of the converted data by the different decision level of the hierarchy. Thus, the Secretary of the Air Force requires certain OR/SA effort for his role as the PDM, which is different from what he requires for his subPDM role, which is still different from what he requires for his role as sub-subPDM. How can an OR/SA effort be made which simultaneously satisfies the requirement of the three roles?

One of the first decisions that has to be made is the *importance* of the three different roles. It is rarely that all the three would be equally important. It is even rarer that the three demands would be equally *frequent*. What is required is the specification of the relative importance of each of the three roles and the relative frequency with which they are played. It is quite likely that the role of sub-subPDM is the least frequent; but it may also turn out to be the most important. In other words, when the national policy *de*-emphasizes the role of superiority in technological options, the preponderant emphasis upon the technological capability in his PDM role would quite possibly leave the Secretary of the Air Force high and dry. However, his principal assignment is that of the PDM, and he must argue persuasively for his point of view. If he doesn't argue, nobody else will.

9. APPLICATION 15: Perspective of the SubPDM – Subcorporate Level

Turning from the cabinet to the corporate level, we find the various roles assigned to the decision-makers at the various levels of the hierarchy to be inherently conflicting. For instance, each of the heads of the functional activities in a corporation is charged with the responsibility of looking after his own. His staff is *not* to be mindful of the corporate organismic objective of survival and growth of the corporation. He must diligently and persistently argue for his own particular parochial interest.

9.1. Vice-President for Production – Raise Production Inventory

If he is the Vice-President in charge of Production, his role as the PDM is to make the production a cost-effective process. If the production is an assembly line process, he would require that the employment of his assembly line workers be steady so that they can gain from their own experience, thereby improving the quality and quantity of production. In other words, the Vice-President for Production as PDM requires persuasive arguments which will insure that the assembly line production proceeds on an uninterrupted and uniform basis, which would quite possibly *increase* the volume of production. His facts and figures should enable him to persuade the President of the corporation that the assembly line production must continue unruffled.

Let us assume that, while the production is maintained at a high and uniform rate, the demand for the product does not keep pace. That would result in the accumulation of high inventory: inventory being goods that could be readily converted into liquid cash. The high inventory means that a sizable portion of the resources of the company is tied up in finished goods, decreasing the turnover of the money that is so invested. The money that does not turnover does not bring in returns. On the contrary, it absorbs additional resources in the form of storage space and inventory maintenance and the cost of interest for the money that is frozen in the form of finished goods.

9.2. Vice-President for Finance – Reduce Inventory

Consider the position of the Vice-President for Finance in his role as PDM. His primary concern is with turning over the money as fast as possible, so that profits are acquired and payments, in the form of interest for the money that is frozen in the form of finished goods, are minimized. The arguments that the Vice-President for Finance requires for his role as PDM are those which will enable him to persuade the President that as little money should be tied up in inventory, and as much money should be invested in products that are readily sold.

9.3. President of the Corporation – Ignore the SubPDM's and the Vice-Presidents

Both the Vice-President for Production and the Vice-President for Finance are subPDM's with respect to the corporation President. His interest is in the growth and survival of the corporation represented by its human and physical resources. Therefore, he would want to *ignore* the points of view of the Vice-Presidents for Production and Finance, the former urging for more production, and the latter urging for less production (assuming the situation that the market demand is much less than the volume of production). The President may decide that the rapidity of the turnover of the money invested is less important than the availability of those products which would permit the uninterrupted flow of goods to the market. Or he may decide that the high inventory of the particular set of goods suggests that the corporation should change its production line.

This conflict between the perspective of the PDM and the subPDM, whether of the corporation, or of the nation, is built in. The basic premise is that of free enterprise. We hold that competition is conducive to efficiency. Therefore, each man is given a specific area of responsibility, e.g., production, finance; defense, health; and is assigned a measure of performance which will put him in direct conflict with his peers. This inherent conflict inevitably extends itself to the contributions of the OR/SA effort that each builds for his own purpose.

10. Index of Importance of PDM Roles

In Section 8, brief reference has been made to: (1) the importance, and (2) the frequency of the three roles of PDM, subPDM, and sub-subPDM. Recognizing that the data are basically the same whether they are drawn upon by the PDM, subPDM, or sub-subPDM, but the decisions are different, the mix of the decisions to be supported by the OR/SA effort needs to be identified.

We have found in Section 8.3 that the Secretary of the Air Force is simultaneously: (1) PDM for the Air Force; (2) subPDM to the Secretary of

Defense; and (3) sub-subPDM to the President. Similarly, the Production Manager of a Product Group is simultaneously: (1) PDM for his Product Group; (2) subPDM to the Vice-President for Production; and (3) sub-subPDM to the corporate President.

The frequency of the role, e.g., the percent of working time devoted to decision-making in the PDM, subPDM or sub-subPDM role, becomes a poor measure when multiple roles are involved. Since higher hierarchies can be highly critical to the very survival of the lower order hierarchies, the frequency of utilization must be qualified by the criticality of the decisions. The combination of the criticality of decision with its frequency of occurrence together yields an index of importance of that role.

The use of the OR/SA effort for the PDM and subPDM roles is probably much more frequent than at the sub-subPDM level, because the primary role is that of the PDM. Therefore, the OR/SA effort should be designed to satisfy primarily the PDM role, secondarily the subPDM role and thirdly the sub-subPDM role. The index of importance indicates the extent of resources that need to be committed to the preparation of information appropriate to each of the three roles. These roles change in time and space; therefore *flexible* allocation of OR/SA effort should be planned. Modifying the *in*frequency (say once a year) of the sub-subPDM level by its criticality to the organismic survival (say 100 on a scale of 0−100), we get (1 × 100=) an index of importance of 1 000. The subPDM level may get an index of importance of (once a month or 12 times a year multiplied by its criticality to the organismic survival of say 60: 12 × 60=) 720. The PDM level may get an index of importance of 100. The subPDM level may get an index of impor-organismic survival of say 20: 52 × 20=) 1040.

The OR/SA effort allocation would then be:

100/1860	=	5.37%	Sub-subPDM.
720/1860	=	38.71%	subPDM.
1040/1860	=	55.92%	PDM.
		100.00%	

PROBLEMS

The three chapters, 3, 4 and 5, of Part II deal with the substance and sequence of OR/SA effort. What OR/SA prescribes needs to be implemented; and to implement, resources must be committed by appropriate authority. The purpose of the following questions is to highlight the perspective of the decision-maker who has to implement the prescriptions of the OR/SA effort.

A. *Principal Decision-Maker (PDM) Roles*

1. Indicate the inherent conflict in the three different PDM roles of any decision-maker.

2. In allocating internal resources to affect outcomes external to him, what safeguards can the PDM institute to avoid grave errors?

B. *Defense and Non-Defense Objectives*

3. Discuss the basic difference between defense and non-defense activities in the nature of credibility.

4. Develop operational measures of survival as an objective in the defense and non-defense sectors.

C. *Conflicting Information Demands*

5. The conflicting PDM roles, whether in the defense or non-defense areas, impose upon the PDM different requirements for the information he needs to make up his mind. Discuss this conflicting demand for information with respect to a PDM.

6. To resolve the inherent conflict in the alternative demands that are placed upon the same PDM at the same time, the relative importance of the different roles must be identified. Suggest an approach to devise such an index of importance of PDM roles.

PART THREE

**LARGE, UNSTRUCTURED PROBLEMS
IN THE PUBLIC SECTOR**

CHAPTER 6

OR/SA PROTOCOL APPLIED TO PUBLIC SECTOR PROBLEMS: (1) ECOLOGICAL INVESTMENT

TECHNICAL OVERVIEW

The OR/SA protocol, developed in Chapter 4, is applied to a public sector problem.

As we move from the military to the urban frontier, we leave behind the reasonably well-defined system objectives and sub-system performance characteristics (e.g., the cost effectiveness of Weapon System I compared with Weapon System II, the circular error of probability, etc.). Instead, there arise system objectives which have not only not been well-defined, but also, by and large, are not even definable (e.g. quality education, good health).

Yet, the 51-man committee of the U.S. House of Representatives, the Committee on Appropriations, has to appropriate funds for the operation of the Cabinet Departments and Government Agencies. Can OR/SA protocol offer any assistance in evaluating the many competing requirements for the same federal dollar? A preliminary study was undertaken in 1970 which was limited to a very small segment of the entire U.S. budget.

With the National Environmental Policy Act of 1970 focusing legislative attention on the problem of the environment, the general theme of concern for the environment was chosen to be explored with reference to the budget for the Department of the Interior. A portion of the budget was studied, accounting for 54.7% of the 1970 budget, and 55.5% of the 1971 budget.

The choice of an overall study theme was undertaken to give coherence to the budgetary evaluation. After examining several alternatives for the common objective, one was chosen with which an operational penalty for non-fulfillment could be identified: Averting Ecological Disaster by Improving the Environment.

To determine the allocation between the different components of the activities of the Department, it is found necessary to translate the general objective into operational measures. What constitutes the improvement of the environment — more grass; more plants; more trees; less industry?

The five elements of the Department of the Interior Budget: (1) forest protection and utilization, (2) acquisition of land, (3) national park service, (4) bureau of land management, and (5) bureau of outdoor recreation, had each to interpret the implications of the overall objective of averting ecological disaster, and improving the environment. Each objective could be accomplished by means of a number of activities, which could be grouped into a collection of concerted activities. Given each sequence, its components can be identified.

The budgetary requests (e.g., funds for forest fire prevention and the funds for policing strip mining) have to be converted into the objectives at the tactical level. More often, two tactical objectives may be parts of two different strategic objectives. The relative importance of the competing budgetary requests cannot be determined until they are related to a level at which the competing requests are part of the same sequence. To find the common highest level, the various budget requests had to be related to the strategic level, and sometimes to the organismic level.

Among the many tactical objectives, illustrative ones were selected to establish illustrative scores to represent the penalty for non-fulfillment, the less critical choices receiving the lower scores. Competing objectives at the tactical level were identified, and related to the same strategic objective. Corresponding to several strategic objectives, a single organismic objective was identified. The process continued in successive rounds, the organismic objective of one round being the tactical objective for the next round upward. Several rounds were found to be necessary in some cases to relate a budgetary request item (e.g., state assistance for land acquisition) to the overall objective of averting ecological disaster.

The highest common penalty was set up for the nonfulfillment of the organismic objective for the entire study.

In terms of the non-fulfillment penalty for the highest organismic level, the relative importance of each tactical level objective of interest to the study was determined. A total of 14 tactical choices was identi-

fied as competing for the achievement of the overall objective. The weighted penalties for the 14 tactical choices together came to 30 712. One tactical choice, viz., improved fire prevention/fighting techniques, with its score of 7 500 claims 24.2% of the total budget. Similarly, the tactical choice: prevent strip mining, with its score of 9 500, claims 30.9% of the total budget allocation, and so on.

The initial allocation shows that 65% of the resources are allocated to regulate the use of the environment, and only 1.5% to facilitate the enjoyment of the environment. A small computer program was developed which could reallocate the resources according to the new direction. The reallocation required changing not one, but all of the ordering of the objectives. The human judgments are preserved at every stage of the process, and the effect of an increase or decrease in an appropriation item can be shown promptly in terms of an overall budgetary objective which has been selected at the start. The selection of new objectives remains, of course, a viable option of the Congressional decision-maker.

EXECUTIVE SUMMARY

The method of conducting an OR/SA effort, developed in Chapter 4, is applied to an initial study of the evaluation of U.S. budget appropriations.

The objectives of the study have been rather modest: to illustrate how the competing claims for funds from the different activities of the federal agencies could be evaluated in a comparable and consistent manner.

A small portion of the entire U.S. Budget was chosen; and about 55% of the Budget of the Department of the Interior for 1970 and 1971 was selected for study.

Given two competing appropriation items, such as forest fire prevention and state assistance for land acquisition, how much money should be allocated to each activity? The question cannot be answered by simply comparing the amount of the budget requests, the research findings advanced by proponents of both activities, and/or the strength of the lobbying that each can provide. Instead, their individual potential contribution to the achievement of the objectives of the Department of the Interior has to be determined.

It means that the two competing items have first to be translated in terms not of what they will spend, but of what they will achieve. It requires the specification of what the Department wants to achieve, alternative ways of achieving it, and the contribution that the fire prevention can make toward the achievement of that objective, versus the contribution that assistance for land acquisition can make toward the achievement of the objective. The contribution may indeed be of different kinds, i.e., fire prevention contributing a negative value in not losing the forests that are already in existence, while the land acquisition contributing a positive value in creating new land.

While both the positive and negative elements are important, how much weight should be given the one over the other? That, in turn, requires the specification of the objectives at a higher level, which can treat the positive and negative elements as part of the same objective. Such an objective cannot be directly found; in which case additional progress upward in the hierarchy of objectives will become necessary.

The object is to make explicit the hidden assumptions about the objectives of the organism, as opposed to the budgetary requests of administrative units. By focusing their attention upon the objectives, the administrative units will have to establish their claims for appropriations allocations on the basis of what they will achieve to further the objectives of the organism.

There are two sets of comparisons that are made: (1) horizontal, and (2) vertical. The horizontal comparison requires that each request for funds be identified as competing at the same level, i.e., fulfilling the same objective in a different way. When two or more objectives at the same level are identified, they can be related to a higher level of objective of which they are each a component. The procedure has the advantage that it can be started anywhere within the organism. No matter where it is started, its final decision has to reckon with the contribution of the particular objective to that of the organism as a whole.

The relative merits of each means of achieving the objective can be weighted and expressed in terms of the total, overall objective. The improved fire prevention/fighting techniques received a score of 7 500

out of a total weighted score of 30 712. Therefore, according to the
share of the tactical choice in the total picture, fire prevention/fighting
technique is allocated 24.2% of the total budget. Similarly the tactical
choice to prevent strip mining with its score of 9 500 claims 30.9% of
the total budget allocations, and so on.

The initial allocations shows that 65% of the resources are allocated
to regulate the use of the environment, and only 1.5% to facilitate the
enjoyment of the environment. The Congressional Decision-Maker may
decide that this allocation is incongruent; therefore he would like to see
the priorities changed from say, 65% to 37% for regulation, and in-
creased from 1.5% to 25% to facilitate the enjoyment of the environ-
ment. A small computer program was developed which could reallocate
the resources according to the new direction. The reallocation would
require changing not one, but all of the elements of the objectives. The
human judgments are preserved at every stage of the process, and the
effect of an increase or decrease in an appropriation item can be shown
promptly in terms of the overall budgetary objective which has been
selected at the start. The selection of new objectives remains, of course,
a viable option of the decision-maker.

The shift in emphasis of national concern from the military and space problems of the '60s to the urban and social problems in the '70s is perhaps most
dramatically reflected in the Fiscal Year 1972–73 budget of $79 billion for
the U.S. Department of Health, Education and Welfare which exceeded the
corresponding figure for the U.S. Department of Defense by as much as $1.3
billion.

As we move from the military to the urban frontier, we leave behind the
reasonably well-defined system objectives and subsystem performance characteristics (e.g., the cost effectiveness of Weapon System I compared with
Weapon System II, the circular error of probability, the probability of kill,
etc.). Instead, there arise system objectives which have not only *not* been
defined but also, by and large, are not even definable, (e.g., quality education).
With undefinable system objectives, the contribution of the subsystem performances to the accomplishment of the system objectives becomes even
more intractable. Yet, $79 billion are there to be spent on penalty of for-
feiture if not spent within the fiscal year.

Can OR/SA protocol offer any assistance in making the problem tractable, so that competing demands for the same limited resources can be equitably allocated among the numerous subsystems, so that the organismic objective of improvement in the well-being of the majority of Americans in the long run has a reasonable chance of accomplishment?

1. APPLICATION 16: Systems Approach to Appropriations Evaluation

Every single dollar of the $79 billion appropriated for HEW did have to compete with the demands of the other Cabinet Departments: Defense, State, Interior, Transportation, etc. Since the money bills originate in the House of Representatives, the power of the purse is clearly constitutionally vested in the people's representatives. The 435 Congressmen are assigned to 19 legislative committees, all of which propose budgetary appropriations (except the Committee on Rules and the Committee on Standards of Office Conduct), after reviewing the Administration requests for funds. All requests for budget appropriations are processed by a single committee, the U.S. House Committee on Appropriations. The 51-man committee is an exclusive Committee in the sense that the members cannot hold any other committee assignments, while the legislative committee assignments are nonexclusive. The Appropriations Committee is organized into sub-committees, more or less as counterparts to the legislative committees.

Can OR/SA protocol offer any assistance to systematically evaluating the multitude of requests for the limited funds — from the different departments and from the components of each department? Understandably, the systematic evaluation of the multitude of requests from within the same Department exerts enormous pressure upon the Congressional Members of the Appropriations Committee who have to evaluate not only the merits of each claim, but also the merits of their counterparts; further, the evaluation has to take into account not only the immediate and the obvious impact of the funds, but also the long-term and the invisible impact.

During the spring of 1970, an opportunity arose to apply OR/SA to a problem faced by policy-makers of the U.S. House of Representatives. A preliminary study which was limited to a very small segment of the entire United States budget was undertaken. The Study was performed under the author's direction by a Seminar on Operations Research offered in the spring of 1970 at the American University, Washington, D.C.

Recalling the operations research desiderata in Chapter 2, Section 2.4, of the "homely" communication, we were particularly sensitive to what the policymaker thought of our offerings. We were particularly gratified that the Honorable John O. Marsh, Jr., who invited us to this exploratory effort, read the entire report into the Congressional Record with the following gracious remarks:

> Under Dr. Chacko's direction, a preliminary study, using the systems approach, was made of several elements of the Interior Department budget. It should be understood that this sample study involved arbitrary choices as to specific subject matter. The chief interest is in the methodology, which involves an integrated approach to all of the alternatives for reaching selected objectives, so that changes in approach, or in elements of it, necessarily affect all other elements.
>
> I was impressed by the fact, that, once the technique has been mastered, it seems particularly adaptable to the assistance of computers. The human judgments are preserved at every stage of the process, but the adjustments, reflecting the interaction of these judgments on other elements of the budget, can be worked out speedily by the computer, and the effect of an increase or decrease in an appropriation item shown promptly in terms of the overall budgetary objective which has been selected at the start.
>
> Because this voluntary effort of Dr. Chacko and his seminar associates, Harry Birnkrant, Jay S. Brown, Abdelhai Chouikha, James E. Crownover, Jr., Bert R. Francis, Lt. Col. Francis S. Logan, Tamara Luzgin, and Frederick T. Martin, represents, I believe, a useful introduction to the systems approach as applied to the congressional budget-management reponsibility, I include a portion of the study report, as follows:[1]

2. Systems Approach to Appropriations Evaluation – Introduction

The massive documents of the U.S. Budget, as submitted by the Executive Branch of the Government to the Legislative Branch, demand of the latter in general, and the Appropriations Committee in particular, at least the wisdom of Solomon, supported by the access to modern abacuses with nanosecond capabilities for retrieval, analysis and recalculation.

Information, by itself, cannot offer judgment. As a matter of fact, more often information may have to be superceded. As the elected representatives

[1] Honorable John O. Marsh, Jr., "The Systems Approach", *Congressional Record,* May 28, 1970 p. E 4808.

of 200 million people, how can the Congressional decision-makers effectively evaluate the minutest line items in the budget in terms of their contribution to achieving national goals and objectives?

If some method can be found by which the central theme of achieving national goals can be pursued by Congressional decision-makers by allocating appropriate resources at the appropriate time, then they shall have strengthened the working of the democratic process in no small measure. Can such an approach be conceivably evolved is the ambitious question examined in this very preliminary and exploratory study.

3. Rationale and Process of Selection of Study Theme

An effort was made to relate the current national concerns with the exploration of the applications of systems methodology to the allocation of resources to meet these concerns.

3.1. Selection Criteria of Study Theme

The interest of the Honorable John O. Marsh, Jr., a member of the Appropriations Subcommittee on Department of the Interior and Related Agencies, facilitated the choice of the particular segment of the U.S. Budget in which the application of systems approach could be explored.

With the National Environmental Policy Act of 1970 focusing legislative attention on the problem of the environment, with the environmental teach-in on Earth Day observed on April 22, 1970, and with the widespread awareness of, and concern for, the problems of the environment, it is not difficult to choose as the general theme the concerns of the environment insofar as they are within the purview of the budgetary provisions of the Department of the Interior.

Further, the study of the environment provides a multi-agency focus involving agriculture, industry, recreation, pollution, and allied problems in which the various agencies of the government have a direct interest. It was felt that the choice of the environment as the primary element which would give cohesion to the exploration of the application of the systems approach to the appropriations process would identify a function which has many applications beyond the immediate purview of the Interior budget.

3.2. Study Elements and Interior Budget

As currently constituted, the Department of the Interior budget does not identify any single source whose exclusive concern is the preservation and protection of the environment. Instead, the environmental responsibility can be read into virtually all units of the Department of the Interior. For purposes of initial identification the Seminar Team selected five study elements. They are:

      1. Forest Protection and Utilization.
      2. Acquisition of Lands.
      3. National Park Service.
      4. Bureau of Land Management.
      5. Bureau of Outdoor Recreation.

NOA (New Obligational Authority) figures for FY 1970 (including supplemental appropriations) and the NOA for FY 1971 then were identified as shown in Table 6.1.

The FY 1970 Interior Budget (NOA) was $997.191 millions and the study elements together accounted for $546.206 millions, or 54.7%. The FY 1971 (NOA) was $1 149.703 millions, and the study elements together accounted for $637.311 millions, or 55.5%.

In addition to NOA, it is important to include both the Federal Funds and Trust Funds to reflect the aggregate amount available to the Interior Budget in FY 1970 and FY 1971. In FY 1970 the NOA was $997.191 millions,

Table 6.1
Study elements (in millions of dollars)

	NOA FY 1970[a]	NOA FY 1971
1. Forest Protection and Utilization	257.676	278.566
2. Acquisition of Lands	108.472	138.500
3. National Park Service	101.817	134.224
4. Bureau of Land Management	74.491	81.996
5. Bureau of Outdoor Recreation	3.750	4.025
	546.206	637.311

[a] Includes supplemental appropriations.

Federal Funds $553.983 millions and Trust Funds $149.151 millions, making a total of $1 700.325 millions. In FY 1971 the NOA is $1 149.703 millions, Federal Funds $418.314 millions, and Trust Funds $109.225 millions, making a total of $1 677.242 millions.

4. Selection of an Overall Objective Common to all Elements

Congress has declared in the National Environmental Policy Act the goals and policies to guide all Federal actions which have an impact on the quality of the environment. Given the national goals and policies, what should be the unifying objective of the study elements selected to focus upon the preservation and enhancement of the environment as part of the budget of the Department of the Interior?

4.1. One Objective: Increase GNP

It is clear that a number of quite acceptable alternative statements can be made of the common objectives connecting the five study elements. For instance, the protection and utilization of our forests can lead to increase in our natural resources, and consequently higher income from the forest resources. Similarly, the National Park Service by attracting more visitors to the different parks would also contribute to higher revenue and additional income to people engaged in the provision of services in the parks.

4.2. Another Objective: Survival

While the income from material resources is an important element of our GNP, one may concentrate upon the opposite side of the coin, as it were: the dimunition of the income-producing forces as well as the substratum of national survival; for, if we do not have clean air to breathe, clean water to drink and clean land to live on, the quality of our life would suffer seriously, which, in turn, would lead to severe repercussions upon the GNP itself.

4.3. Alternative Objectives: Congressional Prerogative

The specific overall objective is to be chosen by the policy makers. Since this choice reflects the will of the people as to the disposition of their environment, it is only right that the overall objective be chosen at the legislative level. The overall objective sets the tenor. Therefore, its selection is quite important.

At the same time, the merit of the systems approach is the *flexibility* of choosing different objectives to be accomplished by means of the five study elements mentioned here, or any other operational measures open to the Department of the Interior.

4.4. Change the Objectives; Change the Consequences

Change the overall objective(s); and you change everything else with it. Because of its *flexibility* the systems approach offers a series of alternative courses of action and their consequences in allocating the available resources to meet the specific objectives.

4.5. One Objective Chosen for this Study

The seminar Team discussed several alternative statements of a common objective to be accomplished through the five elements chosen for the study. The entire analysis follows from the overall objective so identified. It bears repetition that this one objective is by no means an *exclusive* one, much less *exhaustive*. The same Seminar Team may well choose another statement of the overall objective incorporating five different elements of study at another time; anyone else may offer an entirely different statement of the overall objective for the same set of five elements. The methodology does *not* rise or fall with the different objectives; it is independent of them. What the methodology offers is a consistent derivation of the courses of action from a single overall objective, as well as all the consequences that flow from the single choice. When the choice of the overall objective changes, so will the courses and consequences; the method of consistent derivation of courses and consequences remains unchanged.

For purposes of this discussion the overall objective of the five study elements is *"Averting Ecological Disaster by Improving the Environment."*

5. Perspective of the Congressional Decision-Maker

This objective, which sets the tone for the present study, emphasizes one aspect of the several legislative roles of the Congressional decision-maker. He is the representative of a district; he is the law-maker of a nation; he is the key member of a political party. He is definitely influenced by his personal and professional background in exercising his responsibilities as a decision-maker.

5.1. Law-Maker of a Nation

It is inevitable that conflicts arise between the different demands that are made upon the Congressional decision-maker when he faces legislative problems. For purposes of this study, it will be assumed that one particular role, viz., that of the *law-maker of a nation* will be the predominant role. Any conflicts will be resolved in favor of this particular role.

5.2. Appropriations Assignment Instead of Legislative

As a law-maker of a nation, the Congressional decision-maker will have either legislative or appropriations assignments. The present study, being under the auspices of a member of the Appropriations Committee, will specify that its perspective is that of the appropriations function, instead of the legislative. Even given the same overall objective, the results of the study from a legislative committee point of view would quite likely be different from that of the present study.

6. Ordering of Study Elements for Allocation of Resources

Given the appropriations point of view of the accomplishment of the overall objective by allocating resources to the five study elements, the first question that has to be resolved is: Is one element more important than another? For example, is forest protection more important than acquisition of land? Again, is acquisition of land more important than National Park Service? Is outdoor recreation more important than forest protection? etc.

6.1. Two-By-Two Comparisons Will Not Do

These questions cannot be answered pair-wise. Instead, they each have to be related to the same overall objective.

6.2. Identify Next Higher Level of Objectives

To determine whether forest protection is more important than acquisition of land, it is necessary to identify the next higher level of objectives. One may say that the next higher level of objective for forest protection is: Averting ecological disaster. Similarly, one may say that the next higher level of objective for the acquisition of land is: Improving the environment.

Both the acquisition of land and forest protection are desirable objectives. As a matter of fact, for the purposes of this study, the overall objective combines both of them as part of the same, viz., averting ecological disaster by improving the environment.

How can a choice be made between the two?

It is crucial to identify some criterion which will permit establishing the choice of one over the other. For instance, one could think of a measure for the improvement of the environment. The question then is: What constitutes improvement of the environment — more grass; more plants; more trees; less industry?

How can this be determined — by counting the additional growth of grass; the additional number of trees; the additional number of plants; a reduction in the number of industrial plants?

While the index of an improvement in the environment is desirable, it easily becomes intractable. On the other hand, a negative approach, if employed, could more clearly identify the averting of clear disasters, e.g., acres of forest burned up by fire. One could compare the number of acres being ravaged by fire one year with that in the subsequent years; and relate the improvement of the environment to the lesser number of acres of forest that were burned.

Turning to the overall objective itself, the avoidance of disaster is easier to identify. In 1966, on Thanksgiving Day, New York City experienced an atmospheric inversion, to which was attributed a significant increase in the number of deaths. The avoidance of an episode such as that can be recognized in successive years, much more readily than the decrease, say, in the SO_2 content of the atmosphere. The stark predictions of impending ecological doom allow readier identification of the measures for averting ecological disaster. Thus, though less palatable, averting ecological disaster can be compared with improving the environment to the advantage of the former. The key question is *not* how desirable improving the environment is, but rather how bad is the *nonfulfillment* of averting ecological disaster.

The choice has to be made between the two higher level objectives; further, one has to decide how much worse is nonfulfillment of the given objectives. Is the nonfulfillment of averting ecological disaster, say 100; is improving the environment, say 80?

6.3. Three Levels of Objectives

The highest level of objectives identified for the segments of the Department of the Interior Budget under study was the unit comprising man and the environment in the U.S.

6.3.1. Organismic objectives
It should be emphasized that there are several characteristics associated with this highest level objective. They are:

1. The objectives relate to people.
2. Systems involving people can foul up neat solutions.
3. The people are animate.
4. The people interact.
5. The interaction generates a whole *larger* than the sum of parts or a whole *smaller* than the sum of parts.

To emphasize the fact that the decision-affecting and decision-affected entities are both unamenable to any neat theoretical solutions, the word organism is used in the present discussion. As stated elsewhere:

> The decision-affecting and decision-affected entities are organisms. The term "organism" denotes the fact that the constituents are animate, that they interact, that their dynamic interrelationships tend to generate intangibles which can sometimes make the whole considerably larger or considerably smaller than the sum of its parts. Thus, a well-motivated team of workers produces much more than the arithmetic sum of their individual capabilities, measured in common units like

salaries, years of training and experience, etc., whereas a poorly motivated team produces much less than their individual capabilities.

Organismic viewpoint underlies operations research. It is the art of applying the scientific method to executive-type decision problems. It is also the practice of translating progressively what-can-be into what-is in industrial, commercial, military and/or institutional environments. Thus operations research is indispensable to identify the potentials of alternate solutions to meet the challenges of the environment as well as to implement them.[2]

6.3.2. Strategic objectives

Just as the score of 100 was assigned to the organismic objective of averting ecological disaster and 80 to the organismic objective of improving the environment, a consistent set of scores need to be assigned to the second highest level of objectives: Strategic objectives.[3] The term "strategic" connotes a sequence of actions as opposed to a single specific action. Thus, forest protection and utilization is a strategic objective because the activity envisioned by the element calls for a large number of coordinated activities directed toward the achievement of the goal. Similarly, acquisition of land for forests is also a strategic objective, which can be accomplished by means of a number of activities directed toward the same goal.

Distinguishing the two organismic objectives of averting ecological disaster and improving the environment, the five strategic objectives may be illustratively listed as shown in Table 6.2.

6.3.3. Tactical objectives

The organismic objectives are pursued through strategic objectives, each of which is a sequence of action. To implement the strategic objectives, each sequence of actions must have logical components which are the action items. These are called tactical objectives.[4]

The tactical objectives pinpoint the specific actions that must be taken, such as improving fire prevention/fighting techniques; improving the access to national park sites.

---

[2] George K. Chacko, *Today's Information for Tomorrow's Products — An Operations Research Approach*, Thompson, Washington, D.C., 1966, pp. 5–6.
[3] *Ibid.*, pp. 32–42, 55, 208.
[4] *Ibid.*, pp. 34–42, 55, 207, 208.

Table 6.2
Ordering of organismic-strategic objectives

	Averting Ecological disaster Score 100	Improving the environment Score 80
Element 1. Forest Protection and Utilization		
Element 2. Acquisition of Land		
Element 3. National Park Service		
Element 4. Bureau of Land Management		
Element 5. Bureau of Outdoor Recreation		

7. Successive Rounds to Relate Hierarchies of Objectives

Which is more important: Fire prevention/fighting techniques or access to national park sites?

It is necessary to compare alternative means of accomplishing each strategic objective with each other and with the overall objective.

7.1. Round 1

Consider Element No. 1: Forest Protection and Utilization. How is this element related to averting ecological disaster?

One could start at the *international* level of ecological disaster and work one's way down to averting *national* ecological disaster. In this case averting international ecological disaster is the organismic objective, and averting national ecological disaster is the strategic objective.

National ecological disaster may be averted by preserving our oxygen source or purifying our oxygen supply. Just as oxygen is critical for averting national ecological disaster; so is water; so is land. Therefore, corresponding to the strategic objective of averting national ecological disaster, one could go to the tactical objective geared to preserving oxygen and water. Both the alternatives are shown in Fig. 6.1.

7.2. Round 2

The tactical objectives of Round 1 become the organismic objectives of

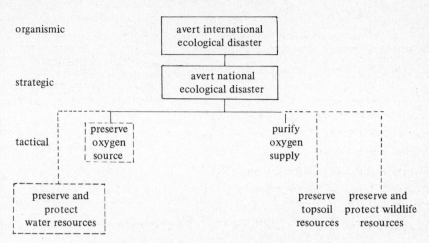

Fig. 6.1. Element 1. Forest protection and utilization (Round 1).

Round 2. Thus, the organismic objectives in Round 2 are: Preserve oxygen source; preserve and protect water resources (which are boxed in Fig. 6.1).

Corresponding to the objective of preserving oxygen sources there are three strategic objectives identified in Fig. 6.2. They are:

  1. Prevent further loss of trees.
  2. Increase existing stands of trees.
  3. Build oxygen generators.

Similarly, one could identify three strategic objectives corresponding to the organismic objective: Preserve and protect water resources. They are:

  1. Prevent lowering the water table.
  2. Improve watershed holding capacity.
  3. Prevent natural/man-made pollution of water resources.

At the tactical level there are five choices to accomplish the objective of preventing further loss of trees. They are:

  1. Improved tree farming.
  2. Eliminate SO_2 in atmosphere.
  3. Selective cutting and reforestation.
  4. Improve fire prevention/fighting techniques.
  5. Decrease lumber demand via substitute.

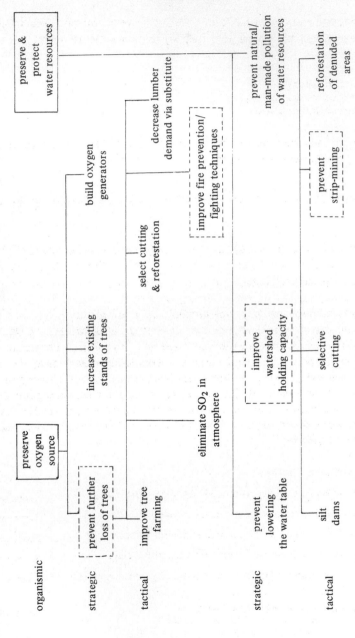

Fig. 6.2. Element 1. Forest protection and utilization (Round 2).

Similarly, one could identify four tactical objectives corresponding to the strategic objective of improving watershed holding capacity. They are:

1. Silt dams.
2. Selective cutting.
3. Prevent strip mining.
4. Reforest denuded areas.

The process may be repeated in further rounds until the action item levels and/or budget line items are reached.

7.3. Successive Rounds to Assign Illustrative Scores to Hierarchies of Objectives

Next comes the question of deciding the gravity of not fulfilling each of the tactical choices. Consider the tactical choices open to fulfilling the objective of preserving the oxygen source.

7.3.1. Horizontal relationships – one tactical choice to another

Let it be said that decreasing the lumber demand via a substitute is the least critical choice, and better tree farming is the next least critical choice. In a *horizontal* comparison of tactical choices – comparing each tactical choice with all the remaining tactical choices – the least critical tactical choice gets a *lower* score than the most critical choice, say score 8 for decreasing lumber demand via a substitute and score 10 for better tree farming. All the five technical choices may be given illustrative scores, on the basis of successful comparisons, as follows:

Of the five Tactical Choices:

Decrease lumber demand via substitute is the least critical choice.	Score 8
Better tree farming is the next least critical choice.	Score 10
Eliminate SO_2 in atmosphere is the next least critical choice.	Score 12
Select cutting and reforestation is the next least critical choice.	Score 13
Improve fire prevention/fighting techniques is the next least critical choice.	Score 15
Total Tactical Level (8 + 10 + 12 + 13 + 15 =)	Score 58

Table 6.3

Element 1. Forest protection and utilization: penalty values for nonfulfillment

Round	Hierarchy	Penalty	Choice	Score	Weighted penalty
2	Tactical	10	Improve fire prevention/fighting techniques	15	$10 \times 15 = 150$
	Strategic	10^2	Prevent further loss of trees	100	$10^2 \times 100 = 10\ 000$
	Organismic	10^5	Preserve oxygen source	300	$10^5 \times 300 = 30\ 000\ 000$
1	Tactical	10^5	do	300	$10^5 \times 300 = 30\ 000\ 000$
	Strategic	10^6	Avert national ecological disaster	1 000	$10^6 \times 1\ 000 = 1\ 000\ 000\ 000$
	Organismic	10^7	Avert international ecological disaster	10 000	$10^7 \times 10\ 000 = 100\ 000\ 000\ 000$

By similar reasoning, one can arrive at the following illustrative tactical scores for preserving and protecting water resources:

Silt dams.	Score 10
Selective cutting.	Score 15
Reforestation of denuded areas.	Score 19
Prevent strip mining.	Score 20
Total Tactical Level (10 + 15 + 19 + 20 =)	Score 64

In Table 6.3 at tactical level in Round 2: Improving fire prevention/fighting techniques of Fig. 6.2 (Table 6.3) is given a penalty level of 10, which, when associated with its score of 15, provides a weighted penalty of $(10 \times 15 =)$ 150. This tactical choice is a component of the strategic choice: Prevent further loss of trees. Giving a penalty level of 10^2 to the strategic choice, it is found that the weighted penalty is $(10^2 \times 100 =)$ 10 000.

Assigning a penalty level of 10^5 to the organismic level of preserving the oxygen source, the weighted penalty is $(10^5 \times 300 =)$ 30 000 000.

All these weighted penalty figures relate to Round 2 of Fig. 6.2.

The preservation of the oxygen sources, which is the organismic choice in Round 2, becomes the tactical choice in Round 1 in Table 6.3. The tactical choice of preserving the oxygen source has a penalty level of 10^5; therefore its next higher level of strategic objective is given a penalty level of 10^6. The strategic choice of averting national ecological disaster gets a weighted penalty of $(10^6 \times 1\ 000 =)$ 1 000 000 000. The corresponding organismic objective of averting international ecological disaster gets a weighted penalty of $(10^7 \times 10\ 000 =)$ 100 000 000 000.

No effort has been made to make the total tactical choice scores to reach 100 or 50 or 10, or any predetermined level. The only rule followed was that the *less critical tactical choices receive the lower scores.*

7.3.2. Vertical relationships – one tactical choice to organismic objective

The five tactical choices corresponding to the preservation of oxygen sources listed in Fig. 6.2 and the four tactical choices corresponding to the preservation and protection of water resources relate to two strategic choices.

These tactical choices have to be related *up-ward*. The first five relate to

Table 6.4

Element 2. Acquisition of land: penalty values for nonfulfillment

Round	Hierarchy	Penalty	Choice	Score	Weighted penalty
3	Tactical	10	Create new cities in semiwild forests	5	$10 \times 5 = 50$
	Strategic	10^2	Create new cities in forests	9	$10^2 \times 9 = 900$
	Organismic	10^3	Create new surface cities	25	$10^3 \times 25 = 25\ 000$
2	Tactical	10^3	do	25	$10^3 \times 25 = 25\ 000$
	Strategic	10^4	Create new environment	90	$10^4 \times 90 = 900\ 000$
	Organismic	10^5	Improve conditions	200	$10^5 \times 200 = 20\ 000\ 000$
1	Tactical	10^5	do	200	$10^5 \times 200 = 20\ 000\ 000$
	Strategic	10^6	Ameliorate urban irritants	500	$10^6 \times 500 = 500\ 000\ 000$
	Organismic	10^7	Avert ecological disaster	800	$10^7 \times 800 = 8\ 000\ 000\ 000$

Table 6.5

Element 3. National park service: penalty values for nonfulfillment

Round	Hierarchy	Penalty	Choice	Score	Weighted penalty
2	Tactical	10	Improve routes to more distant areas	30	$10 \times 30 = 300$
	Strategic	10^2	Maximum 1-day round trip from metro areas	70	$10^2 \times 70 = 7\ 000$
	Organismic	10^5	Recreation	600	$10^5 \times 600 = 60\ 000\ 000$
1	Tactical	10^5	do	600	$10^5 \times 600 = 60\ 000\ 000$
	Strategic	10^6	National Park Service	4 000	$10^6 \times 4\ 000 = 4\ 000\ 000\ 000$
	Organismic	10^7	Improve the environment	5 000	$10^7 \times 5\ 000 = 50\ 000\ 000\ 000$

Table 6.6

Element 4. Land management: penalty values for nonfulfillment

Round	Hierarchy	Penalty	Choice	Score	Weighted penalty
2	Tactical	10	Preserve trees by better farming	9	$10 \times 9 = 90$
	Strategic	10^2	Conserve land	40	$10^2 \times 40 = 4\ 000$
	Organismic	10^5	Prevent land depletion	90	$10^5 \times 90 = 9\ 000\ 000$
1	Tactical	10^5	do	90	$10^5 \times 90 = 9\ 000\ 000$
	Strategic	10^6	Prevent further depletion of land and minerals	200	$10^6 \times 200 = 200\ 000\ 000$
	Organismic	10^7	Avert ecological disaster	1 000	$10^7 \times 1\ 000 = 10\ 000\ 000\ 000$

Table 6.7

Element 5. Outdoor recreation: penalty values for nonfulfillment

Round	Hierarchy	Penalty	Choice	Score	Weighted penalty
3	Tactical	10	State assistance for land acquisition	2	$10 \times 2 = 20$
	Strategic	10^2	Federal acquisition of land	4	$10^2 \times 4 = 400$
	Organismic	10^3	Acquire recreational land	20	$10^3 \times 20 = 20\ 000$
2	Tactical	10^3	do	20	$10^3 \times 20 = 20\ 000$
	Strategic	10^4	Improve recreational land	100	$10^4 \times 100 = 1\ 000\ 000$
	Organismic	10^5	Improve land	100	$10^5 \times 100 = 10\ 000\ 000$
1	Tactical	10^5	do	100	$10^5 \times 100 = 10\ 000\ 000$
	Strategic	10^6	Improve environment	500	$10^6 \times 500 = 500\ 000\ 000$
	Organismic	10^7	Avert ecological disaster	1 200	$10^7 \times 1\ 200 = 12\ 000\ 000\ 000$

the strategic choices of preventing the further loss of trees. That is one of the three strategic choices, all of which are alternative means of fulfilling the preservation of the oxygen source, the organismic choice.

To relate the choices up-ward, it is necessary to establish *penalty levels* by hierarchy. These penalty levels will modify the scores assigned to the tactical, strategic and organismic choices, so that each tactical choice will be related to the overall objective of averting ecological disaster.

7.3.3. Relative allocation of resources

Now, the tactical objective of improving fire prevention/fighting techniques can be related to the overall organismic objective of averting national ecological disaster by the ratio of their weighted penalties: 150 : 1 000 000 000.

Considering another tactical choice at the same level, viz., selective cutting and reforestation, the allocation would be in the ratio: 130 : 1 000 000 000. In other words, if one billion dollars were spent to avert national ecological disaster, $130 would be allocated to selective cutting and reforestation, and $150 to improving fire prevention/fighting techniques.

8. Organismic Allocation of Interior Budget — Tactical Level

A similar systematic process of reasoning was applied to the other five elements of the study. The penalty value tables are shown in Tables 6.4, 6.5, 6.6, and 6.7.

8.1. Assume Each Element Hierarchy to be Equally Consistent

As was mentioned earlier, no attempts were made to straightjacket illustrative scores at the horizontal or vertical levels. The members of the Seminar had very little knowledge of the preferences that the administrative personnel of the Department of the Interior would have employed in either achieving the goals that have been set, or in weighting them. Nevertheless, each Study Team Group that pursued the different hierarchical choices corresponding to the elements tried conscientiously to relate it in a responsible manner to the overall objective of averting national ecological disaster. Owing to the differences in professional and personal background, the nonfulfillment of the organismic objective of averting ecological disaster was given a penalty rang-

Table 6.8

Equalizing the 5-budget element penalties for nonfulfillment: set organismic objective nonfulfillment penalty at 50×10^9

---

1. Tactical Choice: Improve Fire Prevention/Fighting Techniques

$$\frac{50 \times 10^9}{1 \times 10^9} \times 150 = \qquad\qquad 7\ 500$$

2. Tactical Choice: Create New Cities in Semi-Wild Forests

$$\frac{50 \times 10^9}{8 \times 10^9} \times 50 = \qquad\qquad 311$$

3. Tactical Choice: Improve Routes to More Distant Areas

$$\frac{50 \times 10^9}{50 \times 10^9} \times 300 \qquad\qquad 300$$

4. Tactical Choice: Preserve Trees by Better Farming

$$\frac{50 \times 10^9}{10 \times 10^9} \times 90 = \qquad\qquad 450$$

5. Tactical Choice: State Assistance for Land Acquisition

$$\frac{50 \times 10^9}{12 \times 10^9} \times 20 = \qquad\qquad 83$$

Total for Five Tactical Choices   8 644

---

ing from one billion to 50 billion. Assuming that the protagonist of each element was equally consistent, how would the Congressional decision-maker decide among the competing claims for the same limited resources?

8.2. Set Organismic Objective Nonfulfillment Penalty at 50×10^9

The preferred tactical choice in Element 1 was: Improve fire prevention/fighting techniques with a weighted penalty of 150, compared with the weighted penalty for nonfulfillment of the organismic objective of one billion.

To make a valid comparison between the claims of this particular tactical choice and, say, the tactical choice of improving routes to more distant areas in the national forests, its weighted penalty score of 300 must be related to the corresponding penalty for nonfulfillment of not one billion but 50 billions. Although the weighted penalty score itself is twice that of the first tactical choice, the much larger base against which it has to be compared in fact reduced the resource allocation for the same. In Table 6.8 the organismic objective nonfulfillment penalty is set at the highest level of 50 billion. Accordingly, the tactical choice of fire prevention/fighting techniques gets a score of 7 500 compared with only 300 for improving the roads to more distant areas.

8.3. Computer Program

Once the tactical choices are each related to the organismic objective of averting national ecological disaster, the relative allocation of resources to each can be determined on the basis of:

1. Penalty score.
2. Weighted penalty.

Table 6.9
Tactical objectives

I. Avert ecological disaster	100
II. Improve the environment	80

Element 1. Forest Protection Utilization
    Improve fire prevention/fighting techniques
    Prevent strip mining.
    Prevent strip logging.

Element 2. Acquisition of Land
    Create new cities in semiwild forests.
    Move to suburban areas with civil systems electronic products.

Element 3. National Park Service
    Improve routes to more distant areas.
    Education of the public on fire protection.
    Demonstration of effects of violating environmental ethic.

Element 4. Bureau of Land Management
    Preserve trees by better farming.
    Establish criteria on fossil fuel (e.g., oil) mining.
    Improve seed inventory replenishment to restore land.

Element 5. Bureau of Outdoor Recreation
    State assistance for land acquisition
    State assistance to acquisition of urban land for recreation.
    State assistance to acquisition of industrial land for recreation.

The change by the Congressional decision-maker of the organismic objectives would change the organismic level penalties and corresponding tactical level penalty scores. Should the agencies of the Government change the number and/or importance or alternative strategic and tactical choices to accomplish the organismic objective, that would be reflected in the penalty scores and/or penalty levels by hierarchy.

It bears repetition that:

1. The Congressional decision-maker decides what the organismic objectives should be, and can change them;

2. The agencies of the Government decide upon the best means of accomplishing the organismic objectives and can change them.

In this study, there are 14 tactical choices identified as competing for the achievement of the overall objective. They are listed in Table 6.9. The weighted penalty scores for the 14 tactical choices together came to 30 712.

As a first approximation, consider that the 14 tactical choices are the only measures open to the Department of the Interior to accomplish the organismic objective. In that case, improved fire prevention/fighting techniques with its score of 7 500 claims 24.2% of the total budget.

Similarly, prevent strip mining with its score of 9 500 claims 30.9% of the total budget allocation, and so on.

For illustrative purposes, a simplified computer program was written, and the budgetary allocation based on these hypothetical hierarchic objectives was made for both FY 1970 and FY 1971.

8.4. CREED

Turning now from the tactical choices open to the pursuit of the organismic objective to their logical groupings, what can be said about the 14 tactical choices employed in this study?

Improving fire prevention/fighting techniques; preserving trees by better farming; and improving seed inventory replenishment clearly CONSERVE natural resources. Similarly, prevention of strip logging, strip mining and the establishment of criteria on fossil fuel mining are designed to REGULATE. The education of the public on fire prevention and the demonstration of the effects of violating environmental ethics are designed to EDUCATE. The tactical choices to improve roads to more distant areas, state assistance for land acquisition in general and urban and industrial land in particular, accent

Table 6.10
CREED

CONSERVE 27.19%	Improve Fire Prevention/Fighting Techniques	24.42%
	Preserve Trees by Better Farming	1.47%
	Improve Seed Inventory Replenishment to Restore Land	1.30%
REGULATE 65.43%	Prevent Strip-Logging	32.55%
	Prevent Strip-Mining	30.93%
	Establish Criteria on Fossil Fuel (e.g. Oil) Mining	1.95%
EDUCATE 4.88%	Education of the Public on Fire Prevention	3.74%
	Demonstration of Effects of Violating Environmental Ethic	1.14%
ENJOY 1.50%	Improve Routes to More Distant Areas	0.98%
	State Assistance for Land Acquisition	0.26%
	State Assistance to Acquisition of Urban Land	0.13%
	State Assistance to Acquisition of Industrial Land	0.13%
DEVELOP 1.00%	Create New Cities in Semi-Wild Forests	0.98%
	Move to Suburban Areas with Civil Systems Electronic Products	0.02%

the facility to ENJOY. Finally, the creation of cities in semi-wild forests and the move to suburban areas of electronic products industries are designed to DEVELOP the environment.

Combining the first letter of these five activities, the acronym CREED is evolved.

The Congressional decision-maker can look at the allocation of resources under each of these categories as shown in Table 6.10 and decide, for instance, that the allocation of 65% of resources to regulate the use of the environment may be too much and the allocation of 1.5% to facilitate the enjoyment of the environment too little. He could instruct that certain other percentages, say 37% and 25% may be more appropriate. He can ask for the decreasing of the allocation to regulatory activities from 65% to 37%, and the increase of the allocation for the facilitation of the enjoyment of the environment from 1.5% to 25%. The methodology of the present study requires the indication from the decision-maker as to where he would want to make the change, so that the total of resources to all of CREED is 100%.

9. Systems Approach to Appropriations Evaluation — Conclusion

The purpose of this introductory study has been to explore the use of the systems approach to help the systematic evaluation of budget requests by the Congressional decision-makers on the Appropriations Committee. The Department of the Interior Budget figures for FY 1970 and FY 1971 were selected, and some 55% of the total budget (NOA) represented in five elements was identified for analysis.

Using the organismic, strategic and tactical hierarchy of objectives, the five elements were associated with a single, overall objective: Averting national ecological disaster. Alternative measures of meeting this overall objective were systematically developed for each of the five elements.

A systematic comparison was made of different tactical level choices, horizontally; and also of each tactical choice with its higher level of objectives at the strategic and organismic level, vertically.

The consequences of nonfulfillment of each of the tactical level choices upon the organismic objective were illustratively put into numerical terms. Based upon the relationship of each tactical objective to each other and each tactical objective to the corresponding strategic and organismic objectives, the allocations of the Interior Budget were demonstrated.

The strength of the systems approach explored with respect to the appropriations evaluation lies in the consistency of methodology which forces the user to make explicit his hidden assumptions and values, so that alternative means of accomplishing the same objective can be identified and evaluated; as can courses and consequences corresponding to altogether different sets of overall objective themes.

PROBLEMS

The three chapters, 6, 7 and 8, of Part III deal with the application of OR/SA Protocol to large, unstructured problems in the Public Sector. This chapter deals with the problem of Ecological Investment. *The purpose of the following questions is to develop an appreciation for the specific demands of the substance of the* particular *problem in applying the* general *sequence.*

A system Context.
1. The Objective of any System is to fulfill User Objectives. Therefore, the relevance of the study would, to a large extent, depend upon the realism of

the User Objectives identified as the guideline. Discuss how an operational measure of the User Objective can be arrived at for the U.S. Budgetary Appropriations.

2. Given such an operational objective, how can the progress toward that goal be monitored?

3. In requesting appropriations for any activity, what are the minimum competitive and hierarchical considerations that should be taken into account? Illustrate with respect to a particular choice in U.S. Budgetary Appropriations.

4. If the Congressional decision-makers, representing the User, were to assign greater weight to the objective of providing enjoyment of the environment than to the objective of enforcement of restrictions on the misuse of the environment, how would the change in the System Objective influence the allocation of resources to fulfill the Objective?

B. *System Cost*

5. What is the cost of Opportunity Acquired with respect to the environment that may be included in discussing ecological investment?

6. How would the cost of opportunity foregone be incorporated into the choice of alternatives open to an Administrative Division of the Department of the Interior?

7. Illustrate the use of the cost of penalty for non-fulfillment in arriving at resource allocation to a particular activity.

C. *System Effectiveness—Absolute*

8. Discuss a way of justifying the investment of $1 in ecological investment in preference to $1 investment in national defense.

9. What is the principal limitation in making the resource allocations dependent upon the penalty scores as a fraction of the total penalty for the non-fulfillment of the Organismic Objective?

D. *System Effectiveness—Relative*

10. Illustrate how the subsystem performance will contribute to the change in the rate of achievement of the System Objective in ecological investment.

11. The decision is based on *ordinal* choices but the analysis is based on *cardinal* criteria. Discuss the limitations in applying the method to ecological investment.

CHAPTER 7

OR/SA PROTOCOL APPLIED TO PUBLIC SECTOR PROBLEMS: (2) HEALTH CARE ALLOCATION

TECHNICAL OVERVIEW

The OR/SA protocol, developed in Chapter 4, is applied to a second public sector problem.

The National Advisory Commission on Health Manpower, and the National Advisory Commission on Health Facilities, in presenting their Reports respectively in 1967, and 1968, concluded that more people could be employed in health activities, and more money spent, only to obtain less care from the increased manpower and dollar resources — unless a systems approach was employed.

As in the first application of the OR/SA protocol, the objectives of the system are first identified, in the light of the historical developments dating back to the 1900s. Health is no longer confined to the cure of ailments; its concerns extend back to the pre-illness environment through the post-illness reentry into the work force.

Given the extended concept of health, what is the appropriate form of organization? Different concepts of organization are examined and applicable concepts are identified.

Whatever be the method of organizing the health services, there must be a measure of effectiveness of the organization. Good health is defined as a situation where everyone who is willing to work is mentally and physically able to do so.

Thirteenth-century Europe offers an instructive parallel to the integrated health care and cure approach. However, unlike the thirteenth-century Europe there is considerable mobility in the twentieth-century United States, approximately 1 in 5 changing his place of residence every year. So provision has to be made for not only developing valuable individual medical data, but also for easy transmittal of the same to wherever the need may be for diagnostic and prescriptive purposes. Eight elements are identified as basic to a health care and cure system: (1) health base of individual data, (2) education base of individual care, (3) diagnosis screening of individual ailment, (4) pathologists' diagnosis of individual ailments, (5) auxiliary hospitals for ambulatory care, (6) central hospitals for major care, (7) technological advances for health systems, and (8) administrative arrangements for health systems.

Using the 8 elements as the principal means of insuring the development and administration of an integrated health care and cure system, the validity and the consistency of the 8 elements is tested by an inquiry into the allocation of resources for two competing claims: (1) a new wing of an auxiliary hospital in a county and (2) research on cancer chemotherapy. The first activity is included under the Element 5: auxiliary hospitals, while the second activity is included under element 7: technological advances – production of cure. Ordinal orderings of the objectives are developed first; and cardinal orderings are developed subsequently. The weighted value of the cardinal ordering for the auxiliary wing at county level is 51 100 000 while for the cancer chemotherapy research at the Federal Level it is 78 300 000 000; resulting in the allocation of $2 412 for the auxiliary wing, and $3 497 588 for cancer chemotherapy.

The specifics of the allocation are much less important than the method which neccessitates the recognition of the explication of objectives and preferences in such a way that each alternative competes for the allocation of resources in a consistent and comprehensive scheme; and the changes in the allocation or evaluation of one will affect directly all the other elements which are part of the same hierarchy.

EXECUTIVE SUMMARY

The method of conducting an OR/SA effort developed in Chapter 4, is applied to a study of the U.S. Health Services.

As in the previous study on the evaluation of the appropriations for the different activities of the Department of the Interior, an overall objective for the U.S. Health Services is developed and its major elements identified.

What constitutes health? It is more than paying medical bills. Tracing the development of the concepts of health in the United States and in Europe, an operational definition of good health is made. Good health is defined as the situation in which everyone who is willing to work is mentally and physically able to do so.

To achieve good health for the U.S. population, 8 elements are found to be essential. The value of the 8 elements thus identified is tested by raising the question of a hypothetical allocation of $3.5 million between two competing claims, one for the building of a new wing at a county hospital and another for the research in cancer chemotherapy.

To make the two competing demands comparable, higher levels of objectives have to be identified, as was done in the resource allocation for the components of the Department of the Interior. The two claims are made comparable at the highest level of care and cure. Based on the weighted score, the county hospital wing is allocated $2 412, and cancer chemotherapy is allocated $3 497 588, out of the total $3.5 million.

---

1. APPLICATION 17: An Ordering Approach to Organizing the Health Services

The largest appropriations in the U.S. budget now go to HEW, the first responsibility of which, as the H in HEW indicates, is the maintenance and improvement of the health of the people of the United States. Two Presidential Commissions, the National Advisory Commission on Health Manpower, and the National Advisory Commission on Health Facilities, concluded their deliberations with the concurring observation that more people could be employed in the health activity, and more money spent; but that there would be *less* care provided by the increased manpower and dollar resources *unless* the concept of systems is applied to the understanding, solution, and implementation of the solution of the problem of health care production and delivery.

The Operations Research Society of America held a Symposium on Health, May 14–16, 1969, in Washington, D.C., to respond to the efforts of the two Presidential Commissions, and their challenge to the profession to apply a systems approach to the health problem. Five half-day sessions were held, each devoted to one of the Panels of the Commission: The Role of the Consumer; Health Manpower; The Role of Technology; Hospital Care; and Organization of Health Services. The Chairman of the Panel, or a Member of the Panel, addressed the Symposium describing the special problems uncovered during the Commission work, as well as his updated thinking on the respective problems and approaches to solution. In an earnest effort to fulfill the public responsibility of the professional soceity, the operations research/-systems analysis viewpoint was then presented by a speaker, followed by two discussants who opened the floor for lively discussions.

In her presentation to the Symposium, Mary Lee Ingbar, Ph.D., M.P.H., who served as a Member of the Panel on the Organization of Health Services of the National Advisory Commission on Health Manpower, referred to the 14 recommendations which were concerned with: (1) the encouragement of competitive large-scale integrated health services systems; (2) the development of specially organized ambulatory care centers; and (3) the development of automatic diagnostic and laboratory services.[1] She pointed out that even when new techniques were being applied to develop a variety of reports, ranging from those designed for billing patients to those used for accounting purposes, "our increased knowledge is not being designed to relate to the system as a whole."[2]

William L. Kissick, M.D., who served as the Executive Director of the National Advisory Commission on Health Facilities, discussed the systems approach in terms of systems and authority:

> A systems conceptualization and approach to the health enterprise is recommended by both the referent commissions. However, the authority to implement the alternatives is the critical factor that is seldom given adequate emphasis in discussions of the systems approach. We often become so preoccupied with the problems of analysis that we ignore the prerequisite of authority in decision-making. I shall discuss these issues – *systems* and *authority* separately ... .
> In my opinion, *institutionalization*, i.e., structuring of authority, must accom-

[1] National Advisory Commission on Health Manpower, *Report*, Vol. II., U.S. Government Printing Office, Washington, D.C., 1967, pp. 186, 189, 190, 191–196.
[2] Mary Lee Ingbar, "Organization of Health Services: Challenge to Operations Research", in George K. Chacko (ed.), *The Recognition of Systems in Health Services,* Operations Research Society of America, Health Applications Section, Arlington, Va., 1969, p. 21.

pany operations research, if we are to have improved decision-making in the health enterprise. Both must be ranking items on the health agenda as we attempt to effect the transition to the comprehensive health care systems of the future.[3]

In responding to the challenge to the profession by both Doctors Kissick and Inbgar who served on the National Commission, the author asked three questions: (1) What are the *objectives* of the system; (2) what does it mean to organize the health services; and (3) since the best organization in the world is of no use unless it delivers what it is supposed to deliver, how do you *measure the effectiveness* of this organization? A test case was made of a hypothetical allocation of $3.5 million between two competing health projects, viz., building a new wing for an auxiliary hospital versus investing in cancer chemotherapy for a possible cure.

2. Introduction

The National Advisory Commissions on Health Manpower and on Health Facilities have both stressed the need for a systems perspective on health. In discussing the "wide-spread and serious talk of a 'health crisis' in the country", the Commission on Health Manpower emphasized that "the crisis, however, is not simply one of numbers ... unless we improve the system through which health care is provided, care will continue to become less satisfactory, even though there are massive increases in cost and in numbers of health personnel."[4]

To counter the situation where more and more money and manpower means less and less medical care, the Panel on the Organization of Health Services of the Health Manpower Commission proposes "more effective and efficient use of personnel. To achieve some improvement, however, existing patterns in the organization of health services must be restructured in major ways."[5]

---

[3] William L. Kissick, "Organization of Health Services", in George K. Chacko (ed.), *The Recognition of Systems in Health Services, op. cit.,* pp. 53, 55, 73.
[4] National Advisory Commission on Health Manpower, *Report,* Vol. I, U.S. Government Printing Office, Washington, D.C., 1967, pp. 1, 2.
[5] National Advisory Commission on Health Manpower, *Report*, Vol. II, U.S. Government Printing Office, Washington, D.C., 1967, p. 181.

The "effective and efficient use of personnel" cannot be separated from the effective and efficient use of health facilities. Therefore, the National Advisory Commission on Health Facilities, under the leadership of its Executive Director, William L. Kissick, M.D., focused attention on three general areas: "(1) Design and Construction; (2) Financing; and (3) Planning, Community Responsibility, and Consumer Participation... The Commission defines comprehensive health care as a system of services, for individuals and families, including four essential components:

health education,

personal preventive services,

diagnostic and therapeutic services, and

rehabilitative and restorative services."[6]

What can operations research contribute to the "effective and efficient use of personnel?" The key lies in the improvement of the system through which health care is provided, as the Health Manpower Commission has pointed out. The challenge to operations research is: how can the health services be organized as a system, which, among other things, permits the effective and efficient use of personnel?

3. Objectives of the System

The Health Facilities Commission defines the comprehensive health care as a system of services for individuals and families. Since these services are provided by the private and public sectors, and since public health services have to compete with all other public sector commitments, ranging from outer space to inner cities, both the scope of and the need for such services have to be well established.

Perhaps the greatest impetus to the role of the public sector in the delivery of health care has been provided by the participation of the Federal Government in the last five years in which more than 30 pieces of health legislation were passed to expand health resources and to improve health services. A student of private and public financing of health services in the United States points out that the rapid enactment of workmen's compensation laws provided

[6] National Advisory Commission on Health Facilities, *Report*, U.S. Government Printing Office, Washington, D.C., 1968, pp. 4–6, 8.

the stimulus for government health insurance drives in 16 states from 1915 to 1920:

> Those formulating legislative policy in this country, at both federal and state levels of government, simply did not have a concept for the individual, short of the individual who was indigent or who had other special problems. Moreover, government did not have the power to tax until 1914, nor did the precedents set for separation of specific federal and state functions permit official action. Perhaps a more deep-seated reason was that elected representatives did not become cognizant of the medical revolution that was taking place until the whole health services structure was established; then government began to be a buyer rather than a provider of services, a very important differentiation that remains with us to this day.[7]

3.1. Public Purchase of Private Production

The aforementioned differentiation, viz., the government being a buyer of health services, rather than a provider, has immense implication for any effective organization of personnel and facilities. Insofar as health has indeed become a constitutional right which entitles claims to be made for the widespread and timely provision of the same to the public, not as a function of ability to pay, but as a *right to be respected,* thanks to the impressive amount of legislation on the books, the Federal budget provision for health services has to answer the question: What services is the government buying; for whom?

It is too easy to look at the immediate and the obvious, and identify health services with simply the care and cure of those who are ill. This identification would be as shortsighted as was the pre-World War I concept of government responsibility: something confined to the indigent individual.

The broad objectives of the role of the government as a buyer of health services are twofold: (1) to foster health which is more than healing; and (2) to provide the protection to all the people.

However, the history of medical legislation shows that neither objective has been the guideline for legislation. The very first piece of health legislation was an Act of Congress in 1798 which was addressed to a very specific

---

[7] Odin W. Anderson, *The Uneasy Equilibrium*, College and University Press, New Haven, 1968, p. 53.

segment of the population, namely the seamen; and it was designed specifically for curative measures with no concept of health as anything more than healing. Following the precedent established by Great Britain to provide care for seamen who were such an integral part of the trade-based British economy, the U.S. Congress wanted to provide for the merchant seamen who came into port after long stretches of service on the seas with little provision for care when they became sick or destitute. The 1798 Act established the Marine Hospital Service and provided for a payroll tax of 20¢ a month on all American seamen, with no contribution to be made from the National Treasury. The next year the benefits of the Act were extended to all Naval personnel, and 20¢ a month was deducted from their pay. It took nearly a 100 years to lift the requirement that seamen contribute to the financing of the Merchant Marine Hospital Service, which was legislated in the Act of Congress in 1884. Instead of the 20¢ levy, a special tonnage tax became part of the source of revenue, the other part being met by general taxation. The tonnage tax, in turn, was eliminated in 1905 and henceforth the Merchant Marine Hospital Service was run on funds from the U.S. Treasury.[8,9,10]

3.2. From Private Segments to Public Health; From Cure to Prevention

Perhaps the first movement away from the care of the ill in particular population segments to the population as a whole, and from the limited concentration upon the cure of illness to its prevention came in 1911. According to Odin Anderson:

> It was in 1911 that one of the great pioneers in public health, then Commissioner of Health of New York, first coined the motto which appeared in the *Monthly Bulletin* of the health department and stood for many years thereafter. "Public health is purchasable. Within natural limitations, a community can determine its own death rate."[11]

---

[8] Robert Straus, *Medical Care for Seamen; The Origin of Public Medical Service in the United States*, Yale University Press, New Haven, 1950, pp. 5ff.

[9] Ralph C. Williams, *The United States Public Health Service, 1798–1950*, U.S. Public Health Service, Bethesda, Maryland, 1951, pp. 31–32.

[10] Harry S. Mustard, *Government in Public Health*, Commonwealth Fund, New York, 1945, p. 27.

[11] Odin W. Anderson, *op. cit.*, p. 24.

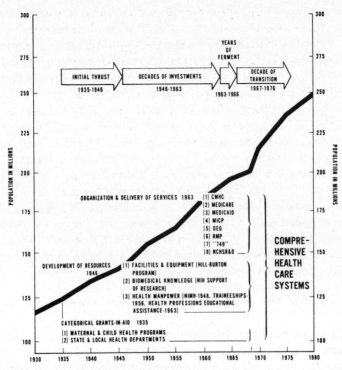

Fig. 7.1. Major health programs of the federal government: transition to healing systems.

From these bold beginnings in the early days going back to the 1900s, the nature and magnitude of governmental interest and involvement in public health as applied to the population as a whole, and as no longer limited to the mere cure of ailments, proceeded at an increasing, if not uniform, pace as depicted in Fig. 7.1, reproduced from the Report to the President from the National Advisory Commission on Health Facilities. The milestone pieces of legislation, such as Medicare and Medicaid, appear in the early '60s, which the Commission refers to as "the years of ferment". This fermentation is viewed as the background for the "decade of transition, 1967–76".

3.3. Federal Overview: "Improvement in Well-Being"

What is the rationale for the public purchase of private production of health services? Alice Rivlin[12] has proposed a "social report" which reflects the aggregate impact upon human living of the various forces which are at work, both in the public and in the private sector, the harmonious coordination of which is the acknowledged objective of any effective government. It is one thing to propose that such a report be attempted; it is quite another for it to be accepted – particularly at the highest levels of government where it counts most. Hence, one was pleasantly surprised to find in the Economic Report of the President transmitted to the Congress in January 1967, what appears to be the closest to such an aggregate index of the quality of life of the people as a whole. Before introducing the concept itself, which provides us with the clearest statement at the national governmental level of the overview of health in the broadest sense, we may look at the parallels between 1957 – post-Korea – and 1971 – post-Vietnam. In the words of the Report:

> *The Economic Report* transmitted to the Congress in January 1954 called attention to the opportunity afforded by the ending of the conflict in Korea to turn the productive capacity of the Nation increasingly to peaceful purposes, and thereby to undertake a sustained improvement in living standards. It also set forth the main lines along which the Federal Government proposed to move toward this goal and to seek to fulfill its mandate under the Employment Act of 1946 to promote maximum employment, production, and purchasing power.[13]

Given the post-Korean background, and the change in attention from war to peace – which we hope can be applied to the post-Vietnam situation – the President referred to "Improvement in Well-Being, 1952–1956". Fig. 7.2 reproduced from the Report summarizes the 30 tables in Appendix D, the titles of which are reproduced in Table 7.1.

It is significant that in Fig. 7.2 half of the six bargraphs refers to health in

---

[12] Alice Rivlin, *Toward a Social Report*, Department of Health, Education and Welfare, Government Printing Office, Washington, D.C., 1968.
[13] *Economic Report of the President,* Government Printing Office, Washington, D.C., 1957, p. 4.

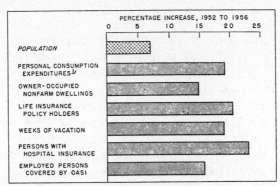

Fig. 7.2. Improvement in well-being, 1952 to 1956.

the broadest sense: "life insurance policy holders", "persons with hospital insurance", and "employed persons covered by OASI". The 30 tables listed in Table 7.1 upon which Fig. 7.2 was based indicate a similar emphasis upon health: "population, paid civilian employment, and employment covered by old-age and survivors insurance benefits", "civilian hospital beds", "hospital, surgical, and medical expense coverage", "injury-frequency rates in manufacturing industries", and "life insurance". The Economic Report emphasized its theme: "To help extend prosperity into the future, to strengthen competitive enterprise, and to increase our ability to achieve further improvement in national well-being."[14]

3.4. From Federal Overview to Individualized Cure and Care

What does the "improvement in well-being" mean in operational terms? Doubtless, it has to be translated in terms of the individual's well-being. In a negative sense, individual well-being can be considered the absence of illness. However, the mere absence of illness would not thereby insure the ability of the individual to achieve or enjoy well-being. To count well-being in terms of merely the reduction in the number of hours of hospital confinement is comparable to measuring the improvement in fire hazards merely in terms of

[14] *Economic Report of the President, op. cit.*, p. 3.

Table 7.1
Statistical tables relating to diffusion of well-being, 1946–56

1.   Population growth and vital statistics, 1946–56
2.   Total and per capita gross national product, in current and 1956 prices, 1946–56
3.   Civilian employment, 1946–56
4.   Total and per capita personal income, in current and 1956 prices, 1946–56
5.   Total and per capita disposable personal income, in current and 1956 prices, 1946–56
6.   Distribution of personal income disbursements, 1946–56
7.   Average family personal income, before and after Federal individual income tax liability, in current and 1956 prices, 1946–47 and 1950–55
8.   Distribution of families by family-income groups, 1946–47 and 1950–55
9.   Average gross hourly earnings of production workers in manufacturing industries, in current and 1956 prices, 1946–56
10. Average weekly earnings, gross and net spendable, of production workers in manufacturing industries, in current and 1956 prices, 1946–56
11. Average gross weekly earnings in selected industries, in current and 1956 prices, 1946–56
12. Work stoppages, 1946–56
13. Total and per capita personal consumption expenditures, in current and 1956 prices, 1946–56
14. Vacations and vacation activities, 1946–56
15. Families owning automobiles, 1948–49 and 1950–56
16. Home ownership, 1947, 1950 and 1952–56
17. Married couples with and without own household, 1946–56
18. Homes with selected electrical appliances, 1946–56
19. Life insurance, 1946–56
20. Selected financial assets of consumers, 1946–56
21. Shareowners in public corporations, 1952, 1954 and 1956
22. Fall school enrollment, 1948 and 1950–56
23. Percent of civilian noninstitutional population 5 to 34 years of age enrolled in school, by age group, October of each year, 1946–56
24. Selected measures of educational achievement and costs 1946–56
25. Population, paid civilian employment, and employment covered by old-age and survivors insurance and railroad retirement, 1946–56
26. Old-age and survivors insurance benefits, 1946–56
27. Unemployment insurance benefits, 1946–56
28. Civilian hospital beds, 1946–56
29. Hospital, surgical and medical expense coverage, 1946–56
30. Injury-frequency rates in manufacturing industries, 1946–56

the reduction in the property damage from fire. Even as the damages done by a fire are much more devastating in terms of its impact upon the commercial and industrial interrelationships that were built around a certain physical locale, so also, the damaging effects of serious illness are both preceded by and followed by significant reduction in the capability to achieve and enjoy well-being. Therefore, in discussing the implementation of the Federal overview of "improvement in well-being", the loss in the ability to achieve well-being must be operationally considered. To the individual, this would mean not only *cure* from illness, but also the *care* following the illness, and more importantly, preceding an illness which can even prevent its occurrence.

We present in Fig. 7.3 an overview of the illness problem in terms of individualized cure and care. The purely "medical" part of the health concern would deal with the "treatment" segments shown in Fig. 7.3. In a secondary sense, admissions and diagnostics would also play a role. However, the ecological environment from which the patients arrive, and the post-morbid environment which they enter, are usually treated as unrelated to the handling of illness. One implication of the concept of individualized cure and care would be to recognize the antecedents and the sequel to the merely "medical" aspects of health.

Having indicated the extension in space and time of the medical aspects of health, we shall nevertheless be confined to concentrating upon precisely the medical aspects of the health problem in the present discussion. However, the relationship of the ecological environment with the prevention of disease, and the relationship of the post-morbid environment with the return of the patient to achieve and enjoy well-being will be explicitly recognized in the analysis of the organization of the health services to achieve the goal of individualized cure and care.

4. Concepts of Organization

The Health Manpower Commission states that its emphasis throughout its deliberation and its Report has been "to put the needs of the patient first". Says the Report:

> Our recommendations for improving access to the medical care system, assuring high quality care, and controlling costs are all in keeping with this philosophy.

health concerns	population	patients	diagnostics	treatment			discharge	performers
methodology	ecological environment	admissions		medical	ambulatory and in-patient	dietary		post-morbid environment
formulation problem, methods	pollution: air, water, solids; hazards, accident proneness	multiphasic screening	computer-aided diagnosis; dynamic programming and cancer diagnosis	organization of research on leukemia, cancer	group nursing care			
data collection, processing	common survival rates, morbidity parameters	patient-day population	patient record, community data		poisson, log-normal, gamma arrivals	menu planning		
evaluation, cost-effectiveness	cost effectiveness of prevention vs cure		cost of wrong diagnosis	cost of length of stay				bonus payments to early discharge

Fig. 7.3. An overview of the health problem.

> Less than perfect use of resources is, of course, not unique to health. Yet in our opinion, the organization of health care has been less responsive to rapidly changing national needs than have many other aspects of society, and unless major changes are accomplished more quickly than has ever been possible in the past, a more serious "crisis" will be inevitable.
>
> We are convinced that just as it is true for so many of our nation's gravest difficulties, *government alone is not big enough to solve the problems of health care for the American people.*[15]

The "rapidly changing national needs" in part must refer to the change that has taken place in the realm of health, from being somewhat of a luxury to a necessity: a necessity guaranteed as an individual right. When the Commission points out that the organization of health care has been less responsive than many other aspects of society, the reference is to the *rate* of responsiveness of the health care system to the *rate of change in national needs* with respect to health. The Commission very clearly states that the situation will not change unless "the combinated resources and experience of the private sector" are organized in conjunction with those of the government.

4.1. Organizing for War (Machiavelli); Organizing for Peace (Pope John)

What is the "organization" that is envisaged? The Commission does not state what level of organization would be considered a desirable goal for the working together of the private and public sectors. The applicable meaning of the term seems to be: "A number of individuals systematically united for some end or work: *military organization.*"[16] The association of "organization" with the military is perhaps the easiest to recognize. In fact, Niccolo Machiavelli (1469–1527) said that the study of the organization and discipline of war should be the sole aim of a prince: "A prince should therefore have no other aim or thought, nor take up any other thing for his study, but war and its organization and discipline, for that is the only art that is necessary to one who commands."[17]

Whether we agree with this emphasis or not, the making of war is by no means indispensable to the success of the concept of organization. It can be

[15] National Advisory Commission on Health Manpower, *Report,* Vol. I, *op. cit.,* p. 3.
[16] The Reader's Digest, *Great Encyclopedic Dictionary*, Pleasantville, New York, 1966, p. 951.
[17] Niccolo Machiavelli, *The Prince*, (tr. W.K. Marriott) Chapter 14.

equally central in peaceful pursuits. Pope John XXIII refers to the Universal Declaration of Human Rights, approved by the General Assembly of the United Nations Organization, December 10, 1948, as an important step toward organizing the world community. In the words of his Encyclical:

> The document represents an important step on the path towards the juridical-political organization of the world community. For in it, in most solemn form, the dignity of a person is acknowledged to all human beings; and as a consequence there is proclaimed, as a fundamental right the right of free movement in search for truth and in the attainment of moral good and of justice, and also the right to a dignified life.[18]

In the context of peaceful pursuits, the concept of organization recognizes the requirements of political rules of conduct, which have to be governed by judicial review. The protection afforded the members of the organization is also judicial. Unlike in the case of the military organization, political factors are of the essence in the nonmilitary organization. This fact makes for less coercion and more cooperation on a voluntary basis. When left primarily to voluntary cooperation, what can be the guidelines for both creating and fostering the mechanism by which collective good, such as the capability of the largest number of people to pursue and enjoy well-being, be pursued on a national scale? It is clear that coercion as the basis of organization is at least conceptually unacceptable. The sense of the Health Manpower Commission was that the capabilities of the Federal Government in the health field must be complemented by the capabilities of the private sector. The underlying theme is that of cooperation.

4.2. Economic Integration of Latin America as an Organizational Framework

A parallel would be helpful. The Latin American countries, for some time now, have been discussing a form of institutionalized cooperation among themselves for the collective economic development of their region. The term used in this connection is "economic integration". In fact, the Inter-American Development Bank has been approvingly referred to as "the Bank of Latin American Integration".[19] Among the recent formal expressions of this con-

[18] Pope John XXIII, *Pacem in Terris*, Rome, Italy, April 11, 1963.
[19] Felipe Herrera, President's Statement before the Second Committee of the United Nations General Assembly, New York, December 12, 1968, p. 6.

cept of economic integration is Resolution AG-6/68: Physical Integration of Latin America, which says in part:

> WHEREAS:The Charter of Punta del Este, in establishing the Alliance for Progress, emphasized the need to proceed with economic integration as a condition for the acceleration of economic development of Latin America... .
> The Bank has been assigned the primary responsibility for implementing, within its sphere of competence, the measures agreed upon by the Presidents of America, including physical integration and the Preinvestment Fund for Latin American Integration.
> The Board of Governors RESOLVES: That the Bank undertake promptly, in conjunction with CIAP to initiate the establishment of a task force to develop a five-year plan and action program for physical integration projects in Latin America.[20]

To suggest that the organization framework of the health services in the United States is some form of integration of private and public sector activities, will appear to be a direct violation of the basic tenets of free enterprise. It should be emphasized that the institutional framework of Latin American economic integration has been used only as a parallel; not as a prototype. Since the desired objective of the organization of health services is to provide for a vigorous and concerted use of public and private resources of health, and since this result has to be obtained in conformity with the forces of independent decision by different entities each of which exercises control over parts of the total health resources, the concepts of organization that the Latin American countries have found necessary to develop and employ bear further scrutiny. Should the features appear undesirable, we could learn from experience to avoid either the structure as a whole, or in part. On the other hand, if there are desirable features, they would provide us with some guidelines as to what may be expected of the effective organization of the health services.

4.3. From Cooperation to Coordination to Integration

In his presentation before the Fourth Annual Meeting of the Board of Governors of the Inter-American Development Bank, Mr. Javier Marquez, the Direc-

---

[20] Inter-American Development Bank, PROCEEDINGS: Ninth Meeting of the Board of Governors, Bogota, Columbia, April 1968, pp. 197–198.

tor of CEMLA (Center for Latin American Monetary Studies) made useful distinctions between cooperation, passive coordination, active coordination and interaction. According to him:

> The essence of COORDINATION is that it is an *independent and harmonious activity resulting from an express or tacit agreement and carried out for mutual benefit or for the benefit of others.* It is much more complex and subtle than COOPERATION ALONE... .
>
> It is COORDINATION by express agreement if the countries involved decide to discuss whether the discipline regulating them is the kind they want; to persuade each other to submit to it; to press one another's securing of suitable instruments to carry out this adjustment; to help each other in this process, etc. If, on the other hand, these countries actually accept the discipline without any system of coordination, the result is SPONTANEOUS COORDINATION, or by TACIT agreement... .
>
> The problem of whether INTEGRATION is or is not involved in [any country in the area obtaining resources from another or several others in the same region] does not arise when they are received from another country in the same area, since one country's access to the capital market in another country or countries itself constitutes economic integration of a kind, that is to say, a capital market integration, whatever the outcome of utilization of such resources.[21] (capitals supplied)

4.4. Resource Organization Parallels: Economic Development and Health Services

There are several parallels between the Latin American economic development and the U.S. Organization of Health Services as shown in Table 7.2.

It bears repetition that the parallelism by no means suggests an outright adaptation with the reasoning: what is good for Latin American economies is good for United States Health. However, the fierce adherence to their independence by the different countries as a welcome parallel to the insistence on maintaining their independence by private institutions in the health field. Similarly, the deliberate delays that have been introduced into the active coordination to mobilize regional resources in Latin America may also be expected to quell the fears of a federal takeover tomorrow of the entire

---

[21] Javier Marquez, "Coordination of Policies for Mobilizing Resources on the Regional Level", in *Financial Aspects of Economic Integration in the Hemisphere*, Caracas, Venezuela, 1963, pp. 4, 6, 9.

Table 7.2
Resource organization parallels: economic development and health services

	Organizing for economic development	Organizing for health services
1. Overview	acceleration of economic development	improvement in well-being
2. Prerequisite	economic integration	the recognition of systems in health services
3. Participants	independent countries	independent institutions
4. Exchange elements	Producers: countries C_1, $C_3, C_5, ..., C_{n+1}$	Producers: private institutions
	Purchasers: countries $C_2, C_4, ..., C_n$	Purchasers: public institutions
5. Past history	voluntary cooperation unsuccessful	voluntary cooperation imperative
6. Present precepts	tacit coordination: free trade between Columbia and Venezuela	Tacit coordination
	Active coordination: LAFTA (Latin American Free Trade Association)	Active coordination: Medicare, Medicaid
7. Future profile	Fiscal integration: access by one country to another's capital	Fiscal integration: central funds for medical facilities, new technologies, etc.
	Physical integration: "[establish] interconnection, and expansion of land, sea, river and air transportation ... telecommunications and electric power systems and pipelines." (Resolution AG-6/68)	Physical integration: "integrated health services systems under a variety of auspices including physicians in private practice, universities, hospitals, voluntary agencies, and government." (Health Manpower Commission Report, Vol. I, p. 75)

network of private institutions and resources engaged in the production and distribution of health services in the United States.

An important difference between the Latin American integration and the health services organization is that unlike the Latin American countries which both produce and purchase goods and services, the Federal *Government* remains a *purchaser* of health services, while the private sector remains the producer of health services. Another difference between the Latin American integration and the health services organization is the significant capability of the Federal Government to condition, and to some extent determine, the course of the production of health services in the private sector. This control can be exercised both with respect to the construction of medical facilities, e.g., Hill-Burton Funds, and the undertaking of basic research into health services. No single agency exerts such power with respect to the Latin American economic integration.

The question now is: how can the vast resources, both public and private, of the United States, be mobilized in such a way that individualized cure and care of health may be made available to the maximum number of people with the minimum of interference with the free enterprise system?

5. Effectiveness Measures for Health Resources Allocation

Whatever be the method of organizing health services, there must be a measure of the effectiveness of the organization. It should indicate if the organization has accomplished what it was supposed to accomplish; and it should also measure the interim progress towards this accomplishment or regress away from the accomplishment.

5.1. Misplaced Emphasis Upon Cure-of-Illness Costs

In this context, the cost reduction in hospital care can be not only an inadequate, but also an erroneous measure of effectiveness. Its error lies in the misplaced emphasis upon reducing the money costs of hospital care; or the cost of *illness* instead of *health*. If this caveat is borne in mind, then the specific measures of limited value can be accorded their proper place in the system of health services as a whole. One estimate puts the reduction in the total cost of patient care in American hospitals as a result of reducing the average length of stay by one day to be over $8 000 000, all other things being equal.[22]

[22] H. Smalley and J. Freeman, *Hospital Industrial Engineering,* Reinholt, New York, 1966.

The limitation in the use of cost reduction as a measure of effectiveness is brought into sharp focus by the Health Manpower Commission Report which projects the patient-days from 1965 to 1975 and points out the effect of Medicare in significantly raising the utilization of hospital services by the over 65 age group. The length of stay has also shown a proportionate increase. Therefore, from a purely cost reduction standpoint, the results of Medicare has been negative. However, cost reduction was *not* the intent of the Medicare legislation. Its focus was health, not illness. What Medicare made possible was for a number of the over 65 group to improve their well-being. If the effectiveness of individual cure and care is used as a measure of effectiveness of the organization of health services, then that measure would show a positive result for Medicare. The immediate area of impact of Medicare is the hospital; its nature and magnitude is outlined in the words of the Commission:

> AHA (American Hospital Association) surveys indicate that the *length of stay* for the over 65 group increased about 20 percent in the first 6 months of the program. The Social Security Administration has estimated that overall utilization of hospital services by the over 65 group increased 15–20 percent in the 1st year of the program... . A minimum estimate of the increase in hospital admissions and patient-days from 1965–1975... is perhaps 45 percent as a result of longer lengths of stay by the over 65 age group. This means that by 1975 *hospital admissions* in the neighborhood of 36.5 million per year and an average daily census of about 820 000 patients can be expected... . The Nation will need about 1 075 000 beds in non-federal short-term general hospitals... approximately 45 percent over 1965 levels... .
>
> It appears likely that by 1975 average short-term *hospital costs* will exceed *$100 per patient day* unless some significant changes in the way of producing hospital services are introduced. This would mean that expenditures for care in non-federal short-term general hospitals will rise to about $3.2 billion a year by 1975. This is almost four times the 1965 private consumer expenditure for hospital care and not quite 2½ times the national expenditure for hospital care in 1965.[23] (italics supplied)

A *narrow* view of the measures of effectiveness would include:
maintaining 1965 patient-day cost of $44.48 in 1975,
keeping the average daily hospital admissions below 820 000 in 1975,
keeping the demand for beds below 1 075 000 in 1975.

[23] National Advisory Commission on Health Manpower, *Report*, Vol. II, *op. cit.*, pp. 253, 254, 256.

The reason why these measures of effectiveness are narrow is because they focus attention upon the wrong question, viz., on illness instead of health; on cure, instead of care.

> Broader view — Care of health
> Good Health: Everyone who is willing to work is able to do so.
> Good Health: *Not* zero ill health.
> Age group Indices:
> > Under 17: Everyone who is willing to go to school is able to do so.
> > 17—65:   Everyone who is willing to work is able to do so.
> > Over 65: Everyone who is willing to relax is able to do so.

5.2. *Required Emphasis upon Care of Health*

When attention is turned to an individual's health as an integral element of his well-being, we do not ask the question: How long was he ill?; but instead: How well can he function? An equal, if not greater, emphasis will be placed upon keeping the individual out of the hospital, and preventing him from becoming sick. If this emphasis is followed through, he will probably make a much more significant contribution to the reduction of the cure of illness costs. The notion here is that of well-being and its extension: Well-Being Extension.

What could be a tangible measure of individualized care of health? For the 17—65 age group, the criterion can be the *capability to work*. From the point of view of health services, whether the individual does work, whether he chooses not to work or whether he is technically competent to work is besides the point. The only question is: is he physically able to work?

5.3. *Good Health and Full Employment*

The parallel between this concept and the concept of full employment is apparent. Under full employment, everyone who is able and willing to work is able to find work. Under the concept of what we call good health *everyone who is willing to work is able to do so*.

When Lord William Beveridge[24] drew up the blueprint for full employ-

---

[24] William Beveridge, *Full Employment in a Free Society,* Norton, New York, 1945.

ment for Great Britain, he provided for 5 percent unemployment. At lunar landing time, the U.S. unemployment stood at 4.1 percent.[25] In other words, full employment is *not* zero unemployment; so also good health is *not* zero ill health.

5.4. Ill Health and Unemployment

Without discussing the merits of the current measures on employment, we can say that it does provide a numerical index upon which national policy can be based. There are unresolved questions of underemployment, unproductive employment, etc., but the point is that there is a *consistent* base for comparing the percentage of unemployed working force.

With respect to the concept of *good health*, the absence of good health can take even greater variations and forms than the absence of employment. A number of people currently in the work force may be adjudged by psychologists to be too unhealthy to be in the work force. This refinement is not a luxury we can afford in trying to establish a gross working index of good health. It may well be a desirable refinement to the concept of good health itself; but for the moment, it will deny the possibilities of arriving at an initial numerical measure of good health.

5.5. Good Health: Macro and Micro Measurements

So far, good health has been discussed in macro terms, in terms of the national good health. While the discussion has been confined to the 17–65 age group because of the direct implications for the work force, it can be extended to those under 17 and over 65. Under 17, good health would mean that those who want to go to school can do so; over 65, good health would mean that those who want to relax can do so. Still, the concept refers to the entire population in each group – under 17, 17–65, over 65.

How can this macro concept be applied to *micro* segments of the U.S. population? We can talk about the percentage of people in a particular plant, firm, industry who are able to report to work for a week, a month, a year, etc. By categorizing the absence from work into health and other reasons, the experience of the individual plant, firm, industry, etc., can be recorded over

[25] "Economic Indicators", *The New York Times,* July 20, 1969, p. F 5.

different periods of time. The variations within plants and between plants can
be investigated; so can variations within and between industries. The effect of
seasonal fluctuations can also be standardized, in much the same way as provision is made for the seasonal employment in summer, when the labor force
is swelled temporarily by the influx of high school and college students. The
concept of good health can thus be measured meaningfully both at the macro
and the micro level, the latter permitting the monitoring of the implementation of policy at the level of the former.

5.6. Available Resources for Care of Health

What are the resources available for the care of health; how much?

The question: "how much" should be modified to reflect the emphasis
upon health. Thus, it is worth the while of the plant, the firm, the industry to
have as many of its personnel on the rolls to work as many days in the year
as possible. The question should be: how much is it worth to the plant, firm,
industry to have its work force report to work for the entire work year? In
calculating the work year, allowance must be made for legal holidays, personal vacations, and any other similar expected period of absence from
work. On a 40-hour week basis, the 52-week period has 2 080 hours. Allowing for 9 days of holidays, the work year reduces to 2 008 hours. If the
personal vacation is counted as part of the work year, the objective of the
plant, firm, industry is to increase for the majority of its employees the work
year from whatever be the past record to 2 008 hours. What is it worth to the
plant, firm, industry to accomplish this?

At the national level, the increase in the effective work hours would be
reflected in a continuing increase in the Gross National Product. The national
budget for health services could thus be directly related to the Increase in
Income.

6. Elements of Health for Individualized Care and Cure

Thirteenth-century Europe offers us an instructive parallel to the integrated
health care and cure approach. It also offers a workable arrangement between
the public and private sectors. In the words of Will Durant:

Good schools of medicine existed in the thirteenth century at Bologna, Padua, Ferrara, Perguia, Siena, Rome, Montpellier, Paris, and Oxford. In these schools the three main medical traditions of the Middle Ages – Greek, Arabic, and Judaic – were merged and absorbed, and the entire medical heritage was reformulated to become the basis of modern medicine.

As the supply of trained physicians increased, governments began to regulate medical practice. Roger II of Sicily, probably influenced by old Moslem precedents, restricted the practice of medicine to persons licensed by the state. Frederick II (1224) required for such practice a license from the School of Salerno... .

Every city of any importance paid physicians to treat the poor without charge. Some cities had a measure of socialized medicine. In Christian Spain of the thirteenth century a physician was hired by the municipality to care for a specified part of the population; he made periodically a medical examination of each person in his territory, and gave each one advice according to his findings; he treated the poor in a public hospital, and was obliged to visit every sick person three times a month; all without charge, except that for any visit above three in any month he was allowed to ask a fee. For these services the physician was exempted from taxes, and received an annual salary of twenty pounds, equivalent to some $4000 today. In the laws of Visigothic Spain the physician was not entitled to a fee if his patient died.

As licensed physicians were not numerous in thirteenth century Christian Europe, they earned good fees, and had high social status. Some amassed considerable fortunes; some became art collectors; several won an international reputation.[26]

6.1. Element 1: Health Base of Individual Data (ID)

It is clear that the physician provided health services of care and cure both under public and private aegis. Under the public aegis, he has a "specified part of the population" whom he had "to care for". Under the private aegis, he presumably had his own practice from which he "earned good fees". The key to the public practice of medicine lay in the fact that "he made periodically a medical examination of each person in his territory." The comprehensive medical checkup which the individual physician was providing to every citizen in the thirteenth-century Europe could now be provided by means of *multiphasic screening*.

Unlike the thirteenth-century Europe, there is considerable mobility in

[26] Will Durant, *The Story of Civilization*, Vol. IV, Simon and Schuster, New York, 1950, pp. 998, 999.

twentieth-century United States – approximately 1 in 5 changing his place of residence every year. This makes it impossible for an individual physician to be the repository of the Individual Data (ID) on health of a specified number of people in a given territory. Therefore, provision should be made for ID's to be carried by each individual for use whenever and wherever he may need medical aid. Such an ID could include but not necessarily be limited to:

Complete medical history,
Physical examination,
Chest X-ray,
Electrocardiogram,
Sigmoidoscopy,
Complete blood count,
Complete urine analysis,
Sedimentation rate,
Blood cholesterol,
Post-prandial blood sugar,
Blood urea nitrogen,
Uric acid,
Protein bound iodine.

Since the ID constitutes the essential data base for any organization of health services designed for individualized care, and since the ID's ought to be universal, the initial development of ID's should properly be facilitated at the Federal level. The cost for the ID's should be shared three ways: the Federal Government; the employer; and the employee.

6.2. Element 2: Education Base of Individual Care (IC)

Given the base of ID, the individual should be educated to recognize discomforts and ailments, and be prepared to take the first step in handling them. The intent here is for the individual to make use of drugs under medical advice on a care basis instead of a cure basis. It may well be that the ID's can contain specific instructions as to the drugs that can be obtained without prescription which may be used a limited number of times prior to consulting a physician. Part of the education for Individual Care (IC) would be a requirement that the individual keep up with periodic checkups. Simple rules on health habits would also be part of IC.

The cost of the education base of IC, like other costs of education, would largely devolve upon the government. The private sector can cooperate with the health educational process, by making both the premises and the personnel available for the conduct of such health classes after work hours. This will be a logical sequel to the practice in many corporations of providing innoculations to their employees at cost on the premises of the plant or firm.

6.3. Element 3: Diagnostic Screening of Individual Ailment (DS)

A function of advancing technology and health education would be the awareness by the individual of the limits within which the measures of ID can move. It is conceivable that, even as today laboratory tests are performed in locations physically separated from the diagnostic centers, so also the multiphasic screening results can be used in different time periods; and either the individual and/or the physicians be alerted to the divergence in measurements which suggests one or more possible ailments.

While such an eventuality is in the future, the tremendous advantage provided by the creation of a health base of ID's can be put to efficient use by utilizing auxiliary health personnel. In other words, instead of a machine alerting the patient and/or the physician to a possible ailment, a nurse or a nurse's aid could do so for the present. The difference between the present practice of an individual talking to the nurse of his discomforts and the new procedure is twofold: (1) both the individual and the nurse shall have the ID in front of them when they talk, and (2) the laboratory shall have recorded the latest measurements of ID which are also available both to the individual and the nurse. On the factual basis, the nurse can suggest intermediary steps of care and/or cure; she may further suggest that the patient consult with a physician.

This extension of the use of auxiliary health personnel to perform Diagnostic Screening (DS) of individual ailments can simultaneously relieve the load on the physician and provide timely care and/or cure to the individual. For this, the major prerequisites are ID and IC.

6.4. Element 4: Pathological Diagnosis of Individual Ailments (PD)

One of the predicted phenomena of the next decade is the increasing complexity of technical innovations pertaining to the functioning of the human organism. The more we understand its inner workings, the more likely are we to recognize warning symptoms earlier, and therefore be able to take preventive action. However, both the increased knowledge of the human organism and the workings of its enemies are quite likely to call for increasingly complex devices of detection. Here the setup costs would be much heavier by comparison than the operating costs. It is somewhat similar to the use of a computer to solve a problem. Once the program is written and debugged, the time taken for the solution of a number of problems by changing the values of the variables is comparatively miniscule. So also, to gear up to perform a host of specialized tests upon the human subject would take years of experience and an array of equipment. Having once set it up, the diagnostic machinery can be operated again and again for individual cases with miniscular costs in comparison with the initial setup.

Based on the present expanding trends in medical technology, it is inevitable that diagnostics become more and more specialized. A benefit of this specialization is that ailments will be more accurately identified: a cost of this improved accuracy is the investment in training and equipment. A necessary division of labor between the specialized pathological diagnosis (PD) and diagnosis screening (DS) is also in the cards, so that the specialized training and talent of the pathologist would be used most effectively in the most demanding situation.

6.5. Element 5: Auxiliary Hospitals for Ambulatory Care (AH)

Once the need for hospital care — ranging from exploratory observation to intensive care — has been established, there must be a screening mechanism to distinguish between types of hospital care. The purpose of the screening is similar to that of the diagnosis screening; viz., effectively use the specialist's time or the specialized facilities by reducing the pressure of demands for the nonspecialized services. Clearly, there is no need to tie up a specialized hospital bed for exploratory observation. Low cost alternatives to the hospital bed may be efficiently utilized for selected types of ailments. Further, medical services relating to opthalmology, pediatrics, urology, etc., can be provided in an Auxiliary Hospital (AH) for ambulatory care. It may well be that two or more auxiliary hospitals could be satellites to a central hospital for which the auxiliary hospitals function as a diagnostic screening setup, similar to the role of the auxiliary health personnel with respect to the pathologist.

6.6. Element 6: Central Hospital for Major Care (CH)

Elements 1 through 5 are intended to release the Central Hospitals (CH) for their specialized functions. Unless this is done, it will be necessary to build more hospital beds and still end up with less individual care.

6.6.1. Construction costs

The Health Manpower Commission projects the need for an additional 1 075 000 beds in nonfederal short-term general hospitals in 1975. The costs, according to the Commission, are going to be twice the hospital construction expense in the previous decade. The Commission says:

> If spending for construction of medical facilities lagged 1 year is compared with the number of short-term general hospital beds added over the 1955–65 period, we find that total spending was at the rate of about $82 500 per new bed added. This figure, coupled with the estimate of net new beds to be added (285 000–335 000) [assuming that hospital beds are retired at the rate of 3 percent per year], yields an estimate of $23.5–$27.5 billion that will have to be spent on new medical facilities over the 1965–75 decade.[27]

An effectiveness measure of Elements 1 through 5 will be the decrease in the costs of hospital bed construction from $23.5–$27.5 billion. If, for instance, that cost is reduced by half, Elements 1–5 can be allocated between $11.75–$13.75 billion. The chances are that what would have taken $11.75–$13.75 billion in central hospital bed construction would be more than adequately met by a smaller investment in Elements 1 through 5.

6.6.2. Community management

The key to the accomplishment of the objectives of individualized cure and care in the central hospitals is community management. If there is successful community management, then Elements 1–5 would be imaginatively implemented, thereby increasing considerably the chances of meeting the objective of well-being extension by means of individualized cure and care.

The Health Manpower Commission said:

[27] National Advisory Commission on Health Manpower, *Report*, Vol. II, *op. cit.*, p. 254.

> We recommend that *the highest priority should be given by community health councils to developing methods which will assure access to adequate health care for all those in the community they serve.*[28]

Just like the nation's school system, the ultimate arbiter of the effectiveness of hospitals at the local level is the local community. It is the community which ultimately realizes the extension of well-being, and consequent increase in income. It is the community member who should enjoy individualized care and cure. It is the community member who pays for these service, either directly in fees, or indirectly through taxes. Therefore, it is only logical that each community receives the health services it deserves.

While the exact mix of the management roles would vary from community to community, all community management of health services would necessarily include coordination at the following levels:

Township/City,
County,
State,
Regional,
Federal.

There can be no uniform formula for incorporating all the five levels into any organization of health services. They will necessarily be different. However, the encouragement toward efficiency in terms of a chosen measure, e.g., the Commission's "access to adequate care for all those in the community", can be made effective by means of rewards and punishments, by means of awarding grants or withholding them. If universal access to adequate health care is indeed established as a national criterion, then to the extent that the access is not universal, to that extent withholding of grants is in order in a manner similar to the withholding of grants pending fulfillment of desegregation in the education system.

It is imperative that measurable objectives be identified for gauging the success of community management. Goals, instead of platitudes, should be placed before the community, so that they can work, say over a six month period, towards access for 85 percent of the members of the community to at least an auxiliary hospital within 24 hours of a health-care need.

[28] National Advisory Commission on Health Manpower, *Report,* Vol. I *op. cit.,* pp. 72–3.

6.6.3. Medical staff and hospital management

While the community management deals almost exclusively with social management of the hospital complex, the medical staff deals with the technical
management of hospital facilities. Yet, in a vast majority of hospitals we have
structures offering little or no role in the technical management to the technical staff. In the words of the Health Manpower Commission:

> [The physician] makes the initial decision to admit a patient, and his decisions
> control the vast majority of costs incurred during hospitalization... . Presently,
> most physicians feel little responsibility to a hospital because they pay nothing
> for its use; neither do they suffer any direct consequences when the hospital gets
> into financial trouble... .
>   We recommend that *medical and hospital associations [consider] providing
> physicians with a financial stake in the operation of the hospital and of including
> physicians in the membership of hospital boards of control.*[29]

One of the recommendations of the Commission is to give physicians
financial incentives to improve the efficiency of hospital operations. The
caveat expressed earlier may be repeated here, viz., that the length of hospital
stay can be cut down at the cost of the patient not being well enough to get
back into the work force, but with a demonstrable decrease in the cost of
hospital operations. The physician should be given an incentive award, not for
cutting short the stay in the hospital of the patient, but for not getting him
into the hospital in the first place, and getting him back on his feet in the
second place. Some aspects of the health care arrangement in thirteenth-
century Spain may well be adapted to harness the vast advances of technology in the twentieth century by making it worthwhile to the physicians to
employ their technology not only in the practice of individualized cure, but
also equally in the practice of individualized care.

6.7. Element 7: Technological Advances in Health Systems (TA)

One of the major differences between the thirteenth-century Europe and
twentieth-century United States is precisely the enormous Technological Advances (TA) that have been made in the health field. An integrated system of
U.S. Health Services ought to have provision for systematic incorporation of

---

[29] *Ibid.,* pp. 63–64.

technological advances into both the production and delivery of health care and cure.

6.7.1. Production of cure

Technological advances in the cure of ailments would be more easily recognised. Thus, the cure for cancer, when discovered, will make medical history of the order of the discovery of penicillin for bacterial infections.

6.7.2. Production of care

Once the cure for a disease has been found, attention is likely to be turned to the prevention of its occurrence. The vaccine for poliomyelitis is an illustration. While the discovery of a cure is spectacular, the discovery of a means to care so that the disease would not occur is more dramatic in the long run as far as the improvement of well-being of the population as a whole is concerned.

6.7.3. Delivery of cure and care

It is one thing to produce a cure or a means to care; it is quite another to deliver the same to those in need. Since benefit delayed is benefit denied, the discovery of rapid means of dissemination of the technological advances for cure and care to as wide a segment of the population as possible is equally, if not more, important than sometimes the discovery of the means itself.

6.8. Element 8: Administrative Arrangements for Health Systems (AA)

While technological advances have been rapidly changing the practice of medicine, there has been taking place a slower, but significant change in the ways of the Administrative Arrangement (AA) for the delivery of health care. The most crucial developments have been in the financing of health care. Two major changes in the administration of health care were brought about simultaneously: one, the physician would be paid a "salary" from some form of insurance, instead of a "fee" as thereunto; two, there will be protection against the cost of illness, so that help would be available when needed most for restoring health. According to Odin Anderson:

> Health insurance was considered the next logical step after workmen's compensation. Compensation protected workmen from the economic loss associated with

illness and accidents incidental to employment; health insurance would protect the worker against the cost of illness and accidents outside of employment... . The decade from 1910 to 1920 represents the first clearly delineated period in the history of health insurance in this country... . [However] there was a double confusion at the time: (1) regarding health insurance as a health service or as a method of payment from a pool fund; and (2) regarding the role of health insurance in relieving poverty or in helping middle income groups to pay for services in an orderly manner.[30]

The confusion was gradually resolved and the principles of health insurance were adopted during 1933–52. No integrated U.S. health services system can ignore the decisive role of administrative arrangements for the payment of health care that are offered by insurance companies, voluntary associations, governments and other institutions. We have so far considered:

Element 1: Health Base of Individual Data (ID).
Element 2: Education Base of Individual Care (IC).
Element 3: Diagnostic Screening of Individual Ailment (DS).
Element 4: Pathological Diagnosis of Individual Ailment (PD).
Element 5: Auxiliary Hospitals for Ambulatory Care (AH).
Element 6: Central Hospitals for Major Care (CH).
Element 7: Technological Advances in Health Systems (TA).
Element 8: Administrative Arrangements for Health Systems (AA).

7. Allocation Mechanism of Aggregate Resources for Individualized Care and Cure

An integrated system of health services for the United States will by no means come into being overnight. Even if a Council of Health Advisors, similar to the Council of Economic Advisors, were to be formed as recommended by the Health Manpower Commission, that agency, being by and large an advisor on the purchase of health services which are predominantly produced in the private sector, is unlikely to implement an effective integration of national health services.

It can, however, provide a most useful function by both structuring and maintaining an overview of the national health services. When applied, such

[30] Odin W. Anderson, *op. cit.,* pp. 60–61, 86.

an overview would provide an operational ordering of objectives, so that the Council can recommend the choice between the allocation of say \$3.5 million for the building of an auxiliary wing of a hospital, on the one hand, and for the research into cancer chemotherapy, on the other. The merit of the operations research approach in this context is in that it shall provide an ordering — ordinal or cardinal — on the basis of which the interrelationship between individual decisions and the overall objective of improvement in individual well-being can constantly be kept in view.

Competing Objectives: \$3.5 million for (1) a new wing of an auxiliary hospital in a county, and (2) research on cancer chemotherapy. How should \$3.5 million be allocated between (1) and (2)?

7.1. Identify Next Higher Level of Objectives

The construction of a new wing of an auxiliary hospital in a county is much more visible than the result of research on cancer chemotherapy. Before a determination can be made as to which objective merits what allocation, it is necessary to ascertain the *next higher level* of objectives. For the auxiliary wing, it is Element 5: Auxiliary Hospitals for Ambulatory Care. Similarly, for cancer chemotherapy, the next higher level of objective is Element 7: Technological Advances — Production of Cure. Is Element 5 > Element 7? Or, Element 7 > Element 5?

7.2. Ordinal Ordering of the Highest Level of Objectives

To decide whether Element 5 > Element 7 or vice versa, we have first to decide whether cure > care or care > cure.

To decide upon the priorities between care and cure, let us consider the terms of reference of the two National Advisory Commissions:

> The President established the National Advisory Commission on Health Manpower to "develop appropriate recommendations for action by government or by private institutions, organizations, or individuals for improving the availability and utilization of health manpower."[31]
>
> In establishing the National Advisory Commission on Health Facilities on October 6, 1967, President Lyndon B. Johnson said: "... The whole structure of

[31] National Advisory Commission on Health Manpower, *Report*, Vol. I, *op. cit.*, p. 1.

health care delivery must be considered as we design the buildings and facilities of tomorrow."[32]

Clearly, the emphasis in both the Presidential charges is upon cure, rather than care. The number one objective is cure; the number two objective is care.

To emphasize the fact that these objectives relate to people, and systems involving people who can, consciously or unconsciously bring to naught the most carefully laid plans for effective functioning, we may term the highest level of objectives: *organismic objectives.* As said elsewhere:

> The decision-affecting and decision-affected entities are *organisms*. The term "organism" denotes the fact that the constituents are animate, that they interact, that their dynamic interrelationships tend to generate intangibles which can sometimes make the whole considerably larger or considerably smaller than the sum of its parts. Thus, a well-motivated team of workers produces much more than the arithmetic sum of their individual capabilities, measured in common units like salaries, years of training and experience, etc., whereas a poorly motivated team produces much less than their individual capabilities. Organismic viewpoint underlies operations research. It is the art of applying the scientific method to executive type decision problems. It is also the practice of translating progressively what-can-be into what-is in industrial, commercial, military, and/or institutional environments. Thus operations research is indispensable to identify the potentials of alternate solutions to meet the challenges of the environment as well as to implement them.[33]

7.3. Cardinal Ordering of the Highest Level of Objectives: Organismic Objectives

The *hypothetical* score of 100 to cure and 80 to care is assigned to reflect the Presidential priorities.

Ordinal ordering is converted into cardinal ordering:

Cure is prefered to care.

Cure is "20 points" higher than care.

Allocation of resources between cure and care is in the ratio 5 : 4.

---

[32] National Advisory Commission on Health Facilities, *Report, op. cit.*, p. 5.
[33] George K. Chacko, *Today's Information for Tomorrow's Products – An Operations Research Approach,* Thompson, Washington, D.C., 1966, pp. 5–6.

7.4. Cardinal Ordering of Second Highest Level of Objectives: Strategic Objectives

Just as we assigned the score of 100 to the organismic objective of cure and 80 to the organismic objective of care, we need to assign a consistent set of scores to the second highest level of objectives: *strategic objectives*,[34] which would permit the consistent scoring of Element 5 and Element 7 within the same scheme. The term "strategic" connotes a sequence of actions as opposed to a single specific action. Thus, "Health Base of Individual Data (ID)" is a strategic objective because the building up of the health base of ID's calls for a large number of coordinated activities directed towards the accomplishment of building up the health base for the nation as a whole. Similarly, the objective of "Education Base of Individual Care (IC)" is also a strategic objective, which can be accomplished by means of a number of interrelated activities, each of which is concerned with the formation and development of widespread education in health practices.

In order to assign consistent scores to Element 5: Auxiliary Hospitals for Ambulatory Care and Element 7: Technological Advances − Production of Cure, we have to rank *ordinally* all the eight elements. Which among the eight are so basic to the accomplishment of health cure that the failure of its accomplishment would spell disaster? it would seem that Element 6: Center Hospitals for Major Care (CH) would easily qualify for one, if not the, top spot. For, irrespective of the inefficiencies of the care administered through central hospitals, their very existence is counted upon by the population in general as the assurance that, in an emergency, they shall receive help.

Next to the *existence* of health care facilities is the *access* to them when needed. This is an area where the administrative arrangements for financing health care assume increasing significance. For, what is the use of the central hospitals if one cannot avail of them in times of need? It would thus seem that among the strategic objectives, Element 6 would rank first, followed by Element 8. Elements 3, 4, and 5 are essential preparations for meeting the explosive demand for health care. The key element in this proposed new development is Element 1: Health Base for Individual Data (ID). Since, without proper ID's, the successive screening of need for medical cure by the

---

[34] *Ibid.*, pp. 32–42, 55, 208.

auxiliary health personnel, by the pathologist, and the auxiliary hospitals, is without its necessary foundation, Element 1 would appear to qualify for Rank 3.

The development of ID's is essential to the nationwide basis of the national health services system. This data base is developed to respond to the new capabilities provided by advances in technology. Therefore, the efforts to take advantage of technological advances must be explicitly recognized as ranking either immediately above or immediately below the health base of Individual Data (ID) itself.

Distinguishing the two organismic objectives of cure and care, the eight strategic objectives may be illustratively ranked as shown in Table 7.3.

The scores incorporating the interaction of organismic *and* strategic objectives at the federal level (i.e., organismic × strategic) are as follows:

Element 6: Central Hospitals   100 × 100 = 10 000
Element 8: Administrative Arrangements   100 × 95 = 9 500
Element 7: Technological Advances:
            Production of Cure   100 × 90 = 9 000
Element 4: Pathological Diagnosis   100 × 80 = 8 000
Element 5: Auxiliary Hospitals   100 × 70 = 7 000

Table 7.3
Ordering of organismic–strategic objectives

Strategic objectives	Organismic objectives	Cure 100 Rank 1 Score 100		Care 80 Rank 2 Score 80	
		Rank	Score	Rank	Score
Element 6: Central Hospitals		1	100		
Element 8: Administrative Arrangements		2	95		
Element 1: Health Base				1	85
Element 7: Technological Advances:					
Production of Cure		3	90		
Production of Care				2	75
Element 3: Diagnostic Screening				3	60
Element 4: Pathological Diagnosis		4	80		
Element 5: Auxiliary Hospitals		5	70		
Element 2: Education Base				4	50

Element 1:   Health Base   80 × 85 = 6 800
Element 7:   Technological Advances:
              Production of Care   80 × 75 = 6 000
Element 3:   Diagnostic Screening   80 × 60 = 4 800
Element 2:   Education Base   80 × 50 = 4 000

On the basis of the absolute scores, the most critical objective is Element 6: Central Hospitals with a score of 10 000; the least critical is Element 2: Education Base with a score of 4 000. Therefore, the resources allocation between Central Hospitals and Education Base should be in the ratio of 5 : 2.

7.5. Cardinal Ordering of Third Highest Level of Objectives: Tactical Objectives

Now we come to the third dimension of objectives in an integrated scheme, viz., *tactical objectives*.[35] The "tactical" objectives are the logical components of the strategic objectives. They would pinpoint the specific actions that must be taken, such as the building of a wing of an auxiliary hospital in a community, the discovery of a chemotherapy cure for cancer.

The two *tactical* level *objectives* introduced in our discussion are: hospital wing, and cancer chemotherapy. They are respectively related to the strategic objectives of Element 5: Auxiliary Hospitals, and Element 7: Technological Advances (Production of Cure).

Under the strategic objective of Auxiliary Hospitals may be identified several tactical objectives such as:

Ambulatory care categories for auxiliary hospitals
Manpower for auxiliary hospitals and central hospitals
Physical equipment for auxiliary hospitals
Physical plants for auxiliary hospitals

If these four tactical objectives are in fact in decreasing order of importance to the accomplishment of the given strategic objective, they may be illustratively given the following scores:

	Score
Ambulatory care categories for auxiliary hospitals	100
Manpower for auxiliary and central hospitals	90
Phisical equipment for auxiliary hospitals	85
Physical plants for auxiliary hospitals	73

[35] *Ibid.*, pp. 34–42, 55, 207, 208.

Table 7.4
Cardinal ordering of organismic–strategic-tactical objectives

Auxiliary Hospital Wing Construction	Cancer Chemotherapy Research
Objectives Hierarchy	Objectives Hierarchy

Cure 100	Cure 100
Element 5: Auxiliary Hospitals 70	Element 7: Technological Advances:
Physical Plants 73	Production of Cure 90
$100 \times 70 \times 73 =$ 511 000	Cancer Chemotherapy Research 87
	$100 \times 90 \times 87 =$ 783 000
Administrative Hierarchy:	Administrative Hierarchy:
County 100	Federal 100 000
(Objective)(Administrative) =	(Objective)(Administrative =
$100(100 \times 70 \times 73) =$ 51 100 000	$100\ 000(100 \times 90 \times 87) =$ 78 300 000 000

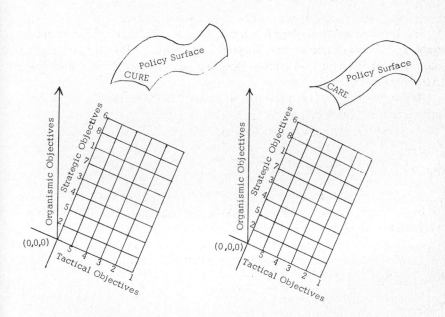

Fig. 7.4. Three-dimensional policy surface and component elements

7.6. Cardinal Ordering of the Policy Surface

We have now identified three successive levels of objectives in decreasing order:
   Organismic,
   Strategic,
   Tactical.

The consistent *ordinal* ordering we have arrived at to discuss the allocation between the construction of an auxiliary wing and conduct of research in cancer chemotherapy permits the *cardinal* ordering shown in Table 7.4.

It should be noted that both the activities pertain to cure, in the sense of curing disease rather than preventing its occurrence. The strategic objectives, comprising *both* care and cure, were ranked in Table 7.3. This ordering is graphically presented in Fig. 7.4. It shows the three-dimensional policy surface with the organismic, strategic, and tactical objectives arranged in increasing order as they move away from the origin.

7.7. Cardinal Ordering of Administrative Hierarchy

What is lacking in Fig. 7.4. is the weighting of the different levels of objectives by the administrative hierarchy with which it is associated. Five levels were identified earlier, viz., federal, regional, state, county, township/city. The highest policy level objectives in each of the administrative hierarchies have a specific, but different, contribution to make to the United States health services system as a whole. How can this interrelationship be structured?

In Table 7.5 such a scheme is presented. The lowest level of objectives hierarchies (tactical) of the lowest level of administrative hierarchies (township/city) is given a weighting of 10. The next higher level of objectives hierarchies (strategic) is given a weighting of 100; and the highest level of objectives hierarchies (organismic) is given a weighting of 1 000. The implication is that at the lowest administrative hierarchy level (township/city) the *failure* to accomplish the objectives would provide a minimum *penalty* of 10, and a maximum of 1 000.

What happens at the next higher level of administrative hierarchy (county)? The penalty at the tactical level for nonaccomplishment is 100, which means that it is as grave to fail at the *lowest* objectives hierarchy

Table 7.5
Ordering of objectives—administrative hierarchy matrix

Administrative hierarchy	Objectives hierarchy	Organismic	Strategic	Tactical
Federal		50 000 000	5 000 000	100 000
Regional		4 000 000	400 000	10 000
State		300 000	30 000	1 000
County		20 000	2 000	100
Township		1 000	100	10

level for the *county* as it is to fail at the *middle* level of objectives hierarchy for the *township/city*.

The penalty rates go up at a faster rate at the county level. Thus, at the tactical level the penalty is 100, but at the strategic level it jumps to 2 000. At the organismic level, the jump is even higher to 20 000.

At the third level of administrative hierarchy (state) the penalties for nonaccomplishment increase even more rapidly: 1 000; 30 000; 300 000.

At the fourth level of administrative hierarchy (regional), the penalties are even more severe: 10 000; 400 000; and 4 000 000.

At the fifth and highest level of adminstrative hierarchy (federal), the penalties mount furiously: 100 000; 5 000 000; 50 000 000.

The construction of a wing to the auxiliary hospital in a county occurs at the *county* level, with a weight of 100; the research and cancer chemotherapy occurs at the *federal* level with a weight of 100 000.

7.8. *Application of the Cardinal Ordering to Resources Allocation*

In Table 7.5 the score for cancer chemotherapy research is weighted by the administrative hierarchy with which it is associated. Cancer chemotherapy research was assigned an illustrative score of 87 (compared to the illustrative score of 73 for physical plans of auxiliary hospitals). Since cancer chemotherapy research is a tactical objective under Element 7, which itself has the score of 90, and since Element 7 is a strategic objective of the organismic objective of cure, with a score of 100, the total score for cancer chemotherapy research is $100\,000(100 \times 90 \times 87) = 78\,300\,000\,000$. Similarly, the construction of a wing at an auxiliary hospital is assigned an illustrative score of 73. Since the construction of the wing is a tactical objective under Element 5, which itself has the score of 70, and since Element 5 is a strategic objective of the organismic objective of cure, with a score of 100, the total score for construction of a wing at an auxiliary hospital is $100(100 \times 70 \times 73) = 51\,100\,000$.

Thus, we come to the final evaluation of the significance of the auxiliary wing vis-a-vis cancer chemotherapy in the U.S. National health services systems:

Auxiliary Wing at County Level	Cancer Chemotherapy at Federal Level
$(100 \times 70 \times 73)100 = 51\,100\,000$	$(100 \times 90 \times 87)100\,000 = 78\,300\,000\,000$

On this basis, the resources allocation should be:

Auxiliary Wing : Cancer Chemotherapy :: 511 : 783 000.

which would represent dollar allocation from $3.5 million of:
$2 412   for auxiliary wing,
$3 497 588   for cancer chemotherapy.

8. Conclusion

The purpose of this application outline is to identify, in gross outline, some contributions that operations research may make, first to understanding the nature and magnitude of the organization of the United States health services system as a whole, and second to delineate a workable strategy for devising a modular approach to the evolution of the system itself, taking advantage of insights gained from earlier years.

The thesis of this chapter is that operations research can in fact offer assistance in devising strategies of policy-making for an integrated health service system for the United States.

The concept of "good health" has been developed as an operational guideline for the health services system at the federal level, even as "full employment" has been the guideline at the federal level for economic activities.

Kissick's view is that we should provide *maximum care* for the maximum number.[36] We say that instead it must be the improvement in *well-being* for the maximum number. Secondly, instead being on cure the emphasis, it should be on *care*. In order to provide care, we must have individual medical data, which must be updated; we must have consumer medical education and a few other things. Reflecting these needs for medical data, medical education and others, there are four elements for the cure part; so also four for the care part. Any request for funds must be imbedded in its immediately higher objective and the process repeated until imbedded in the cure or care objective. Given that structure, you find that there is not a single penny that will go out of the total funds without your knowing why. You gave only \$2 412 to the hospital wing — not just because the man shouted the loudest, but because there was an integrated determination in which that and some other objectives were weighed. The plea here is simply that we open the black box and start finding where a particular health measure belongs so that we can allocate funds in an integrated manner making explicit our decisions and our preferences and take the consequences. Then, instead of having a system that costs more and cares less, in more than one sense, we will have a system which costs less and cares more.

PROBLEMS

The three chapters 6, 7 and 8, of Part III deal with the application of OR/SA Protocol to large, unstructured problems in the Public Sector. This chapter deals with the problem of Health Care Allocation. *The purpose of the following questions is to develop an appreciation for the specific demands of the substance of the* particular *problem in applying the* general *sequence.*

A. *System Context*

   1. Distinguish between the User Objective of health care and the User Objective of ecological investment. Compare the operational measures applicable to these two different Public Sector Problems.

   2. The National Advisory Commission on Health Manpower concluded: "Government alone is not big enough to solve the problems of health care for

[36]William L. Kissick, *loc. cit.*

the American people." If both the Public and Private Sectors need to work together to accomplish the national delivery of health care, what type of problems would be encountered at the System Objective level?

3. From the point of view of OVERVIEW, what parallels does the organizing of resources for economic development have with the organizing of health services?

B. *System Cost*

4. The National Advisory Commission on Health Manpower estimated that by 1975 the cost per patient per day would be $100. What additional cost(s) should be included to arrive at the cost of opportunity foregone?

5. How would you apply the cost of Opportunity Acquired in the national delivery of health care?

C. *System Effectiveness—Absolute*

6. Develop an operational concept of effectiveness of health care delivery.

7. What is the inherent difficulty in devising an operational measure of health care delivery, compared with that of ecological investment?

D. *System Effectiveness—Relative*

8. The value of research in preventing illness or curing it lies in the implementation of the results. Since the implementation is at least twice removed from investment, how can the rate of change of implementation be related to the rate of change in investment?

9. By how much should you increase the investment in the basic datá on individual health in order to improve the rate of change in the national delivery of health care?

10. The ordinal preferences have to be translated into cardinal orderings before the appropriate allocation to achieve a desired objective can be identified. Discuss the decision-making in the context of a physical construct, such as an auxiliary hospital wing, contrasted with a research concept, such as cancer chemotherapy.

CHAPTER 8

OR/SA PROTOCOL APPLIED TO PUBLIC SECTOR PROBLEMS: (3) AIR POLLUTION REDUCTION

TECHNICAL OVERVIEW

The OR/SA protocol, developed in Chapter 4, is applied to a third public sector problem.

The Air Quality Act, 1967, is examined to arrive at the highest level of objectives (organismic objectives). Three organismic objectives which emerge are: (1) Public Health, (2) Public Welfare, and (3) Public Productivity. These three objectives are explicitly ranked, and the published long-range goals for FY 1969–74 of the National Air Pollution Control Administration (now part of Environmental Protection Agency) are related to the organismic objectives as strategic objectives. The strategic objectives of: (1) motor vehicle emission reduction (2) stationary source emission reduction (3) non-Federal regulatory efforts, and (4) air quality criteria publication, are ranked within the first of the three organismic objectives: Public Health.

The Department of Health, Education, and Welfare prepared a list of industries and pollutant categories to be considered first in developing national emission standards. It will be noted that the stationary sources pollution reduction is ranked second among the strategic objectives.

At the tactical level, the particulate characterization is identified with respect to 6 primary and 7 secondary particulate matter sources by industry. These 13 tactical objectives of particulate characterization are given a consistent ranking. Not only particulate characterization but also emission control devices are identified at the tactical level – although with different scores. Integrated steel mills, a subset of particulate matter characterization, and scrubbers-venturi, which are a subset of operational emission control devices, emerge as activities of equal weight in air pollution reduction on the basis of the consistent scoring for the different levels of objectives.

253

In order to overcome serious deficiencies in knowledge of the nature of important particulate pollution sources, (1) total tonnage of emissions by important sources, (2) objectionable properties of important sources, and (3) contribution to particulate pollution problems by minor sources, are studied. Both from the point of view of higher tonnage of particulate emissions, and higher rate of particulate emissions, industry emerges as the prime area where particulate emission control should be effective. Kraft Pulp mills are ranked 6 in terms of total tonnage of particulate pollution, while iron and steel mills are ranked 1.

Equally, if not more, important than the tonnage are the toxicity, corrosiveness, and soiling properties of pollutants. The abnormally high concentration of 54 micrograms of benzo(a) pyrant per 1 000 cubic meters (over ten times the urban average) in 1959 in Saint Louis emphasized the need for monitoring the concentration of this pollutant, whose toxicity could alter the ranking based only on tonnage. In addition, the added cost of living in a dirty environment which in a 1960 study ranged from $86 per family (Do-It-Yourself) to $338 (non-Do-It-Yourself) must be taken into account in the allocation of resources for air pollution reduction.

How should research and development related to air pollution control be allocated resources?

We find that cyclones with large diameters are more than 8 times as effective as coal cleaning plants as far as implementation effectiveness is concerned. However, when the implementation effectiveness is weighted by the probability of success (which has to be assigned on a "best guess" basis), the cyclones emerge as only more than 4 times as attractive as the coal cleaning plants.

In addition to the considerations of effectiveness of implementations and probability of success, at least three types of cost: (1) direct, (2) indirect, and (3) cost over time, must be considered in ranking the particulate R and D products. In addition, the technological gap in the understanding of the nature of particulate pollution must also be incorporated into the final ranking.

The illustrative scheme of integrated ordering of objectives of, and means for, air pollution control has several advantages. (1) It makes explicit the hidden objectives and preferences. (2) It classifies the type of R and D insights by technological gaps in our understanding of the mechanism of air pollution. (3) It relates operational measures of effectiveness with the probability of success of related research. (4) It helps integrate the success of the operation at the tactical level with the hierarchy of objectives at the organismic level. (5) It provides a method to relate the highest levels of policy guidance which the legislators would like to see, with the lowest operational *level of whether we should allocate funds to study a $20 emission control device for automobiles, or spend more money studying how to measure a particulate which contributes to air pollution in the form of sulphur dioxide.*

EXECUTIVE SUMMARY

The method of conducting an OR/SA effort developed in Chapter 4, is applied to a study of an aspect of implementing the Air Quality Act of 1967.

The emphasis in this study is in the allocation of resources to research *on control devices versus the precise measurement of what causes pollution.*

This emphasis upon the allocation to a potential *result in the future, is different from the allocation of resources to a* present *activity as in the allocation of funds to the different elements of the Department of the Interior, discussed in Chapter 6.*

To arrive at a hierarchy of objectives, the Air Quality Act, 1967 is examined. The perspectives of both the legislative and the executive branches are studied; and a resolution is made in favor of not 1, but 3 policy objectives: (1) public health, (2) public welfare, and (3) public productivity. On the basis of the study of statements by the Department of Health, Education, and Welfare, the National Air Pollution Control Administration goal and related documents, the strategic objectives are identified as motor vehicle emission reduction by 20% by 1974, and reducing the emission from stationary sources by 30% by 1974.

To implement these strategic objectives, the ordering of pollutant categories and industries prepared by the Department of Health, Education and Welfare, is studied in arriving at an initial ranking of tactical objectives, including the operation of emission control devices, and particulate matter characterization. A total of 13 tactical objectives of particulate characterizations, and 11 types of emission control devices are considered.

Since there are important gaps in the knowledge of particulate pollution sources, additional considerations, such as emissions by important sources, objectionable properties of emissions, etc., are taken into account.

Four major elements are brought together in arriving at a method of allocating research funds: (1) implementation effectiveness, (2) probability of success, (3) existing technological knowledge gaps, and (4) research life-cycle costs. A method is developed which can relate the highest level of policy guidance at the legislative level with the lowest operational level *of implementation, so that the allocation of funds to study $20 emission control device for automobiles and the allocation of funds for measuring the concentration of a particulate, could both be weighed in terms of their contribution to the organismic objective of air pollution reduction.*

When one considers the contribution of OR/SA protocol to problems such as environmental pollution, there are three elements which may offer insights to the problem and perhaps help develop an operational approach * (see Fig. 8.1).

Perspective	How to look at the problem **as a whole.**
Process	Which underlying **interactions** exert decisive influence.
Practice	What to **do** today.

Fig. 8.1. Contributions of OR/SA methodology.

1. Three Levels of Objectives — Organismic, Strategic, Tactical

The overriding consideration of the application of OR/SA protocol to air pollution is to contribute significantly to the implementation of the Air Quality Act of 1967.[1] One concrete means, i.e., further particulate control

*An earlier version of this discussion appears in Robert L. Chartrand (ed.), *Hope for the Cities,* Spartan, New York, 1971.

[1] House of Representatives Hearings, *Air Quality Act of 1967,* Serial No. 90–10, Government Printing Office, Washington, D.C., 1967, August 15–24, 1967, p. 9.

technology, finds its justification – in fact its *raison d'etre* – in the probability of contributing to the accomplishment of the Air Quality Act objectives.

The Air Quality Act itself is a single instance in the entire spectrum of concerted measures designed to improve the quality of our environment. This view is shared by the executive branch as well, as shown in Fig. 8.2, which created the new Environmental Protection Agency, now headed by Train.

"An *overall* policy for the environment
which *integrates* these purposes and objectives,
which provides for *choice* when they are incompatible." (italics supplied)
  Daddario Committee Report *Managing the Environment,* 1968, p. 5.

"Presidential Special Assistant for Environmental Affairs
who would serve as a 'focal point' for
the Government's scattered environmental concerns."
  (Russell E.) Train, Task Force on Resources and the Environment as
  reported in *Science,* 7 Feb. 1969, p. 549.

Fig. 8.2. Organismic perspective – legislative and executive view

Turning from executive agency to present legislation, what are the primary objectives of the Air Quality Act?

"... integrates these *purposes and objectives*"

AIR QUALITY ACT, 1967
Title I

(1) Protect and enhance the quality of the Nation's air resources,
(2) initiate and accelerate a national research and development program,
(3) provide technical and financial assistance to state and local governments in
    air pollution prevention and control, and
(4) assist the development and operation of regional air pollution control programs.

"So as to promote the public *health* and
                      welfare and the
                      productive capacity of its population."

Fig. 8.3. Organismic perspective – Air Quality Act, 1967.

Paraphrasing the purpose of Title I of the act, the highest level of objectives are shown in Fig. 8.3.

The overriding objective is the first one, viz., protect and enhance the quality of the nation's air resources. The other three are only some of the means by which the primary objective can be attained.

What is the measure of the implementation of the Air Quality Act?

The Title says, "So as to promote the public health and welfare and the productive capacity of its population."

To keep things in perspective, it is essential that the Commissioner of the National Air Pollution Control Administration fix his attention upon the end result of promoting: (1) public health, (2) public welfare, and (3) productive capacity of the public.

This highest level of objectives, from the perspective of management, constitutes the policy essentials which judge every element of accomplishment of the implementation process. To emphasize the relationship of these policy objectives to people, and systems involving people, we may term the level of objectives: *organismic objectives.*[2] The term *organism* emphasizes the element of life which would both help and hinder the implementation of the Air Quality Act. It also serves to remined one that the best solutions can go wrong when confronted by the human element.

The second level of objectives deals with concrete elements of implementation. This level must be consistent with the higher level of organismic objectives. The specifics of implementing the organismic objectives are the concern of the second level of objectives: *strategic objectives.*[3] The term *strategy* connotes a sequence of actions, as opposed to a single specific action.

The third level in the hierarchy of objectives is *tactical objectives.*[4] Tactical objectives are the logical components of strategic objectives. They pinpoint the specific actions to be taken.

There are thus three levels of objectives: organismic (policy), strategic (sequence of actions), and tactical (individual actions). This classification scheme is:

flexible,
adaptive,

[2] George K. Chacko, *Today's Information for Tomorrow's Products,* Thompson, Washington, D.C., 1966, pp. 5–6.
[3] *Ibid.,* pp. 34–42, 55, 208.
[4] *Ibid.,* pp. 34–42, 55, 207, 208.

comprehensive,
logical,
self-correcting.

1.1. Ordering of Objectives: Organismic

There can be no straight line from the policy perspectives of the Air Quality
Act to the installation of devices in automobiles to control air pollution. The
best safeguard that can be provided is assuring a logical sequence of actions
related to policy perspectives. There are many alternative ways in which an
action sequence can be planned and executed. It may become necessary, from
time to time, to alter or augment any sequences of actions in progress. How
can these choices be made at each of the three hierarchies of policy-making
and policy implementing?

One method is to rank the various objectives as part of the entire scheme
of activities, not individually. How can this ranking be made self-consistent?

By focusing attention upon the end result, policy goals, one might precipitate a choice from among the major policy objectives. This can be done by
ranking the three objectives, promoting the public health, promoting public
welfare, and promoting the productive capacity of the population in some
order of preference. For instance, public health may be ranked more important
than productive capacity, and productive capacity more important than public welfare. Or, the order may be reversed. It is meaningless to say that all
three have to be accomplished at all times in the same manner.

To ascertain which of the three is most important, the acid test would be:
what would produce the worst effect if not accomplished? Is it health or
welfare or productivity? A case could be made for public health being more
important than productive capacity, because there can be no productive capacity without health. Given health, should the priority be productivity or
welfare? The democratic reflex would be to choose public welfare over public
productivity. However, it may be argued that there would be no public welfare without public productivity. Ranking objectives in order of preference
may create a dilemma similar to having to rank life, liberty, and the pursuit of
happiness in descending order. Of the three, life undoubtedly would be the
primary objective; without it the other two would be irrelevant. Similarly, a

Ranking	Organismic objectives	Public health	Public welfare	Public productivity
Rank		1	2	3
Score		100	90	80

Fig. 8.4. Organismic perspective − Air Quality Act implementation

case could be made for the enhancement of public health as the primary objective of the Air Quality Act. Thus, we may use an initial ranking scheme as shown in Fig. 8.4.

The score of 100 to public health, and 90 to public welfare, and 80 to public productivity is an illustration. The point is, there must be an explicit recognition of implicit preferences. Without such explicit preferences, there is no logical way of arbitrating alternatives that multiply rapidly, as we progress down the hierarchy of objectives from organismic to strategic to tactical.

1.2. Ordering of Objectives: Strategic

Where do the primary goals adopted by the National Air Pollution Control Administration fit in? To illustrate, the published long-range plans for FY 1969−1974 stated that: "The Center is currently directing its activities at four primary goals:

1. Reduce emissions from motor vehicles 20 percent by 1974.

2. Reduce emissions from stationary sources 30 percent by 1974.

3. Expand regional, state, and local air pollution regulatory efforts to 75 percent of the necessary level of activity by 1974.

4. Publish air quality criteria for the 20 most harmful pollutants by 1974."[5]

The foregoing four goals are admittedly not organismic objectives. They are, in our terminology, strategic objectives. To identify their role in imple-

---

[5] National Center for Air Pollution Control, "Long-Range Plans: FY 1969−1974", Washington, D.C., April 1968, p. 1.

menting the Air Quality Act, it is necessary to relate these four strategic objectives to one or more organismic objectives.

At the House Hearings on the Act, the HEW testimony emphasized the health aspect of the problem. The Surgeon General concluded his testimony saying: "Mr. Chairman, may I conclude by *stressing again the magnitude of the air pollution challenge as a national health problem.*"[6] (italics supplied)

The four primary goals of the National Air Pollution Control Administration are strategic objectives related to the organismic objectives of health.

How can the strategic objectives be ranked?

The fourth goal, publishing air quality criteria, appears to have the least priority. Part of the reason is the difficulty in establishing criteria. At the congressional hearings. Drs. Middleton, Blomquist, and Stewart stated:

> It is true that it took about three and one-half years to become organized, to get the framework established, to understand what criteria should be, and how one could bring about the resources of the nation to bear on this particular problem ...
>
> ...one air quality criterion has been promulgated with regard to sulfur oxide.
>
> The other criteria under consideration are photochemical oxidants, particulates, carbon monoxide, nitrogen oxide, and hydrocarbons.
>
> These are on the drawing board. We hope to have this completed by the summer of 1968. After that we expect to start on such pollutants as lead, fluorides, hydrogen sulfide, asbestos.
>
> In the reorganization of the Center in January 1967, all activities relating to criteria and standards development, including economic and health effects research, were brought together under the supervision of a single associate director. Currently, seven professional staff members are engaged in criteria development; before the end of fiscal 1968, the staff assigned to this work will be increased to 35. In addition, services of fourteen scientists are being employed by means of contracts.[7]

The publication of air quality criteria has the lowest priority, the reduction of emission from motor vehicles has first priority, followed by the reduction of emissions from stationary sources. The strategic objectives may be ranked initially as shown in Fig. 8.5.

The numerical score associated with the strategic objectives is clearly illustrative.

[6] House Hearings, *op. cit.,* p. 54.
[7] House Hearings, *op. cit.,* pp. 162–65.

Organismic objectives　　　　Strategic obejctives	Public health		Public welfare	Public productivity
	1		2	3
	Score	100		
	Rank	Score		
Motor vehicle emission reduction	1	100		
Stationary source emission reduction	2	95		
Non federal regulatory efforts	3	85		
Air quality criteria publication	4	75		

Fig. 8.5. Strategic perspective—air qualtity implementation

1.3. Ordering of Objectives: Tactical

The specific study and advancement of particulate control technology, mentioned as a concrete means of implementing the Air Quality Act, is directly concerned with stationary source emission reduction and motor vehicle emission reduction via the development and installation of devices. The contribution of the particulate control study to the first and second phases would be in the area of tactical (individual) efforts to successfully select fruitful sources of research and development. Particulate characterization would also aid in establishing emission criteria and eventually national emission standards. The Department of Health, Education, and Welfare prepared a list of industries and pollutant categories to be considered first in developing national emission standards. The Department published another list of industries and categories most likely to receive the next highest priority. Following the ordering of pollutant categories and industries, prepared by HEW, we initially rank in Table 8.1 the tactical objectives.

Numerical ordering—tactical objective: particulate matter characterization

Organismic objectives	Strategic objectives	Public health (Score 100)				
Tactical objectives		Motor vehicle emission reduction S-Score 100	Stationary source emission reduction S-Score 95	Nonfederal regulatory efforts S-Score 85	Air quality criteria publication S-Score 75	
Operation of emission control devices			T-Score 100			
Manufacture of emission control devices			T-Score 97			
Development of prototypes of emission control devices			T-Score 90			
Research into emission control device characteristics			T-Score 80			
Selection of areas for research on control characteristics			T-Score 70			
Particulate matter characterization:			T-Score 60			
11 integrated steel mills			ST-Score 100			
12 Large steam electric generating station			ST-Score 96			
13 Portland cement plants			ST-Score 92			
14 Gray iron and steel foundries			ST-Score 90			
15 ferroalloy plants			ST-Score 85			
16 Kraft pulp mills			ST-Score 70			
21 soap and detergent plants			ST-Score 55			
22 caustic and chlorine plants			ST-Score 53			
23 calcium carbide manufacturing			ST-Score 50			
24 phosphate fertilizer plants			ST-Score 45			
25 lime plants			ST-Score 40			
26 aluminum ore reduction plants			ST-Score 30			
27 coal cleaning plants			ST-Score 20			

The numerical score associated with the tactical objectives is clearly illustrative.

1.4. Numerical Values for Tactical Objectives

Four levels in the hierarchy of objectives are shown in Table 8.1. Their respective scores are identified in Fig. 8.6. To devise a consistent numerical scale to recognize the relative contributions made by the activities at each level simultaneously, we may assign weights to the different hierarchies, also shown in Fig. 8.6.

These weights reflect the gravity of the consequence of *not* fulfilling the objectives at each respective level. If the particulate characterization of coal cleaning plants is not fulfilled, Air Quality Act implementation would be impaired by 20 X 10 = 200 weighted units. If, on the other hand, the particulate characterization of the ferroalloy plants is not fulfilled, Air Quality Act implementation would be impaired by 85 X 10 = 850 weighted units.

The gravity of nonfulfillment of objectives rises dramatically with the hierarchy. If the research objective of emission control device characteristics is not fulfilled, it would impair the Air Quality Act implementation by 80 X 100 = 8 000 weighted units. Similarly, if the manufacture of emission control devices is not fulfilled, it would impair the Air Quality Act implementation by 97 X 100 = 9 700 weighted units.

The penalty for nonfulfillment of the objective of particulate characterization of manufacture of emission control devices (T-Score 97) is *not* just five times as grave as the nonfulfillment of the objective of particulate characterization of coal cleaning plants (ST-score 20), but 48.5 *times* as grave.

1.5. Numerical Values for Contribution of Control Devices

In Table 8.1 the particulate characterization is outlined with respect to six

Organismic	—	Highest policy level	— Air Quality Act
Strategic	—	Next highest policy level	— NAPCA
Tactical	—	Implementation level	— Industry

Organismic Score	O-Score, weight 10 000
Strategic Score	S-Score, weight 1 000
Tactical Score	T-Score, weight 100
Sub-tactical Score	ST-Score, weight 10

Fig. 8.6. Scores for organismic, strategic and tactical objectives

Table 8.2

Numerical ordering of tactical objective: emission control devices

Organismic objectives				
	Strategic objectives	Public health (O-Score 100)		
Tactical objectives		Motor vehicle emission reduction S-Score 100	Stationary source emission reduction S-Score 95	Nonfederal regulatory efforts S-Score 85	Air quality criteria publication S-Score 75

Operation of emission control devices:	T-Score 100
11 CYCLONES–large diameters	ST-Score 100
12 CYCLONES–multiple	ST-Score 97
21 FILTERS–deep bed	ST-Score 90
22 FILTERS–fabric	ST-Score 86
23 FILTERS–reverse jet	ST-Score 82
31 ELECTROSTATIC PRECIPATORS–high voltage	ST-Score 80
32 ELECTROSTATIC PRECIPATORS–low voltage	ST-Score 75
41 SCRUBBERS–simple	ST-Score 70
42 SCRUBBERS–medium energy	ST-Score 65
43 SCRUBBERS–venturi	ST-Score 60

primary and seven secondary particulate matter sources by industry. These 13 tactical objectives of particulate characterization have been given a consistent ranking procedure. It is admittedly illustrative, but the principle holds.

There are 10 types of emission control devices which will logically be subtactical objectives under the tactical objective of "operation of emission control devices" listed in Table 8.1, Row 1. We present in Table 8.2 a concept to develop a scoring device for the operation of emission control devices.

In Table 8.1 particulate characterization was accorded a T-score of 60, while the operation of emission control devices was given the T-score of 100. Since the weighting factor for T-score was 100, and for the ST-score was 10, the lowest objective in the category, "operation of emssion control devices", emerges as equal to the *highest* in the category, "particulate matter characterization".

This is because the former has an ST-score of 60 with a weight of 10, making the category SCRUBBERS-venturi equivalent to $60 \times 10 = 600$ weighted units. Since the 600 weighted units are part of the T-score which has $100 \times 100 = 10\,000$ weighted units, SCRUBBERS-venturi represent $600 \times 10\,000 = 6\,000\,000$ *double* weighted units.

In the case of particulate characterization, integrated steel mills has an ST-score of 100 with a weight of 10, making the category equivalent to $100 \times 100 = 10\,000$ weight units. Since the 10 000 weighted units are part of the T-Score which has $60 \times 100 = 6\,000$ weighted units, integrated steel mills represents $600 \times 10\,000 = 6\,000\,000$ *double* weighted units.

Thus, both operational emission control devices and particulate matter characterization have *equal* weight in air pollution control at the tactical level objectives of SCRUBBERS-venturi for the former, and integrated steel mills for the latter.

2. Ordering of Particulate Pollution Sources — Tonnage, Objectionable Properties, Related Minor Sources

In order to overcome serious deficiencies in our knowledge of the nature of important particulate pollution sources, any particulate study should take into account:

total tonnage of emissions by important sources,
objectionable properties (toxicity, corrosiveness, visibility effects, etc.) by

important sources,
contribution to particulate pollution problems by minor sources.

2.1. Ordering of Particulate Pollution Sources by Total Tonnage

Fig. 8.7 indicates the total tonnage of emission by important sources. An estimated 11.5 million tons of particulate matter, about 10 percent of all pollutants, were emitted in the U.S. in 1966.[8]

A measure of the nature and extent of particulate matter in the U.S. in 1966 may be obtained by relating the particulate emission to energy consumption by select consumers:

household and commercial,
industrial,
power generation.

The energy usage and total tonnage of particulate matter for 1966 are shown in Fig. 8.7.

Both from the point of view of higher tonnage of particulate emissions − 6 tons − and higher rate of particulate emission − more than twice the household and commercial segments − industry emerges as the prime area where particulate emission control should be effected. In Table 8.3, several industries are listed that release large quantities of particulate matter. Considering only the annual potential in tons, the industry or process can be ordered according to its tendency toward particulate emission. In addition to the annual capacity, the number of plants should also be taken into account in ordering

	Energy consumption 1966 − 10^{15} BTU	Particulate emission 1966 − 10^6 Tons
Power Generation	12	3
Industrial	10	6
Household and Commercial	10	2.5
Total	32	11.5

Fig. 8.7. Sources of particulate matter: Ton/Yr.

[8] National Center for Air Pollution Control, *The Sources of Air Pollution and Their Control*, PHS Publication No. 1548, Cincinnati, Ohio, 1966.

268 *Applied OR/SA*

Table 8.3.
Total tonnage ranking—industrial sources of particulate pollution

Industry or process	Annual capacity, 1000 tons (except as noted)	Number of plants	Total tonnage rank	PHS ranking
Iron and steel mills	149 000[1,2]	184	1	1
Gray iron foundries	17 350[3,4]	1 052	2	4
Metallurgical Nonferrous smelters and furnaces	2 721[3,5]	2 500	3	
Petroleum refineries and asphalt blowing	3 650 × 10^{6}bbls.[a3,6]	318	4	
Portland cement	500 × 10^{6}bbls.[b3,7]	180	5	3
Kraft pulp mills	300 000[9]	40	6	6
Acid manufacture				
Phosphoric	2 300[9]	66	7	
Sulfuric	20 513	223	8	
Coke manufacturing	54 278[1]	60	9	
Carbon black	1 496[10]	37	10	

[a] Barrel = 42 gallons.
[b] Barrel = 376 pounds.

[1] J.J. Schueneman, *Air Pollution Aspects of the Iron and Steel Industry*, PHS Publication No. 99-AP-1, National Center for Air Pollution Control, Cincinnati, Ohio, 1963.
[2] Directory of Iron and Steel Works of the United States and Canada, 31st edition; American Iron and Steel Institute, New York, 1967.
[3] J.M. Von Bergen, *Profile of Industry Costs for Control of Particulate Air Pollution*, unpublished manuscript, 1967.
[4] *A Marketing Guide to the Metal Casting Industry*, Pentan, Cleveland, Ohio, 1959.
[5] *Statistical Abstract of the United States*, 85th edition, U.S. Department of Commerce, Bureau of the Census, Washington, D.C., 1964.
[6] *Standard Industrial Classification Manual*, Bureau of the Budget, Washington, D.C., 1964.
[7] *Atmospheric Emissions from the Manufacture of Portland Cement*, PHS Publication No. 999-AP-17, National Center for Air Pollution Control, Cincinnati, Ohio, 1967.
[8] *Air Pollution and the Kraft Pulping Industry*, an annotated bibliography, PHS Publication No. 999-AP-4, Division of Air Pollution, Cincinnati, Ohio, 1963.
[9] *Atmospheric Emissions from Sulfuric Acid Manufacturing Processes*, PHS Publication No. 999-AP-13, Division of Air Pollution, Cincinnati, Ohio, 1965.
[10] H. Drogin, "Carbon Black", *Journal of Air Pollution Control Association*, April 1968, pp. 216–28.

particulate pollution sources in terms of tonnage. The ordering so obtained is shown against the earlier ordering in Table 8.1 based on Public Health Service priorities for particulate matter characterization wherever applicable.

We see that the Kraft pulp mills are given the same rank – rank 6 – in terms of total tonnage of particulate pollution, as well as PHS priorities for particulate characterization; so too are iron and steel mills. This agreement on the basis of two separate sets of criteria suggests that an ordering scheme can be evolved which will reflect both the industrial contribution to particulate pollution and the government's view of its gravity. Again, these two rankings are only illustrative.

2.2. Ordering of Particulate Pollution Sources by Particle Size, Shape, Density

While total tonnage is a directly perceivable property of particulate pollution, it should be recognized that the tonnage figure is the cumulative total of all particle sizes composing the heterogeneous, polydisperse aerosol being released to the atmosphere.

In addition to the total tonnage, attention must be paid to the effects most commonly associated with particulate air pollution. Routine air pollution measurement techniques sample only a segment of the particle sizes which contribute to air pollution effects.

Particle size, an important correlate of air pollution effects in the community, needs to be standardized as a unit of measure. The British Steel Castings Research Association was the first to make particle size the prime parameter considered in a single dust test, with the intent to generalize.[9]

Available data on particulate pollution in terms of collector performance and aerosol size characteristics need to be sorted out. Using the British approach to summarize comparative results, we need to organize available U.S. data to determine where comparisons can be properly made. It is also hoped that particulate emission size data would be amenable to statistical theoretical distributions, such as the log normal distribution commonly used to characterize dispersions. Should the particulate study disclose that data warrant the use of one or two theoretical distributions to represent them, it would greatly facilitate the handling of particulate size data.

[9] The British Steel Castings Research Association, *Data Sheets on Dust Collectors,* Sheffield, England, 1958.

In addition to size, the shape of the particle affects the packing properties of particles. Some work has been done on the effect of shape on particle settling,[10] area and weight conversions,[11,12] and on morphological identification of particles.[13] Shape factors have been assigned to certain dusts,[14] but at this point the relation to collector performance is not determined.

The significance of particle shape in the particulate study is that given the particle shape, one needs only to determine the area distribution of emitted particulates to derive the number distribution.

Apart from size and shape, the particle density is also a significant parameter that assists in the ordering of particulate pollution sources. If particles are classified by their terminal settling velocity, the parameters of shape and density are removed from consideration. However, they are needed in the equation defining particle terminal settling velocity in air. To convert particle data from a weight basis to an area or number basis, it is necessary to have information on particle density. The discovery of patterns or relationships between collector performance and aerosol density would enable the ranking of generic dust, and thus permit a sharper distinction between pollution sources.

2.3. Ordering of Particulate Pollution Sources by Objectionable Properties

To overcome "serious deficiencies in our knowledge regarding the nature of important particulate pollution sources", any particulate control study should take into account total tonnage of emissions by important sources. In the discussion above, it was found that total tonnage ranking had to be supplemented by considerations of particle size, shape and density or particle pervasiveness.

[10] J.F. Heiss and J. Coull, "Effect of Orientation and Shape on the Settling Velocity of Non-Isometric Particles in a Viscous Medium", *Chemical Engineering Progress*, Vol. 48, 1952, p. 133.
[11] J. Cartwright, "Particle Shape Factors", *Annals of Occupational Hygiene*, Vol. 163, 1962.
[12] J.R. Hodkinson, "The Effect of Particle Shape on Measures for the Size and Concentrations of Suspended and Settled Particles", *American Industrial Hygiene Association Journal*, Vol. 26, 1965, p. 64.
[13] W.C. McCrone, R.C. Draftz, and J.G. Delly, *The Particle Atlas*, Ann Arbor Sciences Pub., Ann Arbor, 1967.
[14] J.M. Dallavalle, *Micromeritics*, Pitman, New York, 1948, p. 65.

Much more than tonnage, and pervasiveness, properties such as toxicity, corrosiveness, and soiling may weigh heavily in the implementation of the Air Quality Act. For this reason, it is conceivable that a different ordering of particulate pollution sources may be arrived at on the basis of objectionable properties.

The cumulative and joint effect of toxicity and other properties upon the health of the community is reflected in the summary statement by the Assistant Chief of the Division of Air Pollution of Los Angeles, E.T. Blomquist:

> It was found, 9 years after the fact, that some 200 excess deaths occurred in New York City in 1953 during a period of air stagnation... .
>
> In the long run, however, there is even greater significance in the health hazards associated with levels of air pollution to which millions of urban dwellers are exposed almost constantly ... The results [of investigations covering a broad range from correlations between urban air pollution and the incidence and mortality rates for various respiratory diseases to the effects produced by exposure of animals and, in some cases, human beings, to controlled amounts of specific air pollutants] can be summed up by saying that air pollution is associated with the occurrence and worsening of many serious respiratory diseases, including asthma, chronic bronchitis, lung cancer, and emphysema.[15]

The primary mechanism through which air pollution encourages and accelerates the serious health problems listed by Dr. Blomquist is the toxicity in the particulate pollution. According to T.F. Hatch and P. Gross:

> Particles larger than 10 microns in diameter are partially removed in the nasal passages. Upper respiratory efficiency in removing particulate matter decreases as the size of particles decreases and becomes practically nil for 1-micron-diameter particles... . Upper respiratory trapping increases with faster breathing as the rate of inspired air-flow increases.[16]

As a result of the upper respiratory trapping of particulate matter, acid mists, silica, and beryllium, as well as benzo(a)pyrene, introduce and aggra-

---

[15] E.T. Blomquist, M.D., Public Address, Los Angeles. 1965, quoted in J.D. Williams et al , *Interstate Air Pollution Study,* National Center for Air Pollution Control, Cincinnati, Ohio, December, 1966, p. 21.

[16] T.F. Hatch and P. Gross, *Pulmonary Deposition and Retention of Inhaled Aerosols,* Academic Press, New York, 1964, p. 68.

vate toxicity, as found in the general study of the overall air pollution problems in the St. Louis-East St. Louis metropolitan area, reported in 1966.
The sample average of benzo(a)pyrene in St. Louis was 10.2 g/1 000 m^3
during the winter of 1964, with the range between sites from 1.4 to 28.0,
compared with the United States urban average value of 5.

The significance of the toxicity of particulate matter lies in its role in altering the weights that are associated with particulate pollution sources. The
abnormally high concentration of 54 micrograms benzo(a)pyrene per 1 000
cubic meters (over 10 times the urban average) in 1959 in St. Louis emphasized the need to continue measuring the concentration of this pollutant. As a
consequence, the ranking for the source of this pollutant could very well be
much higher than that based on tonnage, particle size, shape, and density.

Similarly, unusual soiling properties may elevate the ranking of a source
of pollutant contributing to damage of building exteriors. A study conducted
in the upper Ohio River Valley in 1959–60 revealed important differences in
the cost of four categories of cleaning in communities subjected to different
levels of air pollution.

In Table 8.4, the added cost of living in a dirty environment as shown by
the study is presented. In general it shows the necessity for greater frequency
of cleaning and maintenance operations and costs of air pollution.[17]

As in the case of toxicity, the unusual soiling properties can again push a
particulate pollution source(s) to a much higher rank than would be warran-
ted by tonnage, particle size, shape, or density.

3. From Ranking to Allocation

It was shown earlier that the objectives of the application of OR/SA methodology to air pollution are twofold: first, to indicate the development of a
ranking procedure to order all significant sources of particulate pollutants in
decreasing importance as contributors to the overall particulate pollution
problem; and second, to indicate the development of an *allocation procedure*

---

[17] Il. Michelson and B. Tourin, *Economic Effects of Air Pollution* (unpublished draft),
Environmental Health and Safety Research Associates, January 1965.

Table 8.4
Added costs of living in dirty environment (Downtown Stuebenville, Ohio, 383 $\mu g/m^3$
Versus Uniontown, Pa., 115 $\mu g/m^3$) for 28 Activities, 1960

	Income group [a]	Per family	
		Do it yourself	Non do it yourself
Inside maintenance	(1)	$ 29	$162
	(2)	44	227
Outside maintenance	(1)	21	49
	(2)	337	368
Laundry and cleaning	(1)	27	79
	(2)	129	186
Hair and facial care		9	48
		―	―
Totals per family			
In private homes	(1)	86	338
	(2)	519	829
In apartments (no inside painting or decorating, no outside maintenance)	(1)	47	263

[a](1) Annual income under $8 000, (2) Annual income $8 000 or more.

to order potentially significant cost-effective research and development projects needed to advance particulate control technology.

The ranking procedure has been developed. Now we turn to the development of an *allocation procedure.*

3.1. Ordering of Research and Development Products by Implementation Effectiveness

The data collection function of the particulate study can well be to provide a reference source of all available information on the "distinguishing particulate characteristics likely to be of value in the selection of control systems." The measure of success of the "optimum control systems" resulting from research and development efforts is directly related to the implementation of The

National Air Pollution Control Administration objectives in the successive hierarchies.

Using the illustrative ranking procedure developed in Tables 8.5 and 8.6 a comparison of the products which will result from research and development efforts can be made. Two illustrative outputs are: (1) particulate matter characterization, and (2) operation of emission control devices. Admittedly, there are other products which will result from the research and development programs. However, there needs to be evolved a consistent scheme by which the expected outputs of the research and development programs can be compared on a uniform basis. We present in Table 8.5 the comparative double weighted units.

3.2. *Ordering of Research and Development Projects by Probability of Success*

As seen from Table 8.5, the success of the subtasks under emission control devices operation has decidedly higher value when implementing the objectives of the air pollution control system. However, it is a long way from success in identifying particulate characterization to the effective operation of an emission control device. The former has a much greater probability of success than the latter. In recommending research and development projects, implementation effectiveness has to be weighted by the probability of success.

In Table 8.6 a scheme is presented of illustrative probabilities with respect to 23 subtasks considered in Table 8.5.

The triple weighted units shown in Table 8.6 provide quite a different ordering of the different projects than heretofore. To illustrate the unique ranking of each R and D output, we distinguish among the different size CYCLONES; large diameters cyclones, rank 7.

In addition to the rank ordering, the triple weighted units show the quantitative basis for resources allocation. Aluminum reduction plants' particulate characterization and coal cleaning plants' particulate characterization differ by only one rank. However, the former is one and a half times as desirable as the latter from the point of view of the air pollution control system, the triple weighted units for the former being 150 percent those of the latter.

Table 8.5

Double weighted units—R&D outputs

Particulate matter characterization	Double weighted units	Rank
integrated steel mills	5 700 000	10
large steam electric generating station	5 472 000	11
Portland cement plants	5 244 000	12
Gray iron and steel foundries	5 130 000	13
ferroalloy plants	4 845 000	14
Kraft pulp mills	3 990 000	15
soap and detergent plants	3 135 000	16
caustic and chlorine plants	3 021 000	17
calcium carbide manufacturing	2 850 000	18
phosphate fertilizer plants	2 535 000	19
lime plants	2 280 000	20
aluminum ore reduction plants	1 710 000	21
coal cleaning plants	1 140 000	22

Operation of emission control devices	Double weighted units	Rank
CYCLONES—large diameters	9 500 000	1
CYCLONES—multiple	9 215 000	2
FILTERS—deep bed	8 550 000	3
FILTERS—fabric	8 170 000	4
FILTERS—reverse jet	7 790 000	5
ELECTROSTATIC PRECIPATORS—high voltage	7 600 000	6
ELECTROSTATIC PRECIPATORS—low voltage	7 125 000	7
SCRUBBERS—simple	6 650 000	8
SCRUBBERS—medium energy	6 175 000	9
SCRUBBERS—venturi	5 700 000	10

Table 8.6

Triple weighted units—R&D outputs

	(1) Implementation effectiveness	(2) Probability of success	(3) (1) × (2)	(4) Rank
CYCLONES–large diameters	9 500 000	0.45	4 275 000	7
CYCLONES–multiple	9 215 000	0.48	4 423 200	4
FILTERS–deep bed	8 550 000	0.51	4 360 500	5
FILTERS–fabric	8 170 000	0.56	4 983 700	1
FILTERS–reverse jet	7 790 000	0.58	4 528 200	3
ELECTROSTATIC PRECIPATORS–high voltage	7 600 000	0.60	4 560 000	2
ELECTROSTATIC PRECIPATORS–low voltage	7 125 000	0.60	4 275 000	8
SCRUBBERS–simple	6 650 000	0.65	4 322 500	6
SCRUBBERS–medium energy	6 175 000	0.65	4 013 750	9
SCRUBBERS–venturi	5 700 000	0.65	3 695 000	10
integrated steel mills	5 700 000	0.55	3 135 000	14
large steel electric generating station	5 472 000	0.57	3 119 040	15
Portland iron and steel foundries	5 244 000	0.60	3 146 400	13
Gray iron and steel foundries	5 130 000	0.65	3 334 500	11
ferroalloy plants	4 845 000	0.68	3 294 600	12
Kraft pulp mills	3 990 000	0.70	2 793 000	16
soap and detergent plants	3 135 000	0.75	2 351 250	17
caustic and chlorine plants	3 021 000	0.75	2 265 750	19
calcium carbide manufacturing	2 850 000	0.80	2 285 000	18
phosphate fertilizer plants	2 535 000	0.81	2 053 350	20
lime plants	2 280 000	0.85	1 938 000	21
aluminum ore reduction plants	1 710 000	0.85	1 453 500	22
coal cleaning plants	1 140 000	0.85	969 000	23

3.3. Ordering of Research and Development Projects by Total Costs

Three types of cost elements are to be considered with respect to each of the research and development projects. They are:

direct costs,

indirect costs,

costs over time.

The direct costs are measured in direct monetary units paid out for man years, materials, experimentation, etc. Overhead expenditures required to maintain the research and development projects are also included under direct costs.

The indirect costs are related to the projects that were foregone in order to permit those chosen for exploration. The alternate costs depend very much upon subsequent knowledge of technology which may suggest that Project Q, which was abandoned in favor of Project N, was likely to have succeeded. This would make the entire direct costs of Project N a greater liability if Project N failed, or failed to yield significant results which Project Q could have provided.

While this particular element of indirect costs is hard to estimate, and would necessarily involve subjective and scientific judgment, another element of indirect costs is not as difficult to determine. The cost of technological exchanges between air pollution researchers (indispensable to avoid duplication and to provide cross-fertilization of ideas) must be included under indirect costs.

A third type of cost relates to research and development over the entire life span of the chosen programs. Thus, it would be inadequate merely to consider the expenses in the first year of an R and D project. Usually, the development or improvement of devices is *not* envisaged in a particulate study. Therefore, the terminal point would be the recommendation for *prototype* development of devices. Realism requires costs to cover the research and development program through prototype recommendation.

3.4. Ordering of Research and Development Projects by Technical Gaps

In addition to the criteria of effectiveness, probability of success, and costs discussed earlier, it is critical to introduce the potential contribution to the state-of-the-art on control of important particulate pollution sources as a principal criterion in selecting R and D projects.

One of the objectives of the OR/SA protocol study is to overcome serious deficiencies in our knowledge of the nature of important particulate pollution sources. What are some of the more serious deficiencies? The knowledge of particulate pollution sources is not an abstract addition to human knowledge. It is a vital input to the pollution control technology. The deficiencies in our knowledge ought to have as clear and direct a relation to the advances in pollution control technology as possible.

The first step is to order problem severity, employing criteria such as tonnage, pervasiveness, objectionable properties. The weighted severity criteria are applied to the available data on particulate pollution sources to yield different orders of deficiencies.

There will be not one but several options of severity ordering. The alternate options are obtained by ranking the available data on particulate pollution sources in different combinations of severity criteria. Thus, if tonnage, pervasiveness, and objectionable properties are given equal weight, they would produce one set of ranking of particulate pollution sources. If, on the other hand, the weight of objectionable properties is, say, ten times that of total tonnage, this would quite possibly yield a different ranking for the particulate pollution sources.

The several options of severity ordering of particulate pollution sources have to be classified according to the nature of deficiencies. One may, at one level, consider the nature of deficiencies with respect to the particulate control devices now in existence, or that ought to be in existence. If, for instance, the 0.5–5 micron range has very few particulate control devices and 6.0–20 micron range has a plethora of particulate control devices, it could suggest that the particulate characterization in the range 6.0–20 will be considered an important candidate for R and D work, after weighting factors relating to objectionable properties are applied.

A second level of deficiencies may be related to the applications engineering that may result from R and D explorations. Using the same illustration as in previous paragraphs, further work on 6.0–20 micron range may more readily yield information on particulate structure than on the translation of that information into particulate control devices. A separate consideration is apropos to all size ranges. It is the translatability of the knowledge of the structure of particulate matter into particulate control devices, or briefly, with respect to ease of application and engineering.

Yet a third level of deficiencies would be the particulate characteristics themselves. It is upon the particulate characteristics that both applications engineering and particulate control technology should basically depend. Therefore, the potential contribution to particulate characterization could be given a ranking in its own right as a contribution to knowledge on the nature of important particulate pollution sources.

It is clear that the final ranking of particulate R and D projects would be the result of:

implementation effectiveness,
probability of success,
total costs,
technological gaps.

4. Conclusion

The illustrative scheme of integrated ordering of objectives of, and means for, air pollution control has several advantages. One, it shows unequivocally that every allocation to one activity means that by so doing, we are taking away the resources from some other means of reducing pollution. Two, given this integrated scheme by which we could rank each of these elements, we are able to see every single demand for resources as elements of the same sub-group. How much money should we spend in deciding what is the particulate that will be most detrimental, and how precisely ought we measure it? Should we measure it with respect to steel mills; should we measure it with respect to ferroalloy plants; should we measure it with respect to carbon and pulp companies? The insight we get from collecting data in measuring the particulate characteristics in one of the mills or one group of mills, has to be immediately related to the next higher level of objectives, viz., that of establishing criteria of permissible levels, which in turn will help establish standards, which in turn will help cut the emission down. Should we spend more money, energy, and time on CYCLONES, on FILTERS, and other means of cleaning the air; or should we spend money devising more precise measurements of what it is that causes pollution? Whatever be our pleasure, OR/SA protocol can show us that there has to be an ordering. If we do not like this ordering, that is no problem; we can immediately change it, as only a rank ordering is involved. This ordering is something that we do every day; and it is done by

default if we do not do it by design. Our illustrative scheme shows only that
we can do it without waiting for all the normative questions and preferences
to be settled. Without a final determination, we could still say that certain
objectives are more desirable than others. Herman Kahn makes the point in
the book *The Year 2000* that we could agree upon an interim ordering. While
income increases, so does, to some extent, juvenile delinquency and crime.
However, we could say that it is more desirable to have an average income of
$17 000 per capita than $3 000. It is this type of judgment which our ordering scheme makes explicit.

  All of this discussion so far has been simply illustrative. In a sense, it has
been very much like using Bufferin merely to relieve one's symptoms, because
here the symptom has been that of polluted air and our discussion has been
how we shall go about removing pollution, or controlling it. We have *not*
taken the much larger perspective; namely, not only to look at a national
policy for the environment, but also at an ecological policy for not merely
the United States, but the entire world. We have looked at only a very small
problem, but it has given us enough perspective to see that we could relate
the highest levels of *policy guidance* which the legislators would like to set, to
the lowest *operational level* of whether we should allocate funds to study a
$20 emission control mechanism for automobiles, or spend more money
studying how to measure a particulate which contributes to the pollution in
the form of sulphur dioxide.

PROBLEMS

*The three chapters, 6, 7 and 8, of Part III deal with the application of OR/SA
Protocol to large, unstructured problems in the Public Sector. This chapter
deals with the problem of* Air Pollution Reduction. *The purpose of the following questions is to develop an appreciation for the specific demands of the
substance of the* particular *problem in applying the* general *sequence.*

A. *System Context*
  1. Distinguish between the User objective of Air Pollution Reduction and
the User objective of health care.
  2. What are the major elements that go into an index of pollution control,
with particular reference to air pollution?

3. The standard of pollutants in coal used for energy purposes were relaxed at the time of the energy crisis in 1973. How does the relaxation jibe with the User objective of air pollution?

B. *System Cost*

4. The Council of Environmental Quality has estimated that the cost of effectively controlling air pollution is of the order of $120 billion. What additional cost(s) should be included to arrive at the cost of opportunity foregone?

5. How would you apply the cost of opportunity acquired in the national reduction of air pollution?

6. It has been suggested that (air) pollution is a problem created by the private sector, which should therefore, be assigned to the private, and not the public, sector to solve. Comment on the system cost aspects.

C. *System Effectiveness—Absolute*

7. Outline the elements of effectiveness that can be associated with research on air pollution control.

8. Discuss a way of justifying the investment of $1 billion in air pollution reduction in preference to a $1 billion investment in health care delivery.

D. *System Effectiveness—Relative*

9. How would you relate the increase in investment in automobile emission reduction to the potential decrease in the number of deaths in an air pollution episode like the one in New York City on Thanksgiving Day, 1966?

10. It has been suggested that the techniques for air pollution reduction are available, the primary problem being political. Develop an argument to convince political decision-makers that the investment in research to control automobile emission is relatively more important than the investment in research on stationary source emission reduction.

PART IV

UNSTRUCTURED PROBLEMS IN THE PRIVATE SECTOR

CHAPTER 9

NATIONAL DATA FOR PRIVATE SECTOR PROBLEMS: STANDARD INDUSTRIAL CLASSIFICATION (SIC) BASIS

TECHNICAL OVERVIEW

The first of the private sector problems *studied is a general business problem: how to increase sales?*

In the particular problem, a number of "Textbook" solutions is found to be simply inapplicable. The management has no idea of the profitability of products; they have no patience with sales training; and they have no interest in, or inclination to streamline the production in the plants. The inapplicability of 9 illustrative approaches in (1) financial, (2) sales, and (3) manufacturing activities is discussed.

What are the requirements of an organismic index for management decision-making? The effective management hierarchy is identified; and alternative classifications of decision-making levels are established with particular reference to the given problem.

Three major requirements are established for an operational index of performance: (1) independence of present performance, (2) industrial and regional sales potentials, and (3) action indicators at the different hierarchical levels. The first requirement is necessitated because the 53 salesmen compare their present performance with that of the previous year or month, whichever shows their present performance to be better; and the management has no convincing arguments to induce improved sales. The second requirement underlines the need for a relationship between the external demands for the company products for groups of sales territories, instead of individual territories, so that there is a group measure against which the individual performance can be measured. The third requirement highlights the fact that the management has no action signals which indicate to them when remedial action is called for at the managerial or the salesman level.

285

The requirement to develop some objective measure of the sales potentials is not a requirement peculiar to the particular company under discussion. In fact, it may be considered a universal requirement, especially applicable to corporations which deal in physical products. A wealth of information is available in the form of U.S. Government publications which publish data on the basis of the Standard Industrial Classification (SIC) Code which incorporates every single economic activity, and every single economic unit in the United States. Under U.S. Code Title 13 every establishment is required to file certain types of information with the Bureau of the Census which conducts the Census of Manufactures in the years ending in 2 and 7, which is supplemented by the Annual Census of Manufactures.

The results of the Census of Manufactures are available in three principal volumes: (1) Summary and Subject Statistics, (2) Industrial Statistics, and (3) Area Statistics. The Industrial Statistics are compiled by states and couties; but in addition, they are also available for Standard Metropolitan Statistical Areas (SMSAs). The SMSA data are updated by private organizations, such as the publishers of Sales Management, *who make available detailed data on 41 000 "key plants" with 100 or more employees using the SIC code and sources.*

How can a business organization take advantage of the National Data Base? In one of the publications of the Bureau of the Census, Concentration Ratios in Manufacturing, *the shipments of approximately 1 200 classes of products, and the fraction of shipments accounted for by 4, 8, 20, and 50 largest companies manufacturing each class of product in 1967 are given, with comparative statistics for 1963, 1958, and 1954. On the basis of these concentration ratios, one could place oneself within the industry, and calibrate one's rank fairly closely.*

Another comparison is the profitability of each enterprise. The Federal Trade Commission and the Securities and Exchange Commission have published Quarterly Financial Reports for Manufacturing Corporations *since 1947 based on a sample representing about 88 percent of a composite frame based on the Internal Revenue Service Form 1120 returns and the Social Security Administration Applications for Employer Identification Number. Among the 10 Tables published in the Quarterly Financial Report are rates of change in sales and profits by industry, profits per dollar by sales by industry, annual rates of profit on stockholders equity by industry, etc. These industry statistics provide yardsticks of comparison for business enterprises.*

The application of the national data to an individual company is illustrated with respect to the Mattresses and Bedsprings Industry. The national data, by themselves, are inadequate to set up an organismic index of performance. For instance, the particular company would be only one among the 939 companies engaged in the shipment of Mattresses and Bedsprings. If the company were not a single product company, but a multi-product company, then the chances are the associated products would make the company one in 9 518 companies, all of which are included in the larger group: Furnitures and Fixtures. The financial data are on the basis of not mattresses and bedsprings, but on Furnitures and Fixtures.

The demand to custom-tailor the national data to the individual company needs is clear. With respect to the company whose problems we started out with, the SMSA data updated by private organizations is found to be quite important in determining the sales potential. To arrive at the group *basis for sales performance potential, the very meager data for only 6–9 months of the current year have to be used to redraw the map of the United States in terms of the company sales. It has been possible to divide the United States into five regions, Regions I and II being comparable to each other, Region III half the size of Region I, and Regions IV and V approximately equal to each other.*

Using the internal *classification into regions, the* external *indicators of sales potentials are explored in terms of percent of U.S. retail sales volume in Urban Trading Centers with over 100 000 population in each of the states in the five regions.*

Two external characteristics are considered: (1) percent of U.S. retail sales volume, and (2) percent of effective buying income on the basis of SMSA. The question is: given the values for the percentage share of U.S. retail volume, and U.S. effective buying, can the share of company bookings in a given state be predicted? This is explored further in Chapter 10.

EXECUTIVE SUMMARY

Two major problems which face any manufacturing and sales organiza-

tion: (1) sales, and (2) production, are examined with respect to a real life multi-plant, multi-product manufacturing and sales corporation. The sales question is studied in Chapters 9, 10, and 11; and the production question is studied in Chapter 12.

The 53 salesmen of the company sell through some 5 000 dealers who have direct access to the end-users. The 315 products that this durable goods manufacturer sells are organized into 12 administrative divisions, each with a sales manager. The salesmen handle different groups of products; and depending upon the particular type of product handled, they will be in the purview of a particular sales manager.

The top management wants to increase sales. The salesmen are on commissions; therefore, presumably they have sufficient motivation. But there is no way of knowing whether the company sales are at the peak of their potential, or at the bottom, or in between.

To develop a yardstick, advantage is taken of the extensive data that are collected and disseminated by the U.S. Bureau of Census. The Census of Manufactures collects data from establishments every fice years; and the Federal Trade Commission and Securities and Exchange Commission publish financial data every quarter, the data on rates of change in sales and profit by industry, profits per dollar by sales by industry, etc. These national data provide a valuable basis for comparison of any corporation's own performance.

National Data have to be adapted. For the present problem, two series of data are considered: (1) percent of U.S. retail sales volume, in urban trading centers and (2) percent of effective buying income in the Standard Metropolitan Statistical Areas. These two variables are associated with the company bookings.

The large, unstructured problems, of ecological investment, health care allocations, and air pollution reduction, have been made conceptually manageable by the application of the OR/SA protocol developed in Chapter 4. It should be remembered that each application is but one instance of utilizing the protocol; the structure, as well as the substance, of the decisions could well be different in another application of the same protocol to the same problems. However, what the protocol contributes is a systematic approach to tackling large, unstructured problems, which yields a consistent structure and a consistent scheme of allocation.

The ecological investment of $2 billion by the Department of Interior in one year discussed in Chapter 6, and the organization of the health services in the United States for the production and delivery of health care which involved $79 billion dollars in 1972, discussed in Chapter 7, as well as the air pollution reduction discussed in Chapter 8, are Public Sector problems of prominence. We now turn to the Private Sector; and consider two major problems which are vital to any manufacturing and sales operation: Sales and Production.

1.Statement of the Problem

A multi-plant, multi-product durable goods manufacturing and sales organization is acquired by three partners in the 57th year of operation. This is the first exposure of the owners to the idea of dealing in goods, whose use has to be "sold" to the customers; their success having been in trading surplus goods in bulk, never having to bother with the merits of the items, but simply having to find a buyer who would match the purchase price of the bulk quantities with a slight margin of profit.

During the 57 years of operation, the company has grown to five manufacturing plants in the United States and two in Canada. Each plant maintains its own line of products, sold by its own group of salesmen. The acquisition by the three owners of the company, the first experience of corporate consolidation, presents major problems to the individual salesmen who have been successful in selling the products manufactured at each plant, but who have never before had the need to be part of any larger entity.

On the part of the management, there is full recognition that the entire success or failure of the new asset literally depends upon the 53 salesmen. For it is they who sell the products; and only they know the customers. The sales are not made directly by the salesmen, but *in*directly through the medium of dealers who exhibit sample products from this particular company, as well as those of its competitors, in their showroom. The showrooms may be elaborate; but more often, they are just a single room, or part of a room. The theory is that prospective customers would be exposed to the company product at the dealers' location, and, being "sold" on the merits of the company's line of products, would place order(s) for a number of units of one or more products. The customer could be someone like the local school; and the order could mean, say, 500 school desks.

The major resource of the company obviously is the 53 salesmen, without whom none of the products would find their way to the customer. The salesmen themselves depend upon the medium of the dealers (and the dealer salesmen) both to create an image of the company, and to maintain it in a favorable light. The company salesmen decide who becomes a dealer for the company; and who does not. The "setting up" of a dealer does not carry with it any serious contractual obligations. It essentially amounts to a gentleman's agreement that the dealer will think kindly of the company product(s) and, if he so choses, will display the company product(s). Should a sale be made, he gets a commission for his services.

The administrative mechanism to control the salesman activities is the sales managers. The control is *in*direct because the sales managers are responsible for the sales of products *only* of their *division*. The sales managers receive salaries which are a direct percentage of the sales of each division. More accurately, the sales managers draw their compensation *not* on the sales of the division, but the *bookings* of each division. The distinction is important, because the actual sales can be about 10% below the bookings, and the company bookings are approximately $18 million a year.

At the time of the acquisition of the company by the three partners, there were 12 divisions and 12 sales managers. The divisions do *not* correspond to the products manufactured in the different plants. As a matter of fact, some products can be sold by every salesman; and some others only by the specialty salesman. But since the orders placed by the customers are for a group of products, they seldom obey the administrative distinction between the divisions. Thus, for instance, if a school were placing an order, it may order 500 school desks, some office chairs, some coat racks, etc. The coat racks in this example could normally be sold by a division which has nothing to do with supplying schools. This gives rise to the question of which division should get credit for the particular booking.

Careful tracking of the assignment of credit for bookings to divisions reveals the interesting fact that the assignment is as arbitrary as the administrative classification of the division itself. Former Secretary of Defense McElroy is said to have gotten his start in the mailroom of Proctor & Gamble from where he rose to be the President of the company. If he were the mailroom clerk in this company, it would not be hard to see how one could rise from the mailroom to the executive suite. For, the mailroom clerk happens to be the arbiter of the assignment of credits to each administrative division; which explains the track shoes that each assistant to the sales manager wears out in chasing the mailman so that his particular division can be credited with the orders, all of which arrive by mail. It is not unusual for serious squabbles to occur between the assistants to the sales managers in each division over the assignment of a particular order to their own division.

The new management decides to move the corporate headquarters from its location in Chicago to the East Coast. They discover that about the only company-wide data available are the bookings by divisions for the nine months preceding the takeover. The comptroller assures them that he would not guarantee the accuracy of the bookings figures beyond the last six months or so.

The assignment is rather straightforward: what should the management do to increase the sales?

2. Practical Limitations Upon Many Plausible Theoretical Approaches

A number of "textbook" solutions is simply not applicable. We will consider nine illustrative approaches to solutions falling into three classes: (1) Financial, (2) Sales, and (3) Manufacturing.

2.1. Financial: (1) No Idea of Product Profitability

Thus, the management does not have any idea as to which products are profitable, and which are not. As a matter of fact, they do not have the vaguest notion even as to how many products the company is producing.

The financial records, such as the profit and loss statement, are closely held by the three partners. There is no record of per unit profitability of any of the products. The taxes paid on earnings are unavailable.

2.2. Financial: (2) No Increase in Sales Incentives

The suggestion to increase the inducement to the salesman by raising the percentage of commission on their sales is ruled out. It should be recalled, however, that at this point, the management needs the salesman more than the salesman needs the management.

2.3. Sales: (1) No Concept or Measure of Sales Potentials

The "productivity" of the salesman is virtually unknown. By digging into the individual records of payments to salesmen, it would be possible to get an approximate idea of the bookings in *dollars*, but not in units of products. In other words, it is possible to construct gross total figures for the bookings of salesmen. But is a salesman whose bookings for the year are $25 000 doing well or poorly compared with another salesman whose bookings total only $5 000? Numerically the answer is clear; but the question is *not* whether $25 000 is greater than $5 000, but whether one salesman is better than another.

Consider that the first salesman is in New York City; and the second salesman is in Huntsville, Alabama. There is clearly a difference between the two locations in what the sales territory is capable of yielding. If there were some figure which indicated that the territory of the New York City salesman could yield say, $50 000 a year, while the territory of the Huntsville salesman could yield only $7 500, then the first salesman while producing 5 times the bookings of the second salesman, is doing a poorer job, because he is doing only 50% of the potential of his territory, while the second salesman is doing 67% of the potential of his territory.

2.4. Sales: (2) No Concept of Salesmanship

You turn to the sales managers as the repositories of wisdom, and ask them who their best salesmen are, so that you may discover what makes them tick. The sales manager of the largest division tells you whom he considers to be the best salesman. But you protest that the bookings figure of the particular salesman has sharply declined from last year to this year. The sales manager adamantly insists that his choice is still the best salesman. It is obvious that the sales manager thinks only of the absolute magnitude of the bookings figure, and not the relative rate of change, or more importantly, any index of relative achievement compared with the potentials that the territory holds.

2.5. Sales: (3) No Idea of Sales Training

The suggestion that the company salesmen be given an intensified indoctrination in a series of training sessions cuts no ice with the management because as mentioned in Section 1, they have little orientation to the need to "sell" the use of any product. They are convinced that the seven plants that they acquired are a profit-making venture; they could not care less as to how the profits are made, whether the salesmen think of themselves as essentially salesmen of ideas of use of the company products, or of pig-in-a-poke; whether the salesmen consider themselves as salesmen of each of the plants, or of a single corporate structure. The sales managers who would be expected to educate the salesmen to do a better job, have almost no concept of sales-manship in the analytical sense; their view is simply that the higher the bookings, the better the salesman. Thus, the management is not concerned with the creation of a corporate image in the minds of their salesmen; and even if they wished to train the salesmen in improved salesmanship there is no readily available material or talent for such training.

2.6 Sales: (4) No Concept of User Views

It may be suggested that an extensive survey be made of the users, and their views of the company products solicited. The thought is almost totally alien to the owners, because they have prospered in selling surplus goods, the significance to the users of which, was a matter of total unconcern; yet they prospered. Therefore, the suggestion that a user survey be made to determine what the likes and dislikes of the customers of the company products are strikes the management as a clearly avoidable large expenditure.

2.7. Sales: (5) No Concept of User Needs

How about a market survey, not of the user attitude, but of the user interest and needs? Again, the management feels that the 53 salesmen know their market, and know it well. The question is therefore not one of additional knowledge, but of direct application of that knowledge. No money for any fancy market research!

2.8. Production: (1) Rational Production Allocation

If you try to sell the management on the idea that there is duplication in the manufacture of the same products, and that production efficiency could be improved by allocating the production of each product to one plant, and only one plant, that argument induces little action. For, one of the plant managers, having been with the company the longest, has secured the title of Vice-President of Production. However, he has no interest in, or inclination towards, streamlining the production in all the plants. In fact, he functions as the plant manager of one of the seven plants; however, because of his title of Vice-President for Production, any allocation of products to or away from his plant would be considered a direct challenge to the way that he has been running the business. The management is in no mood to pick a quarrel with the oldest production manager of a business they have virtually no knowledge of.

2.9. Production: (2) No Rhyme or Reason in Product Numbers

One of the consequences of the unrelated growth over the years of the manufacturing and sales operation in the different plants has been the inconsistency in the designation of the different products. Just as in the Biblical story of creation, where "what Adam called became its name", so also what each plant foreman called out became the number of the product. Thus, it is not unlikely that two products which are essentially similar would have two different numbers if they are manufactured in two different plants. Further, with each modification of the product may come a new number; or an alphabetical annex to the number, which again, is a function of the mood of the foreman of the particular plant at the particular time. This situation contributes enormously to confusion because it is virtually impossible to recognize the same product in all its variations, so that the attitude of the user toward the product may be reasonably ascertained or a reasonable measure be made of the costs of production and of profits.

2.10. Caution: Speak Plainly
A word of caution on the OR/SA study and recommendations. The three partners have not seen the inside of a high school. They are extremely pragmatic and will listen if they can see a direct relationship between what you recommend and the ring of the cash register. Any persuasion must run in terms of perceivable profits, and not analytical abstractions.

3. APPLICATION 19: Organismic Index for Management Decision-Making

The top-management directive that the sales of the company be increased raises the question of the structural relationships governing the implementation of the directive.

3.1. The Company Decision-Making Hierarchy

The *organismic* level comprises the President and Executive Vice-President, who are the two partners actively participating in the affairs of the company, the third partner being essentially "silent".

The *strategic* level comprises the Vice-President—Operations, who acts as the National Sales Manager, the Vice-President for Production, the National Merchandizing Manager, and as the head of other allied operations. Administratively, a labor relations specialist holds the rank of Vice-President, but his primary involvement is in the area of labor negotiations at the different plants. As such, his role in the identification and realization of increased sales is negligible. As stated in Section 2.8, the senior-most manager among the plant managers has also been given the title of Vice-President, but he has no direct input in the production processes of the other six plants; and even in some matters affecting the production in his own plant, he reports to the Vice-President—Operations.

The *tactical* level comprises the 12 sales division managers and the 53 salesmen. Normally, the managers would be at least one decision-making level above that of the salesman. However, with respect to the identification and realization of sales potential, the managers play a relatively passive role, in some cases even secondary to that of the salesmen whose bookings constitute the basis of sales commission paid to the sales manager. Further, because the salesmen can, in effect, sell the products of most, if not all divisions, the shoe is on the other foot, as it were, in that the sales manager has to depend on the good will of the salesmen in promoting the sales of the particular divisions.

Instead of a single triad comprising the organismic, strategic, and tactical decision-making levels comprising respectively of: (1) President and Executive Vice-President, (2) Vice-President—Operations, and (3) Sales Manager and Salesmen, the administrative changes that took place during the first two years of operation under the new management could be reflected by developing two triads instead of one. Since the tactical level of one triad in Round One would be the organismic level of Round Two in developing a top-down hierarchy of objectives, as shown in Chapter 6, Section 7, the hierarchical allocation of company effort can be represented as follows:

Round One
    President and Executive Vice-President   Organismic
    Vice-President—Operations   Strategic
    National Sales Manager   Tactical

Round Two
    National Sales Manager   Organismic
    Division Sales Manager   Strategic
    Salesmen   Tactical

The National Sales Manager level of operation also includes the National Merchandizing Manager, who, during his short tenure, played little role in the identification or realization of sales potential. At the Division Sales Manager level there is also a quasi-*regional* sales manager for the West Coast. Again, his influence on sales potentials identification and realization has been negligible. At the tactical level, the salesmen themselves could be divided into two categories: (1) general salesmen, and (2) specialty salesmen, the latter handling some of the products exclusively.

3.2. Requirements of an Operational Index of Performance

How should the scarce resources, viz., the effort of the 53 salesmen, be allocated so that the sales of the company in the coming year(s) would be increased?

3.2.1. Requirement (1): independence of present performance
To merely ask the salesmen to increase their bookings would be a superfluous exercise, because the salesmen are grown men and know that their earnings would increase with their sales.

The slender data in the form of bookings by divisions themselves arrive three to four months late. Therefore, whenever a salesman is confronted with a decrease in the bookings in any given month compared with the preceding month, he could either say: "Ah, but you haven't seen what I did this month"; or he would say: "Ah, but you should have seen how terrible things were this month last year, or the year before."

If the management cannot achieve its aim by looking at either the present performance, or the past performance, then something new has to be devised. This new device must be one that would give the management the unequivocal targets for the performance of each salesman. These targets should also make the necessary distinction between the bookings of $25 000 by the New York City salesman and the $5 000 bookings by the Huntsville salesman in the example in Section 2.3. In other words, the organismic measure of performance should provide an outside criterion to evaluate the bookings other than its own absolute size.

3.2.2. Requirement (2): industrial and regional sales potentials

The organismic measure of performance should reflect not only the potential of the sales territory of each salesman, but also the potential of a *group* of territories compared with another group. In other words, if it were possible to say that the potentials of the *two* groups of territories are equivalent, then the comparative performance of each of the salesmen within that group of territories has an added objective basis, so that if all the salesmen in one group were to perform poorly, that would be thrown into sharp relief by comparison with the performance of the salesmen in the comparable group of territories.

The concept of a region is introduced to permit the groupings of sales territories by their potential. It is recognized that the region is introduced as an abstract aggregation. Its purpose is to provide an input to the organismic index of performance.

3.2.3. Requirement (3): action increment at the three hierarchical levels

It is found that the allocation of the scarce resource of time presents a problem not only at the tactical level of salesmen, but also at the *strategic* level of division sales managers. Ask a sales manager why he makes a trip to a particular sales territory and he will say: "To tell the salesmen to sell more." But, it was pointed out in Section 3.2.1 that any such urging would be superfluous because the salesmen are grown men who know that their earnings depend directly upon their sales. Therefore, it stands to reason that the visiting fireman in the form of a sales manager would hardly induce further action on the part of the salesmen. This is all the more true when no salesman really works exclusively in any single division and hence does not owe allegiance to any particular division sales manager.

One of the requirements of an effective sales potential index is that it should indicate how the activities of the division sales managers should be allocated. In other words, if they were to be asked why they made a trip to

Sales Territory 5 instead of Sales Territory 17, there should be a better justification than better weather conditions in Sales Territory 5.

In addition to providing a signal for action at the tactical level (salesmen) and the strategic level (the Division Sales Manager) the organismic index of performance should also induce action at the organismic level (National Sales Manager). In other words, while focusing upon the increase of sales for the company as a whole, the organismic index of performance should also be able to identify necessary actions at all the three levels: at the organismic level, the national sales manager should be able to recognize what he should do, and which divisions should show different results in the next time period; at the strategic level, the division sales manager should be able to identify the particular sales territories which need immediate attention to stimulate the sales performance in the coming periods; and at the tactical level, the salesmen should be able to gauge their own performance periodically against some standard which is both realistic and operational and which the company should expect him to maintain.

4. National Data on all Manufacturing and Nonmanufacturing Activities

The requirement to develop some objective measure of the sales potentials is not a requirement peculiar to the particular company under discussion. In fact, it may be considered a universal requirement, especially applicable to corporations which deal in physical products. An enormous amount of data is available from the U.S. Federal Government sources, some of which would be applicable to any industry or activity within the United States. Therefore, it is essential that the nature and magnitude of data be appreciated to enable its proper utilization.

Every economic activity, whether manufacturing or nonmanufacturing, is required under the U.S. Code Title 13 to file certain types of information with the Bureau of the Census. The first census of manufactures was taken in 1810. Under the latest legislation enacted in 1964, the census of manufacturers will be taken in the future in years ending in 2 and 7. The publication of the results of the 1967 Census of Manufacturers was completed by the end of 1971, although some of the results were available soon after the completion of the Census in November 1967.

4.1. Standard Industrial Classification (SIC)

In order to assess the extensive data available, it is necessary to understand the structure of the code governing the collection and processing of data:

> The structure of the [Standard Industrial] Classification makes it possible to classify establishments by industry on either a two-digit, a three-digit, or a four-digit basis, according to the degree of detail in information which may be needed. ... An "establishment" is an economic unit which produces goods or services, for example, a farm, a mine, a factory, a store. In most instances, the establishment is at a single physical location; and it is engaged in only one, or predominantly one, type of economic activity for which an industry code is applicable.[1]

The highest hierarchy of SIC is the Division. In 1972 the first major revision since 1957 was undertaken which recognized the importance of ecological and social concerns.

The single numbers of 1967, for Federal Government (9190), State Government (9290), Local Government (9390), and International Government (9490), have blossomed into many in 1972. The Executive Offices are 9111; Legislative bodies are 9121; and the Executive and Legislative combined is 9131. The Administration of Public Health Programs is 9431; Air, Water, and Solid Waste Management is 9511. Space Research and Technology is 9661; while National Security and International Affairs are respectively 9711 and 9721. The changes in 1972 from the preceding classification of 1967 are as follows:

> There was a total of 976 classified industries (excluding Division J, Public Administration, with 27 industries) in 1972 compared with 917 industries (excluding Division I, Government) in 1967. In 1967, Public Administration was included in the classification for Government, which was represented by a 4-digit code: first two digits (91–94) for the level of government (Federal, State, local, and international) and the last two digits being the 73 Major Groups in 01–89.
>
> In 1972, government establishments engaged in activities paralleling those of the private sector are classified in Major Groups 01–89 by kind of activity in the

---

[1] Executive Office of the President, Bureau of the Budget, *Standard Industrial Classification Manual*, U.S. Government Printing Office, Washington, D.C., 1957, pp. 1–3.

same codes as for private sector establishments. Division J, Public Administration, in 1972 is limited to activities not covered in Major Groups 01 89.[2]

1972 SIC Divisions	1972	1967
Total, including public administrations	1,004	(N/A)
Total, excluding public administrations	977	918 [a]
A. Agriculture, forestry, fishing	61	38
B. Mining	42	53
C. Construction [b]	26	21
D. Manufacturing	452	422
E. Transportation and other public utilities	70	72
F. Wholesale Trade	61	48
G. Retail Trade	64	67
H. Finance, insurance, real estate [b]	70	80
I. Services		
Major Groups 70–79	88	84
Major Groups 80–89	42	32
J. Public Administration	27	(N/A)
K. Nonclassifiable Establishments	1	1

(N/A) Not available.
[a] Does not include government-owned and -operated establishments.
[b] Operative builders were classified as Industry 1531 (Division C) in 1972, and as Industry 6561 (Division H) in 1967.

The relationship between the highest element in the hierarchy, viz., the Division, and the lowest, viz., the product, is illustrated in Fig. 9.1, with respect to Division D: Manufacturing, under which falls Major Group 20: Food and Kindred Products.

The finest level of detail used in SIC is the "product" which is not necessarily synonymous with the use of the term in the marketing sense. For instance, all grades of automobile gasoline are reported as a single "product".

[2] Harold T. Goldstein, *From the Old to the New 1972 Standard Industrial Classifications for Establishments*, Tech. Paper 28, U.S. Department of Commerce, Bureau of the Census, Washington, D.C., October 1972, pp. 1, 3.

DIVISION D: MANUFACTURING

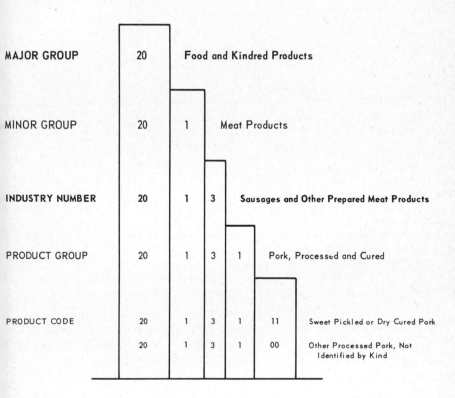

Fig. 9.1

Table 9.1

1967 numerical list of manufactured products

Code	Ck. dg.*	Industry and product description	Quantity measure
251		HOUSEHOLD FURNITURE	
2514		METAL HOUSEHOLD FURNITURE - MC - 25C	
25142		METAL KITCHEN FURNITURE	
		Kitchen furniture (excluding breakfast furniture reported as "dining, dinette, and breakfast furniture")	
25142 11	8	Cabinet, such as base, top and base wall, utility, etc.	....
25142 51	4	Stools, padded and plain	Units
25142 71	2	Tables, including hostess carts	Units
25143		METAL PORCH, LAWN, AND OUTDOOR FURNITURE	
		Tubular aluminum	
25143 12	4	Chairs, rockers, benches, chaise lounges and settees	Units
25143 14	0	Other cast and wrought iron porch, lawn, and outdoor furniture, including gliders, swings, and hammocks	....
		Cast and wrought iron	
25143 22	3	Chairs, rockers, benches, chaise lounges and settees	Units
25143 24	9	Other cast and wrought iron porch, lawn, and outdoor furniture, including gliders, swings, and hammocks	....
25143 98	3	Other metal porch, lawn, outdoor, and casual furniture, including picnic tables	....
25144		OTHER METAL HOUSEHOLD FURNITURE	
24144 33	8	Folding cots, rollable cots, army cots, and other metal beds	Units
25144 37	9	Metal bed frame (complete metal bed frames, sold separately, with or without a headboard)	Units

* Check digit − the 8th digit inserted to provide a check in computer processing.

Table 9.1 (Continued)

Code	Ck. dg.	Industry and product description	Quantity measure
25144 55	1	Upholstered metal household furniture	...
25144 71	8	Card tables and chairs	...
25144 75	9	Medicine cabinets, including "wall type" and "insert type"	Units
25144 91	6	Metal radio, phonograph, TV, and Hi-Fi cabinets	Units
25144 93	2	Infants' and children's metal furniture, including high chairs and tables	Units
25144 95	7	Metal folding tray tables	Units
25144 98	1	Other metal household furniture	...
2515		MATRESSES AND BEDSPRINGS - MC - 25D	
25151		INTERSPRING MATTRESSES, OTHER THAN CRIB SIZE	
25151 15	0	Interspring mattresses, other than crib size, including those with polyurethane or rubber topper pads and those sold as part of Hollywood beds	Units
25152		OTHER MATTRESSES, INCLUDING CRIB MATTRESSES	
25152 01	8	Spring cushions, (excluding air-cooled auto seat cushions)	...
25152 11	7	Crib mattresses, all types, including crib size mattresses made with inner-springs, polyurethane, latex foam, hair, cotton felt, etc.	Units
25152 31	5	Latex foam core mattresses, other than crib size	Units
25152 37	2	Polyurethane foam core mattresses, other than crib size	Units
25152 45	5	Other mattresses, including those made of cotton felt, hair, etc.	Units
25153		BEDSPRINGS	
25153 11	5	Box springs, including those sold with or without legs as parts of Hollywood beds	Units
25153 41	2	Coil springs and flat springs, including springs for bunk beds but excluding crib springs	Units
25153 71	9	Hospital bedsprings, all types, including hospital bedsprings, manual or motorized, shipped at such as this establishment. (Excluding bedsprings incorporated at the location into hospital beds)	Units

Table 9.1 (Continued)

Code	Ck. dg.	Industry and product description	Quantity measure
25154		CONVERTIBLE SOFAS	
25154 21	2	From purchased mattresses, including interplant transfers	Units
25154 31	1	From mattresses produced at this location	Units
25155		JACKKNIFE SOFA BEDS AND CHAIR BEDS	
25155 21	9	Jackknife sofa beds and chair beds (back lowers to seat level by means of jackknife hinge and forms half the sleeping surface)	Units
25156		STUDIO COUCHES	
25156 11	8	Studio couches	Units
2519		HOUSEHOLD FURNITURE, N.E.C.* - MC - 25A	
25190		HOUSEHOLD FURNITURE, N.E.C.	
25190 11	7	Plastic cabinets, radio, phonograph, TV hi-fi and combinations thereof	No. of cabinets
25190 32	3	Reed and rattan furniture, including willow, wicker, and cane	....
25190 98	4	Other household furniture, including plastic furniture	....
252		OFFICE FURNITURE	
2521		WOOD OFFICE FURNITURE - MC - 25E	
25210		WOOD OFFICE FURNITURE	
25210 11	3	Chairs, including upholstered	Units
25210 21	2	Sofas, couches, settees, stools, etc., including upholstered (except factor and institutional)	Units
2522		METAL OFFICE FURNITURE - MC - 25E	
25221		METAL OFFICE FURNITURE	
		Chairs, Stools, couches, etc.	

* N.E.C.: Not Elsewhere Classified.

Table 9.1 (Continued)

Code	Ck. dg.	Industry and product description	Quantity measure
25221 11	0	Chairs, including upholstered	Units
25221 51	6	Sofas, couches, settees, stools, etc., except factory and institutional including upholstered	Units
25222		DESKS	
25222 21	7	Executive type	Units
25222 31	6	Clerical and secretarial with or without typewriter mechanism	Units
25223		CABINETS AND CASES	
		Vertical filing cabinets, noninsulated, nonmechanical, nonvisible; including security files	
25223 11	6	Letter	Units
25223 14	0	Legal	Units
25223 16	5	Other (card, jumbo, ledger, document, ledger trays, transfer cases, computer tape and micro-film cabinets, etc.)	Units
25223 19	9	Mechanical filing equipment (other than visible), letter, legal, card, etc., manually or electrically operated	Units
25223 23	1	Insulated filing cabinets (except safes including security files, insulated ledger trays and insulated computer tape and microfilm cabinets)	Units
		Visible equipment (other than insulated), including vertical and rotary units	
25223 24	9	Nonmechanical (including cabinets, reference panel type, chart boards, book type)	Units
25223 26	4	Mechanical (including card size and reference type, manually or electrically operated)	...

Table 9.1 (Continued)

Code	Ck. dg.	Industry and product description	Quantity measure
25224		OTHER METAL OFFICE FURNITURE, INCLUDING TABLES, STANDS, ETC.	
25224 11	4	Tables and stands	Units
25224 21	3	Modular service units (except desks) including "L" and "U" returns, desk extensions, stand attachments, platforms, etc.	Units
25224 98	1	Other metal office furniture, including bookcases, storage cabinets, costumers, etc.	...
253		PUBLIC BUILDING FURNITURE	
2531		PUBLIC BUILDING FURNITURE - MC - 25E	
25311		SCHOOL FURNITURE, EXCEPT STONE AND CONCRETE	
		Single pupil units	
25311 12	7	Desk seat combination with book box (swivel or fixed seat)	Units
25311 15	0	Desk seat combination without book box (including study top)	Units
25311 22	6	Chair desk	Units
25311 24	2	Tablet arm chair	Units
25311 29	1	Other single pupil units (including single pupil table desks)	Units
25311 33	3	Two or more pupil desks and tables	Units
25311 36	6	Chairs, all purpose (nonfolding)	Units
25311 38	2	Combination folding tables and benches	Units
25311 37	4	Storage cabinets	No. of cabs.
25311 39	0	Other school furniture, designed specifically for use in schools (including tables, teachers' desks, chalk boards, study carrels, etc.)	...

Table 9.1 (Continued)

Code	Ck. Dg.	Industry and product description	Quantity measure
25312		PUBLIC BUILDING AND RELATED FURNITURE, EXCEPT SCHOOL FURNITURE	
25312 11	7	Seats for public conveyances, automobiles, trucks, aircraft and buses	No. of seats
25312 31	5	Church pews	Lin. ft.
25312 39	8	Other church furniture (pulpits, altars, lecterns, etc.)	.....
25312 41	4	Folding tables, including folding banquet tables	No. of tables
		Chairs and seats	
		Theatre and auditorium	
25312 51	3	Fixed	No. of chairs
25312 55	4	Portable folding chairs, single or ganged	No. of chairs
25312 61	2	Stadium and bleacher seating, including grandstands	.....
25312 71	1	Library furniture, all types (including chairs, charging desks, study carrels, reading tables, etc.)	.....
25312 98	4	Other public building furniture	.....

Table
General statistics for establishments

| | | 1967 | | |
| | | | Establishments* | |
Code	Industry group and industry	Com- panies* (number)	Total (number)	With 20 employees or more (number)
24	Lumber and wood products	35 573	36 795	5 803
2411	Logging camps, logging contractors	16 265	16 334	598
242	Sawmills and planing mills	11 058	11 461	2 355
2421	Sawmills and planing mills, general	10 016	10 271	1 916
2426	Hardwood dimension and flooring	613	665	331
2429	Special product sawmills, nec**	454	525	108
243	Millwork, Plywood, related prod	4 308	4 558	1 496
2431	Millwork	3 292	3 342	767
2432	Veneer and Plywood	516	667	515
2433	Prefabricated wood structures	519	549	214
244	Wooden containers	829	905	304
2441	Nailed wooden boxes and shook	567	596	182
2442	Wirebound boxes and crates	118	134	63
2443	Veneer and Plywood containers	81	84	39
2445	Cooperage	67	91	20
249	Miscellaneous wood products	3 319	3 537	1 050
2491	Wood preserving	278	375	177
2499	Wood products, nec**	3 044	3 162	873
25	Furniture and fixtures	9 518	10 008	3 449
251	Household furniture	5 948	6 306	2 366
2511	Wood household furniture	2 934	3 084	1 011
2512	Upholstered household furniture	1 582	1 644	727
2514	Metal household furniture	464	486	251
2515	Mattresses and bedsprings	939	1 013	341
2519	Household furniture, nec**	75	79	36
252	Office furniture	334	365	189
2521	Wood office furniture	172	178	69
2522	Metal office furniture	166	187	120
2531	Public Building furniture	428	438	188

see footnotes at end of table

9.2
by industry groups and industries: 1967

All employees		Production workers			Value added by manufacture	Value shipments
Number	Payroll	Number	Man-hours	Wages		
(1,000)	(million dollars)	(1,000)	(millions)	(million dollars)	(million dollars)	(million dollars)
554.0	2 798.9	495.7	977.0	2 290.6	4 973.4	11 205.7
70.6	338.8	67.5	125.9	306.8	695.1	1 476.3
215.5	1 028.3	196.5	385.0	874.5	1 783.9	3 997.8
180.5	884.6	164.7	322.7	754.8	1 556.4	3 506.4
27.9	115.1	25.2	51.5	94.4	176.8	373.5
7.1	28.5	6.7	10.9	25.4	50.7	117.9
154.0	896.3	132.0	268.8	697.3	1 505.4	3 653.2
64.8	373.0	53.9	106.6	274.1	636.4	1 472.4
72.9	420.6	66.2	138.4	361.9	678.1	1 687.2
16.3	102.6	11.9	23.8	61.2	190.9	493.7
31.3	134.5	28.3	55.6	109.5	238.6	529.5
15.9	70.9	14.4	27.8	56.9	123.0	273.8
9.4	36.5	8.5	17.2	29.8	71.1	144.9
3.3	11.6	3.0	5.9	9.8	18.4	32.0
2.7	15.5	2.4	4.7	13.0	26.1	78.8
82.6	401.2	71.3	141.6	302.5	750.3	1 548.8
12.2	61.9	10.3	21.7	47.1	135.6	344.2
70.4	339.3	61.0	119.9	255.4	614.8	1 204.6
425.3	2 258.3	357.5	715.7	1 653.7	4 169.5	7 749.8
297.8	1 456.1	257.3	513.1	1 101.0	2 649.5	5 111.0
157.4	738.1	139.7	283.9	582.8	1 322.0	2 438.9
75.2	376.2	64.8	125.9	287.0	670.3	1 266.4
31.0	155.5	25.8	50.3	109.6	291.3	605.3
31.2	171.5	24.4	47.8	110.7	335.5	745.1
3.0	14.8	2.6	5.2	10.9	30.4	55.3
35.2	225.0	28.0	57.2	160.9	478.1	781.2
8.2	46.4	6.9	14.3	35.6	88.8	158.3
27.0	178.5	21.1	42.9	125.3	389.3	622.9
22.6	132.2	17.5	36.3	89.2	233.6	421.2

Table 9.2

		1967		
			Establishments*	
		Com-panies*	Total	With 20 employees or more
Code	Industry group and industry	(number)	(number)	(number)
254	Partitions and fixtures	1 947	1 970	526
2541	Wood partitions and fixtures	1 463	1 470	338
2542	Metal partitions and fixtures	491	500	188
259	Misc. Furniture and fixtures	898	929	180
2591	Venetian blinds and shades	581	605	61
2599	Furniture and fixtures, nec**	317	324	119
26	Paper and allied products	3 913	5 890	3 813
2611	Pulpmills	45	61	43
2621	Papermills, except building paper	203	354	313
2631	Paperboard mills	148	283	264
264	Misc. Converted paper products	2 030	2 492	1 284
2641	Paper coating and glazing	334	397	202
2642	Envolopes	172	228	163
2643	Bags, except textile bags	466	557	310
2644	Wallpaper	74	77	31
2645	Die-cut paper and board	368	440	189
2646	Pressed and molded pulp goods	43	58	45
2647	Sanitary paper products	91	125	86
2649	Converted paper products, nec**	566	610	258
265	Paperboard containers and boxes	1 681	2 606	1 835
2651	Folding paperboard boxes	476	569	393
2652	Setup paperboard boxes	418	454	295
2653	Corrugated and solid fiber boxes	568	1 071	803
2654	Sanitary food containers	144	244	184
2655	Fiber cans, drums, related material	165	268	160
2661	Building paper and board mills	43	94	74
27	Printing and publishing	36 431	37 989	8 035
2711	Newspapers	7 589	8 094	2 029
2721	Periodicals	2 430	2 510	454

(Continued)

All Employees		Production workers		Wages	Value added by manufacture	Value of shipments
Number	Payroll	Number	Man-hours			
(1,000)	(million dollars)	(1,000)	(millions)	(million dollars)	(million dollars)	(million dollars)
48.0	323.6	37.6	76.0	220.1	587.0	1 010.7
25.3	170.7	20.7	40.9	124.1	284.6	498.6
22.7	152.9	17.0	35.1	96.0	302.5	512.0
21.6	121.4	17.0	33.0	82.5	221.2	425.7
11.6	62.1	8.6	15.9	37.7	122.3	246.8
10.1	59.4	8.4	17.2	44.8	98.9	179.0
638.9	4 436.2	507.7	1 071.2	3 205.5	9 756.3	20 969.9
15.1	125.6	12.2	25.4	96.0	333.7	730.5
140.0	1 120.7	112.3	249.2	849.2	2 356.3	4 844.0
67.0	533.5	53.8	118.2	405.9	1 508.8	2 907.0
186.6	1 187.4	146.8	298.8	819.1	2 833.3	6 210.1
37.1	260.8	27.0	56.4	165.6	728.0	1 566.5
22.5	141.9	18.1	37.6	98.0	253.1	470.3
46.3	278.3	37.1	75.6	197.4	563.7	1 375.6
2.3	14.6	1.8	3.6	9.9	27.0	48.6
18.6	117.3	14.7	29.4	79.9	247.3	577.5
6.7	44.8	5.4	11.4	33.0	97.8	145.9
22.0	154.2	18.3	37.6	119.2	540.2	1 293.4
31.1	175.5	24.4	47.2	116.2	376.1	732.2
218.6	1 386.5	172.6	358.2	967.9	2 540.5	5 937.3
49.3	322.6	39.5	82.1	228.8	563.2	1 216.2
21.1	100.4	18.3	35.4	73.3	160.2	282.4
97.1	656.0	73.0	152.5	435.0	1 130.0	2 959.6
35.3	213.8	28.5	60.2	157.8	506.1	1 093.9
15.7	93.7	13.3	27.9	72.9	181.1	385.2
11.7	82.5	10.0	21.5	67.4	183.7	341.1
1 031.0	7 151.5	631.6	1 196.1	4 011.3	14 355.1	21 738.4
335.9	2 223.7	169.2	302.0	1 121.5	4 184.7	5 757.1
79.1	633.7	14.5	25.2	80.5	1 868.7	3 095.9

Applied OR/SA

Table 9.2

		1967		
			Establishments*	
Code	Industry group and industry	Com-panies*	Total	With 20 employees or more
		(number)	(number)	(number)
273	Books	1 673	1 766	603
2731	Book publishing	963	1 022	287
2732	Book printing	720	744	316
2741	Miscellaneous publishing	1 433	1 493	204
275	Commercial printing	19 162	19 497	3 216
2751	Commerical printing, exc. litho	11 955	12 098	1 439
2752	Commerical printing, lithographic	6 718	6 822	1 648
2753	Engraving and plate printing	569	577	129
2761	Manifold business forms	454	542	295
2771	Greeting card publishing	203	222	92
278	Blankbooks and bookbinding	1 409	1 462	527
2782	Blankbooks and looseleaf binders	402	444	193
2789	Bookbinding and related work	1 008	1 018	334
279	Printing trade services	2 366	2 403	615
2791	Typesetting	1 518	1 535	365
2793	Photoengraving	732	735	193
2794	Electrotyping and stereotyping	124	133	57

* An establishment is a single physical location at which business is conducted. An establishment is not necessarily identical with the "company" or "enterprise" which may consist of one or more establishments.
** nec: not elsewhere classified.

(Continued)

All Employees		Production workers		Wages	Value added by manufacture	Value of shipments
Number	Payroll	Number	Man-hours			
(1,000)	(million dollars)	(1,000)	(millions)	(million dollars)	(million dollars)	(million dollars)
96.5	688.0	49.9	98.1	304.5	1 967.4	2 922.1
51.8	390.1	13.2	24.7	76.6	1 456.5	2 134.7
44.7	297.9	36.7	73.4	227.9	510.9	787.4
31.1	197.4	15.0	25.6	79.7	417.5	605.3
330.6	2 357.9	261.8	511.1	1 689.3	3 944.4	6 532.8
175.1	1 186.0	142.3	273.2	880.1	1 947.9	3 255.5
146.5	1 113.2	112.2	223.3	766.5	1 897.7	3 139.4
9.0	58.7	7.3	14.6	42.7	98.8	137.9
34.4	240.2	25.3	51.4	158.9	550.5	932.3
27.6	150.6	16.4	31.3	75.0	372.3	517.9
53.5	294.2	46.6	88.7	225.6	506.0	721.9
23.2	130.3	19.4	38.4	94.5	245.4	381.3
30.3	163.9	27.2	50.3	131.0	260.6	340.6
42.2	365.8	32.9	62.7	276.4	543.7	653.1
25.5	208.3	20.9	40.2	164.1	304.3	356.7
13.2	126.2	9.4	17.5	89.8	191.7	234.3
3.6	31.3	2.6	5.0	22.5	47.7	62.0

The SIC has a seven-digit code for the product. There were 7 000 product items in the 1964 census and in the 1967 census which is the current basis of classification.

In addition to the seven-digit code, there is an eighth digit that is inserted to provide a check in computer processing. Its purpose is to ensure the accuracy of the seven-digit code by signalling any error in coding so that the error may be corrected before the data are processed. There is a numerical list, as well as an alphabetical list, of the products; a page from the former is reproduced as Table 9.1. In order to qualify for a "line" in the *Census of Manufactures,* the minimum requirement is approximately 5 000 000 units or

$5 000 000 worth of sales of the particular product in the year in which the census is taken.

4.2. The Census Publications

The results of the census of manufactures now carried out in the years ending with 2 and 7 are made available in three principal volumes:

Volume I: Summary and Subject Statistics,
Volume II: Industry Statistics,
Volume III: Area Statistics.

In Volume I, the manufacturing establishments are reported in terms of: (1) size of establishments; (2) type of organization; (3) manufacturers' inventories; (4) expenditures for new plant and new equipment; (5) materials consumed; and (6) water used in manufacturing.

In Volume II, the industrial statistics are reported for major groups 19–39, and in Volume III, the data are shown by states, Standard Metropolitan Statistical Areas (SMSA), counties, seleceted cities and industry groups and industry.

In Table 9.2, the general statistics are shown from Volume I for major groups 24–27. In Fig. 9.2 the map of the United States is shown with the SMSAs identified as they are enforced at present.

4.3. Updating of Data by SMSA

The notion of the SMSA is a particularly significant one from the point of view of the identification of sales potential. For use by a particular company, interested primarily in a yardstick against which to assess how well the company is doing with respect to what it could be doing, the information by the states would generally be too gross a figure to serve the purpose; and the information by counties may not be realistic enough to reflect the potential market for the product(s). The notion of the SMSA fills the particular need of the business community by identifying a unit of population in terms of its contiguous economic operations cutting across political boundaries, such as those of county and state.

Even the SMSAs, like the political/administrative divisions of county and state, tend to remain static; therefore, market research firms have elaborated

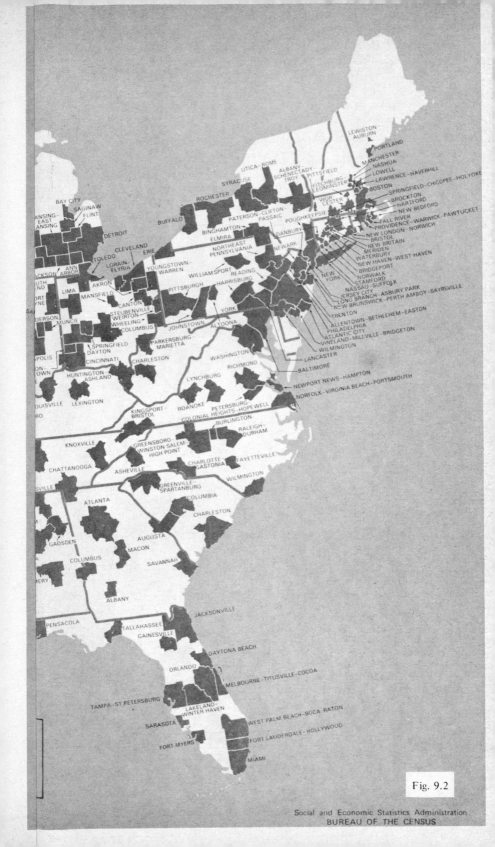

LEWISTON–AUBURN
PORTLAND
MANCHESTER
NASHUA
LOWELL
LAWRENCE–HAVERHILL
PITTSFIELD
FITCHBURG–LEOMINSTER
BOSTON
SPRINGFIELD–CHICOPEE–HOLYOKE
BROCKTON
HARTFORD
NEW BEDFORD
FALL RIVER
PROVIDENCE–WARWICK–PAWTUCKET
NEW LONDON–NORWICH
BRISTOL
NEW BRITAIN
MERIDEN
WATERBURY
NEW HAVEN–WEST HAVEN
BRIDGEPORT
NORWALK
STAMFORD
NASSAU–SUFFOLK
JERSEY CITY
LONG BRANCH–ASBURY PARK
NEW BRUNSWICK–PERTH AMBOY–SAYREVILLE
TRENTON
ALLENTOWN–BETHLEHEM–EASTON
PHILADELPHIA
ATLANTIC CITY
VINELAND–MILLVILLE–BRIDGETON
WILMINGTON
LANCASTER
BALTIMORE
NEWPORT NEWS–HAMPTON
NORFOLK–VIRGINIA BEACH–PORTSMOUTH

UTICA–ROME
SYRACUSE
ALBANY–SCHENECTADY–TROY
ROCHESTER
PATERSON–CLIFTON–PASSAIC
POUGHKEEPSIE
BUFFALO
BINGHAMTON
ELMIRA
DANBURY
NORTHEAST PENNSYLVANIA
NEWARK
WILLIAMSPORT
READING
NEW YORK
PITTSBURGH
HARRISBURG
JOHNSTOWN
ALTOONA
YORK
PARKERSBURG–MARIETTA
WASHINGTON
CHARLESTON
RICHMOND
LYNCHBURG
HUNTINGTON–ASHLAND
LEXINGTON
KINGSPORT–BRISTOL
ROANOKE
PETERSBURG–COLONIAL HEIGHTS–HOPEWELL
KNOXVILLE
BURLINGTON
RALEIGH–DURHAM
CHATTANOOGA
GREENSBORO–WINSTON SALEM–HIGH POINT
FAYETTEVILLE
ASHEVILLE
CHARLOTTE–GASTONIA
WILMINGTON
GREENVILLE–SPARTANBURG
ATLANTA
COLUMBIA
CHARLESTON
GADSDEN
AUGUSTA
COLUMBUS
MACON
SAVANNAH
ALBANY
JACKSONVILLE
PENSACOLA
TALLAHASSEE
GAINESVILLE
DAYTONA BEACH
ORLANDO
MELBOURNE–TITUSVILLE–COCOA
TAMPA–ST PETERSBURG
LAKELAND–WINTER HAVEN
SARASOTA
WEST PALM BEACH–BOCA RATON
FORT MYERS
FORT LAUDERDALE–HOLLYWOOD
MIAMI

BAY CITY
SAGINAW
LANSING–EAST LANSING
FLINT
DETROIT
CLEVELAND
TOLEDO
ERIE
LORAIN–ELYRIA
ANN ARBOR
JACKSON
AKRON
YOUNGSTOWN–WARREN
SOUTH BEND
LIMA
MANSFIELD
FORT WAYNE
CANTON
STEUBENVILLE–WEIRTON
ANDERSON
MUNCIE
WHEELING
COLUMBUS
SPRINGFIELD
DAYTON
INDIANAPOLIS
CINCINNATI
YOUNGSTOWN
LOUISVILLE

Fig. 9.2

Social and Economic Statistics Administration
BUREAU OF THE CENSUS

upon the U.S. classification of SMSA. The publication, *Sales Management* updates the SMSA classification in the light of annual data on population, income, employment, and spending. Therefore, the count of SMSAs in *Sales Management* tends to be higher than the government classification because they propose "potential SMSA" on the basis of the annual figures.

4.4. Annual Survey of Manufactures

One of the sources that updates data by SMSA is the Annual Survey of Manufactures, initiated in 1949, and conducted for years not covered by the Census of Manufactures. It provides data on employment, payroll, manhours, value added by manufactures for geographic divisions, states, and SMSAs:

> The survey currently covers approximately 65 000 plants out of a total of about 300 000. Included in the sample are all large manufacturing plants, which account for more than two-thirds of total employment of all manufacturing establishments in the United States, and a sample of the more numerous medium- and small-sized establishments. [3]

4.5. Key Plant Data

There are about 300 000 plants in the United States, and insofar as the sales of products depend upon their manufacture in these plants, it would be most valuable to business interests to know the plants by SIC classification. The publishers of *Sales Management* who publish data by SMSAs also publish the identity of the plants, their address, and their respective number of employees by SIC code. The total number of plants identified in the 1970 publication includes 41 000 "key plants" with 100 or more employees, both the book and the entire deck of cards on the 41 000 plants being available for purchase. Notice how the SIC numbers in the excerpt from *Market Statistics: Key Plants 1970-71*, shown as Table 9.3, correspond to those in Table 9.2.

4.6. Key Company Data

One of the several industries which appears in Table 9.2 is Industry 2515:

---

[3] Bureau of the Census, *Catalogue 1971*, U.S. Department of Commerce, Washington, D.C., Part I Publications, p. 65.

Table 9.3

Market statistics: key plants 1970–1971

State	County code	Plant name	Address	Zip code	Employ't thous.
2519		**HOUSEHOLD FURNITURE NEC**			
ARK	131	Arkansas Best Corp-Twin Rivers Fur		72901	.1
CAL	037	Aeon Industries Inc Pride Prod Div		90209	.3
CAL	037	Finkel Outdoor Prods of California		90023	.1
KY	067	Vogue Rattan Mfg Co Inc		40505	.1
MO	105	Independent Stave Co		65536	.3
OHI	061	Ficks Reed Co		45227	.3
TEX	113	Interlake Steel-Falcon Mfg Co Inc		75006	.2
2521		**WOOD OFFICE FURNITURE**			
CAL	037	Hiebert Inc	23606 Telo Ave Torrance	905095	.1
CAL	037	Brown Saltman Co	15000 S Figuerrou Gardena	90247	.1
CON	003	Dettenborn L F Woodworking Co	337 Sheldon St Hartford	06106	.2
FLA	025	Simkins Industries-Benner Box Div	N W 28th St & Simkins Miami	33147	.3
FLA	079	Madison House-Furniture	Madison	32340	.1
ILL	031	Vertiflex Co	630 W 41st St Chicago	60609	.2
ILL	031	Interior Crafts Inc	2513 W Cullerton Ave Chicago	60608	.2
ILL	201	Rockford National Furniture Co	2400 Kishwaukee St Rockford	61108	.1
IND	037	Jasper Desk Co	501 East 6th Street Jasper	46546	.2
IND	037	Jasper Seating Co	932 Mill Street Jasper	47546	.1
IND	037	Jasper Office Furniture Co	402 East 13th Street Jasper	47546	.1
IND	037	United Manufacturing Co	Box 190 Jasper	47546	.1
IND	037	Hoosier Desk Co	310 S Mill St Jasper	47546	.1
IND	037	Indiana Desk Co Inc	1226 N Mill St Jasper	47546	.1
IND	037	Jasper Chair Co	Box 311 Jasper	47546	.1
IND	163	Imperial Desk Co Inc	1312 W Florida St Evansville	47707	.1

Mattresses and Bedsprings. From Table 9.2 it is seen that there were 939 companies in the industry in 1967 with 31 200 employees and a payroll of $171.5 million. The value of the shipments by the industry is $745.1 million. As one of the 939 companies, are you performing as well as could be expected? Knowing nothing else, one could take a stab at what one's shipment "ought" to be by simply dividing $745.1 million into 939, giving approximately $739 400. However, averages imply "above average" and "below average". Therefore, the mere fact that your shipment is say $800 000, does not give much cause for comfort.

On the other hand, suppose that the share of the market of some of the 939 companies were known. That would provide a yardstick with which to compare your own performance. For instance, is your performance closer to the highest or lowest or middle group of companies in your industry? If not in the highest group, should you try to be, and if so, how?

Fortunately, such a yardstick is indeed available. It is published in the Bureau of the Census publication, *Concentration Ratios in Manufacturing*:

> Information on the shipments of approximately 1 200 classes of products and the proportion accounted for by the 4, 8, 20, and 50 largest companies manufacturing each class of product. Data are given for 1967, with comparative statistics for 1963, 1958, and 1954. [4]

A page out of the *Concentration Ratios* is reproduced as Table 9.4. It is found that in the Mattresses and Bedsprings Industry, the four largest companies accounted for 26 percent of the 1967 shipments; the remaining 935 sharing 74 percent of the 1967 shipments. The eight largest companies accounted for 34 percent of the shipments. Or, the 5th, 6th, 7th, and 8th largest companies each shipped an average of 2.0 percent of the industry shipments compared with an average of 6.5 percent of the industry shipments by the 1st, 2nd, 3rd, and 4th largest companies. The next twelve largest companies, viz., 9th through 20th, each average 0.83 percent. The average share of the next thirty largest companies, viz., 21st through 50th, is even smaller at 0.47 percent.

On the basis of these concentration ratios, if one were in the group of

---

[4]. Bureau of the Census, 1971 Census of Manufactures, *Concentration Ratios in Manufacturing*, Part II: Product Class Concentration Ratios, U.S. Department of Commerce, Washington, D.C. 1971, pp. 61–62.

the 21st to the 50th largest companies, the yardstick would be the average share of the shipment, viz., 0.47 percent of $745.1 million or $3.5 million. Of course, the $3.5 million is an average figure. Therefore, the higher ranking companies in the lowest group of 21st through 50th may be closer to the average of the 9th through 20th largest companies, or 0.83 percent representing $6.2 million.

4.7. Key Financial Data

It is one thing to arrive at a yardstick to compare one's performance in shipment (sales) with that of one's industry; it is quite another *to know how profitable* the performance is.

If sales figures are closely held by the companies, profit figures are even more so. However, corporations are required to file U.S. Corporation Income Tax Form 1120. The Federal Trade Commission and the Securities and Exchange Commission have published Quarterly Financial Reports for Manufacturing Corporations since 1947 based on a sample representing about 88 percent of a composite frame. The component parts of the sample frame are the Internal Revenue Service Form 1120 returns and the Social Security Administration applications for Employer Identification Number. The sample covers the companies accounting for the bulk of the corporate assets — the 9 500-10 500 manufacturing companies included in the Quarterly sample accounting for approximately 88 percent. In the second quarter in 1971, the 9665 manufacturing companies included in the sample had corporate assets of $584 253 000 000.

The *Quarterly Financial Report for Manufacturing Corporations* publishes 10 tables. They are:

Table 1: Rates of Change in Sales and Profits by Industry.
Table 2: Profits per Dollar by Sales by Industry.
Table 3: Profits per Dollar by Asset Size and Industry Group.
Table 4: Annual Rates of Profit on Stockholder's Equity by Industry.
Table 5: Annual Rates of Profit on Stockholder's Equity by Industry Asset Size and Industry Group.
Table 6: Financial Statements in Ratio Form by Industry.
Table 7: Financial Statements in Ratio Form by Asset Size and Industry Group.
Table 8: Financial Statements in Dollar Amounts by Industry.
Table 9: Financial Statements in Dollar Amounts by Asset Size and Industry Group.
Table 10: Composition of the Sample by Total Assets.

Percent of selected statistics accounted for by the 4, 8, 20 and 50 larg

Item	Number of		Value of shipments	All employees	
	Com-panies	Estab-lishments		Number	Payroll
	(a)	(b)	(c)	(d)	(e)

Industry 2515 — Mattresses and bedsprings

Item	(a)	(b)	(c)	(d)	(e)
Total (columns c, e, g, h to m in millions d and f in thousands)	939	1,013	$745.1	31.2	$171.5
Percent of above totals accounted for by					
4 largest companies	(x)	3	26	26	28
8 largest companies	(x)	5	34	33	36
20 largest companies	(x)	8	44	44	47
50 largest companies	(x)	12	58	55	58

Industry 2519 — Household furniture, N.E.C.

Item	(a)	(b)	(c)	(d)	(e)
Total (columns c, e, g, h to m in millions d and f in thousands)	75	79	$55.3	3.0	$14.8
Percent of above totals accounted for by					
4 largest companies	(x)	8	36	26	29
8 largest companies	(x)	13	53	47	49
20 largest companies	(x)	29	82	74	75
50 largest companies	(x)	68	98	98	98

Industry 2521 — Wood office furniture

Item	(a)	(b)	(c)	(d)	(e)
Total (columns c, e, g, h to m in millions d and f in thousands)	172	178	$158.3	8.2	$46.4
Percent of above totals accounted for by					
4 largest companies	(x)	4	29	23	24
8 largest companies	(x)	8	48	42	44
20 largest companies	(x)	15	71	68	68
50 largest companies	(x)	32	88	87	87

4

ompanies ranked on value of shipments in each industry: 1967

roduction workers			Value added by manufacture	Capital expenditures, new			Cost of materials
umber	Man-hours	Wages		Total	Structures and additions to plant	Machinery and equipment	
)	(g)	(h)	(i)	(j)	(k)	(l)	(m)
dustry 2515 — Mattresses and bedsprings							
4.4	47.8	$110.7	$335.5	$10.3	$4.3	$6.0	$408.8
	25	31	30	22	21	23	23
2	32	39	37	29	24	31	30
3	44	48	47	43	40	45	42
3	54	58	60	58	58	59	55
dustry 2519 — Household furniture, N.E.C.							
6	5.2	$10.9	$30.4	$1.3	$0.7	$0.6	$24.7
	28	29	35	10	(D)	(D)	36
	48	48	51	81	(D)	(D)	54
	75	75	80	94	(D)	(D)	83
7	98	98	98	99-	99-	99-	98
dustry 2521 — Wood office furniture							
9	14.3	$35.6	$88.8	$5.7	$2.8	$2.9	$71.7
	24	23	26	45	46	45	33
	42	42	46	70	68	72	52
3	69	67	68	89	93	85	74
	87	87	88	94	95	94	90

Tabl

	Number of		Value of shipments	All employees	
	Com-panies	Estab-lishments		Number	Payr
	(a)	(b)	(c)	(d)	(e)

Industry 2522 — Metal office furniture

Total (columns c, e, g, h to m in millions d and f in thousands)	166	187	$622.9	27.0	$17
Percent of above totals accounted for by					
4 largest companies	(x)	7	38	31	37
8 largest companies	(x)	11	52	47	52
20 largest companies	(x)	20	75	71	75
50 largest companies	(x)	38	92	88	91

Industry 2531 — Public building furniture

Total (columns c, e, g, h to m in millions d and f in thousands)	428	438	$421.2	22.6	$13
Percent of above totals accounted for by					
4 largest companies	(x)	1	23	21	27
8 largest companies	(x)	3	36	31	37
20 largest companies	(x)	7	54	49	54
50 largest companies	(x)	14	72	67	70

Industry 2541 — Wood partitions and fixtures

Total (columns c, e, g, h to m in millions d and f in thousands)	1,463	1,470	$498.6	25.3	$17
Percent of above totals accounted for by					
4 largest companies	(x)	(Z)	6	4	5
8 largest companies	(x)	1	10	8	9
20 largest companies	(x)	2	20	16	17
50 largest companies	(x)	4	36	31	33

(Z)   Less than half of 1 percent.
—   Represents zero.
(D)   Withheld to avoid disclosing figures of individual companies.
(x)   Not applicable.
r   Revised.

ontinued)

oduction workers			Value added by manufacture	Capital expenditures, new			Cost of materials
ımber	Man-hours	Wages		Total	Structures and additions to plant	Machinery and equipment	
	(g)	(h)	(i)	(j)	(k)	(l)	(m)

lustry 2522 – Metal office furniture

.1	42.9	$125.3	$389.3	$31.5	$15.9	$15.6	$239.5
	31	37	37	26	28	25	38
	48	54	53	74	79	69	51
	71	75	76	84	85	83	73
	88	91	93	94	94	94	91

lustry 2531 – Public building furniture

,5	36.3	$89.2	$233.6	$10.0	$4.4	$5.6	$194.7
	18	25	26	18	13	22	21
	28	34	38	29	28	30	34
	47	52	56	48	43	53	53
	66	68	73	68	65	69	72

lustry 2541 – Wood partitions and fixtures

,7	40.9	$124.1	$284.6	$8.1	$3.8	$4.3	$214.8
	4	6	7	8	11	5	5
	8	9	10	(D)	(D)	(D)	10
	15	17	20	28	37	21	20
	32	32	35	51	61	43	37

N.E.C.   Not Elsewhere Classified.
N.S.K.   Not Specified by Kind.

Furniture and Fixtures

	2Q 1970	3Q 1970	4Q 1970	1Q 1971	2Q 197
INCOME	(percent of sales)				
Sales (net of returns, allowances, and discounts)	100.0	100.0	100.0	100.0	100.
Deduct: Costs and expenses (net of purchase discounts)	95.1	94.5	95.0	96.0	93.
Net profit from operations	4.9	5.5	5.0	4.0	6
Add: Other income or deductions (net)	−0.1	−0.2	−0.1	0.0	−0
Net profit before Federal income taxes	4.9	5.3	4.9	3.9	6
Deduct: Provision for Federal income taxes	2.5	2.4	2.5	2.2	2
Net profit after taxes	2.4	2.9	2.4	1.7	3
Depreciation and depletion included above, including accelerated amortization of emergency facilities	1.8	1.7	1.8	1.9	1
ASSESTS	(percent of total assests)				
Cash on hand and in bank	5.7	6.3	6.7	6.4	6
U.S. Government securities, including Treasury savings notes	1.7	1.5	1.8	1.7	1
Total cash and U.S. Government securities	7.4	7.8	8.5	8.0	7
Receivables from U.S. Government, excluding tax credits	0.4	0.2	0.1	0.2	0
Other notes and accounts receivable (net)	24.9	26.1	25.4	24.6	24
Total receivables	25.2	26.3	25.5	24.8	24
Inventories	31.9	30.3	29.2	29.6	29
Other current assests	3.0	3.1	3.0	3.4	3
Total current assests	67.5	67.4	66.2	65.9	64
Property, plant and equipment	50.6	50.9	51.7	52.9	53
Deduct: Reserve for depreciation and depletion	23.6	23.8	23.7	24.5	24
Total property, plant and equipment (net)	26.9	27.0	28.0	28.4	28
Other noncurrent assets	5.6	5.5	5.8	5.7	6
Total assets	100.0	100.0	100.0	100.0	100

nufacturing corporations by industry

mber and Wood Products, cept Furniture					Instruments and Related Products					Miscellaneous Manufacturing, and Ordnance				
3Q	4Q	1Q	2Q	2Q	3Q	4Q	1Q	2Q	2Q	3Q	4Q	1Q	2Q
70	1970	1970	1971	1971	1970	1970	1970	1971	1971	1970	1970	1970	1971	1971
rcent of sales)					(percent of sales)					(percent of sales)				
).0	100.0	100.0	100.0	100.0	100.0	100.0	100.0	100.0	100.0	100.0	100.0	100.0	100.0	100.0
.8	94.9	96.4	94.8	92.7	85.9	85.2	86.1	88.4	85.9	93.5	93.4	92.8	93.7	92.4
5.2	5.1	3.6	5.2	7.3	14.1	14.8	13.9	11.6	14.1	6.5	6.6	7.2	6.3	7.6
).3	−0.2	−0.2	−0.3	0.0	−0.3	−0.6	−0.5	−0.5	−0.4	0.0	−0.3	−0.2	0.0	−0.5
.9	4.9	3.4	4.8	7.3	13.8	14.2	13.4	11.1	13.6	6.5	6.3	6.9	6.2	7.1
2.1	2.1	1.6	1.8	2.6	6.6	6.6	5.8	5.4	6.2	3.0	2.8	3.1	2.9	3.3
2.9	2.8	1.8	3.0	4.7	7.2	7.6	7.6	5.7	7.4	3.5	3.6	3.8	3.3	3.3
.3	4.2	4.5	4.6	4.5	4.5	4.4	4.9	5.6	5.3	2.0	2.0	2.1	2.3	2.3
rcent of total assests)					(percent of total assests)					(percent of total assests)				
.0	4.0	4.1	4.0	4.2	4.2	4.7	5.2	5.4	4.4	5.3	5.7	6.5	5.5	5.9
.3	0.4	0.4	0.3	0.2	1.8	1.8	2.1	1.7	1.6	0.4	0.2	0.4	0.3	0.3
.3	4.4	4.5	4.3	4.4	6.0	6.4	7.3	7.1	6.0	5.8	5.9	6.8	5.8	5.2
.0	0.0	0.0	0.0	0.0	1.3	0.9	1.1	1.3	1.3	0.3	0.3	0.4	0.4	0.3
.0	13.9	12.7	13.8	13.8	20.1	20.9	19.4	18.4	19.1	27.1	28.8	27.7	25.9	26.3
.0	13.9	12.7	13.9	13.8	21.3	21.8	20.5	19.7	20.4	27.4	29.1	28.1	28.3	26.3
.5	19.5	19.2	19.1	18.6	26.4	25.7	24.2	24.0	24.2	30.4	29.3	28.9	30.5	30.4
.1	3.2	2.9	3.4	4.3	5.8	5.8	5.8	6.2	5.6	2.7	2.6	2.5	2.6	2.9
.0	41.0	39.3	40.7	41.0	59.6	59.8	57.8	57.0	56.2	66.4	66.9	66.3	65.1	66.9
.7	79.2	81.6	80.2	79.7	61.5	61.6	65.3	66.9	68.2	45.1	44.8	46.8	47.1	46.7
.2	29.8	30.5	30.4	30.5	27.0	27.2	29.0	30.0	30.8	21.0	21.2	21.9	22.5	22.2
.5	49.4	51.2	49.8	49.2	34.5	34.4	36.2	36.9	37.4	24.0	23.6	24.4	24.5	24.6
.5	9.6	9.6	9.4	9.7	5.9	5.8	6.0	6.1	6.4	9.6	9.6	9.2	10.2	9.1
.0	100.0	100.0	100.0	100.0	100.0	100.0	100.0	100.0	100.0	100.0	100.0	100.0	100.0	100.0

Furniture and Fixtures

	2Q 1970	3Q 1970	4Q 1970	1Q 1971	2Q 197
LIABILITIES AND STOCKHOLDERS' EQUITY					
Short-term loans from banks (original maturity of 1 year or less)	5.7	5.5	5.2	5.1	4
Advances and prepayments by U.S. Government	0.0	0.0	0.0	0.0	0
Trade accounts and notes payable	10.5	10.7	10.0	9.4	9
Federal income taxes accrued	1.5	1.7	1.6	1.6	1
Installments, due in 1 year or less, on long-term debt					
(a) Loans from banks	1.2	1.0	0.7	0.8	0
(b) Other long-term debt	1.1	1.0	1.0	1.1	1
Other current liabilities	5.9	6.0	6.0	6.0	5
Total current liabilities	25.9	26.0	24.6	23.9	22
Long-term debt due in more than 1 year (a) Loans from banks	3.5	3.4	3.1	3.1	3
(b) Other long-term debt	8.7	8.5	8.9	9.4	9
Other noncurrent liabilities	1.0	1.1	0.9	0.9	1
Total liabilities	39.1	39.1	37.5	37.3	36
Reserves not reflected elsewhere	—	—	—	—	—
Capital stock, capital surplus, and minority interest	18.4	18.4	19.0	18.8	19
Earned surplus and surplus reserves	42.4	42.5	43.5	43.9	44
Total stockholders' equity	60.9	60.9	62.4	62.7	63
Total liabilities and stockholders' equity	100.0	100.0	100.0	100.0	100
(percent)					
OPERATING RATIOS					
Annual rate of profit on stockholders' equity at end of period —					
Before Federal income taxes	15.4	17.0	15.8	11.4	19
After taxes	7.6	9.2	7.8	4.9	10
(times)					
Current assets to current liabilities	2.60	2.59	2.69	2.76	2.
Total cash and U.S. Government securities to total current liabilities	.28	.30	.34	.34	.
Total stockholder's equity to debt	3.02	3.12	3.30	3.22	3.

ontinued)

nufacturing corporations by industry

	mber and Wood Products, cept Furniture				Instruments and Related Products					Miscellaneous Manufacturing, and Ordnance				
70	3Q 1970	4Q 1970	1Q 1971	2Q 1971	2Q 1970	3Q 1970	4Q 1970	1Q 1971	2Q 1971	2Q 1970	3Q 1970	4Q 1970	1Q 1971	2Q 1971
4.8	4.5	3.7	3.7	3.4	5.7	5.5	5.2	5.2	5.3	11.1	12.3	10.5	9.2	11.0
0.0	0.0	0.0	0.1	0.1	0.6	0.5	0.4	0.4	0.4	0.0	0.0	0.0	0.0	0.0
6.7	7.1	6.5	6.3	6.3	5.3	5.6	6.0	5.5	5.4	10.3	10.4	10.7	9.5	9.1
1.2	1.1	1.1	1.1	1.0	3.5	3.7	3.3	4.0	3.2	1.9	2.2	2.5	2.7	2.2
1.5	1.4	1.6	1.5	1.6	0.6	0.6	0.6	0.7	0.6	0.6	0.5	0.6	0.6	0.5
1.4	1.4	1.5	1.3	1.3	0.6	0.5	0.9	1.0	1.0	1.2	1.2	1.4	1.4	1.2
5.8	6.5	5.2	6.2	6.1	8.0	8.2	8.6	8.0	8.0	6.3	6.1	6.4	6.9	6.4
1.5	22.1	19.6	20.2	19.8	24.3	24.6	25.1	24.7	24.0	31.4	32.5	32.1	30.3	30.5
5.4	6.2	6.2	7.2	7.0	3.4	3.5	2.0	1.7	2.3	2.3	2.1	2.9	3.2	3.6
9.7	19.3	21.9	20.6	21.9	8.5	8.5	11.2	10.9	10.2	12.1	12.2	12.2	11.9	11.9
2.5	2.5	2.6	2.1	2.2	2.9	3.0	3.2	3.4	3.3	1.7	1.9	1.8	1.8	2.3
0.1	50.2	50.3	50.1	51.0	39.1	39.5	41.6	40.8	39.9	47.6	48.8	49.0	47.1	48.3
—	—	—	—	—	—	—	—	—	—	—	—	—	—	—
0.6	20.2	20.8	21.6	20.9	20.8	19.8	19.6	20.0	20.2	18.3	18.2	18.6	18.7	18.2
9.3	29.6	28.9	28.3	28.2	40.1	40.7	38.8	39.2	39.9	34.1	32.9	32.4	34.1	33.5
9.9	49.8	49.7	49.9	49.0	60.9	60.5	58.4	59.2	60.2	52.4	51.2	51.0	52.9	51.7
0.0	100.0	100.0	100.0	100.0	100.0	100.0	100.0	100.0	100.0	100.0	100.0	100.0	100.0	100.0
rcent)					(percent)					(percent)				
2.3	12.2	8.1	10.8	19.3	26.5	27.5	27.4	19.9	26.0	19.3	18.8	21.3	16.2	19.7
7.1	7.1	4.3	6.7	12.4	13.9	14.8	15.5	10.2	14.2	10.3	10.7	11.7	8.6	10.6
nes)					(times)					(times)				
90	1.85	2.01	2.02	2.08	2.45	2.43	2.30	2.31	2.34	2.11	2.05	2.07	2.15	2.17
20	.20	.23	.21	.22	.25	.26	.29	.29	.25	.18	.18	.21	.19	.20
48	1.52	1.43	1.45	1.39	3.24	3.28	2.92	3.05	3.09	1.91	1.81	1.85	2.01	1.83

A portion of one of the tables is reproduced as Table 9.5. The first column gives the data for Furniture and Fixtures. Industry 2515: Mattresses and Bedsprings whose shipments were discussed in the previous Section is part of the Major Industry Group 25: Furnitures and Fixtures. Its breakdown, as shown in Table 9.2, is as follows:

		Value of Shipments
25	FURNITURE AND FIXTURES	$7 749.8
251	*Household Furniture*	5 111.0
2511	Wood Household Furniture	2 438.9
2512	Upholstered Household Furniture	1 266.4
2514	Metal Household Furniture	605.3
2515	Mattresses and Bedsprings	745.1
2519	Household Furniture, NEC	55.3
252	*Office Furniture*	781.2
2521	Wood Office Furniture	158.3
2522	Metal Office Furniture	622.9
2531	Public Building Furniture	421.2
254	*Partitions and Fixtures*	1 010.7
2541	Wood Partitions and Fixtures	498.6
2542	Metal Partitions and Fixtures	512.0
259	*Misc. Furniture and Fixtures*	425.7
2591	Venetian Blinds and Shades	246.8
2599	Furniture and Fixtures NEC	179.0

In Table 9.5, financial statements in ratio form for Major Industry Group 25: Furnitures and Fixtures is shown. In other words, the figures relate to an industry group with 1967 shipments of $7 749.8 million, of which Mattresses and Bedsprings shipments account for 9.5 percent at $745.1 million.

It is seen that the net profit after taxes increased from 2.4 percent of sales in the 2nd quarter of 1970 to 3.3. percent in the corresponding quarter of 1971. The 2nd quarter figure is even more impressive when compared with the preceding quarter — a figure of 1.7 — almost double!

In using these figures as a yardstick for the profits in Mattresses and Bedsprings, it bears repetition that Mattresses and Bedsprings is only 9.5 percent of the Major Industry Group whose net profit figures are published.

If one were contemplating investment in the most profitable industry group, Instruments and Related Products is clearly the choice from among the four groups in Table 9.5.

5. APPLICATION 20: National Data Input to Company Potentials

The national data, of shipments, financial ratios, etc., are by themselves *in*adequate to set up the organismic index of performance.

5.1. Shipment Data: Single Product Company, One Among 939

The reason why the national data do not readily lend themselves to the development of a company organismic index of performance is that if it were a single product company, say, Matresses and Bedsprings, it is only one among 939 companies engaged in the shipment of that product, as seen from Table 9.2. The key company data on shipment would be a point of departure for the potentials of the particular company under discussion, as pointed out in Section 4.6. However, the adaptation of the data on the 939 companies to the single company is neither ready nor direct.

5.2. Shipment Data: Multiproduct Company, One Among 9 518

More often than not, the company is likely to be multiproduct rather than single product. Even if Mattresses and Bedsprings were treated as a single product, the associated products which the company deals in would probably include it in the Furniture and Fixtures group, which is the Major Industry Group 25 of which the Industry Group 2515: Mattresses and Bedsprings is a component. This would mean that the company is one not among 939, but one among 9 518 companies; therefore, even using the indices of concentration discussed in Section 4.6, it would be much harder to translate the national data into an organismic index of performance for the company.

5.3. Financial Data: Multiproduct Company, One Among 9 518

Turning from the shipment data to financial data, the national data relating
to manufacturing corporations are based on a large group of companies. For
instance, the net profit after taxes, expressed as percentage of sales, applies to
the entire Furniture and Fixtures industry. Therefore, the comparison of the
net profit after taxes of the particular company with the industry figure of
2.4 percent in the second quarter of 1970, rising to the figure of 3.3 percent
in the second quarter of 1971, must be seriously qualified. Nevertheless, if
the company activity justifies including it within the Furniture and Fixtures
Group, the net profit after taxes for the 9 518 companies would be a useful
starting point.

5.4. Area Data: Company Products, Components of Amorphous Aggregates

More than the gross shipment figures for the nation as a whole, the company's
interests would be in the specific shipments to particular areas of the country.
For, the improvement in shipment(s) to the country as a whole is made up of
improvements in the shipments to the various segments of the country.

At this level, the national data tend to become less reliable. The reason is
that the shipment data are no longer for the entire line of Mattresses and
Bedsprings treated as a unit, but different kinds of mattresses and bedsprings.
In terms of the SIC numbers, the level of detail increases from 4 to 7 digits —
from 2515 to 2515115 — which introduces errors in reporting. It is not that
the figures at the 4-digit level are more accurate, but simply that the classifi-
catory errors at the lowest level are less likely to affect the overall figures at
the gross level than at the finer detail. Thus, the distinction between ortho-
pedic, regular, heavy duty, and firm mattresses would be most significant at
the 7-digit level if each of the products does, in fact, have a single product
"line". But, the errors in reporting at this level do not affect the usefulness
of the 4-digit figure for mattresses and bedsprings as a whole.

To a multiproduct company the product information made available by
Tracts for Industry (and its successors) is not likely to be very useful because
of the tendency towards error in reporting at the finest level of detail, which
is redistributed by apportioning the total figures to the different area groupings in the country. Yet, this is precisely the level at which the information is
most important to the company which wants to establish its sales potentials
and to compare them with actual shipments accomplished.

6. Custom-Tailoring of Company Potentials

The limitations of the national data when applied to individual company potentials as discussed in Section 5 does not rule out their judicious use of the national data. This may be accomplished by recognizing the two basic elements in an organismic index of performance of the company.

6.1. Two Principal Elements: (1) Sales Potentials; (2) Salesmanship

The first of the two basic elements is the sales potential in any given geographic area. Without the existence of these potentials, *external* to the company ability to realizing those potentials, no amount of effort on the part of the company would yield satisfactory results. The national data, whether by product, industry, industry group, or shipment, provides a starting point for *Element (1): Sales Potentials*.

Given the Sales Potentials, the question is: How can the potentials be realized? The end result is that the customers, through the medium of the particular company, satisfy their real and/or imagined needs. The entire process leading to this may be called "salesmanship". Included in the "salesmanship" is the direct and personal efforts of the salesmen themselves, as well as the indirect and impersonal efforts of advertising campaigns and public relations releases, both of which aim at creating a favorable disposition toward company products in the mind of the potential customer. Direct and financial inducements to purchase the products of the company, such as coupons, trading stamps, etc., are also classifiable under "salesmanship". Being internal to the company, the data on *Element (2): Salesmanship* come from *within* the company. More often than not, the internal salesmanship data are much harder to acquire than the external data on sales potentials.

7. Element (1): Sales Potentials by Territory – Data Basis

The particular company under discussion is a multiproduct, multiplant company, with 12 administrative divisions with overlapping products. The 12 divisions of the company suggest that the company may be engaged in several industries; and as such, may find itself on a nation-wide data comparison with several thousand companies, with each of which a particular set of products of each division may be effectively competing. Prior to modifying the national data to derive the *external* basis for an organismic index of performance for the company sales, attention was focused upon the *internal* basis for the projection of the company potentials.

7.1. Internal Basis: (1) Aggregation of Company Data On Past Performance

Considering the fact that the available data barely go back one full year, in spite of the company being in its 57th year of operation, the internal basis for sales potentials suggests the aggregation of the available data into suitable larger units. The purpose of such an aggregation is to develop a viable concept which does not hinge upon the accuracy of the individual elements of data.

Such a concept is that of the *region*, made up of a collection of geographically contiguous areas in which sales efforts were made in the past. It should be recalled that the company sales are through the 53 salesmen, and only through them. By devising a region as the standard of comparison for present with potential sales, the variability of individual salesmen efforts becomes less significant. Even if there are errors in the figures, and even when salesmen vary in their performance, the aggregation of the sales by the different salesmen in the same geographic area assumes that not all the figures are equally wrong all the time.

The records of bookings of company salesmen by dealers were individually aggregated for the latest year. The salesmen territories cut across state lines; therefore, adjustments were made to reflect the company bookings on a state basis. The total figure of bookings is used as the basis for dividing the United States into five regions to which the organismic index of sales performance could be applied.

By juggling the different states which are contiguous, Regions I and II are made comparable to each other. Region I represents 30.9297 percent of the total bookings, and Region II represents 30.2955 percent.

The bookings of Region III represent 15.4502 percent, which makes it almost $\frac{1}{2}$ of Region I. Since the bookings of Region II are 99.98 percent of Region I, Region III bookings may be considered as $\frac{1}{2}$ of Region II as well. Thus, there are two comparisons that are possible for each of the three Regions.

Region IV accounts for 11.7436 percent of the total bookings, and Region

V accounts for 11.5810 percent. These two Regions can be compared one against another.

The division of the United States into five Regions, two of which are equal to two others, and one of them equal to $\frac{1}{2}$ of two other Regions, provides an acceptable starting point to the management because the Regional configuration is based upon the latest available data, viz., latest year of bookings.

Having agreed upon a starting point, the question is: On what should the management peg its organismic index of performance? In the light of the scant data available from the SIC records, the company sales potentials should be related to some outside criteria.

The company's business is, by and large, wholesale, but it runs across many classifications of end users so that a functional relationship between some set of variable(s) describing the United States economy and the company bookings is hard to find.

On the other hand, by virtue of the diversity of the products manufactured and marketed, it is likely that a justifiable relationship could be established between indicators of general economic activity and company bookings.

7.2. External Basis: (1) Retail Sales Volume in Trading Centers

Reference was made in Section 4.3 to the updating of SMSA data by incorporating information from the annual census of manufactures and other national data. It was mentioned that the publication *Sales Management* not only updates the SMSA data, but also proposes the "potential SMSA" on the basis of the annual figures.

Another modification of the U.S. National data has been made in terms of the Urban Trading Centers. The Urban Trading Centers of McKinsey Company reflect two basic concepts:

1. That each major center of population in the United States serves the residents of a relatively small surrounding geographic area, and
2. that these trading center areas can be categorized into a relatively small number of classes because they have certain commercial characteristics in common that are reflected in the population and retail sales volume statistics.[5]

[5] Charles W. Smith, *Targeting Sales Efforts,* Columbia, New York, 1958.

Not all the Trading Center areas were chosen to predict company book-ings. From the Cleartype County Town U.S. Map, all points representing a population of over 100 000 were chosen as reflecting locations of the sales of the company, and the McKinsey data for the Trading Center located around and about these chosen points were studied.

The advantage in using the Trading Center method is that the 311 Urban Trading Centers listed in the McKinsey study provide the company with a definite number of points with which the sales potential for the company products could be specified for the whole state. The data relating to *selected* places with over 100 000 population in the State are aggregated to give an estimate for the percent of the United States retail sales volume in that particular State. Thus, in one region, the State of Connecticut is represented by three places with over 100 000 population each: Hartford, Bridgeport, and New Haven—Waterbury.

According to the McKinsey classification, Hartford is the 41st market in order of importance in the United States; Bridgeport is the 42nd; and New Haven—Waterbury is the 43rd. Their respective shares of U.S. retail sales volume are: 0.4405 percent; 0.4147 percent; and 0.4019 percent. These three together give 1.2571 percent which is taken to be the percentage of U.S. retail sales volume in the State of Connecticut. The Urban Trading Centers used in the study are given in Table 9.6. Since there are only 35 States with Urban Trading Centers with over 100 000 population in the table, and since the data are keyed to such Urban Trading Centers, the effective national data basis for the company potentials will comprise 35 states.

7.3. External Basis: (2) Effective Buying Income

The *Sales Management* reports "effective buying income" which is the same as disposable income (personal income less taxes) available for spending. Since the McKinsey data give the volume of retail sales, they may be con-sidered the result of disposable income invested in retail purchases. Not all of the disposable income is spent in retail buying; therefore, it may be advisable to use the effective buying income as a predictor of the company bookings, separate from the retail sales volume. The *Sales Management* buying power figures are given by SMSA which do not correspond exactly to the Urban Trading Centers. However, with respect to each state as a whole the effective buying income can be estimated from the data for SMASs.

Table 9.6
U.S. Urban Trading Center areas as basis of company sales potential calculations by state and region

State	Trading Center	Trading Center Area in order of importance w/Population & Ret. Sales
Region I: Eastern States		
Connecticut	Hartford	41
	Bridgeport	42
	New Haven–Waterbury	43
Maine	No place w/over 100 000 population	
Massachusetts	Boston	7
	Worcester	48
	Springfield	49
	Fall River–New Bedford	52
New Hampshire	No place w/over 100 000 population	
Rhode Island	Providence	28
Vermont	No place w/over 100 000 population	
Middle Atlantic		
New Jersey	Newark	41
	Camden	54
	Trenton	71
New York	New York City	1
	Buffalo	15
	Rochester	32
	Albany	45
	Syracuse	56
	Utica	75
Pennsylvania	Philadelphia	5
	Pittsburgh	9
	Allentown	51
	Scranton	52
	Reading	79
	Erie	82

Table 9.6 (Continued)

State	Trading Center	Trading Center Area in order of importance w/Population & Ret. Sales
Region II: North Central States		
East North Central		
Illinois	Chicago	2
	Peoria	76
Indiana	Gary	22
	Indianapolis	26
	South Bend	83
	Fort Wayne	86
	Evansville	96
Michigan	Detroit	6
	Flint	61
	Grand Rapids	62
Ohio	Cleveland	12
	Cinncinnati	18
	Columbus	31
	Dayton	34
	Akron	38
	Toledo	39
	Youngstown	47
	Canton	72
Wisconsin	Milwaukee	19
West North Central		
North Dakota	No place w/over 100 000 population	
South Dakota	No place w/over 100 000 population	
Iowa	Des Moines	74
Minnesota	Minneapolis–St. Paul	14
	Duluth	78
Nebraska	Omaha	40
Region III: West Coast		
Pacific States		
California	Los Angeles	3
	Pasadena	3
	San Francisco–Oakland	8
	San Diego	27
	Sacramento	57

Table 9.6 (Continued)

State	Trading Center	Trading Center Area in order of importance w/Population & Ret. Sales
Oregon	Portland	24
Washington	Seattle	21
	Spokane	73
	Tacoma	77
Mountain States Arizona	Phoenix	54
Colorado	Denver	25
Idaho	No place w/over 100 000 population	
Montana	No place w/over 100 000 population	
Nevada	No place w/over 100 000 population	
New Mexico	No place w/over 100 000 population	
Utah	Salt Lake City	67
Wyoming	No place w/over 100 000 population	
Region IV: Atlantic States North Carolina	Charlotte	81
South Carolina	No place w/over 100 000 population	
Delaware	No place w/over 100 000 population	
Florida	Miami	22
	Tampa	46
	Jacksonville	60
Georgia	Atlanta	23
	Savannah	97
Maryland	Baltimore	13

Applied OR/SA

Table 9.6 (Continued)

State	Trading Center	Trading Center Area in order of importance w/Population & Ret. Sales
Virginia	Norfolk	44
	Richmond	59
West Virginia	No place w/over 100 000 population	
East South States Kentucky	Louisville	30
Tennessee	Memphis	33
	Nashville	64
	Knoxville	70
	Chattanooga	80
Region IV: South		
West South Central Arkansas	Little Rock	89
Louisiana	New Orleans	29
	Shreveport	90
	Baton Rouge	94
Oklahoma	Oklahoma City	58
	Tulsa	68
Texas	Houston	17
	Dallas	20
	Ft. Worth	35
	San Antonio	36
	El Paso	85
	Corpus Christi	88
	Austin	95
East South States Mississipi	No place w/over 100 000 population	
Alabama	Birmingham	37
	Montgomery	98
West North Central Missouri	St. Louis	10
	Kansas City	16
Kansas	Kansas City	16
	Wichita	65

Thus, while the *Sales Management* effective income does not correspond to geographic locations which are identical to the Urban Trading Centers, it has been possible to take three areas for which the effective buying income are respectively 0.1473 percent, 0.1255 percent, and 0.1895 percent, giving a total of 0.4623 percent of U.S. effective buying income for the State of Connecticut.

7.4. External Basis and Internal Potentials

The rationale for seeking two external criteria with which to predict the company sales has been the *in*applicability of SIC data to make such a prediction. Further, insofar as the sales of 12 divisions cut across many product lines, resulting in a large spectrum of end users, it is suggested that a general index of economic activity of the nation as a whole would probably qualify as a predictor of the company bookings.

It has been found in Section 7.2 that the percent of U.S. retail sales volume in the three Urban Trading areas together was 1.2571 percent, and it was seen in Section 7.3 that the percent of effective buying income for the State of Connecticut on the basis of SMSAs was 0.4623 percent. The company bookings in the State of Connecticut were 1.7246 percent.

The question is: Given the values for the percentage share of U.S. retail volume and U.S. effective buying, can the share of the company bookings in a given State be predicted?

The analytical approach consists of postulating a relationship between the percent of U.S. retail sales volume (designated as x) and the percent of U.S. effective buying income (designated as z) on the one hand, and the percent of U.S. bookings of the company (designated as y) on the other. Once such a relationship is postulated between y, x, and z, it can be investigated if a series of values of x and z does provide a close enough basis to arrive at corresponding values of y. If, in fact, x and z together can help predict the corresponding value of y, then the analytical basis of an organismic index of performance for the company bookings by State shall have been established, and action at the three hierarchical levels of decision-making in the company can be initiated.

PROBLEMS

*The four chapters, 9, 10, 11 and 12, of Part IV deal with the application of
OR/SA Protocol to large, unstructured problems in the Private Sector. The
two major problems vital to any manufacturing and sales operation are: (1)
sales, and (2) production. This chapter deals with the national data input to
company potentials, in order to arrive at* sales potentials *by territory for the
company product. The purpose of the following questions is to develop an
appreciation for the considerable amount of data that are available for use by
any private company; as well as the precautions that have to be taken in
adapting national data to company needs.*

A. *System Context*

1. What competitive measure of performance is available for the private
company to compare its system performance with that of its peers?

2. What are the limitations in using the number of units of sales of
products as an index of company performance?

3. If the same salesman reports to different sales managers, each of whom
is responsible for the sale of a *different set* of products, how can the conflicting demands placed upon the individual salesman by the different sales
managers be systematically resolved in favor of advancing the company performance?

B. *System Cost*

4. To utilize the financial data available nationally, it is necessary to identify the particular company as part of a larger group. Illustrate the different
contexts in which the same company appears with respect to key financial
data.

5. If you manufacture a product in 7 plants, would you purchase data on
41 000 "key plants" with 100 or more employees at a price of $3 000?

6. How would you allocate $10 000, between the updating of trading
center area figures and the standard metropolitan area center figures?

CHAPTER 10

MULTIPLE REGRESSION
IN PRIVATE SECTOR PROBLEMS:
(1) SALES POTENTIALS STANDARDS

TECHNICAL OVERVIEW

To utilize the national data base, available through publications based on the Standard Industrial Classification (SIC), the company sales (bookings) are explored first with reference to a single external variable; and second with reference to two external variables.

The theoretical basis of the relationship between 1 or 2 variables and another variable is developed through a discussion of the notion of a function and of transformation.

In addition, the measures of association between a group of values of x and corresponding values of y are developed conceptually and defined computationally. Correlation is developed as "groupwise togetherness" and regression as "pairwise togetherness".

Two linear regression equations are fitted to the company bookings. One predicts the company bookings in terms of the retail sales volume; another predicts the bookings in terms of the effective buying income. Which of the two equations is the better predictor? It is found that the first equation is a better predictor of the bookings for the different regions.

Can the two variables be used together to predict the bookings? When the two variables are taken together, it is found that the effective buying income, considered by itself without the retail volume, predicts the company bookings very poorly. The predicted values using both the variables for each region are compared with those obtained, using the first variable by itself, and the second variable, by itself. On the basis of the results, it is concluded that the percent of U.S. retail volume in urban trading centers is an effective predictor of the percent of U.S. bookings of the company by states.

EXECUTIVE SUMMARY

We find that when company bookings are predicted in terms of the retail sales volume, it is a better predictor of the bookings for the different regions of the country than when the company bookings are predicted in terms of the effective buying income.

The two variables are used together to predict the company bookings. It is found that effective buying income, considered by itself without the retail volume, predicts the company bookings very poorly. On the basis of the different predictive efforts, it is concluded that the percent of U.S. retail volume in urban trading centers is an effective predictor of the percent of U.S. bookings of the company by states.

To utilize the national data basis to predict the sales potentials for a given company, it is necessary to postulate a relationship between the national data basis, on the one hand, and the company sales potentials, on the other. The two elements of the national data base identified in Chapter 9 are: (1) percent of U.S. Retail Sales Volume (designated as x); and (2) percent of U.S. Effective Buying Income (designated as z). The percent of the U.S. Bookings of the Company (designated as y) is to be predicted on the basis of the corresponding values of x and z.

1. Linear Relationship, a Hypothesis*

The two elements of the national data base can either jointly or separately be postulated to be related to the company bookings. In other words, given a particular value of x, what is the corresponding value of y? Or, given a particular value of z, what is the corresponding value of y?

It should be emphasized that to postulate a relationship between x and y, or z and y does *not* imply causality. For the purpose of utilizing the postulated relationship, it is only necessary that there be some significant degree of relationship between the sets of values of x and y; or the sets of values of z and y. The two variables can designate any two sets of activity or entity. Thus, x could designate height, and y could designate weight; or, x could

---

* Those familiar with statistical relationships expressed in linear form may wish to skip this section and proceed to Section 2.1.

designate age, and y could designate height or weight. Similarly, z could designate the pressure, and y could designate the volume of a gas. Again, z could designate the number of storks in Sweden, and y the number of babies born. Just as easily, z could designate the number of blondes in New York City and y could designate the price of chili pepper in Mexico City, and so on.

If x were to designate the number of people brushing teeth, and y were to represent the number of people going to sleep; based on contemporary American practice, given the value of x, the corresponding value of y can be rather closely estimated. However, it by no means implies that x "causes" y: the act of brushing teeth does not "cause" the act of going to sleep. However, because of the cultural association between the two activities, the information on one of them serves as a good predictor of the other: if brushing teeth is here, can slumbering be far behind?

The general relationship can be stated simply as: y is a function of x, or $y = f(x)$. Similarly, y can be stated as a function of z, or $y = f(z)$. Unless both x and z have an identical relationship with y, it would be necessary to show the difference in their respective relationships by utilizing a different representation for the function. This can be accomplished by utilizing f_1 and f_2 respectively: $y = f_1(x), y = f_2(z)$. What does it mean to say that y is a function of x? As Buck puts it:

> It is sometimes said that any equation in x and y defines "y as a function of x". This must be both qualified and explained. What is usually meant is that, given an equation $E(x,y) = 0$, one is often able to "solve for y" at least in theory. Without some restrictions, this is certainly false; the equation
>
> $$y^2 + (x - y)(x + y) - 1 = 0$$
>
> certainly cannot be "solved for y". Moreover, solution of an equation such as $[E(x,y) = 0]$ does not usually yield a single unique solution for y, whereas when we write $y = f(x)$, we require that exactly one value of y correspond to a chosen value of x. The meaning of the original statement can be made a little clearer. If the function E is suitably restricted, then $[E(x,y) = 0]$ defines a collection (with possibly just one member) of functions f such that, if f is one of them, then
>
> $$E[x,f(x)] = 0$$
>
> for all x in the domain of f. [The *domain* of a function is the set of objects to which it may be applied and for which $f(p)$ is defined.] ...
> The *notion* of function is essentially the same as that of mapping. A numeri-

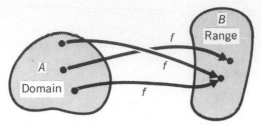

Fig. 10.1.

cal-valued function f assigns to each point p in its domain a single real number $f(p)$ called the value of f at p ... . In all these cases, it is important to bear in mind that the function f itself is the rule or mapping, while $f(p)$ is the value which f assigns to p ... .

More generally, whenever we are dealing with a *mapping* from objects in one set A to objects in a second set B, we are dealing with a function. We can represent this type by a diagram, as in [Fig. 10.1], and sometimes indicate it as

$f : A \rightarrow B$.

The set A is still the domain of f, and the set B will contain the set values (or range) of f. This concept of function is so broad that it permits mathematicians to label things as functions, and to work with them, which do not at all resemble the simple class of numerical-valued functions.[1]

Two important points have been brought out here. One is that a *restricted* view of function stipulates that "exactly one value of y corresponds to a chosen value of y." In other words, the number of babies in Sweden in the year 1975 corresponds to the number of storks in Sweden in 1975. The other is that a more *general* view of the function does not require a one-to-one correspondence; instead, "whenever we are dealing with a *mapping* from objects in one Set A to objects in a second Set B, we are dealing with a function." Nor does this mapping have to be exclusively in terms of numbers. According to Buck:

> It is a serious mistake to think that functions must always have numerical values. The motion of a particle may be described by setting up a correspondence between moments of time and points in space, by means of a function f, with $P = f(t)$. Here the domain of f will be an interval on the time line, and the values of f will

[1] R. Creighton Buck, *Advanced Calculus*, McGraw-Hill, New York, 1965, pp. 16–18, 21–22.

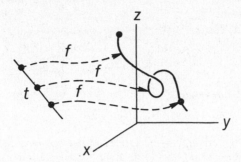

Fig. 10.2. $f : E^1 \to E^3$.

be points in 3-space [Fig. 10.2]. If the moving particle is subject to a magnetic field and we want to indicate the direction and magnitude of the force field at each position of the particle, we may be led to work with a function F which is defined for points on the track of the particle and whose values are vectors [Fig. 10.3].[2]

In Fig. 10.2, the movements are shown along a straight line which is shown in one dimension. The mapping represents the particle motion in three dimensions $x, y,$ and z, instead of one dimension, t. Thus, the mapping involves a

Fig. 10.3. F.

[2] *Ibid.*, pp. 17–18.

change from one into three dimensions as shown in Fig. 10.2. This conversion of a one-dimensional into a three-dimensional representation is called a transformation. John Tukey points out that in statistics today transformations seem to have two sorts of uses:

> (1) providing approximations for theoretical purposes or general convenience;
> (2) aiding in the analysis of data by bending the data nearer the Procrustean bed of the assumptions underlying conventional analyses ... .
>
> In analyzing data which do not match the assumptions of the conventional methods of analysis, we have two choices. We may bend the data to fit the assumptions by making a transformation.[3]

> Or we may develop new methods of analysis with assumptions which fit the data in its "original" form somewhat better. If we can find a satisfactory transformation, it will almost always be easier and simpler to use it rather than to develop new methods of analysis. To judge of its satisfactoriness, we need a criterion. The precise nature of the criterion will depend on the situation – and on what ills we are trying to remove by transformation: nonadditivity of effect, nonconstancy of variance, non-normality of distribution, or what have you.[4]

Consider the convenience of additivity of effect which Tukey mentions first among the factors that permit the process of data analysis. Instead of y being a function only of x, let us add a second variable, z, so that $y = f(x,z)$. We may revise our earlier statement of association between the number of babies born in Sweden and the number of storks in Sweden over a given period of time, and include, say, the number of blondes in Sweden also as associated with the number of babies born over any given period of time. What is the effect of both the number of storks and the number of blondes upon the number of babies? Additivity of effect is a great convenience. We should recognize that additivity is an assumption that we build into the form of the relationship (function) incorporating y, on the one hand, and x and z, on the other. We can express the relationship *linearly* as:

$$y = x + z \quad \text{or} \quad y = 3x + 7z,$$

[3] F.J. Anscombe and J.W. Tukey, "The Criticism of Transformations", paper presented before the American Statistical Association and Biometric Society, Montreal, Canada, September 12, 1954.
[4] John W. Tukey, "On the Comparative Anatomy of Transformations", *Annals of Mathematical Statistics*, September 1956, pp. 602, 603.

assuming that there are no errors of observation. Now we can turn to a definition of a linear function:

> A function g is functionally dependent in [a set] D upon the functions $f_1, f_2, ...,$
> f_m, if there is a function F of m variables such that
>
> $g(p) = F[f_1(p), f_2(p), ..., f_m(p)]$,
>
> for all $p \in D$. When the function F is a *linear* function, g is said to be *linearly dependent* upon $f_1, f_2, ..., f_m$. In this case there are m numbers $C_1, C_2, ..., C_m$ such that g can be expressed in D as a linear combination of the functions f_j:
>
> $g = C_1 f_1 + C_2 f_2 + ... + C_m f_m$. [5]

We notice that in our example of babies, blondes, and storks, $C_1 f_1 = x$, $C_2 f_2 = z$ or, alternatively, $C_1 f_1 = 3x$, $C_2 f_2 = 7z$.

2. "Groupwise" Togetherness: Correlation

Before utilizing x or z to predict y, it would be useful to identify the extent of association between a group of values of x and corresponding values of y or between a group of values of z and corresponding values of y. A measure of association between a group of values of x and y or z and y would indicate if it would be reasonable to use values of x or z to predict the corresponding values of y.

Sir Francis Galton who studied inheritance of stature used the term "correlation" in 1888 in his paper, "Co-relations and Their Measurements":

> Two variable organs are said to be co-related when the variation of one is accompanied on the average by more or less variation of the other, and in the same direction ... . The stature of kinsmen are co-related variables; thus the stature of the father is co-related to that of the adult son, and the stature of the adult son to that of the father; the stature of the uncle to that of the adult nephew, and the stature of the adult nephew to that of the uncle and so on; but the index of co-relation, which is what I ... called "regression", is different in the different cases.[6]

[5] Buck, *op. cit.*, pp. 288–289.
[6] Francis Galton, "Co-relations and Their Measurement", *Proc. Roy. Soc.,* Edinburgh, Vol. XLVII (1888).

Eleven years before the publication of Galton's paper, under the sponsorship of the Massachusetts Board of Health, Bowditch made a study of about 24 500 children. He made six charts, in three of which height in inches was plotted against age in years and, in the other three, weight in pounds was plotted against the age in years. Bowditch appears to have wanted to devise a method to measure the strength of the relationship between his variables.

Turning to the x and z of the national data base under discussion, if the values taken by y (percent of U.S. bookings of the company) exactly correspond to those of x (or z), for instance, then the value of the *coefficient of correlation* will be 1. If the values of x and y were to be plotted on a graph, they would lie on a straight line. For, every increase in the value of x will show a corresponding increase in the value of y; and the increase in the value of y will be exactly the same for identical increases in x. A similar relationship would be obtained between z and y if the coefficient of correlation between z and y is 1.

The ideal value of 1 for the coefficient of correlation does *not* have to be positive. The height, for instance, does not have to increase identically with every increase in age. Similarly, the weight does not have to increase with age. It could decrease with age. It is conceivable to have a coefficient of correlation of -1: for every *increase* in the value of x, there is a corresponding *decrease* in the value of y

Between the values of -1 and $+1$, occurs the value 0. If the coefficient of correlation is 0, it would mean that the values of y can *not* be predicted from the values of x or z, because the increase or decrease in the value of y has little or nothing to do with the increase or decrease in the values of x or z. Therefore, should the coefficient of correlation be close to 0, it could be treated as though the coefficient is in fact 0.

2.1. Computation of Correlation Coefficient

In Table 10.1, the values for the three variables, $x, z,$ and y, for the State of Connecticut are given as follows:

State	% of U.S. bookings of the company	% of U.S. retail vol. in an urban trading center	% of U.S. effective buying income
	y	x	z
Connecticut	1.7246	1.2571	0.4623

The measure of association between x and y, and that between z and y is determined on the basis of the *sums* of the variables Σx over the values of i, written as $\Sigma_i x_i$, and their products, $\Sigma_i x_i y_i$. In addition to these, the squares of the sum of the variables, $(\Sigma_i x_i)^2$, as well as the sum of the squares of the variables, $\Sigma_i x_i^2$, are necessary for the computation. The latter are used to measure the variability of the values of x from each other, as well as the variability of the values of y from each other. The theoretical reasons for these elements in the computation are discussed elsewhere.[7] Therefore, the convenient computational form for correlation will be stated directly:

$$r_{x,y} = \frac{n \sum_{i=1}^{n} x_i y_i - \sum_{i=1}^{n} x_i \cdot \sum_{i=1}^{n} y_i}{\sqrt{[n \sum_{i=1}^{n} x_i^2 - (\sum_{i=1}^{n} x_i)^2][n \sum_{i=1}^{n} y_i^2 - (\sum_{i=1}^{n} y_i)^2]}} .$$

In Table 10.1, the data by State are provided for each of the variables y, x, and z. The first line of the data is the same as it appears earlier in this section. The other sets of data are similarly developed.

The coefficient of correlation between y and x, y, and z, and x and z are now computed for each of the five regions. These values appear in Table 10.2. It is seen that with the exception of Region 4, the correlations between y and x appear to be close to 1. Interestingly enough, it is also found that the two elements of the national data base, viz., x and z, are also highly correlated. This raises the possibility that *either* x or z could be used to predict the corresponding values of y.

3. "Pairwise" Togetherness: Regression

Having established the prima facie reasonableness in using x and/or z as predictive variable(s), the next step is to ascertain the weight that should be given to the predictive variables in order to arrive at the corresponding values of y.

An inspection of the values in Table 10.1 indicates that the values of x could *not* be multiplied by a simple multiple, such as 1, 2, or 3 to arrive at the corresponding value of y. However, in view of the high correlation betwe-

[7] See George K. Chacko, *Applied Statistics in Decision-Making*, American Elsevier, New York, 1971, Chapters 5, 6.

Table 10.1
Multiple linear regression model data

State	% of U.S. bookings of company y	% of U.S. retail volume in an urban trading center x	% of U.S. effective buing income z
Region 1			
Connecticut	1.7246	1.2571	0.4623
Massachusetts	4.9104	3.1122	2.6320
Rhode Island	0.0010	0.4652	0.1613
New Jersey	3.0113	2.9218	0.5095
New York	15.2932	8.9340	6.7838
Pennsylvania	5.5654	4.8615	4.9254
Region 2			
Illinois	10.8644	4.6128	3.2248
Indiana	1.8033	0.9942	0.7936
Michigan	5.1456	2.9601	1.7614
Ohio	4.9612	3.7670	2.3427
Wisconsin	1.2303	0.6747	0.5128
Iowa	0.7984	0.1824	0.0271
Minnesota	4.8692	1.0840	0.6971
Nebraska	0.3758	0.2584	0.1845
Region 3			
California	11.0211	6.6925	3.6768
Oregon	0.5494	0.5312	0.2903
Washington	1.0358	0.9596	0.7206
Arizona	1.1136	0.2893	0.1100
Colorado	0.5206	0.5222	0.3506
Utah	0.4398	0.2162	0.1388
Region 4			
North Carolina	1.0893	0.1527	0.1091
Florida	2.3987	1.1921	0.4300
Georgia	1.1945	0.6531	0.4125
Maryland	1.3105	0.9167	0.5904
Virginia	1.5979	0.6465	0.3800
Kentucky	1.6933	0.3272	0.2669
Tennessee	2.1856	0.9428	0.5355
Region 5			
Arkansas	0.1087	0.1318	0.1763
Louisiana	1.1593	0.6360	0.5754
Oklahoma	1.0053	0.4780	0.3645
Texas	3.1706	2.4028	1.7622
Missouri	3.7846	1.9638	0.9737
Kansas	0.9993	0.9720	0.2310
Alabama	1.1948	0.4035	0.2793

Table 10.2
Correlation values by region

Region	Correlation between y and x	Correlation between y and z	Correlation between x and z
1	0.8903	0.9360	0.9421
2	0.8968	0.9250	0.9133
3	0.9960	0.9908	0.9982
4	0.6812	0.3765	0.9395
5	0.9408	0.8423	0.9139

en y and x, it could be postulated that the values of y can be derived as a multiple of the values of x plus a remainder. Thus, the value of x for Connecticut is 1.2571; and the corresponding value of y is 1.7246. It could be postulated that the y-value is made up of the x-value plus a remainder, which is 0.4675. Similarly, the value of x for Massachusetts is 3.1122; and the corresponding value of y is 4.9104.

It could be postulated that the y-value is made up of the x-value plus a remainder, which is 1.7982. Applying the same reasoning to the third state in Region 1, Rhode Island, the value of the remainder which has been positive for Connecticut and Massachusetts, turns negative: -0.4642.

If, by working with different multiples and remainders for each set of x and y values for Region 1, it were possible to arrive at a *single* value for the multiple, and a *single* value for the remainder, that could be used as a predictive relationship. The advantage would be that given any value of x, the corresponding value of y can be predicted. Naturally, if the prediction were sufficiently close to the actual value of y, that predictive relationship would be most welcome. For that to occur, for every increase in the value of x, there must be a corresponding fixed increase or decrease in the value of y; or, the coefficient of correlation should be 1, or -1, or indistinguishable from either of the values.

Since the coefficient of correlation between y and x for Region 1 is not 1 but only 0.8903 as seen from Table 10.2, it will be necessary to compute both the factor by which x should be multiplied and the remainder which must be added. What should be the criteria for the multiple and the remainder? The purpose of the predictive relationship is to predict the value of y corresponding to the given value of x. Therefore, the predicted value should ideally be the actual value; or, the *expected* value should ideally be the *observed* value. The reason for the word "expected" is the use of probability which specifies the manner in which a variable like *x, y,* or *z* can assume different values such as 1.7246, 4.9104, 0.0010, and so on.

It is now necessary to formally define the term "variable" and the term "random variable". The reason is that the "expected" value pertains to a random variable. In other words, the variables *x, y,* and *z* are *assumed* to be random variables, so that a predictive relationship relating them can be established.

A *variable* is an entity (event, relationship, object, instance) which assumes different values in a prescribed manner. The prescribed manner should state two factors: (1) the range of values that the variable can assume; and (2) the manner in which the different values may be assumed. It is necessary to distinguish between the successive values assumed by any given variable; therefore, the *order* in which the successive values are assumed by the variable *x* has also to be indicated by a subscript *i* (or *j*, or *k*, and so on): x_i, the order of the values indicated by *i* being the order of values of *x* of interest to the study in question. Thus, if *i* were to take the values 1, 2, 3, it would mean that every successive value is of interest: or, the percent of U.S. retail volume in each of the 35 states with Urban Trading Centers over 100 000 population is of interest. Therefore, the first value of *x*, viz., x_1, is the percent of U.S. retail volume in Connecticut which is 1.2571; or, $x_1 = 1.2571$. Similarly, the second value of *x*, viz., x_2, is the percent of U.S. retail volume in Massachusetts which is 3.1122; or, $x_2 = 3.1122$. If, for some reason, only the values of *x* for every third state were of interest, this would be indicated by the values of *i, i* = 1, 4, 7, and so on. If every second state were to be studied, it would be designated by *i* = 1, 3, 5, and so on. There is no reason why the first state should be included in the study. The rule that every third state should be studied can be indicated by *i* = 3, 6, 9, and so on. Similarly, the rule that every second state should be studied can be indicated by *i* = 2, 4, 6, and so on. The end point should also be designated, viz., the last state which should be included in the study, which could be 6 for Region 1 or 35 for the continental United States in the present instance.

The value of the die in a throw is an example of a *random variable*. There are six values − 1, 2, 3, 4, 5, 6 − any one of which can come up in a single throw. If the die is not crooked, any one of the six values may come up. If it is equally likely that any one of the six values may occur, the value of the die in one throw could be 1 once every six times, 2 once every six times, 3 once every six times, 4 once every six times, 5 once every six times, and 6 once every six times. It does not mean that this is exactly how it will occur in practice. All that is required is that in a large number of trials, in fact as the number of trials approaches infinity, equality of the occurrence of each of the values must be obtained. Randomness is fulfilled when (1) equal chance of occurrence of (2) every value in (3) each trial is obtained. When the value of the die, v_i, is a random variable, the different values of $1, 2, 3, 4, 5, 6$ are equally likely to occur in any throw with the relative frequency of $\frac{1}{6}$. Thus, the relative frequency of $v_i = 1$ is $\frac{1}{6}$; the relative frequency of $v_i = 2$ is $\frac{1}{6}$; of $v_i = 3$ is $\frac{1}{6}$; of $v_i = 4$ is $\frac{1}{6}$; of $v_i = 5$ is $\frac{1}{6}$; of $v_i = 6$ is $\frac{1}{6}$. A random variable is an entity (event, relationship, object, instance) which assumes every possible value with equal relative frequency of occurrence every time.

The theoretical discussion of the derivation of the appropriate multiple of x and the appropriate remainder to arrive at the *expected value* of y appears elsewhere.[8] Therefore, the convenient computational form for the regression coefficient will be stated directly:

$$b_{y \cdot x} = \frac{n \sum_{i=1}^{n} x_i y_i - \sum_{i=1}^{n} x_i \cdot \sum_{i=1}^{n} y_i}{n \sum_{i=1}^{n} x_i^2 - (\sum_{i=1}^{n} x_i)^2} .$$

Notice that the *coefficient of regression of y on x*, $b_{y \cdot x}$, has very similar elements to those of the coefficient of correlation between x and y given in Section 2.1. There is a good reason for this. It is the relationship between correlation and regression. The coefficient of correlation *between x* and y is the precise measure of association between x and y. Therefore, there should be a relationship between that measure and the predictive relationship between x and y. There are two such predictive relationships: (1) that which predicts y on the basis of x, $b_{y \cdot x}$; and (2) that which predicts x on the basis of y, $b_{x \cdot y}$. It stands to reason that the measure of association between x and y should be derivable from the two predictive relationships, which are, after all alternative ways of utilizing the relationships between x and y. As a matter of fact, it can be shown that

$$r_{x, y} = \sqrt{b_{y \cdot x} \cdot b_{x \cdot y}} .$$

[8] See George K. Chacko, *Applied Statistics, op. cit.*, Chapter 4.

4. APPLICATION 21: Linear Regression Equation Fitted to the Company Bookings

Having established that x and/or z is sufficiently related to y to warrant developing the regression equations to predict y on the basis of x and/or z, different equations are now developed. On the basis of the different predictive relationships, the corresponding *expected values* of y are computed. For instance, the Equation I: $y = 1.1830 + 1.7448x$ gives the expected percent of U.S. bookings of the company in Region 1 to be 30.5056, compared with the *observed values* of y of 30.5059.

Another equation predicts y in terms, not of x, but of z. Equation II: $y = 0.4625 + 1.7921z$ gives the expected percent of U.S. bookings of the company in Region 1 to be 33.5055, compared with the *observed value* of y of 30.5059.

Which of the two equations is the better predictor? If the bookings in the Region as a whole is the criterion, then for Region 1, Equation I gives a much closer prediction than Equation II. However, the choice will be governed by the values for other Regions, as well as the values for the individual states. For, the object is to determine the sales potentials in each state so that the salesmen can be assigned sales targets to meet in his sales territory. The sales territory does not follow the state lines exactly, but follows them fairly closely. Before comparing the expected and observed values for each state, the comparison by Regions is examined:

Region	Observed	Expected: equation I	Expected: equation II
1	30.5059	30.5056	33.5055
2	30.0482	30.0583	30.0478
3	14.9503	14.9497	14.9833
4	11.4698	11.4692	11.7849
5	11.4266	11.4022	11.3518

5. Multiple Correlation and Regression

Since the expected values using x, in one instance, and using y, in another are fairly close to each other and to the observed values of percent of U.S. bookings of the company by Region, the question may arise: Can the prediction be closer if *both* x and y are used as predictors?

The principle remains the same, as in Simple Correlation or "Group Togetherness", viz., the measure of association among the variables. Only the dimensions change from 2 to 3 when x, y, and z are considered simultaneously instead of x and y or x and z. If x, y, and z represent respectively age, height, and weight of an individual, the requirement for a predictive relationship will be that all the three of them should be related highly to each other, either positive or negative.

The *multiple correlation coefficient* is similar in concept and computation to the simple correlation coefficient. The similarity may best be recognized from the relationship between *simple* correlation, $r_{x,y}$, and its corresponding regression coefficients, $b_{y.x}$, and $b_{x.y}$. To derive the *multiple* correlation coefficient, which measures the relationship of several variables, x, z, and so on to the variable y the respective regression coefficients and the simple correlations must be computed. Thus, if x and z are the two variables used to predict y, the multiple correlation coefficient will be designated $R_{y.xz}$. The notation can be generalized by designating the variables used as predictors by consecutive numbers 1, 2, and so on changing the present multiple correlation coefficient from $R_{y.xz}$ to $R_{y.12}$.

5.1. Partial Correlation and Regression

In using age *and* height to predict the expected values of weight, account has to be taken of the interaction between age and height upon weight. One method is to use age as a predictor, holding the effect of height constant as though height has no effect on weight at all. Similarly, the effect of age is held constant, and height used as the predictor. If age or height has a greater influence as a predictor of weight, this procedure would disclose the nature and magnitude of such an influence.

Using in reverse the argument about the relationship between the two regressions upon their correlation, the multiple correlation coefficient, $R_{y.12}$, can be looked upon as being made up of the *partial* regression coefficient which holds height constant and the simple correlation between weight and age,

$$R_{y.12} = \sqrt{r_{y1}b_{y1.2} + r_{y2}b_{y2.1}},$$

where

$$b_{y1.2} = \frac{r_{y1} - r_{y2}r_{12}}{1 - r_{12}^2}, \qquad b_{y2.1} = \frac{r_{y2} - r_{y1}r_{12}}{1 - r_{12}^2}.$$

The numerator r_{y1} is that portion of y which could be attributed to the relation of y to variable 1, and the demoninator $(1 - r_{12}^2)$ is that portion of y which could not be attributed to the relation of y to variable 1.

6. APPLICATION 22: Multiple Regression Equation I Fitted to the Company Bookings

The multiple regression equation connecting the percent of U.S. bookings of the company (y) on the one hand, and the two elements of the national data base, viz., percent of U.S. retail volume in an urban trading center (x), and percent of U.S. effective buying income (z), on the other, for all the 35 states together is:

$y = 0.4369 + 1.6252x + (-0.2490)z.$

It is found that the two variables x and z *together* explain 90.26 percent of the company bookings by state. Recalling that the y values derived from the multiple regression equation are *expected values*, allowance should be made for the computation of these expected values using the particular predictive relationship. The y values are "estimated" on the basis of the x and z values. In using x and z — individually or severally — there will be errors; hence, the estimate must be modified by an estimation error. This error, the difference between observed and expected values of the variables computed per unit of independent observations, is known as the standard error of estimate which is discussed elsewhere.[9] Therefore, the convenient computational form will be stated directly:

$$s_{y \cdot x} = \sqrt{\frac{\sum_{i=1}^{n} y_i^2 - a \sum_{i=1}^{n} y_i - b \sum_{i=1}^{n} x_i y_i}{n - 2}}.$$

[9] George K. Chacko, *Applied Statistics, op. cit.*, Chapter 5.

The notion of standard error of estimate applies to the estimate of the correlation coefficient also. The value of the correlation coefficient is obtained on the basis of a few values of x, y, and z, 35 sets in the present instance. Therefore, the value of $r_{y.12}$ of 90.26 percent should be modified for the fact that the value is obtained on the basis of the 35 observations. The standard error of estimate of the sample correlation coefficient, $r_{x,y}$, is

$$\frac{1}{\sqrt{n-1}}$$

Applying the standard error of estimate to the value of the *multiple* correlation coefficient on the basis of the sample values of x, y, and z which are only 48 instances of the possible values that the three variables could take, it can be stated that the two variables x and z together explain between 86.55 percent and 93.97 percent of the y-values.

In Section 4, the independent use of x and z to predict y was seen to give values fairly close to each other and to the observed values of y by region. When the two are taken together, another story emerges. It is found that U.S. effective buying income, z, considered by itself without the U.S. retail volume, x, predicts the company bookings, y, very poorly. The partial correlation coefficient which indicates the contribution of z to y when x is held constant, $r_{yz.x}$, has a *negative sign*, which suggests that the higher the effective buying income, the lower the company bookings, and vice versa. Further, the magnitude is very small: -0.0108. The corresponding figure for the retail volume is both positive and high: 0.6832. In other words, when the influence of the effective buying income is held constant, the retail volume accounts for approximately 68 percent of the company bookings in a state. The effective buying income is highly correlated to the retail volume, which association must therefore be considered to account for the predictive power of z.

To complete the considerations of the x and z variables, individually and jointly, a third equation is computed for each Region, in which x and z are simultaneously used to predict y. The first two equations for Region 1 were given in Section 4. They will now be repeated, and the multiple regression equation added to them:

Equation I: $y = 1.1830 + 1.7448x$,
Equation II: $y = 0.4625 + 1.7921z$,
Equation III: $y = -0.6045 + 1.5531x + 0.0427z$.

In Section 4, the comparisons between the observed and expected values were made by region on the basis of Equations I and II, to which the corresponding values of Equation III are now added.

Region	Observed	Expected: equation II	Expected: equation II	Expected: equation III
1	30.5059	30.5056	33.5055	29.5058
2	30.0482	30.0583	30.0478	32.0439
3	14.9503	14.9497	14.9833	13.3378
4	11.4698	11.4692	11.7849	11.8306
5	11.4266	11.4022	11.3518	11.2087

The expected values of y are now shown by states in Table 10.3. Of the three values, that for which the deviation between the observed and expected is a minimum is indicated by an asterisk. It is seen that of the 35 states for which the data sets were complete in all the three variables, Equation I provided the closest prediction for 15 states; Equation II, 8 states; and Equation III, 12 states. Considering the fact that the simple correlation between x and z is 0.9539, it seems reasonable that Equation I could be utilized almost as effectively as Equation II for the 8 states making the total number of states for which Equation I could be utilized as an effective predictor rise to 23 out of 35. Noting the *negative* partial correlation coefficient between the y values and the z values when x is held constant, and further noting the proximity of that value to zero, it can be concluded that percent of U.S. retail volume in urban trading centers is an effective predictor of the percent of U.S. bookings of the company in states.

Table 10.3
Regional predictors

	% of U.S. bookings by company (y observed)	Equation I (y expected)	Equation II (y expected)	Equation III (y expected)
Region 1				
Connecticut	1.7246	1.0104	1.2910*	0.3676
Massachusetts	4.9104	4.2472	5.1793*	4.3414
Rhode Island	0.0010	−0.3713	0.7506	0.1249*
New Jersey	3.0113	3.9150*	1.3756	3.9551
New York	15.2932	14.4050	15.6197*	13.5606
Pennsylvania	5.5654	7.2993	9.2893	7.1562*
	30.5059	30.5056	33.5055	29.5058

Equation I: $y = 1.1830 + (1.7448)x$
Equation II: $y = 0.4625 + (1.7921)z$
Equation III: $y = -0.6045 + (1.5531)x + (0.0427)z$

Region 2				
Illinois	10.8644	8.8718	9.4929	11.5463*
Indiana	1.8033	2.2512*	2.6279	2.4451
Michigan	5.1456	5.8480	5.3607*	5.6085*
Ohio	4.9612	7.3243	7.0021*	7.2692
Wisconsin	1.2303	1.6666*	1.8350	1.6687
Iowa	.7984	.7759*	.4635	.4167
Minnesota	4.8692	2.4155*	2.3577	2.3142
Nebraska	.3758	.9050	.9080	.7752*
	30.0482	30.0583	30.0478	32.0439

Equation I: $y = 0.4322 + (1.8296)x$
Equation II: $y = 0.3870 + (2.8237)z$
Equation III: $y = 0.2466 + (0.6401)x + (1.9684)z$

Region 3				
California	11.0211	10.9723*	10.9009	10.2029
Oregon	0.5499	0.8407	0.7213*	0.7882
Washington	1.3058	1.5452	2.0105	0.9190*
Arizona	1.1136	0.4429	0.1812	0.5530*
Colorado	0.5206	0.8259	0.9020	0.6070*
Utah	0.4398	0.3227*	0.2674	0.2677
	14.9503	14.9497	14.9833	13.3378

Table 10.3 (Continued)

Equation I: $y = -0.0328 + (1.6444)x$
Equation II: $y = -0.1484 + (2.9960)z$
Equation III: $y = 0.3224 + (2.8901)x - (2.5733)z$

Region 4
N. Carolina	1.0893	1.1363*	0.3697	0.4611
Florida	2.3987	2.1074*	1.8749	3.1874
Georgia	1.1945	1.6038	1.7928	1.4704*
Maryland	1.3105	1.8501*	2.6273	2.3275
Virginia	1.5979	1.5977*	1.6404	1.5151
Kentucky	1.6933	1.2994*	1.1100	0.7072
Tennessee	2.1856	1.8745	2.3698	2.1619*
	11.4698	11.4692	11.7849	11.8306

Equation I: $y = 0.99365 + (0.9343)x$
Equation II: $y = -0.1420 + (4.6905)z$
Equation III: $y = 0.1867 + (3.2516)x + (-2.0362)z$

Region 5
Arkansas	0.1087	0.4087*	0.6176	0.4323
Louisiana	1.1593	1.1204*	1.5679	1.0842
Oklahoma	1.0053	0.8974*	1.1463	0.8930
Texas	3.1706	3.5942	3.8275	3.2552*
Missouri	3.7846	2.9946	2.3263	3.0214*
Kansas	0.9993	1.5947	0.8621*	1.7232
Alabama	1.1948	0.7922	1.0041*	0.7994
	11.4226	11.4022	11.3518	11.2087

Equation I: $y = 0.2227 + (1.4115)x$
Equation II: $y = 0.4723 + (1.9040)z$
Equation III: $y = 0.2488 + (1.5310)x + (-0.2403)z$

$R_{y.xz} = 0.9026$ Standard Error of $R_{y.xz} = 0.0371$
$y = a + b_{yx.z}x + b_{yz.x}z$
$y = 0.4369 + (1.6252)x + (-0.2490)z$
Standard Error of the Estimate $\sigma_{y.xz} = 1.0038$

Partial Correlation Coefficients
$r_{yz.x} = -0.0108,$ $r_{yx.z} = 0.6832.$

Simple Correlation Coefficients
$r_{yx} = 0.9512,$ $r_{yz} = 0.9063,$ $r_{xz} = 0.9539.$

* (Observed-Expected)^2 is the lowest for the predictions by the three equations.

PROBLEMS

The four chapters, 9, 10, 11 and 12, of Part IV deal with the application of OR/SA Protocol to large, unstructured problems in the Private Sector. The two major problems vital to any manufacturing and sales operation are: (1) sales, and (2) production. This chapter deals with the predictive mechanisms for Company Bookings. The purpose of the following questions is to develop an appreciation of the potentials and limitations of using statistical methods to arrive at company potentials.

A. *System Effectiveness–Absolute*

1. Why is Bookings chosen as the measure of effectiveness of company performance?

2. Interpret the correlation coefficient of y (Company Bookings) and x (Retail Volume) in a region and the corresponding regression coefficient of y on x.

3. Interpret the correlation coefficient of y and z (Effective Buying Income) for a region and the corresponding regression coefficient of y on z.

B. *System Effectiveness–Relative*

4. In using the *partial* correlation coefficient, what assumptions are made about the effect of the change in subsystem performance upon System Performance?

5. What assumption is made in utilizing multiple regression of y on x and z (instead of one *or* the other)?

6. What is an appropriate criterion to apply when choosing an equation as a predictive mechanism?

CHAPTER 11

EMPIRICAL DISCRIMINANT FUNCTION IN PRIVATE SECTOR PROBLEMS: (2) SALESMAN EFFORT-PERFORMANCE

TECHNICAL OVERVIEW

In Chapter 10, the first of two elements essential to the realization of the management goal to increase sales, i.e., Sales Potentials, has been explored with respect to the national data base in Chapter 9, and with respect to analytical measures of association in Chapter 10. Now we turn to the second element: Salesmanship.

"Salesmanship" is easier to describe than to measure. However, it has to be measured, however imperfectly, if any effort is to be made to develop an objective basis to stimulate company sales by investing in "salesmanship".

The two variables: (1) percent of U.S. retail volume in urban trading center, and (2) percent of company "salesmanship" are together postulated to give rise to the percent of U.S. bookings of company by state. The "salesmanship" is based on merit-rating by 6 "judges" who are sales managers who know the salesmen best. Based on a ranking obtained as a composite of all the 6 rankings, the total company "salesmanship units" are arrived at 141.33. The rank of each salesman is computed as a percentage of the total company "salesmanship". When the salesman has more than one state, the company "salesmanship" is prorated according to the bookings obtained from the states.

It is found that the two variables together explain between 75.26 and 88.64% of the company bookings by state. However, the company "salesmaship" taken by itself, is able to account for approximately 80% of the company bookings. Therefore, it behooves us to study "salesmanship" further.

What do the salesmen do when they get to the company dealership and/or customer? How often does he have to call on the customer who

is the enduser *of the products? Can a relationship be postulated betwe-*
en the particular manner in which the salesman allocates his time, and
the bookings? Or better, to allow for the difference in sales potentials
of territories, we could consider the bookings as percentage of the sales
potentials.

  A salesman call card was developed to determine, in the words of the
salesman himself, the particular type of effort that he expended on
each call. The call card was filled in by the 53 salesmen, and were in use
for a 6-month period. During that time, 14 972 calls were reported.
They were grouped into categories of calls including the customer dis-
position. Some of the salesmen were handling specialty items, and
others handled all the trades. This differentiation gave an additional
means of separation between the salesmen and their bookings/quota
percentages.

  Recognizing that the method of operation of each salesman varies,
and varies with the particular customer, nevertheless, is it possible to
devise some measure on the basis of which the salesman can be divided
into "good" and "bad" on the basis of the percentage of bookings/
quota? The measures are applied not to individual salesmen, as much as
to groups *into which the salesman is assigned. The method of Discrimi-*
nant Function is applied to the data and a linear discriminant function
is derived. It is interesting to note that the discriminant function which
is derived empirically is statistically significant; and that the function
weights active efforts at calls by the salesman three times as much as
the bookings/quota.

  Noting that salesmanship is extremely important, is it possible to
establish the increase in bookings as a result of an increase in "salesman-
ship"? In this instance, we take a concrete measure of salesmanship,
i.e., the commissions earned by the salesmen. The advertisement by the
company of the products may have some beneficial effect upon the
customers. Therefore, we ask the question: what are the returns to scale
of an increase in the investment in the advertising outlay versus an
increase in the outlay of sales commissions?

  On the basis of a Douglas Production Function fitted to the data, it
is found that the company bookings are indeed operating under increas-
ing returns to scale. Therefore, it behooves the company to consider
stimulating the company bookings by increasing the outlay on "sales-

manship" in the form of commissions. For a 10% increase in commissions, the company may expect about 15% increase in bookings.

How can the discriminant function be used to control the quality of "salesmanship"? Decision processes based on the discriminant function are examined from the point of view of quality control to yield a sampling plan of inspection to insure the long run average quality of the decision such that a "bad" salesman is accepted as "good" not more than once in eight times.

EXECUTIVE SUMMARY

In Chapter 10, the sales potentials were established on the basis of the percent of the U.S. retail volume in urban trading centers. Given the sales potentials, converting them into sales is the function of "salesmanship", however defined.

The salesmanship was arrived at on the basis of the ratings by 6 sales managers with personal knowledge of the 25 salesmen selected out of the 53. This salesmanship is allocated on a state-by-state basis, and the effect of the salesmanship and the sales potential in predicting company bookings is determined. It is found that "salesmanship", taken by itself, is able to account for approximately 80% of the company bookings.

Because of its extreme importance, "salesmanship" is studied further. On the basis of 14 972 salesman call cards developed specially for the purpose, and filed by all the 53 salesmen, the allocation of sales efforts by the salesmen is studied. A statistical measure is developed, on the basis of which salesmen can be divided into "good" and "bad", so that management can exercise corrective efforts early in the game.

On the basis of another study, it is found that a 10% increase in the commissions is likely to bring about 15% increase in company bookings, suggesting that it would be a significant stimulus to the salesman's performance.

In Chapter 9, two major problems which are vital to any manufacturing and sales operation, viz., Sales and Production, have been identified in the real-life context of a multiplant, multiproduct, durable goods manufacturing and sales organization. In Chapter 10, the national data have been used to arrive at the sales potentials of the company, leading to the choice of one of the two data elements to be the predictive variable on the basis of simple and multiple correlation analysis and simple and multiple regression analysis.

In Chapter 9, Section 6, *two* principal elements have been identified as essential to the realization of the management goal to increase sale: Element (1): Sales Potentials; and Element (2): Salesmanship. Of the two, only the first element has been considered with respect to the national data base in Chapter 9, and with respect to analytical measures of association in Chapter 10. Now we turn to Element (2): Salesmanship.

1. Toward a Measure of "Salesmanship"

"Salesmanship" is easier to describe than to measure. However, it must be measured, howsoever unsatisfactorily, because the *internal* capabilities of the organization are indispensable to realize the *external* sales potentials which can be predicted on the basis of national data and regression analysis.

The effort here is *not* to isolate all the attributes of "salesmanship"; rather, it is to observe the operation of salesmen in precoded terms, measure the outcome of these operations in terms of changes in sales compared with a predetermined base, and to posit an associative relationship between the operation and outcome.

Over 300 distinct products are sold through a dealership organization which is set up and serviced by the durable goods salesmen as mentioned in Chapter 9, Section 1. The transactions are wholesale, and the different salesmen earn commissions on the basis of the sales to end-users through the dealers. Although the sales as a whole may be classified as durable goods sales, there are distinctive sales techniques which are called for in the handling of the different individual and groups of products. For instance, it is one thing to sell office chairs to a Park Avenue office in New York, and quite another thing to sell hospital beds to Holston Valley Community Hospital in Tennessee. Again, it is quite another thing altogether to sell beauty parlor hydraulic chairs to the State or Federal government. In spite of the variegated nature of the sales techniques involved, the salesman who has "got it" will sell well. How important is this element called "salesmanship", however defined or undefined? The effort is to arrive at some point of departure to determine how the organization should allocate its efforts in realizing as much of the potentials for the company bookings by state as possible.

1.1. Merit Rating of Salesmen

Six of the twelve sales managers who have had personal knowledge of the different salesmen for a reasonable length of time are specifically asked to rate the quality of "salesmanship". The ratings of the salesmen by the managers are translated into five grades: A, B, C, D and E. The letter A is given a value of 4, B–3, C–2, D–1 and the letter E, denoting inadequate acquaintance of the manager with the salesman to give a rating, is given a value of 0. The effect of two or three E's is to reduce the number of judgments, thereby affecting the reliability of the average score arrived at on the basis of the fewer judgments. It should be noted that equal weight is given to the rating by each manager as the number corresponding to the grades given to each salesman is totalled and divided by the number of judges who have given the grades A though D.

1.2. Selection of 25 Salesmen

Out of the 53 salesmen, a smaller number is to be selected for the merit rating by the sales managers. Since the purpose of the analysis is to arrive at a composite description of an "average company salesman", it is necessary to exclude from consideration all the salesmen who handle specialty products, because the specialty sales are presumed to require different, if not additional, "salesmanship" elements from those for the salesmen who handle most of the "general" product lines of the company. Again, since the purpose of the analysis is to identify those characteristics which make up a "good" salesman from the company's point of view, it is only natural that the end product of the salesmanship should be considered, viz., the bookings by the salesman. Twenty-five of the better salesmen, better in terms of their bookings (total volume of gross business) during a selected 6-month period are selected to explore the relationship between the potential of a territory and the salesmanship of the salesman in realizing the potentials by producing the sales volume. In order to achieve generality of result, salesmen who are extreme specialists, like those dealing exclusively with specialty products, are excluded. Among the 25 salesmen chosen, 13 handle all products, 5 handle all but one line of products, and 7 handle all but the specialty lines.

Table 11.1
Data for predictive relationship between sales potential and performance

(1) State	(2) % of U.S. bookings of company	(3) % of U.S. retail vol. in trading center	(4) % of company "salesmanship"	(5) Salesman
	y	x	z	
Region 1, Connecticut	1.8324	1.2571	1.8[††]	Dembner[**]
New Jersey	2.9787	2.9218	2.8	Dembner[**]
New York	4.0214	1.1168	2.7	Hecht[**]
Massachusetts[**]	2.8071	1.5561	2.6	Leeds[†]
Washington, D.C.	1.9114	1.2505[‡]	2.6	Rowland[**]
Maine, Vt., N.H.	0.1328	1.0706[‡]	0.2[††]	Anderson[**]
Virginia	1.9038	0.6465	1.9	Andrews
Pennsylvania[**]	1.4434	0.9723	1.4[††]	Schaum[†]
Region 2, Minnesota	1.6777	1.0840	2.2[††]	Harris
Illinois[*]	1.1263	1.1532	1.4	Barker
Missouri[*]	1.0324	0.9819	1.3[††]	McMurtry
Indiana	1.5635	0.9942	2.1	Larson[†]
Michigan[*]	1.5001	1.4801	1.9	Argelan[†]
Michigan[*]	2.1419	1.4801	1.8	Wois[†]
Ohio[*]	1.8697	1.2557	1.9[††]	Koehn
Region 3, California	0.9860	1.3385	1.6[††]	Mansfield
California[*]	1.2875	1.3385	1.9	Karl[†]
California[*]	0.9253	1.3385	1.4[††]	Iles[†]
Arizona	0.7483	0.2893	1.2[††]	Campbell
Washington, Oregon, Montana, Idaho	2.0571	3.5065[‡]	2.1	Matin
Region 4, Florida	1.7620	1.1921	1.6[††]	Kerr
Alabama[*]	1.0269	0.2017	1.4[††]	Galloway
Georgia	1.4406	0.6531	1.9[††]	Sheridan
Tennessee	2.8747	0.4714	2.0	Blick
Region 5, Texas[*]	1.6388	0.8009	2.3	Brotherton

[*] The sales potential of the state represented by the percentage of U.S. retail volume in the Trading Center is equally divided among the number of salesmen. Thus, N.Y. which had 8.9340% of 1957 U.S. Retail Volume is divided by a total number of eight to give 1.1168, which is recorded against Hecht, the nonspecialist salesman in New York State.

[**] All lines excluding one.

[†] All trades excluding specialty lines.

[††] The Company salesmen were merit rated by six "judges" on the basis of "salesmanship". Based on the ranking obtained as a composite of all the six rankings, the total Company "salesmanship" units were arrived at 141.33. On this composite scale, the higher the score, the better the salesman. The rank of each salesman was computed as a percentage of total Company "salesmanship". When the salesman has more than one state, the Company "salesmanship" was prorated according to the bookings obtained from the states.

[‡] Estimates supplied because it should be recalled that several states included in the sales territories of the top salesmen in this Table do *not* contain Urban Trading Centers of over 100 000 population.

1.3. Allocation of Territorial and "Salesmanship" Potential

The data on the potentials of company bookings are presented by States in Table 11.1. Although the percent of U.S. Retail Volume in Urban Trading Center constitutes the basic data for the company potentials, in Chapter 9, Section 7.2, the potentials have been converted from the Trading Center basis to the State basis by aggregating the percent of Retail Volume for selected Urban Trading Centers in each State.

To present the "salesmanship" factor also by State, the "salesmanship" factor of a particular salesman is allocated among the different States which are included in his sales territory. The basis for the allocation of the "salesmanship" is the actual bookings: which suggest a certain amount of begging of the question; however, in the 12 instances in which such adjustments are made, it seems to be an acceptable procedure.

The "salesmanship" factor is considered to act on the territorial potential to generate the bookings. When more than one salesman works in the same State, the territorial potential is divided equally among the number of salesmen. Thus, New York, which represents 8.9340 percent of U.S. Retail Volume is divided by 8 to give 1.1168, which is recorded against Hecht, the nonspecialist, or "general" salesman in New York State. This is seen in Column 3 of Table 11.1. Applying the same reasoning, the territorial potential of the State of Michigan is divided equally between the two salesmen, Argelan and Wois.

1.4. Sales Potentials and "Salesmanship" Potentials

In Table 11.1, the two major factors which generate bookings are allocated on the basis of States. Thus, the territorial potential is divided equally among the salesmen, and the "salesmanship" of the same salesman in different States is prorated according to the share of his bookings in each State.

In Table 11.1, Column 4, the "salesmanship" of the 25 salesmen is expressed as percent of the company "salesmanship". The 6 judges merit rated the 25 salesmen according to the merit rating scheme in Section 1.1; the resulting total score of company "salesmanship" units was 141.33. The score of each salesman was computed as a percent of the total company "salesmanship". When the sales territory includes more than one State, his percent of company "salesmanship" is prorated according to the bookings achieved in each State.

2. APPLICATION 23: Multiple Regression Equation II Fitted to the Company Bookings

The multiple regression equation connecting the percent of U.S. bookings of the company (y), on the one hand, and the percent of U.S. Retail Volume in Urban Trading Center (x), and the percent of company "salesmanship" (z) on the other, for all the 27 States (including Washington, D.C.) covering the same territories of the 25 top salesmen is:

$$y = -0.4917 + (0.0169)x + 1.1841z.$$

It is found that two variables *together* explain 81.86 percent of the company bookings by State, as is seen from Table 11.2 where the multiple regression coefficient, $R_{y.xz}$, is 0.8186. Applying the standard error of estimate, it could be stated that the two variables, x and z, together explain between 75.26 and 88.46 percent of the y- values.

It is also found that the Retail Volume, considered without company "salesmanship", predicts the company bookings very poorly; the partial correlation coefficient, $r_{yx.z}$, is 0.0237. The correlation between company bookings and Retail Volume, r_{yx}, of 0.3066 must therefore be attributed to the even higher figure of 0.3591 for the correlation between Retail Volume and "salesmanship".

On the other hand, company "salesmanship" taken by itself, is able to

Table 11.2
Company bookings by state—multiple regression coefficient

$R_{y.xz}$ = 0.8186   Standard Error of $R_{y.xz}$ = 0.0660

$y = A + b_{yx.z}x + b_{yz.x}z$,
$y = -0.4917 + 0.0169)x + (1.1841)z$.

Standard Error of the Estimate = $\sigma_{y.xz}$ = 0.4600

Partial Correlation Coefficients
$r_{yz.x}$ = 0.7988, $r_{yx.z}$ = 0.0237 .

Simple Correlation Coefficients
r_{yx} = 0.3066, r_{yz} = 0.8185, r_{xz} = 0.3591.

---

account for approximately 80 percent of the company bookings, as indicated by the partial correlation coefficient between bookings and "salesmanship" when Retail Volume is held constant, $r_{yz.x}$, of 0.7988. Applying the standard error of the partial correlation coefficient, it could be stated that company "salesmanship" by itself accounts for between 72.65 percent and 87.11 percent of the company bookings by the top 25 salesmen.

How good is the multiple regression equation in predicting the company bookings of the top 25 salesmen on the basis of the territory potential and "salesmanship"? During the selected 6-month period, the top 25 salesmen accounted for 42.6898 percent of the total company bookings. When the two factors of territory potential, x, and the "salesmanship", z, are used to predict the percent of U.S. bookings of company, y, the predicted value lies between 42.2298 and 43.1498, which is of the order of 1 percent variation.

2.1. Targeting of Sales Efforts

In view of the closeness of the aggregate prediction by the multiple regression equation utilizing the two variables, x and z, it may be used as a basis for assigning targets of sales efforts, generally known as "Quotas". In Table 11.3, the standard error of the partial regression coefficient is indicated as a modifier of the multiple regression equation. The standard error is *added* to the regression coefficients to yield the upper limit of the quota, and *subtracted* from the regression coefficients to yield the lower limit of the quota.

Table 11.3
Standard error of partial regression coefficients and quota bases

$$b_{yz.x} = \frac{\sigma_{y.zx}}{\sigma_{z.x}\sqrt{N}} = 0.1861, \qquad b_{yz.x} = 1.1841 \ (\pm \ 0.1861),$$

$$b_{yx.z} = \frac{\sigma_{y.zx}}{\sigma_{x.z}\sqrt{N}} = 0.1487, \qquad b_{yx.z} = 0.0169 \ (\pm \ 0.1487).$$

Basis of Calculating the Upper and Lower Limits of Quatas

1. Quota $y = -0.4917 + (0.0169)x + (1.1841)z$,
2. Upper Limit $y = -1.0146 + (0.1656)x + (1.3702)z$,
3. Lower Limit $y = 0.0313 + (-0.1318)x + (0.9980)z$.

3. Empirical Study of "Salesmanship"

In Chapter 10, the territorial potentials were considered with respect of two variables: Retail Volume and Effective Buying Income. On the basis of the overwhelming contribution of Retail Volume toward explaining the percent of company bookings, the decision was made in Section 6 to use U.S. Retail Volume in Urban Trading Centers as the effective predictor of U.S. bookings of the company by State.

Similarly, on the basis of the overwhelming contribution of "salesmanship" toward explaining the percent of company bookings of the top 25 salesmen, it can be concluded that "salesmanship" — or, rather, the percent of company "salesmanship" — is an effective predictor of U.S. bookings of the company by State.

3.1. Design of Salesman Call Card

Recognizing the singular importance of the ill-defined characteristic called "salesmanship", it behooves the management to explore further the components of the characteristic, so that the precious resource of salesman effort can be given as specific a direction as possible to achieve the performance goals.

Granted that the "salesmanship" can be identified, however grossly, by the evaluation of the sales managers, the question is: How do the better salesmen exercise their "salesmanship" capabilities to produce their better results?

Recourse has to be made to the salesmen themselves in trying to construct a profile of better salesmanship in action. The salesmen spend their time in making "calls" on the dealers and/or customers. If the calls can be grouped into categories which are generally applicable to the sales effort in behalf of the different products, then it would facilitate the recording of the calls of not just the top 25 salesmen, but of *all* the 53 salesmen.

What do the salesmen *do* when they get to the dealer and/or customer? How often does he have to call on the customer who is the *end user* of the products?

Both the type of call, and the effort of the salesmen on their calls, depend upon the *disposition* of the end users as well as dealers whom the salesmen service through their calls.

If the three basic characteristics of the salesmen calls, viz., (1) *type* of call;

(2) *efforts* of the salesmen on their calls; and (3) *disposition* of the customers whom the calls are intended to serve, can be traced through the calls made by the salesmen, irrespective of their individual sales abilities and product assignments, then some kind of a quantitative norm can be evolved from the record of the salesmen calls. Clearly, the norm will reflect the strength and weakness of the men, their experience and the lack of it, and definitely the conscientiousness with which they have filled the call cards.

To minimize errors in processing a large number of call cards, it is found advisable to provide room on the same card for mark-sensing the hand written information filed by the salesman. If the salesmen can mark-sense their responses, by darkening the appropriate spaces by a no. 2 pencil, then the salesmen call cards could be directly processed. However, in instituting a procedure for the first time in the 57-year history of the company, making haste slowly is indicated. If the salesmen were to cooperate and send in reasonable records of their calls, that alone would be such a major contribution to the basis upon which action to improve salesmen performance can be based that the mark-sensing activity could well be undertaken at the company offices. The specimen call card, shown in Fig. 11.1, merely asks for check marks, space being provided for short explanations.

3.2. Quid pro Quo

Why should the salesman bother to fill the call cards, something he never had to do before? Without a quid pro quo basis, the best information-gathering device is bound to languish. Careful study and observation indicate that in this company, a frequent complaint of the salesmen is that they can not get the sales manager to respond to the sales needs in the field: whether it is to assuage an angry end user, or to "sell" a prospective customer.

The essence of the quid pro quo is meeting this very need. The salesman can be told: "Write your need or complaint on the call card today; by tomorrow morning your sales manager will get a verbatim copy." To ensure action, the original of the complaints/requests will be on file in the Marketing and Management Research Department, and a complete copy furnished to the national sales manager the same time that the particular division manager receives the complaint/request.

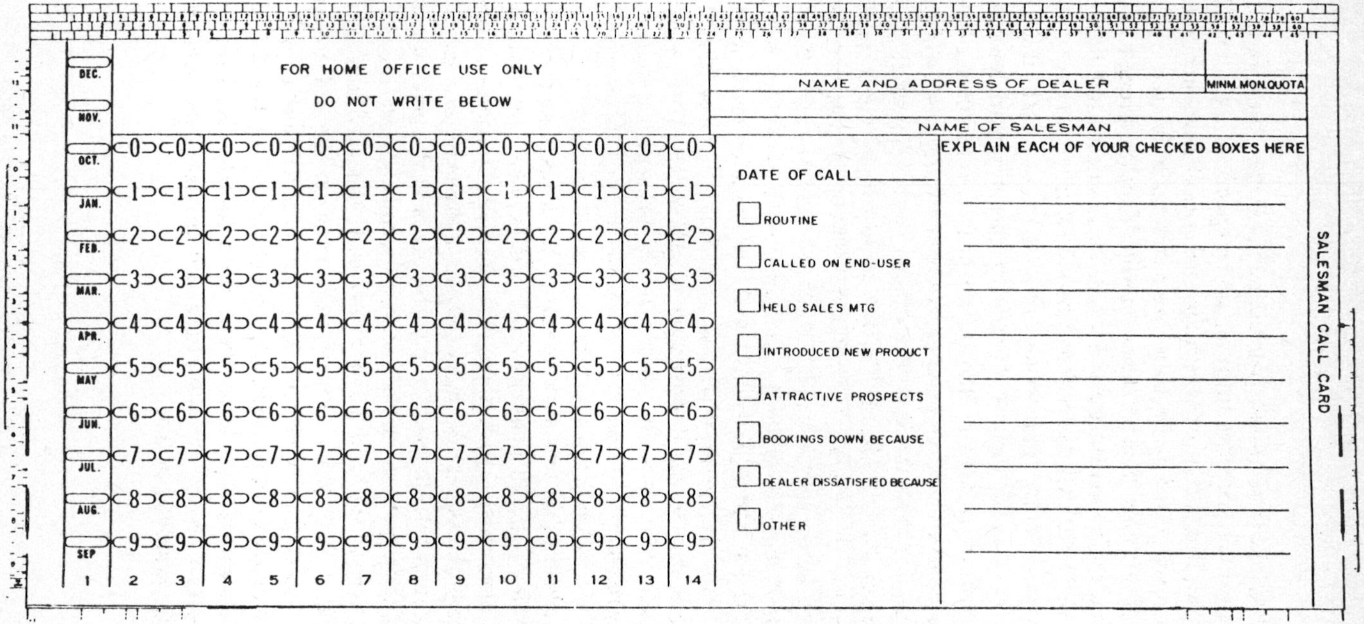

Fig. 11.1. Specimen call card.

3.3. Performance Standard: Bookings/Quota

In order to relate the allocation of sales efforts among the different types of sales calls, it is necessary to know the relationship between sales effort and sales accomplishments, represented by the company bookings. The dollar amounts of bookings by themselves would not be an adequate performance measure; the actual has to be compared with the potential for the given state or sales territory or group of sales territories.

In Section 2.1, an objective method was arrived at to assign targets of sales efforts, generally known as "quotas". The quotas reflect the sales potentials of the sales territories comprising States in whole or part. In Chapter 10, Section 4, the United States was divided into Regions, made up of contiguous States. It was possible to construct the Regions in such a way that the sales potentials in two Regions were equal to each other; and further, the sales potential of one Region was approximately half that of another Region. Since Regions 1 and 2 have potentials of 30.50% each, and since Regions 4 and 5 have both potentials of 11.42% each, and since the potential of Region 3 is 14.95%, which is approximately half that of Region 1, the respective percent of Bookings/Quota for those Regions provide a good performance standard with which to compare the outcome of the salesmen's efforts in allocating their time among the different activities which they deem to be appropriate to realize the sales potentials by applying their sales capabilities.

In Table 11.4, Column 3, the ratio of (*Bookings/Quota*) is shown for the United States as a whole, as well as for each of the Regions. Regions 1 and 2 achieved respectively 90.1 percent and 88.9 percent of their respective quotas during the 8-month period, and Region 3, 129.0 percent of its quota. These three regions, with 42 of the 53 salesmen, exceeded the Bookings/Quota for the United States as a whole, viz., 80.0 percent, while Regions 4 and 5 accomplished 62.5 percent and 62.6 percent, respectively, of their quotas. It is interesting to note that the accomplishment of company bookings in Regions 1 and 2 is approximately 89.0 percent of quota, and in Regions 4 and 5 it is approximately 62.0 of the quota. It would appear that the quotas themselves were reasonable measures of sales potentials; and the differences between the Regions do reflect differences in the sales capabilities, grossly reflected in the "salesmanship" factor.

Table 11.4
Salesman performance and call analysis

(1)	(2)	(3) 6-month average salesman working day calls	(4) Routine	(5) Called on end-user	(6) Held sales meeting	(7) Introduced new product	(8) Attractive prospects	(9) Bookings down	(10) Dealer dis-satisfied	(11) Other	(12) Total
number of salesmen by region											
19	Region I Bkgs/Quota 90.1%	2.28	65.0%	18.2%	1.2%	1.0%	2.7%		0.7%	11.2%	100.0%
14	Region II Bkgs/Quota 88.9%	3.08	68.8%	21.2%	1.1%	2.0%	1.7%		0.1%	5.1%	100.0%
7	Region IV Bkgs/Quota 62.5%	2.00	69.9%	19.4%	1.3%	0.7%	0.7%		1.8%	6.2%	100.0%
4	Region V Bkgs/Quota 62.6%	2.28	71.4%	21.5%	0.1%	0.3%	0.9%	0.1%	0.3%	5.4%	100.0%
9	Region III Bkgs/Quota 129.0%	2.23	62.6%	24.1%	1.2%	2.4%	3.4%		1.1%	5.2%	100.0%
53	USA Bkgs/Quota 80.0%	2.17	66.9% equals 10,010 Calls	20.2% equals 3,036 Calls	1.1% equals 162 Calls	1.4% equals 210 Calls	2.1% equals 312 Calls	0.0% equals 4 Calls	0.7% equals 107 Calls	7.6% equals 1,130 Calls	100.0% equals 14,972 Calls

3.4. Data on the Salesman Allocation of Effort

Even though the institution of salesman call cards is an unprecedented event in the 57-year history of the company, the response of the salesmen to the system has been gratifying. Every one of the 53 salesmen sent call cards back from the field. Over a 6-month period, the recording of individual calls by the salesmen varied in quality: a good many filled the cards faithfully; a few casually; and a small minority filled the cards slovenly. Although the coverage of the individual call cards thus varied, the internal structure of allocation of time between the different components of the calls itself provides a consistent basis to construct a profile of salesman effort allocation.

3.5. Stratification by Trade

It will be recalled that for the purposes of identifying a profile of the "average company salesman" a small group of 25 out of the 53 salesmen was selected which essentially excluded salesmen handling specialty trades (see Section 1.2). However, the salesman call cards have been filled by all of the 53 salesmen. Therefore, the effect of the salesman effort has to be studied with reference both to the territory (as in the case of Regions) and trades (as in the case of "General" salesmen handling all trades, and "Specialty" salesmen who handle specialties I, II, etc.).

3.6. Stratification by Performance

In addition to the stratification by trades and territories, a third, by performance, is also employed to identify the elements of a general norm. The 53 salesmen are divided into three groups: (1) those who exceed their quotas, irrespective of territory and trade; (2) those who achieve between 80 and 99 percent of the quota; and (3) those who achieve below 80 percent of the assigned quota.

3.7. Classification of Data

During the 6-month period 14 972 calls are reported by the 53 salesmen. These calls are reported in eight categories shown in Fig. 11.1: (1) routine calls; (2) end user calls; (3) sales meeting calls; (4) new product introduction calls; (5) prospective customer calls; (6) bookings decline investigation calls; (7) dealer dissatisfaction investigation calls; and (8) other category calls. It is seen from Table 11.4 that the 53 salesmen, taken as a whole, spend 66.9 percent of their calls in the first category which shows the enormous significance that all the salesmen attach to the need for maintaining continuous liaison with the dealers so that they would promote the sale of the company products in preference to competitive products. Next in importance is the category of end user calls: 20.2 percent.

In Table 11.5 the calls are stratified by specialty trades. Three major specialties are identified, the salesmen handling the respective specialties accomplishing respectively 109.7 percent of quota, 88.2 percent of quota, and 73.7 percent of quota. The different categories of calls are grouped by three characteristics: (1) *type* of call; (2) *efforts* of the salesmen on their calls; and (3) *disposition* of the customers whom the calls are intended to serve. These three characteristics, it will be recalled, were identified in Section 3.1 in setting forth the desirable descriptors of salesmen calls.

Table 11.5
Comparative components of specialty trade salesmen calls

	Specialty I	Specialty II	Specialty III
Type			
Bookings/Quota	109.7	88.2	73.7
Routine	81.3	52.5	87.1
End User	11.9	25.2	4.9
	93.2	77.7	92.0
Effort			
Held Sales Meeting	1.1	1.7	0.8
Introduced New Product	1.1	3.2	0.0
	2.2	4.9	0.8
Disposition			
Dealer Dissatisfied	0.6	2.1	0.7
Attrative Prospects	1.5	8.3	2.3
	2.1	10.4	3.0
Subtotal	97.5	93.0	95.8
Other	2.5	7.0	4.2
Total	100.0	100.0	100.0

Table 11.6
Elements of call effort by specialty trades and all trades

(1)	(2)	(3)	(4)	(5)	(6)	(7)
	Specialty trades			All trades		
	Specialty I	Specialty II	Specialty III	Group I	Group II	Group III
Bookings/quota	109.7%	88.2%	73.7%	120.3%	86.0%	65.7%
call	N=12	N=4	N=3	N=20	N=12	N=21
Routine	31.3%	52.5%	87.1%	65.3%	70.5%	64.2%
Called on End User	11.9	25.2	4.9	22.9	14.0	23.8
Held Sales Meeting	1.1	1.7	0.8	1.1	0.9	1.3
Introduced New Product	1.1	3.2	0.0	1.6	1.1	1.7
Attractive Prospects	1.5	8.3	2.3	3.2	0.7	2.1
Dealer Dissatisfied	0.6	2.1	0.7	0.7	0.8	0.7
Other	2.5	7.0	4.2	5.2	12.0	6.2
	100.0%	100.0%	100.0%	100.0%	100.0%	100.0%

The stratification by trade of the salesmen is used as the basis for comparison of the allocation of the sales efforts in Table 11.6. It is seen, for instance, that Specialty II salesmen spend 25.2 percent of their efforts in end user calls, compared with 11.9 percent of Specialty I salesmen and 4.9 percent of Specialty III salesmen, which compares with 20.2 percent for all the 53 salesmen taken together shown in Table 11.4, Column 5.

In addition to the stratification by trade, stratification by performance is also shown in Table 11.6. The percent of calls on the end users is approximately the same for both the 20 salesmen in Column 5 who exceeded their quotas, and for the 21 salesmen in Column 7 who achieved less than 80 percent of their assigned quota. The middle group of salesmen who accomplished between 80 and 99 percent of the quota spend 14.0 percent of their calls on end user calls.

4. APPLICATION 24: Discriminant Analysis of Salesman Effort-Performance Data

Of the two elements essential to the realization of the management goal of increased sales, the "salesmanship" element is found to be able to account for approximately 80 percent of the company bookings as seen in Section 2. In the next section, data on the exercise of "salesmanship" have been gathered in the form of the characterization of their efforts by the salesmen themselves. The question now is: Can any rules of procedure be evolved to guide salesmen effort in order to accomplish sales performance goals?

4.1. Criterion for "Good" and "Bad" Salesmen

In Section 3.6, the sales performance is stratified into three strata on the basis of Bookings/Quota. It is seen from Table 11.4, Column 3, that the Bookings/Quota figure for all the 53 salesmen in all the trades and in all the Regions is 80.0 percent. It could be that the quotas are pegged too high, or that the quotas are realistic, but the sales efforts are not up to par. The realistic nature of the quota is directly related to its predictability from the predicting variables: percent of U.S. Retail Volume in Urban Trading Centers, and the percent of U.S. Effective Buying Income. Of the two, on the basis of the analysis in Chapter 9.0, Section 6.0, the first variable, viz., Retail Volume, accounted for 68 percent of the company bookings in the preceding 8-month period for which company data were available. If the Retail Volume is found to have such a high and direct relationship with the company bookings, it is reasonable to consider the quota figures as realistic, having been derived from such close relationship with an "outside" source. Of course, no causal relationship of any kind is implied, only one of association.

If the quotas are realistic, then it would seem that the company is realizing sales well below its potentials. If the quotas are considered the norm, then Bookings/Quota should be 100 percent. Given that criterion, 33 out of the 53 salesmen are under achievers, or "bad" from the company sales point of view because Table 11.6, Column 5, shows that only 20 out of 53 achieve or exceed the quotas.

Sales by design, rather than by default, is a novel idea introduced for the first time in 57 years. Therefore, while 100 percent for Bookings/Quota may be highly desirable from the company point of view, a concession may be made by utilizing the Bookings/Quota figure for the United States as a whole, viz., 80.0 percent as seen from Table 11.4, Column 3. The concession is not to the derivation of the quotas themselves, but instead to the lack of design in sales efforts for 57 years, which lack cannot be reasonably expected to be remedied overnight, utilizing the salesmen who have never have been told in their 15, 20, or 25 years with the company that they were to meet sales targets established on the basis of "outside" criteria other than those of their "gut" feeling.

Using 80 percent of the Bookings/Quota as the criterion for classifying the salesman performance into "good" and "bad", the object is to evolve a method to calibrate the performance of salesmen on the basis of not only *what* they accomplish, but also *how* they accomplish their sales performance. The reason why the *how* is important is because that alone provides the workable corrective measures that can be undertaken in the short run. Reasonable allowance has been made for the differences in territorial potentials when the comparison is made, *not* between *absolute* dollar volumes of company bookings by the salesmen, but by the *relative* percent of the territorial potential achieved by each salesman. On that basis, 11 out of the 53 salesmen, in Regions 4 and 5, are found to be meeting less than 80 percent of their quotas. The 80 percent figure itself reflects the modification made by the recognition of the fact that the salesmen have never been told to target their efforts before; therefore, it seems quite reasonable that barring an effective sales training program to teach the salesmen *how* to sell, the immediate remedial measures open to the management consist in identifying the specific modus operandi of the "good" salesmen and suggesting that the "bad" salesmen try to emulate the "good" salesmen. It should be noted that this emulation is only in terms of allocating their effort among the different types of calls, the outcome in the calls themselves being dependent upon the "salesmanship". The identification of the modus operandi has therefore a limited *operational* objective: it tells the management what can be done to possibly increase the chances of meeting the quotas insofar as such improvement depends *only* upon the allocation of sales efforts by the salesmen.

4.2. Discriminating the "Good" From the "Bad" Salesman: Decision Implications

The methodology that is of interest to the management decision problem is that of discriminating the "good" from the "bad" salesman at any given time.

There are at least three levels in which these decision problems arise. They are in terms of:

(1) Salesman X_i (general trades) at time $t_1, t_2, ..., t_n$.
(2) Regions 1, 2, 3, 4, and 5 at time $t_1, t_2, ..., t_n$.
(3) Salesman X_j (specialty trades) at time $t_1, t_2, ..., t_n$.

There is a terminal decision involved in continuous "good" ranking for anyone in any of the three strata. If a salesman is continuously "bad", he may lose his job, whether he is a general trades salesman or a specialty salesman. If a region is continuously "bad", the regional manager stands to lose his job eventually.

While this decision is at the "bad" end of the spectrum, promotions, bonuses, and other rewards can be similarly visualized for successively maintaining a "good" rank, at the other end of the spectrum.

However, a single occurrence does not result in extreme decisions all the time. It is, therefore, necessary to set up a criterion for detecting sales performance situations before they get out of hand, necessitating decisions at the extremes. If, instead of at the extremes, detection is possible in the intermediate part of the spectrum, then, appropriate corrective actions can also be devised so as to ensure the long-term growth of the company.

4.3. Discriminating the "Good" From the "Bad" Salesmen: Assumptions Underlying Discriminant Analysis

In order to deal with the problem of detection, discriminant analysis seems to be appropriate. The method of *discriminant functions* was introduced into mathematical statistics by R.A. Fisher.[1] The present problem is to evolve a criterion to separate the "good" from the "bad", or as it were, the sheep from the goats. Unlike in nature, however, in the present problem, this distinction does not remain unchanged, because the sheep can, under certain circumstances, become goats, and vice versa. The differentiation is made on the basis of some observable measurements. Which *linear combination* of the various empirical measurements that have been made on the salesman's performance and effort will in a certain sense *best* discriminate between "good" and "bad" salesmen?

The simplifying assumptions that enter into the use of the discriminant function must be recognized. First, it is postulated that the differentiation

---

[1] R.A. Fisher, "The Use of Multiple Measurements in Taxonomic Problems", *Annals of Eugenics*, Vol. 7, 1936, pp. 179ff. See also, "The Statistical Utilization of Multiple Measurements", *ibid*, Vol. 8, 1938, pp. 376ff, *Contributions to Mathematical Statistics*, Wiley, New York, 1950, Papers 32 and 33; *Statistical Methods for Research Workers*, 8th ed., London, 1941, Section 49.2, pp. 279ff.

between the "good" and the "bad" can, in fact, be based upon a set of *empirical measurements*; in this case, the reported allocation by the salesman among the different types of calls. The word *empirical* is key to the use of the method. We are saying that what distinguishes the "good" from the "bad" salesmen is in fact the distribution of their effort among the eight types of calls. This assumption should be compared with the analytical result in Section 2 that "salesmanship" is the major factor in accounting for the differences in sales performance. By now concentrating upon the empirical profile of the *observable* pattern of behavior, we are stating that the *unobservable* "salesmanship" is in fact reflected closely by the *observable* pattern of sales calls.

Second, we postulate that the observable pattern which comprises three characteristics relating to: (1) the type of call; and (2) the type of effort (which are controlled in part by the salesmen); and (3) the disposition of the customer (which is *not* controlled by the salesmen) is representable by measurements which are combined one with the other, implying that: (1) the effect of each characteristics is additive; and that (2) the contribution of each characteristic to whatever results in "good" or "bad" is directly *proportional*.

Third, we postulate that some linear combination of the observable pattern of sales calls will separate the salesmen into two groups: "good" and "bad". This discrimination capability of the discriminant function is required to be the "best" in a statistical sense. The discriminant function derived from the empirical data could well arise out of pure chance. One of the characteristics of the "best" discriminant function is that it *not* arise out of pure chance. In other words, the classification of each salesman into "good" and "bad" must follow some rhyme or reason beyond that of a pure whim, whether the whim be that of a sales manager or of an empirical discriminant function.

The properties that the empirical discriminant function should have in order to "best" discriminate between the two categories of salesmen depend upon the statistical behavior of the variables themselves. There are four variables that are used to derive the empirical discriminant function. They are:

(1) X_1: Bookings/Quota for the 8-month period.

(2) X_2: Type of call. In Table 11.4, Columns 4 and 5, the calls made by the salesmen are classified into "routine" and "end user". The two types of calls are combined to give X_2.

(3) X_3: Percentage of calls representing special efforts. In Table 11.4,

holding of sales meetings for the dealer or customer salesmen, and introduction of new products are reported by the salesmen. The combined total of the two kinds of effort is designated as X_3.

(4) X_4: Total number of calls in which dealer dissatisfaction is reported. These calls are also expressed as percent of the total number of calls reported by the salesmen.

We may associate the attributes with the variables as follows: *Performance* (X_1); *type* (X_2); *effort* (X_3); and *disposition* (X_4).

The observations on the four variables X_i ($i = 1, 2, ..., p$; in this case $p = 4$) are assumed to be *normally distributed*. This assumption requires that, among other things, the different values of each X_i such as X_1 would tend to cluster together in the middle, and taper off to the ends. In other words, the Bookings/Quota ratio would have most of the values in the middle range. If the mid-point is 50, then most of the values observed for the different salesmen would be close to 50. The number of salesmen whose Bookings/Quota fraction is close to 100, or to 0, representing the extreme values, would be very, very small. Similar descriptions apply to the distribution of X_2, X_3, and X_4 (or X_p), where p can take any value large or small, the value of p in the present case being 4.

4.4. Discriminating the "Good" From the "Bad" Salesmen: Data for Discriminant Analysis

Since the empirical discriminant function is constructed to separate two groups of observations, and separation is based on differences, it stands to reason that the discriminant function be made up of the *differences* in the values of the observable variables X_i, viz., X_1, X_2, X_3, and X_4. Individual differences in the values of the respective variables would be of little help in deciding whether a given salesman falls into one group or the other. However, the *average* value of X_i for the "good" *group* of salesmen, and the "bad" *group* gives an intuitively acceptable measure. It is seen from Table 11.7, Column 3, that the average value of X_1 for the "good" group, X_1, is 101.7428, and the average value for the "bad" group, X_1^{**}, is 66.1250, giving a difference between the averages of $(101.7428 - 66.1250) = 35.6178$. The general average for both the groups, X_1, together is found to be 88.7909.

While the total number of salesmen is 53, it will be seen in Table 11.7 that the total number of observations is more than 53. The reason is that the

Table 11.7

Salesman effort and performance measurements

(1) Rank order based on X_1	(2) Data source and (number of salesmen involved)	(3) Bookings/Quota X_1	(4) Routine and end-user-type of calls X_2	(5) Active at calls X_3	(6) Customer disposition at conclusion of calls X_4	(7) Z	(8) Rank order based on Z	(9) d_i^2 Col. (1) − Col. (8)
		$X_1 \geqslant 80.0$						
1	Region 3 (9)	129.0	86.7	3.6	4.5	−1.318860	1	0√
2	Overall Group I (20)	120.3	88.2	2.7	3.9	−1.410492	2	0
3	Specialty I (12)	109.7	93.2	2.2	2.1	−1.557268	6	9
4	Region 1 (19)	90.1	83.2	2.2	3.4	−1.479934	3	1√
5	Region 2 (14)	88.1	90.0	3.1	1.8	−1.589586	7	4√
6	Specialty II (4)	88.2	77.7	4.9	10.4	−1.510018	5	1
7	Overall Group II (12)	86.0	84.5	2.0	1.5	−1.487240	4	4
Average	X_i^*	101.7428	86.2143	2.9571	3.9428	−1.479058		
		$X_1 < 80.0$						
8	Specialty III (3)	73.7	92.0	0.8	3.0	−1.812038	10	4
9	Overall Group III (21)	65.7	88.0	3.0	2.8	−1.721578	8	1
10	Region 5 (4)	62.6	92.9	0.4	1.2	−1.861414	11	1√
11	Region 4 (7)	62.5	89.3	2.0	2.5	−1.783230	9	4√
Average	X_i^{**}	66.1250	90.5500	1.5500	2.3750	−1.794565		
Difference	$d_i: X_i^* - X_i^{**}$	35.6178	−4.3357	1.4071	1.5678	+0.315508		
General Average	X_i	88.7909	87.7909	2.4454	3.3727	−1.593788		

salesmen have been grouped by: (1) *territory*; (2) *trade*; and (3) *Bookings/Quota ratio* so that those who equalled or exceeded the criterion selected in Section 3.1 of 80 percent of Bookings/Quota figure appear in different combinations. Thus, in the classification by *territory* the 9 salesmen of Region 3, the 19 salesmen of Region 1, and the 14 salesmen of Region 2 provide three sets of observations, the X_1 figure for the three Regions being greater than 80 percent as seen from Table 11.4, Column 3. In the classification by *trade*, all the 20 salesmen who exceed quotas irrespective of trade in Table 11.6, Column 5, are included as one set of observations called Overall Group I. Similarly, all the 12 salesmen who achieve between 80 and 99 percent of quota irrespective of trade in Table 11.6, Column 6, are included as one set of observations, called Overall Group II. Continuing the sets of observations by trade, the specialty trades in Columns 2 and 3 of Table 11.6 are picked up as two sets of observations respectively called Specialty I and Specialty II. Thus, the three sets of observations by Region, two sets of observations by Bookings/Quota ratio irrespective of trade, and two sets of observations by specialty trade give a total of seven sets of observations of "good" salesmen all of whom have accomplished more than 80 percent of the quota. In Table 11.7, these seven sets of observations numbered 1 through 7, are arranged in Column 3 in decreasing order of the value of the Bookings/Quota. Similar reasoning applies to the sets of observations numbered 8 through 11 in Table 11.7, representing the "bad" group.

4.5. Discriminating the "Good" From the "Bad" Salesmen: Discriminant Function

If we designate the differences between the average value of the variable X_1 between the "good" group and the "bad" group of salesmen by the term d_1, the value of d_1 is 35.6178 as seen in Section 4.4. Similarly, d_2 designates the difference of the means between the group of "good" salesmen and the group of "bad" salesmen for the variable X_2. When there are p variables, the differences for each variable can be designated by d_i $(i = 1, 2, ..., p)$.

   Each of these d_i values has some significance in the quality called "goodness" or "badness" of salesmen. To derive the empirical discriminant function, the value of the contribution of each of the differences to the quality of "goodness" or "badness" needs to be determined. If, for instance, d_1 accounts for say, 43 percent of the quality, d_2 accounts for say, 29 percent, and so on, the discriminant function will have coefficients prefixed to d_1 and d_2 (and others) *reflecting* the respective contributions of the illustrative 43 percent and 29 percent. The linear function that is to be empirically determined is made up of:

(1) the difference of the averages, d_i,
(2) the contribution of each difference reflected in its coefficient, k_i, and
(3) the addition of the weighted contributions, $k_i d_i$.

R.A. Fisher introduced discriminant functions to solve taxonomic problems in genetics.[2,3] One of his students, C.R. Rao, utilized discriminant functions in anthropometric measurements, where multiple measurements were used to classify skeletons by the group to which they most likely belonged.[4] Subsequent applications have been made in different fields, such as "good" and "bad" loans in installment financing,[5] "consumers' goods" and "producers' goods" in business cycles,[6] and so on.

The computational approach is to express each d_i as a linear combination of *all* the k_i's. Thus, k_1 will appear in the equation connecting k_1, k_2, k_3, and k_4 with d_1. It would also appear in the equation connecting d_2 with k_1, k_2, k_3, and k_4. Therefore, the different occurrences of k_1 have to be distinguished one from the other. Since k_i is the coefficient of the first difference, viz., d_1, the occurrence of this first coefficient in the first equation to d_1 may be designated by *two* subscripts, say S_{11}. When the first coefficient k_1 occurs in the second equation to d_2, it will be designated by S_{12}, and so on. The system of equations connecting the k_i's to the d_i's appears as follows:[7]

[2]*Ibid.*
[3]R.A. Fisher, *Contributions to Mathematical Statistics,* Wiley, New York, 1950, Papers 32 and 33; *Statistical Methods for Research Workers,* Oliver and Boyd, Edinburgh, Section 49.2, pp. 279ff.
[4]C.R. Rao, "On Some Problems Arising Out of Discrimination with Multiple Characters", *Sankhya: The Indian Journal of Statistics,* Vol. 9, 1944, pp. 343ff; "The Utilization of Multiple Measurements in Problems of Biological Classifications", *Journal of the Royal Statistical Society*, Series B, Vol. 10, 1948, pp. 159ff.
[5]D. Durand, "Risk Elements in Consumer Installment Financing", in National Bureau of Economic Research, *Studies in Consumer Installment Financing*, New York, 1941, pp. 125ff.
[6]G. Tintner, *Prices in the Trade Cycle*, Vienna, 1935, Table 7, pp. 142ff; *Econometrics*, Wiley, New York, 1954, pp. 99ff.
[7]Gerhard Tintner, *Econometrics*, Wiley, New York, 1952, p. 91.

$$S_{11}k_1 + S_{12}k_2 + \ldots + S_{1p}k_p = d_1,$$
$$S_{12}k_1 + S_{22}k_2 + \ldots + S_{2p}k_p = d_2,$$
$$S_{1p}k_1 + S_{2p}k_p + \ldots + S_{pp}k_p = d_p.$$

The solutions k_i are *proportional* to the estimates of the coefficients of the linear function which, in the population from which the sample is drawn, discriminates best between the "good" and "bad" groups.

In Table 11.7, the data and the calculations to derive the empirical discriminant function are shown. The four equations connecting the four differences each with all the coefficients of the differences are:

$$5194.77k_1 - 150.31k_2 + 126.22k_3 + 134.99k_4 = 35.6178,$$

$$-150.31k_1 + 215.39k_2 - 41.09k_3 - 90.33k_4 = -4.3357,$$

$$126.22k_1 - 41.09k_2 + 15.57k_3 + 23.93k_4 = 1.4071,$$

$$134.99k_1 - 90.33k_2 + 23.93k_3 + 64.48k_4 = 1.5678.$$

The solutions k_i to the four simultaneous equations are proportional to the estimates of the empirical linear discriminant function.

4.5.1. Discriminant function

The linear discriminant function is $Z = 0.00646X_1 + (-0.02410)X_2 + (0.01820)X_3 + (0.02850)X_4$.

The discriminant function tells us that if any Z-value is below the Z-value corresponding to general mean -1.593788, the salesman or region should be classified as "good"; if the Z-value is above -1.593788 it is "bad". In this instance, "good" refers to a specialty salesman, a general trades salesman, or to a region comprising both general and specialty salesmen, and overall classification on a national basis.

4.5.2. Test of significance

We now proceed to test the hypothesis that the empirical discriminant function may have arisen out of pure chance. This will be the case if, in reality, there is no difference at all between the variates in the two groups. H. Hotelling developed in 1931 a test of significance by defining a quantity analogous to the multiple correlation coefficient:[8]

$$R^2 = \frac{N_1 N_2 (k_1 d_1 + ... + k_p d_p)}{N} \, ,$$

then the variance ratio

$$F = \frac{(N - p - 1)R^2}{p(1 - R^2)} \, ,$$

has Snedecor's F-distribution for $n_1 = p$ and $n_2 = N - p - 1$ degrees of freedom.[9]

This test is also related to the distance function discussed by Rao.[10]

Our discriminant function has an R of 0.8961. The F-value of 11.59 is significant at 95% and 99% levels of confidence.

We conclude that the empirical discriminant function derived is an admissible yardstick to differentiate between "good" and "bad".

It is interesting to note in the discriminant function *that approximately three times the weight of Bookings/Quota (X_1) is given for active efforts at calls (X_3).*

4.5.3. Rank order correlation

Can the salesman be rank ordered on the basis of Bookings/Quota? In fact, as a first approximation, X_1 values in Table 11.7 are applied, not only to the evaluation of "all trades" salesmen, but also to the evaluation of Regions and specialty salesmen. It will be recalled from Section 4.4, that the 7 sets of "good" and 4 sets of "bad" sales performance sets are arranged in rank order on the basis of the value of Bookings/Quota from Rank 1 for 129.0 through Rank 11 for 62.5. It is understandable that a sales manager may find it hard

[8] H. Hotelling, "The Generalization of Student's Ratio", *Annals of Mathematical Statistics*, Vol. 2, 1931, pp. 360ff.

[9] For a discussion of degrees of freedom, see George K. Chacko, *Applied Statistics in Decision-Making*, American Elsevier, New York, 1971, Ch. 5.

[10] C.R. Rao, "On the Use and Interpretation of Distance Functions in Statistics", *Bull. Inst. Internat. Stat.*, Vol. 34, 1954, pp. 90–97.

to depend on any criterion other than that of the sales that a salesman "produces" bookings.

The discriminant function is a logical means of evaluation with specified properties and limitations. In order for the discriminant function to be accepted as a management tool, it will generally be necessary to compare the rank orderings arrived at by the *line* organization, including the sales managers, with that of the operations research/systems analysis rank ordering. The merit of a mathematical equation would be, in part, judged by the precision with which *borderline* cases are measured; for, the very best and the worst membership of the two groups — "good" and "bad" — are identified with a great deal of unanimity, the question being mostly with reference to the "borderline" cases.

In Table 11.7, Column 1, the rank order based on Bookings/Quota, and in Column 8, the rank order based on the Z-values of the empirical discriminant function are shown. What is the "groupwise togetherness" of the two ranks?

A preliminary analysis may be made in terms of rank order correlations shown in Columns 1 and 8 in Table 11.7. For this purpose, we combine all the rank orders of measures relating to the five Regions, viz., 4, 5, 1, 11, and 10, according to the rank order based on X_1. The d_2 values in Column 9 corresponding to the five observations marked by $\sqrt{}$, are arrived at by squaring the difference between column 1 and column 8 corresponding to these five entries. The value $\Sigma_j d_j^2$, 10, indicates significant positive correlation at the 5% level in the table of critical values for $\Sigma_j d_j^2$ published by Teegarden.[11]

Similar results are obtained when the 53 salesmen are grouped into three Overall Groups I, II, and III on the basis of their respective percent of Bookings/Quota.

However, when we combine the specialty groups which are identified by entries 3, 6, and 8 in Table 11.7, Column 1, the $\Sigma_j d_j^2$ value of 14 indicates significant negative correlation.

The agreement between the two sets of ranks with respect to the Regions, and to Bookings/Quota, and the disagreement with respect to the specialty salesmen can be explained in terms of the heavy contribution of the d^2 value by one in three, out of the three involved in the latter. Specifically, 64% of the $\Sigma_j d^2$ value of 14 is made up by the group of Specialty I salesmen whose X_1 value is 109.7%.

[11] Klare L. Teegarden, "Critical Sigma d^2 Values for Rank Order Correlations", *Industial Quality Control*, May, 1960, pp. 48–49.

5. APPLICATION 25: Production Function Fitted to Company Outlays on Territory and Salesmen

In Section 3, "salesmanship" has been identified as making the overwhelming contribution toward explaining the percent of company bookings of the top 25 salesmen. The "salesmanship" has been studied in action, in terms of merely the observable allocation of the salesmen's time among different types of calls. It has been possible to develop an empirical discriminant function which separates the "good" from the "bad" sales performance.

5.1. Returns to Scale

Can the management expect to influence the salesman effort performance by rewarding "salesmanship"? If, for instance, the commissions were to be increased by 2 percentage points across the board, will the company bookings increase by 2 percentage points, 10 percentage points, or none? If for a 2 percentage points increase, the sales increase by *more* than 2 percentage points, then *increasing returns to scale* are in operation.

A similar question of returns to scale was studied by Paul H. Douglas and his associates in 1928.[12] The Douglas-type production function is of the form:

$$X_0 = A \cdot X_1^{\alpha} \cdot X_2^{\beta},$$

where

X_0 denotes the annual physical output,
X_1 denotes manpower of a firm,
X_2 denotes capital of a firm,
α denotes elasticity of output with respect to labor,
β denotes elasticity of output with respect to capital.

The advantage of this approach lies in the ease of manipulation of the exponents α and β. If $\alpha + \beta = 1$, then the industry is operating under *constant returns to scale*. It means that a 10 percent increase in the expenditure on each of the inputs, labor and capital, will be accompanied by an increase in

[12] Paul H. Douglas, C.W. Cobb, "A Theory of Production", *American Economic Review*, Vol. 8, 1928, Supplement, p. 139ff.

the value of the output by about 10 percent. If, on the other hand, the sum of the exponents were *greater* than 1, say 1.15, it would mean that a 10 percent in the expenditure on each of the inputs, labor and capital, would *increase* the value of the output by about 15 percent. If, however, the sum of the exponents were *less* than 1, say 0.75, it would mean that a 10 percent increase in the expenditure on each of the inputs, labor and capital, would yield an increase of 75 percent in the value of the output, or a *decrease* in the value of the output by 25 percent.

5.2. Returns to Scale: Company Outlay on "Salesmanship" and Territory Potentials

The company bookings are the result of "salesmanship" acting on the sales potential in the territory. The "salesmanship" of the top 25 salesmen have been identified in Table 11.1, Column 4. The company outlay on "salesmanship" may be considered to be reflected in the commissions paid to the salesmen. Similarly, the company outlay on the territory potential may be considered to be reflected in the advertising outlay. To determine the returns to scale, the two inputs will be: (1) commissions paid to salesmen; and (2) advertising outlay in the sales territory; the changes in one or both of which are postulated to bring about increasing, decreasing, or constant returns to scale in the value of the output, viz., company bookings.

5.3. Preparation of Data

The *bookings* data of the 25 selected salesmen are modified to reflect the fact that some sales territory cuts across more than one state; and some states include more than one sales territory.

The commissions of the 25 selected salesmen have also to be modified to reflect the fact that the total commissions earned are over his entire sales territory which comprises more than one State in some instances. The bookings are prorated to reflect the potentials of the territory which, in turn, are taken to reflect the actual bookings achieved. Further, an adjustment has to be made to ensure that the commissions relate to the period in which they are earned. According to the figures available from the accounting department, the total commissions paid to Dembner was $9 612.46. Since Connecticut represents about 80 percent of Dembner's bookings, 80 percent of the total

Table 11.8
Outlay of 25 selected salesmen and territory: 6-month period

State	Commissions earned Z	Advertising outlay X
Region 1		
Connecticut	7,690	2,105
New Jersey	16,484	4,626
New York	16,787	13,476
Massachusetts	13,936	3,829
Washington, D.C.	8,425	761
Maine, Vt., New Hampshire	1,596	1,266
Virginia	7,719	2,409
Pennsylvania	6,841	8,149
Region 2		
Minnesota	8,013	2,326
Illinois	5,321	7,941
Missouri	4,672	3,068
Indiana	8,364	3,285
Michigan	6,557	5,893
Michigan (Wois)	10,551	5,893
Ohio	9,105	7,245
Region 3		
California (Mansfield)	3,791	4,009
California (Karl)	7,146	4,009
California (Iles)	3,547	4,009
Arizona	3,453	774
Washington, Oregon, Montana, Idaho	8,788	4,230
Region 4		
Florida	6,545	3,041
Alabama	4,654	1,711
Georgia	6,185	2,239
Tennessee	10,830	1,977
Region 5		
Texas	8,088	6,285
	195,088 =	

46.76% of Grand Total of Commissions
to All Salesmen

commissions $(9\,612.46 \times 0.80 =)$ \$7 690 is credited to his bookings in Connecticut during the 6-month period. This figure appears in Table 11.8, Column 2.

The commissions paid by the company to the salesmen are considered the *outlay* by the company on the "salesmanship". This is an over-simplification, for there are other outlays on the "salesmanship", such as the guidance provided by the sales managers, sales training, the analysis of the sales effort performance data, and so on. However, the present question is whether a change made in the commissions is likely to make a more than proportionate change in the bookings by the salesman. Therefore, all other services which enhance the "salesmanship" will be excluded in considering the company outlay on "salesmanship".

The *advertising outlay*, which is the company outlay on territory potential is allocated *retrospectively* among the 27 States in which the top 25 salesmen have their territories. The percent of U.S. Retail Volume in a given State has been used in Chapter 10, Section 6 to represent the territory potentials. The advertising outlay could be allocated among the States on the basis of the Retail Volume. However, other alternative estimates of the territory potentials are explored. The same source that updates the Retail Volume by State, also offers another index:

> "Buying Power Index" assigns five points to "percent of U.S.A. Effective Buying Income", three points to "percent of U.S.A. Retail Sales", and two points to "percent of U.S.A. population"[13].

Thus, the "Buying Power Index" appears to represent the territory potentials more inclusively than Retail Volume by itself. The advertising outlay is accordingly distributed among the States on the basis of the "Buying Power Index" in Table 11.8, Column 3.

5.4. The Douglas Function Fit

The Douglas-type production function, it has been said in Section 5.1, is of the form:

$$X_0 = A \cdot X_1^{\alpha} \cdot X_2^{\beta},$$

[13] Sales Management, *Survey of Buying Power*, May 10, 1958, p. 32b.

equivalently,

$$Y = A \cdot Z^{\alpha} \cdot X^{\beta} .$$

Taking logarithms, it reduces to an equation which is linear in logarithms:

$$\log Y = \log A + \alpha \log Z + \beta \log X .$$

In the present instance, the variables are:
Y = the logarithms of the bookings by the salesman,
Z = the logarithm of the commissions of the salesman,
X = the logarithm of the advertising outlay in the State,

$$\log Y = \log A + \alpha \log Z + \beta \log X,$$

$$\log Y = \log A + \alpha \log Z + \beta \log X \text{ (in logarithms)},$$

$$\log Y = 0.5549 + 1.1708\, Z + (-0.0244)X \text{ (in logarithms)}.$$

In Table 11.9, the *logarithms* of the bookings, commissions, and advertising are shown. The equation fitted to the data in Table 11.9 can be looked upon as a multiple regression equation, similar to the multiple regression equation fitted to company bookings in Section 2.

In the present instance, the "multiple regression equation" is $Y = 0.5549 + 1.1708Z + (-0.0244)X$, where the values are logarithms. The Douglas production function is:

$$Y = 3.588 \cdot Z^{1.1708} \cdot X^{-0.0244} .$$

It is found that the two variables, viz., outlay on "salesmanship" (Z) and outlay on territory potential in the form of advertising outlay (X) *together* explain 94.37 percent of the company bookings by State, as is seen from Table 11.10, where the multiple regression coefficient, $R_{y.xz}$, is 0.9437. Applying the standard error of estimate, it could be stated that the two variables, X and Z, together explain between 92.19 percent and 96.55 percent of the Y values.

It is also found that the advertising outlay, considered without outlay on "salesmanship", predicts the company bookings very poorly; the partial correlation coefficient, $r_{yx.z}$, is -0.0527.

Table 11.9

Data for predictive relationship between bookings and outlays on territory and salesman

State	$\log Y = Y^*$	$\log Z = Z^{**}$	$\log X = X^{***}$
Region 1			
Connecticut	5.064083	3.885926	3.323252
New Jersey	5.274850	4.216957	3.665206
New York	5.405346	4.225051	3.226600
Massachusetts	5.249198	4.144263	3.282169
Washington, D.C.	5.082067	3.925570	2.881385
Maine, Vt., New Hampshire	3.924072	3.203033	3.102434
Virginia	5.080626	3.887561	3.381837
Pennsylvania	4.960280	3.835120	3.308991
Region 2			
Minnesota	5.025715	3.903795	3.366610
Illinois	4.852541	3.725993	3.297761
Missouri	4.814714	3.669503	3.486855
Indiana	4.994977	3.922414	3.516535
Michigan	4.976533	3.816705	3.469380
Michigan–Wois	5.131619	4.023252	3.469380
Ohio	5.072617	3.959280	3.382917
Region 3			
California–Mansfield	4.794767	3.578754	3.381296
California–Karl	4.910624	3.854063	3.381296
California–Iles	4.767156	3.549861	3.381296
Arizona	4.674953	3.538197	2.888741
Wash., Oregon, Mont., Idaho	5.114277	3.943890	3.468200
Region 4			
Florida	5.056905	3.815910	3.483016
Alabama	4.812445	3.667826	2.932474
Georgia	4.961326	3.791340	3.350054
Tennessee	5.259594	4.034628	2.995196
Region 5			
Texas	5.015360	3.907841	3.497344

$^*Y$ is the logarithm of prorated bookings by salesmen in primary states.

$^{**}Z$ is the logarithm of prorated commissions shown in Table 11.8.

$^{***}X$ is the logarithm of company outlay by state divided equally among the number of salesmen assigned to the state.

Table 11.10
Company bookings by state—multiple regression coefficient

$R_{y.xz}$ = 0.9437 Standard Error of $R_{y.xz}$ = 0.0218.
$Y = A + b_{yx.z}X + b_{yz.x}Z,$
$Y = 0.5549 + 1.1708\ Z + (-0.0244)X.$

Standard Error of the Estimate = $\sigma_{y.xz}$ = 0.0890

Partial Correlation Coefficients

$r_{yz.x}$ = 0.9407, $r_{yx.z}$ = −0.0527.

On the other hand, outlay on "salesmanship" taken by itself, is able to account for approximately 94 percent of the company bookings, as indicated by the partial correlation coefficient between bookings and commissions, when advertising outlay is held constant, $r_{yz.x}$, of 0.9407. Applying the standard error of the partial correlation coefficient, it could be stated that the commissions, which are the company outlay on "salesmanship", by itself accounts for between 91.8 percent and 96.36 percent of the company bookings by the top 25 salesmen.

How good is the "multiple regression equation" in *logarithm* in predicting the company bookings of the top 25 salesmen on the basis of company outlay on "salesmanship" and on territory potentials? During the selected 6-month period the volume of total bookings by the top 25 salesmen is $2 669 056 out of a total of $6 322 486 for the company. The addition of logarithms represents the multiplication of the numbers represented. Therefore, the sum of the logarithms representing individual bookings of the 25 top salesmen during the 6-month period, 124.276645, is a mathematical entity. When the bookings are predicted using the variables X and Z, the sum of logarithms of the predicted values is 124.285327 which, when modified by the standard error, lies between 124.1876 and 124.3656: which is of the order of 0.07 percent variation.

In Table 11.11 the expected value of bookings (in logarithms) on the basis of the equation is shown by State. It is seen that for Connecticut, the actual value of bookings exceeds the predicted value, while from New Jersey the actual value is exceeded by predicted value. However, the bookings of the 25 salesmen taken together are almost exactly matched by the predicted totals.

Table 11.11
Expected values of logarithms of bookings in primary states—exponential fit

State	$\log Y = Y$	Y Expected
Region 1		
Connecticut	5.064083	5.023475
New Jersey	5.274850	5.410033
New York	5.405346	5.422895
Massachusetts	5.249198	5.326948
Washington, D.C.	5.082067	5.080685
Maine, Vt., New Hampshire	3.924072	4.229313
Virginia	5.080626	5.023958
Pennsylvania	4.690280	4.964533
	40.040522	40.481840
Region 2		
Minnesota	5.025715	5.043337
Illinois	4.852541	4.836842
Missouri	4.814714	4.766082
Indiana	4.994977	5.061475
Michigan—Argelan	4.976533	4.938859
Michigan—Wois	5.131619	5.180691
Ohio	5.072617	5.107903
	34.868716	50.161312
Region 3		
California—Mansfield	4.794767	4.662408
California—Karl	4.910624	4.984750
California—Iles	4.767156	4.628580
Arizona	4.674953	4.626955
Wash., Oregon, Mont., Idaho	5.114277	5.087800
	24.261777	23.990493
Region 4		
Florida	5.056905	4.937595
Alabama	4.812445	4.777661
Georgia	4.961326	4.912075
Tennessee	5.259594	5.205594
	20.090270	19.832925
Region 5		
Texas	5.015360	5.044880
	5.015360	5.044880
Total all regions	124.276645	124.285327

5.5. Increasing Returns to Scale

The question was raised in Section 5.2 as to whether the company bookings were operating under increasing returns to scale. If it does, then the company could increase the bookings more than in proportion to the increase in outlay on "salesmanship" and/or advertising outlay.

The powers (exponents) of Z (outlay on "salesmanship") is 1.1708, and of X (outlay on territory potentials) is −0.0244. The sum of the two exponents is $(1.1708 - 0.0244 =)$ 1.1464. Since this sum is greater than 1, it would appear that the company bookings are operating under increasing returns to scale. In other words, a 10 percent increase in the company outlays on both "salesmanship" and territory potentials is likely to increase the company bookings by 14.64 percent.

Before the company uses this conclusion to influence its policy, it is necessary to check whether the 1.1464 figure has occurred by chance. For this, a test of significance, similar to the one in Section 4.5.2, is performed.

5.6. New Exponents With the Constraint of Unity on the Sum

We recompute the values of the exponents with the restrictions that their sum be 1. This restriction states that for 10 percent additional investment by the company in both commissions and advertising would bring about a 10 percent increase in company bookings. Under this new restriction, the exponents are 1.0245 for Z and −0.0245 for X.

We now proceed to test the assumption of unity for the sum of the exponents. We compare the sum of the squares of the deviations from the regression equation fitted by the method of least squares *without* the restriction, Q_1, with the sum of squares of the deviations from the other regression equation fitted *with* the restriction, Q_2. The quantity Q_1 is distributed like χ^2 with $N - p$ degrees freedom, where p is the total number of variables. The test function:

$$F = \frac{(Q_2 - Q_1)(N - p)}{Q_1} ,$$

is distributed like Snedecor's F with 1 and $N - p$ degrees of freedom.

It is found that the F-value is significant at 95 percent and 99 percent levels of confidence. We conclude, therefore, that the company bookings are indeed operating under increasing returns to scale.

Therefore, it behooves the company to consider stimulating the company bookings by increasing the outlay on "salesmanship" in the form of commissions. For a 10 percent increase in commissions, the company may expect about 15 percent increase in bookings.

6. APPLICATION 26: Douglas-Type Production Function Fitted to Salesman Effort-Performance by Region

To effectively manage the salesman effort-performance, it is necessary to have: (1) a means of separation of the "good" salesmen from the "bad"; and (2) a measure of the contribution of different factors to the final outcome in such a way that manipulations of the variables can be expected to produce predictable results.

The discriminant function provides an answer to the first requirement. We shall now explore the salesman effort and performance, by region, in order to arrive at an input-output relationship with respect to salesman effort variables and salesman performance using the Douglas-type function employed in Section 5. The exponents of the Douglas-type production function are elasticities, the sum of which is *assumed* to be 1. This form of equation is explored here because it yields elasticities immediately, so that the input-output relationship between salesman effort and salesman performance can be measured directly.

The same variables as in Table 11.7 are used with the exception that X_1 is the "dependent" variable, and X_2, X_3, and X_4 are "independent" variables. The five Regions in which *all* the salesmen are included are studied. This group of data is selected, instead of either the three observations on the specialty salesmen or the three observations on all the salesmen together on a national basis, because the regional classification provides the maximum number of independent observations with respect to the variables in question. There is the additional operational advantage in the Regional basis, because the sales organization is required to evaluate performance of Regions under the responsibility of Regional Managers.

The exponential fit is given by:

$$X_1 = 0.000000005 X_2^{0.44746222} \cdot X_3^{1.42711628} \cdot X_4^{1.21633277}.$$

The F-value shows the sum of the exponents to be statistically significantly greater than 1 at both 95 percent and 99 percent levels of confidence.

The standard error of estimate is 0.0849 to a base of $X_1 = 1.9917$, of 4.26 percent. The explained variation due to the linear relationship is as high as 97.36 percent of the total variation. We conclude that the exponential fit to the salesman effort and performance by region is a valid functional relationship.

Some interesting conclusions follow from the exponential fit. To begin with, the input-output relationship, like the outlay on salesmanship and bookings in Section 5 is operating under *increasing returns* to scale. An increase in the input of X_3 by 1 percent will bring about, other things being equal, an increase of about 1.43 percent in the Bookings/Quota value. Similarly, an increase in the input of X_4 by 1 percent will bring about, other things being equal, an increase of about 1.22 percent in the Bookings/Quota value. An increase in the number of calls by 1 percent, by itself, will bring about, other things being equal, only less than one-half a percent increase in the Bookings/Quota value.

In the light of the discriminant function and the exponential fit, we can state that the sales management should concentrate on improving the *quality* of the calls, in terms of training of the dealer (customer) salesmen and introduction of new products. The calls dealing with dealer dissatisfaction should be reduced as a fraction of the total number of calls made by the salesmen; which reduction requires the improvement in the product, thereby reducing defect complaints.

7. Salesman Efforts From the Viewpoint of Quality Control

The discriminant function is our basis for discrimination between "good" and "bad" salesmen or group of salesmen. In order to utilize this function in the managerial decision process, as suggested in Section 4.2, several assumptions are needed. Among them are the following:

(1) We assume that the quota is a valid yardstick measure, not only for large intervals, but also for small intervals like a month or a week.

(2) We assume that the quota is a realistic yardstick, not only for all the salesmen combined, but also for individual salesmen during the small intervals.

(3) The linear relationship of the discriminant function is assumed to be valid for the individual salesman and in the small intervals.

(4) The variates X_1, X_2, X_3, and X_4 are assumed to be normally distributed although in reality they may not be.

It would be noticed from Table 11.7 that the Z-values close to the Z-values corresponding to the general mean -1.593788 will create a problem of classification. For instance, does the Z-value -1.589586, corresponding to the fifth row in Table 11.7, really indicate a "good" rank?

We come up against the familiar Type I and Type II errors.[14] We can control the Type I error, or rejecting the hypothesis that the salesman or region is "good", when it is actually true, by selecting the level of significance α. We may control the Type II error, of accepting the hypothesis that the salesman or region is "good" when it is not true, by selecting the size of the sample, n. In the foregoing instance, we would be incurring Type I error if Region 2 is classified as "bad", while it is really "good"; at the same time we would be incurring Type II error if we classify Region 2 as "good", while in fact it is not so.

From an OR/SA point of view, the classification of one point is not as important as the *rule of procedure* which can be applied to recurrent situations of salesmen management. Interest centers much more around controlling the average quality of the decisions in the long run.

If we were to accept the Z-value corresponding to the mean of the "bad" group -1.794565 as *above* -1.593788, we are incurring Type II error. In terms of the base value of -1.593788 the error represents 12.60 percent.

It is reasonable to specify that, in the long run, sales performance sets with -1.794565 values (really "bad" ones) should not be accepted more than once in eight times. Sample sales performance sets must be considered drawn from a finite universe.

The mathematical probabilities used in the solutions in Dodge-Romig[15] tables are based on equations corresponding to sampling from either a finite

[14] See George K. Chacko, *Applied Statistics in Decision-Making*, American Elsevier, New York, 1971, Ch. 16.

[15] Harold F. Dodge, Harry G. Romig, *Sampling Inspection Tables*, 2nd ed., Wiley, New York, 1959.

or an infinite universe. In relations involving the determination of the Consumer's Risk, the sample is considered as a sample from a lot of finite number of pieces, and probabilities are correspondingly based on sampling from a finite universe.

The number of pieces in the lot, N, at the different decision levels in successive intervals of four-week periods are set forth in Table 11.12. Consumer's Risk is similar to Type II error. Our objective is to obtain an average outgoing quality limit (AOQL) of 12.60 percent, corresponding to a specified Consumer's Risk. Subject to the limitations of the four simplifying assumptions listed by Grant,[16] any acceptance/rectification plan guarantees that regardless of the ingoing qualities submitted, the outgoing qualities in the long run will not be worse than the plan's AOQL.[17] Where the test is an attributes test, the most common plan is: (a) a single sampling plan with an acceptance number, c, or 0; or (b) a double sampling plan with acceptance numbers c_1 and c_2 equal to 0 and 1. When using the Dodge–Romig Sampling Plan Tables, if there is no basis for estimating the process average, the sampling plan should be selected from the right-hand column of the table.

The single sampling plan for salesmen management is provided in Table 11.13.

We now give a meaning to c, the acceptance number. In a manufacturing plant c is the stated allowable number of defectives in a sample of stated size. In the case of salesmen management, we have to specify what a defective is.

We can do this by specifying that 1 percent range is the Z-value corresponding the general mean, -1.593788 is the area in which Z-values are most likely to lead to wrong classification. Thus any Z-value in the range -1.609726 to -1.577850 becomes a "defective". On this basis, we find that in Table 11.7, row 5 contains the only defective which, according to this criterion is a Z-value falling within the range -1.609726 to -1.577850. In this case $c = 1$ for $n = 11$. Alternate criteria for selection of defectives can be arrived at by specifying different error ranges. This is illustrated in Table 11.14.

Our sampling plan in the fourth row of Table 11.13 merely states that for as high a lot tolerance percent defective as 43.5 percent, with a Consumer's

[16] E.L. Grant, *Statistical Quality Control*, 3rd ed., McGraw-Hill, New York, 1964, pp. 336–337.
[17] See also George K. Chacko, *Applied Statistics, op. cit.*, Ch. 21, 22.

Table 11.12

Lot size N (the maximum number of independent Z-values) by decision levels in successive equal time periods

Decision level	Weeks	1-4	5-8	9-12	13-16	17-20	21-24	25-28	29-32	33-36	37-40	41-44	45-48	49-52	1-52
I. Individual Salesman		1	2	3	4	5	6	7	8	9	10	11	12	13	13
II. All Salesmen		53	106	159	212	265	318	371	424	477	530	583	636	689	689
III. By Region															
Region 1		19	38	57	76	95	114	133	152	171	190	209	228	247	247
Region 2		14	28	42	56	70	84	98	112	126	140	154	168	182	182
Region 3		9	18	27	36	45	54	63	72	81	90	99	108	117	117
Region 4		7	14	21	28	35	42	49	56	63	70	77	84	91	91
Region 5		4	8	12	16	20	24	28	32	36	40	44	48	52	52
IV. By Specialist Trades															
Speciality I		12	24	36	48	60	72	84	96	108	120	132	144	156	156
Speciality II		4	8	12	16	20	24	28	32	36	40	44	48	52	52
Speciality III		3	6	9	12	15	18	21	24	27	30	33	36	39	39

Table 11.13

Single and double sampling table for average outgoing quality limit (AOQL) = 10.0%

Row no.	Lot size	Process average 8.01 to 10%			Process average 8.01 to 10%					
					Trial 1		Trial 2			
		n	c	$P_t\%$	n_1	c_1	n_2	n_1+n_2	c_2	$P_t\%$
1	1–3	All	0	–	All	0	–	–	–	–
2	4–15	–	–	–	3	0	–	–	–	50.0
3	16–50	7	1	43.5	6	0	6	12	2	48.0
4	4–50	12	2	37.5	–	–	–	–	–	–
5	51–100	18	3	33.0	7	0	16	23	4	36.5
6	101–200	23	4	32.0	14	1	24	38	7	32.0
7	210–300	29	5	30.0	19	2	29	48	9	31.0
8	301–400	30	5	29.5	21	2	44	65	12	29.0
9	401–500	36	6	28.5	22	2	53	75	13	27.0
10	501–600	42	7	27.5	28	3	52	80	14	26.5
11	601–800				29	3	56	85	15	26.0

n = sample size; c = acceptance number.

Trial 1: n_1 = first sample size; c_1 = acceptance number for first sample.

Trial 2: n_2 = second sample size; c_2 = acceptance number for first and second samples combined.

"All" indicates that each piece in the lot is to be inspected.

P_t = lot tolerance percent defective with a Consumer's Risk (P_c) of 0.10.

Source: H.F. Dodge, H.G. Romig, Sampling Inspection Tables, 2nd ed., Wiley, New York, 1959, pp. 204, 281.

Table 11.14
Some alternate selections of C-basis

Z error range, %	Z error range	"Defectives"	c	n
±1%	−1.609726 to −1.577850	row 5	1	11
±2%	−1.625664 to −1.561912	row 5	1	11
±3%	−1.641602 to −1.545974	rows 3, 5	2	11
±4%	−1.657539 to −1.530036	rows 3, 5	2	11
±5%	−1.673477 to −1.514099	rows 3, 5	2	11
±10%	−1.753167 to −1.434409	rows 3, 4, 5, 6, 7, 9	6	11

Risk of 0.10, AOQL will be 10 percent. If the number of wrong classifications of "bad" and "good" is only 1 out of 7 in the sample, the sampling plan assures us that in the long run, such decisions will be only 1 in 10.

By way of comparison, the second and third rows in Table 11.13 provide the double sampling plan. For as high a lot tolerance percent defective as 48 to 50 percent with a Consumer's Risk of 0.10, AOQL will be 10 percent. However, the number inspected increases from 7 to 9 if there is no defective found in the first sample. On the other hand, under the double sampling plan, there is the risk of inspecting as many as 15 units.

8. Summary

On the basis of 14 972 calls reported by 53 salesmen who sell 315 durable goods/products to 12 different industries, an analytical tool has been devised to make possible successive evaluations of the performance and effort of the salesmen, both in groups and as individuals.

The intuitive appeal of the discriminant function developed from empirical data is established in terms of the rank order correlation of salesman ranking by sales managers and by the discriminant function.

After developing a precise measure of differentiation between "good" and "bad" sales performances, attention is turned to the development of a technique which would indicate areas where additional effort is most appropriate. The exponential fit to the salesman effort and performance provides a tool which is found to be statistically satisfactory.

The Z-values of the discriminant function answer precisely the question: Who is "good", and who is "bad"? As to what can be done about the situation, the answer is provided by the exponential fit to salesman effort-performance data, which explains 97.36 percent of the total variation. The elasticities of the three independent variables – call type, effort, and disposition – with respect to Bookings/Quota, the dependent variable, provide a basis for definitive action. The fact that the actual Bookings/Quota was 101.96 percent suggests that the dependent variable is a realistic choice.

Decision processes based on the Z-values are examined from the point of view of quality control to yield a sampling plan of inspection to ensure the long run average quality of the decisions such that a "bad" one is accepted as "good" not more than once in eight times.

The executive decisions in the home office regarding the merchandising policy can be viewed as the *pacesetter*, the translations of those policies into targets for territories by the sales managers as the *pacemaker*, and the salesman's calls on each customer as the *pacetranslator*; the three types of which decision-making providing an integrated approach to improving the allocation of the scarce commodity of salesmanship to realize the sales potentials.

PROBLEMS

The four chapters, 9, 10, 11 and 12, of Part IV deal with the application of OR/SA Protocol to large, unstructured problems in the Private Sector. The two major problems vital to any manufacturing and sales operation are: (1) sales, and (2) production. This chapter deals with the measurement *of the elusive quality called "salesmanship", which is essential to convert sales potentials into actual sales. The purposes of the following questions is to develop an appreciation for the difficulties in measuring intangible, but important, elements in system performance.*

A. *Empirical Measures of Effectiveness – Absolute*

1. To use the judgment factor of experience, it is essential that a subjective scale be used. Discuss the use of subjective scales in assessing the intangible quality of "salesmanship".

2. While the external indicator of sales potentials, based on the volume of sales in the trading centers, can be measured by different people to yield the

same results, the internal indicator of "salesmanship" of any group of sales-men cannot be so graded. What is the simplest assumption that relates the external potentials, and the internal potentials with the actual results (sales) obtained? What are its limitations?

B. *Empirical Measures of Effectiveness – Relative*

3. How would you use partial correlation coefficients in determining the "rate of change" of Y (Company booking) with respect to Z ("salesman-ship") to determine if it is better to invest in Z in order to bring about a desired rate of change in Y?

4. How would you determine what particular activity of the salesman would contribute most to improving the sales?

C. *Empirical Measures of Subsystem Performance*

5. How do you discriminate between "good" and "bad" salesmen?

6. How would you determine if it is worthwhile to invest in advertisement or to give higher commissions?

ISOPIECES ACTION CHART IN PRIVATE SECTOR PROBLEMS: (3) PRODUCTION AND INVENTORY DECISIONS

TECHNICAL OVERVIEW

In Chapters 9, 10, and 11, the first of the two major problems which are vital to any manufacturing and sales operation, viz., sales, has been discussed. Now the second major problem, viz., production, *will be discussed with reference to the same real life context of a multi-plant, multi-product, durable goods, manufacturing and sales organization.*

The symptom of the problem was overtime. The total number of 1 484 overtime hours during the specimen week amount of 13.16% overtime. The company management wanted to reduce the overtime.

A study of the causes of overtime shows that it results from inadequate planning from top down. During the specimen week, 51% of the worktime, and 57% of the jobs, are devoted to "Special Assignment" jobs. Had there been better planning this fraction could be considerably reduced, if not eliminated altogether. Since the special assignments really arise from the need for parts which were not in inventory, the management must make decisions regarding the size of the inventory. It will also depend upon the "learning" by the decision-makers at different levels of the need for particular parts to be carried in inventory in order not to have to rush to "special assignment" jobs to fulfill customer orders.

Based on the 1 000 orders that arrive a week from the customers, and the average 3 000 items represented by the orders, the physical correlates of decision processes are identified from the Vice-President for Production down to the individual operator in the plant. Noting that the loss in sales comes to 7.03% of the gross bookings, it is attributed to delays in shipment, and to defects in manufacture.

The two types of delay and defect causes can be made operational.

The number of pieces per job during the specimen week is 164.83. To meet the 1 000 customer orders, 95 700 pieces are required: which when divided into 282 jobs (1 job per week per operator), gives an average production of 339.96 pieces per direct operator. Manufacturing economies are obtained at 500 pieces or more; therefore, we double the average production to 678.72 pieces. When the average number of pieces per job is raised from 164.83 to 672.72, the problem of special assignments leading to overtime payments will be solved.

So far, we have not differentiated between the different plants which can manufacture the products. How should production be allocated among the different plants? The concept of resources-use index is introduced, and illustrated with respect to 10 top selling products which can be made in different plants. It is found that by applying this concept, if all the units of the 10 products now manufactured by plant A were to be manufactured at plant B, it would result in an additional gain of $20 000 to the manufacturer during the 20 weeks.

Whether the loss in sales is due to delay, or defect, the effect is the same. What the management requires is an action signal. If this can be directly related to the number of pieces produced by a direct operator in the plant, then we shall have an objective mechanism for initiating corrective action.

We could relate the 678.72 pieces per job per direct operator per week to represent no customer dissatisfaction, or 0% delay dissatisfaction, and 0% defect dissatisfaction. As the number of pieces decrease, the dissatisfaction percentage will correspondingly increase. For instance, when the average number of pieces is 340, it represents 50% dissatisfaction. By calibrating the efficiency of top management, and the lower level managements in terms of the average number of pieces of production, it is possible to devise an Iso-pieces Action Chart which indicate whenever corrective action is required, whether it be due to defect or delay; or whether it be due to inefficiencies of production or of inventory; or whether it be due to higher or lower management problems.

EXECUTIVE SUMMARY

In Chapters 9, 10, and 11, the first of the two major problems of any manufacturing and sales organization, i.e., sales, was examined. In Chapter 12, the other problem, i.e., production, is examined.

The company has an overtime problem, a specimen week showing 13.16% overtime. More importantly, 51% of the work time, and 57% of the jobs are found to be devoted to "Special Assignment Jobs". These are jobs into which the plant worker is assigned on a rush basis.

To overcome the overtime problem, better management has to be brought about from top down. It is found that 7.03% of the gross bookings are cancelled by customers during the year. This cancellation could be related to dissatisfaction with delay and dissatisfaction with defects. A method is devised by which the combination of defect and delay can be detected on the basis of the average number of pieces per operator per week. This permits the management· to take action to correct the problem whatever may be the origin, in sufficient time to control the situation.

In Chapters 9, 10, and 11 the first of two major problems which are vital to any manufacturing and sales operation, viz., sales, has been discussed. The same real life context of a multiplant, multiproduct, durable goods manufacturing and sales organization used in those chapters will be maintained in the discussion of the second major problem, viz., Production.

1. The Problem of Overtime

Soon after the acquisition of the 57-year old multiplant, multiproduct organization by the three entrepreneurs, the cost accountant collected, for the first time, data on the manufacturing costs of the different plants.

Each plant worker is asked to "punch in" and "punch out" every time he engages in a different operation. Thus, the worker "punches in" on his time card the time at which he starts working on the lathes. He "punches out" when he finishes the lathe operations, and "punches in" at the next work station, and so on.

Based on the time card information provided by the "punching in" and "punching out" of the different work stations, it is possible to develop the distribution of the worker effort-performance. The parallel to the salesman effort-performance in Chapter 11 of the worker effort-performance in this Chapter stems from the common characteristics:

(1) the time card as the worker's report on how he allocated his time among different jobs; the salesman call card as the salesman's report on how he allocated his time among different sales efforts;

(2) the absence of a norm which permits the determination of how the worker effort or the salesman effort should be allocated among different jobs or different sales efforts; and

(3) the need to take immediate corrective action to reduce the overtime in the plants, parallel to the need to increase the Bookings/Quota figure of the salesman.

The dissimilarities between the salesman effort-performance in Chapter 11, and the worker effort-performance in this chapter include:

(1) the establishment of "outside" criteria to set realistic sales targets; there being no comparable "outside" criterion to set realistic production targets;

(2) the separation into "good" and "bad" performance categories on the basis of the four variables, there being no comparable descriptors of worker effort to develop an empirical discriminant function; and

(3) the initiative exercised by the salesman in allocating his time, mostly on his own cognizance, the plant worker having little say in his allocation of effort.

1.1. The Limitations of the Data

The data collected by the cost accountant present a curious phenomenon. Overtime is recorded in each plant. However, even the plants with the worst overtime increased in their productivity almost weekly! In other words, based on the cost accounting data, the workers in the different plants are producing at 135 percent, 140 percent, and so on of their respective production norms. Clearly, if the workers are producing at a very efficient rate, their overtime is either necessitated by the very short time allowed for filling the orders; or, the recorded productivity figures are questionable.

Being the very first ones of its kind, the cost accounting figures are an understandable source of pride to the accounting department. Therefore, any questioning of the basic validity of the figures should be made with extreme circumspection. If, however, the basic validity of the figures is under question, then the entire edifice of profitability that is built upon the cost accounting data crumbles.

The investigation of the data base is, after some study, divided into two parts: One, the recording of the actual time spent on the different jobs by the worker; two, the computation of the productivity by the cost accounting department.

Of the two, the recording of the figures emerges as reasonably straightforward and reliable. The "punching in" and the "punching out" are observed reasonably well. The work station supervisor sees to it that the worker "punches in" at his station before he is allowed on the machine. If this rule is reasonably well enforced, then the worker has to record his entry at the different stations. If the exits are not marked, then that gives a valid basis for questioning; for, it would mean that the worker presumably worked on two machines at the same time!

The second part of the investigation relates to the use made of the time card data of "punching in" and "punching out". It emerges that the reported increase in productivity in fact presumes a standard. For the 23 minutes or 17 minutes recorded by the worker is converted into a productivity index in the cost accounting calculation in terms of the standard. On what basis is the calculation made? "Oh, that is based on time and motion studies," answers the cost accountant. "Who performs these time and motion studies?" "The plant supervisors." "Do the plant workers know that they are being timed?" "Of course, we have to tell them under the union regulations." "You mean that they know that whatever time is registered now with the stop watch is going to be the standard, and that if, instead of 28 minutes, they do the job next time when nobody is timing them, in say 23 minutes, it is recorded as a productivity increase of 18 percent (calculated on the basis that 28 minutes for the job is 100; therefore, 23 minutes for the same job is 82.14, which *reduces* the time required by 17.86 percent, or equivalently, *increases* productivity by 17.86 percent, rounded off to 18 percent)?" "Yes, of course."

It also emerges, on further investigation, that any reduction in the time taken to perform the job from the established standard directly results in correspondingly increased payments to the worker. Since this loads the die, as it were, against the manufacturing activity by motivating the worker to go slow when the norm is established, the entire cost accounting calculations of plant productivity have simply to be scrapped.

Can anything be salvaged out of the time card data? How can they be used to understand the nature of overtime costs? What types of decision process changes are required to bring about a reduction in the costs of overtime?

1.2. The Summarization of Basic Data

The time card data for one of the plants are analyzed to indicate the magnitude of the overtime problem. A clue is provided by the number of "Special Assignment" jobs performed by the plant workers, and, in particular, the number of pieces produced in each such job. A manufacturing operation is associated with mass production; the advantage of machine production being normally reflected in the large number of pieces that are produced at any one time. If, however, in a manufacturing operation, the majority of jobs leads to the production of a few pieces at a time, it would suggest that the plant operations do not take advantage of large scale manufacturing, but instead operate as a sort of custom job shop.

In Table 12.1, a profile of production during a specimen week in terms of both the number of jobs and number of pieces is shown. It will be noticed that out of the 11 280 manhours available from 282 direct operators in the plant during the week, 5 755 hours are devoted to "special assignment" jobs which require pulling the workers off the assembly line and putting them on

Table 12.1
Production profile of special-assignment jobs specimen week

Number of pieces	Number of jobs	Percentage of total jobs	Number of minutes
1 to 9	237	10.63%	16 616
10 to 39	556	24.94%	65 279
40 to 59	211	9.47%	39 918
60 to 99	264	11.85%	47 094
1 to 99	1,268	56.89%	
100 to 199	320	14.36%	58 503
200 to 499	319	14.36%	50 119
500 and up	322	14.39%	67 786
	2,229	100.00%	345 307 = 5 755 hours

282 direct operators × 40 hours = 11 280 man-hours.

special assignments, presumably because some customer orders require just the effort represented in the special assignment jobs to fill them.

The 5 755 hours are devoted to as many as 2 229 "special assignment" jobs. Of the 2 229 jobs, more than half, 1 268 jobs to be exact, each produce lots of less than 100 pieces each.

The small number of pieces per lot indicates the "custom-tailored" job nature of the operations. The manufacturer, however, is not a supplier of custom-made items. It is the degeneration from the manufacturing process that has given rise to the situation in which 57 percent of the jobs each produce lots of less than 100 pieces.

When the advantages of machine production are foregone by making much fewer pieces of a product at a time, it is not surprising that to meet the customer demands on time more time is used up than if the production were made in lots of sizable number of pieces. The fewer lot sizes of production may not be within the powers of the plant manager to control. They may be forced upon him by the short notice given him by the marketing department. If the orders placed by the salesmen to the marketing department are not aggregated to yield requirements for sizable lots, then the production department may well be forced into responding to the customer orders for 5 and 6 pieces of an item, instead of producing with little extra effort 100 or 200 pieces of the same production item.

The *symptom* that has caught the management attention is the overtime. What is the relationship between the number of "special assignment" jobs, and the plant overtime?

From the point of view of the worker, overtime has special attractions. For one thing, he earns more when on overtime. For another, if he were able to produce the same unit of output in less time, he is additionally rewarded for increased productivity. If he were successful in establishing a greater amount of time to accomplish each job, then it is almost certain that he can earn productivity points which, when added to the increased rate of overtime, provide him with greater earnings for the same effort.

However, to justify the overtime activity, he has to be assigned to work on those jobs where he can perform more efficiently outside of the normal working hours. This would require that during his regular working hours, his time has to be occupied otherwise. If the orders come to the production department for a small number of units of each item, then that would be a justification to give the worker "special assignment" jobs during the working

Table 12.2
Overtime payments by department, Specimen week

Department	Number of overtime hours
1	246
2	218
3	139
4	141
5	2
7	121
8	245
10	246
15	51
43	75
	1 484

Average overtime per direct operator per week −5.26 hours = 13.16% of 40 hour week.

day. The fact that more than 51 percent of the specimen week is devoted to "special assignment" jobs reflects a poor flow of demand. Presumably, the 49 percent of the specimen week is devoted to regular assignments, hopefully leading to the machine production of a large number of units on each job.

In Table 12.2, the overtime payments during the specimen week by each of the elements of the plant, called "departments," are tabulated. With the exception of Departments 5, 15, and 43, all the other departments have had overtimes from 121 to 246 hours during the specimen week. The total number of 1 484 overtime hours during the specimen week amounts to 13.16 percent overtime, which works out to 5.26 hours per direct operator per week in the plant.

1.3. Overtime Reduction in Operational Terms

The company management wants to reduce the overtime from its present level of 13.16 percent. To accomplish this objective, it appears that the 51 percent of the specimen week hours devoted to "special assignment" jobs needs to be reduced. It is seen from Table 12.1 that 57 percent of the jobs, 1 268 jobs recorded during the specimen week, produced 1−99 pieces per job. The fewer the number of pieces produced per job, the greater the time required to move from one job to another per number of pieces produced. In other words, to produce 10 pieces or 1 000 pieces, it is necessary for the worker to "punch in" and "punch out". Therefore, if it takes 100 jobs to produce 1 000 pieces, instead of one job to produce 1 000 pieces, there are 99 "punching in"/"punching out" that are *additionally* required over that for the single job producing 1 000 pieces. If it takes only 1 minute to "punch in" and 1 minute to "punch out", that would represent 198 minutes *additionally* required. Over and above this, the worker has to move from one work station to another. If it takes only 2 minutes on the average to move from one work station to another, corresponding to the 99 *additional* "punching in" and "punching out", another 198 minutes are consumed. In other words, to produce 1 000 pieces in 100 jobs, instead of 1 job, *at least* 396 minutes of *additional* time is expended. Nearly a whole day of work more is required!

To reduce the overtime, these extra expenditures of time should be reduced. Since ther are 1 268 jobs producing 1–99 pieces per job, the question is: Can the number of pieces per job be increased from less than 100 to over 100 pieces?

2. Decision Processes by Management Levels

The overtime of 13.16 percent, it has been pointed out in Section 1.2, is the *symptom* that has caught the management attention. Care should be exercised that in seeking relief from the symptoms, the disease itself is not worsened.

2.1. Decisions on Planning Horizon

To reduce the 51 percent of the time now devoted to "special assignment" jobs, it is necessary that the *need* for such "special assignment" jobs be eliminated altogether, or at least reduced substantially. To avoid the plant having to forego mass production to assemble individual products for shipment to the customers, it would be reasonable to carry an *inventory* of either completely finished goods, or partially finished goods. Since inventory represents finished goods or partially finished goods into which the company has invested financial resources and manpower resources, it behooves the company to rapidly turn over the inventory, converting the investment in the inventory into resources which can be used again. Of course, in turning the inventory over, the company normally receives more than what it invested in the inventory; therefore, $100 invested in inventory would probably provide the company with say, $125 when the inventory is liquidated.

To reduce the "special assignment" jobs, the management must make decisions regarding the size of the inventory. The decision should reflect a balance between the costs of investment in inventory, on the one hand, and the capability of the company to meet customer demands, on the other. In what period must the company be ready to meet customer demands? The answer is in the planning horizons of the management. The company may elect not to carry more than a certain minumum level of inventory, enough to meet the customer requirements which demand shipments in "less than 15-days" which may be called *immediate future.* Then, the period 15-30 days could be *intermediate furture,* and the period beyond 30 days, *long term future.* The number of days is, of course, illustrative. Instead of days, other dimensions of time, such as hours or years, could be employed as appropriate. For instance in projecting the demand for Boeing 747 airplanes, the immediate future would probably be 3 to 6 months, if not longer; while in projecting the demand for blasting powder for coal mining, the immediate future would probably be 12 to 15 hours. Irrespective of the particular demand for the particular product, the future in which the demands are to be met can be conceptually classified into three: (1) immediate; (2) intermediate; and (3) indefinite (long term).

2.2. Physical Correlates of Three Levels of Decision

What is the magnitude of the customer orders? It is found that on the average, 1 000 orders a week are placed by the customers with the company. These orders are for the most part transmitted by the 53 company salesmen to the company headquarters.

We shall assume that the company needs an inventory of 1 000 orders in *finished goods,* and another 1 000 orders in *raw materials* on their way to the plant, in order to service the new 1 000 sales orders initiating *manufacturing operations* during the week. The Vice President in Charge of Production will be considered reponsible for the execution of policies designed to meet the various requirements to fulfill the 3 000 orders. Any customer complaint of *delay* in the supply of goods will be directly attributed to the Vice President in Charge of Production, who can maintain the production-distribution flow through three plants, designated A, B, and C.

Table 12.3

Physical correlates of decision processes

Initiating Decisions

Customer   Salesman   →   Headquarters
1 000 Orders → 1 000 Orders   1 000 Orders

Risk Management Decisions

Headquarters → Vice President, Production
1 000 Orders   1 000 Sales Orders +
           1 000 Inventory Orders +
           1 000 Material Purchase Orders

Plant Manager   Plant Manager   Plant Manager
Plant A   Plant B   Plant C
333 Sales Orders   333 Sales Orders   334 Sales Orders
333 Inventory Orders   334 Inventory Orders   333 Inventory Orders
334 Material Purchase   333 Material Purchase   333 Material Purchase
Orders   Orders   Orders

Process Management Decisions

Plant Manager → Plant Production Manager → Plant Foreman → Job Department
Plant A   3 000 items*   95 700 pieces**   Supervisor
1 000 Orders

Process Engineering Decisions

Job Department Supervisor*** → Direct Operator → { Shipping Department → Customer
15 950 pieces   340 pieces   { Inventory Department   1 000 Orders

* 3 items per order.
** 30 pieces per item; 95 700 pieces include the waste allowance of 6.33% on 90,000 pieces required for shipment of 1,000 customer orders.
*** 6 job department supervisors supervise 282 direct operators in Plant A.

In Table 12.3, the physical correlates of decision processes involved in the efficient servicing of the 1 000 customer orders are presented. The Vice President in Charge of Production is shown assigning the 3 000 orders equally among the three plants by means of decisions communicated to the three plant managers. In following through with the decision processes at the plant level, it is noticed that the plant manager has 1 000 *orders* to be taken care of, which, to the plant production manager, are 3 000 *items*. When the decision reaches the plant foreman, the 1 000 orders become 95 700 *pieces*. This is because, on an average, there are 3 items per order, and 30 pieces per item. Allowing a waste fraction of 6.33 percent on 90 000 pieces required for shipment of 1 000 customer orders, the plant foreman has to deal with decisions which will produce 95 700 pieces.

2.3. The Impact of Management Decisions by Levels

The different kinds of decisions involved are classified into three groups: (1) risk management; (2) process management; and (3) process engineering. The vice presidential decisions are classified as predominantly risk management; the plant managerial decisions as both risk and process management. The decisions by the plant production manager and plant foreman are mostly process management decisions.

The plant foreman's decision which will result in the production of 95 700 pieces become decisions involving the production of 15 950 pieces each by the six job department supervisors at the process engineering level. These decisions are communicated to 282 direct operators in Plant A. Each one of them is responsible for decisions relating to 340 pieces.

How important are these decisions at the different levels? Evidently, owing to the vice presidential responsibilities, the consequences of his decisions are generally much more far-reaching than those of the individual direct operator with respect to production. The units of decision, it was seen, vary from orders to units and from units to pieces. For comparison, the equivalent pieces involved at each level can be calculated, although the number of pieces by itself does not provide a basis for the allocation of weights to decision at the three levels.

In Table 12.4, this allocation is presented. Out of a total of 1 760 "operator decision units", 856, or 48.64 percent are allocated to risk management. An equal number belongs to process management and 48 percent belongs to the process engineering level.

Table 12.4

Allocation of weights to decisions at the three levels

(1)	(2)	(3)	(4)	(5)	(6)	(7)
	Risk Management		Process Management		Process Engineering	
	Vice President (R)	Plant Manager (P_1)	Plant Production Manager (P_2)	Plant Foreman (P_3)	Job Dept. Supervisor (E_1)	Direct Operators (E_2)
No. of Persons	1	1	1	1	6	282
Units of Decision	3 000 orders	1 000 orders	3 000 units	95 700 pieces	15 950 pieces	340 pieces
Equivalent Pieces	287 100 pieces	95 700 pieces	95 700 pieces	95 700 pieces	15 950 pieces	340 pieces
Weight of Decision	856	282	282	282	47	1

Risk Management   = 856 = 48.64% of all decisions
Process Management   = 856 = 48.64% of all decisions
Process Engineering   = 48 = 2.72% of all decisions

Decision Function: $k + aR^\alpha + b_1P_1^\beta + b_2P_2^\gamma + b_3P_3^\delta + c_1E_1^\epsilon + c_2E_2^\xi$

Small letters of English alphabet refer to weights of the number of decisions made by decision-makers.
Small letters of Greek alphabet refer to coefficients of learning of decisions made by decision-makers.

In the physical correlates of weekly decision process, all decision makers have perfect learning scores of 1, making
$\alpha = \beta = \gamma = \delta = \epsilon = \xi = 1$

In the present instance, the weights of decision-makers are:

a = 0.4864 c_1 = 0.0267
b_1 = 0.1621 c_2 = 0.0006
b_2 = 0.1621
b_3 = 0.1621
The Decision function in this instance is:
$$k + 0.4864R^1 + 0.1621P_1^1 + 0.1621P_2^1 + 0.1621P_3^1 + 0.0267E_1^1 + 0.0006E_2^1$$

This allocation is admittedly for illustrative purposes. The apportionment of weights to decisions can be worked out statistically on the basis of empirical data.

For this calculation, we need a mathematical model. The simplest is a linear model.

The *number of decisions* made by each participant at the different levels can be assigned a coefficient, and aggregated.

In addition to these coefficients, we need a weighting procedure for the learning process of participants. Perfect learning by the Vice President would mean that there will be 0 percentage of customer complaints with respect to *delays* of shipment of orders. Perfect learning by the process engineering participants would mean that there would be 0 percentage of customer complaints with respect to *defects* of manufacture. When perfect learning is evidenced by all the participants, the index of learning assumes the value of unity.

3. APPLICATION 27: Empirical Index of Learning of Decision Processes

To achieve the management objective of reducing the overtime, action has to be taken at the risk management level, at the process management level, and at the process engineering level. The Vice President for Production is at the risk management level, designated R in Table 12.4, Column 2. At the process management level there is the plant manager, P_1, the plant production manager, P_2, and the plant foreman, P_3, shown in Table 12.4, Columns 3, 4, and 5, respectively. The process engineering level comprises the job department supervisor, E_1, and the direct operator, E_2, shown in Columns 6 and 7, respectively of Table 12.4.

The weight of the decisions at each level in the final outcome, viz., company sales, can be indicated by coefficients prefixed to each of the decision levels, such as aR, b_1P_1, b_2P_2, and b_3P_3, c_1E_1, and c_2E_2.

3.1. Exponents of Learning Function

Clearly, the contribution to the company performance of the decisions at the risk management level is likely to be much greater than that at the process management levels, and process engineering levels. By the same token, the mistakes at the R-level are much more serious than those at the P-level, and much, much more serious than those at the E-level. Consequently, the *index of learning* at the R-level is much more significant to the company sales than at the P- and E-levels.

What are the respective weights of learning by the different decision levels? It may be easier to measure the *loss* in business and relate it to the inadequate learning at the different decision levels than to associate an increase in sales due to adequate learning at the different decision levels. The customer orders received are called "bookings" which have been used in Chapters 9, 10, and 11 as the basic variable.

It should now be modified by considering the *gross sales*, which represent the sales revenue received by the company. There is a difference between the two figures: the gross sales is less than the total bookings; and the decrease in the gross sales figure can be considered as the *loss* in sales. This loss arises out of customer dissatisfaction with the manufacture of the product (*defect* component) and/or customer dissatisfaction with the shipment of the products (*delay* component).

The loss in annual gross sales attributable to defect and delay together is found to be 7.03 percent for the latest year for which data are available. How much of this is contributed by delay, and how much by defect?

A probability sampling of the customer invoices discloses that between 38 and 42 customers during the course of two weeks are irritated because of poor service. At this rate, there will be between 988 and 1092 instances of dissatisfaction due to delay during the year on the basis of the sample values.

The defect component can be attributed to the P and E levels of decisions, and the delay component can be attributed to the R level of decisions. The plant manager, P_1, could be considered to share with R in the delay component, and with the P_2 and P_3 elements, as well as with E_1 and E_2 elements in the defect component. Irrespective of the specific breakdown, it is reasonable to state that the two main components of defect and delay in the loss in sales due to customer dissatisfaction can be allocated to the different decision levels.

The loss in business is due to customer dissatisfaction. If the entire loss were allocated between dissatisfaction due to delays in shipment and defects in manufacture, the respective *negative* weights of index of learning by the decision makers can be empirically ascertained from the following equation:

$$L_0 = g \cdot L_1^\eta \cdot L_2^\theta$$

where,

L_0 is the percentage loss in gross sales,

L_1 is the loss contributed by delays in shipments,

L_2 is the loss contributed by defects in manufacture.

The number of customer complaints during the two week period can be split between delay complaints and defect complaints in the ratio $7 : 1$. In other words, with 40 dissatisfied customers $0.0703 = g \cdot 35^\eta \cdot 5^\theta$. Successive values for L_1 and L_2 can be empirically determined without difficulty. The exponents η and θ indicate the area of effective action. If $\eta + \theta = 1$, the increment in either L_1 or L_2 will bring about only a proportional increment in the L-values. However, if, for instance, η is greater than 1, 1 percent increase in L_1 can bring about more than 1 percent increase in the loss value, L.

It should be noted that the value of η may be considered a weighted average of the exponents of the risk management level learning, α (and part of the respective exponents of the process management levels P_1, P_2, and P_3, viz., β, γ, δ) and θ, a weighted average of the respective exponents of the process engineering levels E_1 and E_2, viz., ϵ and ζ (and part of β, γ, δ), the partitioning of β, γ and δ depending on the share in risk management and process engineering of process management.

Against the background of these two alternate estimates of the index of learning of decisions, there needs to be evolved a criterion for continuing operational measurement and evaluation of decision process changes.

The decision function describes the *input* of decisions which have as *output* satisfied and dissatisfied customers. The input and output can both be expressed as numbers. Out of the 52 000 customers a year, between 988 and 1 092 are found to be dissatisfied.

$$k + aR^\alpha + b_1 P_1^\beta + b_2 P_2^\gamma + b_3 P_3^\delta + c_1 E_1^\epsilon + c_2 E_2^\zeta = 0.19 \text{ or } 0.21,$$

depending on the estimate of dissatified fraction of customers, $988/52\ 000$ or $1\ 092/52\ 000$.

Instead of the annual basis, we can use weekly data, which would thus provide 52 equations instead of one. One set of 19 such equations yields a set of values for the 19 unknowns.

3.2. Empirical Index of Learning in Terms of Number of Pieces

We need to establish a relationship between the number of decisions made at different levels and the number of pieces per job so that an operational evaluation of the production and inventory system is possible.

In our empirical example, 95 700 pieces are required to be made during a week in Plant A, in order to meet the 1 000 customer orders. The data for the specimen week show that 2 229 special assignment jobs are performed. The number of pieces produced is 367 405, giving an average of 164,83 pieces per job during the specimen week.

An identifiable criterion of manufacturing, as opposed to customer-tailoring jobs, is the number of pieces produced per job. In this particular instance, lots of 500 pieces and above may be considered the desired characteristic, although the specific number can be arrived at in the light of production economics.

In arriving at the desired number of pieces per job, we may consider the number of direct operators involved in the process. During the specimen week, an average of 7.90 special assignments per direct operator have been made. It will be simpler if, for instance, an operator could be assigned one job for a week. This would eliminate the necessity of special assignments almost altogether, and as a consequence, the need for overtime payment. If there were to be 282 jobs during the week, it would necessitate an average production of 339.36 pieces per direct operator. Since this number is less than 500, the chosen lot size for purposes of manufacturing economy, we could assign two operators to the same job for the week, thus making 141 jobs, each with an average lot size of 678.72 pieces.

Our rule of procedure in this instance is to raise the average number of pieces per job from 164.83 to 678.72, an increase by 311.77 percent. When this is accomplished, the problem of special assignments leading to overtime payments will be solved.

This objective is to be considered as a probabilistic model. Thus, the increase of 311.77 percent is to be attained asymptotically over periods longer than a week, say a month. Similarly, the number of decisions which enter the equation on the left hand side will have exponents, indicating learning processes of the different levels of decision, approaching the perfect score asymptotically.

4. Modification of Real Life Data to Reflect Profitability of Decision Alternatives

So far the problem has been stated in operational terms, such as customer orders, units, items, and pieces. In Section 2.1, it is assumed that the company needs an inventory of 1 000 orders in finished goods. The customer orders are specific demands for items of specific description. Therefore, some way has to be found to make the specific request translatable into abstract statements such as "inventory of 1 000 orders in finished goods".

4.1. The Concept of Product Classes Instead of Administrative Divisions

Not only is the customer order specific in terms of its identification of the company product, but also specific in terms of color, fabric, and other auxiliary characteristics, so that the delivery of a product in navy blue, instead of the specified light blue, is almost sure to cause customer dissatisfaction. Therefore, the inventory decisions have to be stated in terms of all the appropriate auxiliary characteristics as well as the major characteristics, number of such items of each kind.

It has been stated in Chapter 9, Section 2.9, that the company has no concept of product differentiation, except that of an administrative classification which has grown less distinct over the 57 year history, resulting in each division offering overlapping lines of products. There is no central repository of the products offered by the company. Each division puts out its own promotional pieces when new products are introduced. Direct questioning of the top management brings the definite assurance that they have no idea as to how many products the company is offering. This necessitates an *ab initio* classification study, the purpose of which is to identify each product in one class, and one class only. If such product classes can be identified, then that would permit an operational classification of the products which have to be specified for inventory decisions.

The basis for such a classification of the products (items) is the *primary* end use of the item. The same product is sold at *different discounts* by the different divisions which make one product in reality as many as 12 products from the point of view of the company profits, because each of the 12 divisions can, in fact, offer the same product at a different discount.

4.2. Alternate Measures of Profitability: Sample Values

Using the concept of product classes, an attempt is made to identify the minimum number of groups of nearly homogeneous products which make up a sizable portion of the total dollar volume. These groups are studied with respect to: (1) their contribution to the total dollar volume; and (2) their contribution to total gross profit. These two measures provide the background for further consideration in terms of (3) *average unit gross profit* of individual products.

Every one of the 315 basic products is arranged in order of the percentage contribution to the total sales *volume* in dollars. Two product classes, which will be designated 01 and 02 in this study, together account for 38.49 percent of the total annual dollar volume of bookings in the three United States plants of the manufacturer. Bookings are orders received and thus constitute demand for production, but are subject to cancellation. Product classes 01 and 02 together constitute 42.81 percent of the total gross *profit* in the latest year for which bookings data are available.

The *gross profit* is an accounting entry. It is arrived at by subtracting from the net price of each of the products; (1) inventory factor, (2) direct labor, (3) overhead, and (4) material costs. It should be borne in mind that these costs are based on the manufacture of *100 units* of each product at one time, a situation not always obtained in practice. Further, when a particular product could be manufactured in all the three plants, designated A, B, and C in this study, the cost factors used to arrive at the gross profit are those of B *only*, without any consideration of those of A, B and C in the form of some kind of a weighted average of the three. Products manufactured only in A are assigned costs of manufacture on a 100-unit basis with respect to: (1) direct labor; (2) overhead; and (3) material, without specific reference to the inventory factor.

The two product classes together comprise 28 basic products, each of which becoming conceptually different when sold through the 12 divisions, making a total of 336 products for inventory control. Taking into account the differences in finish entering into each basic product, the number of the two product classes selected becomes 101 physically different products turning into 1 212 products for inventory purposes.

Selection within the two product classes reduce the basic number of products to 10 (120 inventory units), which comprise 23 physically different

Table 12.5

Alternate measures of profitability of 10 top sellers

Product	Contribution to Total Sales	Contribution to Total Gross Profit	Rank in Total Sales	Rank in Gross Profit	Rank in Unit Profit*
011	8.07%	8.17%	1	1	4
021	5.47%	4.52%	2	2	10
022	3.69%	4.39%	3	3	2
023	3.40%	2.96%	4	4	7
012	2.86%	2.67%	5	6	6
024	2.84%	2.81%	6	5	5
013	2.34%	1.95%	7	7	9
014	1.32%	1.38%	8	8	3
015	1.02%	0.88%	9	10	8
016	0.99%	1.23%	10	9	1
Total	32.00%	30.96%			

* The unit profit rank is arrived at on the basis of (gross profit/net price) so that, given the same facility to manufacture each of the 10 products, and the aim to maximize rate of returns on outlay, the unit gross profit index would be the manufacturer's yardstick. The consumers' yardstick of the products is their purchase, translated into sales and profit for the manufacturer.

products (276 inventory units). These ten products, six from product class 01, and four from product class 02, and the *top sellers.* They will be identified as 011, 012, 013, 014, 015, 016, 021, 022, 023, and 024, indicating the product class they belong to and their own number in their respective groups.

Taking into account only (1) the contribution to total dollar volume, (2) the contribution to total gross profit, (3) average unit gross profit, excluding (4) alternate costs of manufacture, (2) may be considered as the weighting by the public of (3). In other words, if all the products were equally demanded by the public, the product with the highest (3) would also contribute the highest to the total gross profit. If, for instance, the number 1 unit gross profit item were found to be the number 10 contributor to total gross profit, it would mean that the quantity of the product bought by the public accounted for the change in rank of the product between (3) and (2). Table 12.5 presents the data.

5. APPLICATION 28: Product Allocation Decisions Among the Plants Using Resource-Use Index

Given the alternative measures of profitability of the 10 top sellers among the company products, the management has at hand the basis to alter the inventory decisions, not on the basis of total sales or total customer demand, but on the basis of contribution to company profits.

This brings about a major change with respect to inventory decisions: *instead of maximizing the total sales, it is the gross profit that is to be maximized.*

The change from sales to profits (preferably net profits) explicitly introduces the basic criterion in management decisions. Granted that some customer dissatisfaction will always be experienced, the emphasis on profitability makes it possible to identify the particular products for which the company management is willing to risk consumer dissatisfaction. Further, when more than one product is involved, the willingness on the part of the management to incur customer dissatisfaction is indicated by the rank of profitability of the product.

The 10 top sellers are all from the same administrative division. The products can be manufactured in the three plants A, B, and C in the United States. How should the production be allocated?

5.1. Demand Considerations

The 10 top sellers belong to two product classes 01 and 02. Taking into account *all* the products in product classes 01 and 02, two-thirds of the total dollar volume for the division have been accounted for by the two product classes on the basis of annual data. The demand for product classes 01 and 02 appears to be distributed fairly evenly: 23 percent in the first quarter of the year; 26 percent in the second quarter; 27 percent in the third quarter; and 24 percent in the fourth quarter.

5.2. Production Allocation Considerations: (1) Minimum Overlap of Service by Plants

Three alternative methods are employed to assess the use of available resources of production of items in the three different plants combined with ease in distribution. The first method divides the United States into three areas with plants A, B, and C as respective centers, the different mileages as radii of the circle to be served by the plants. When the minimum of overlap among the plants and the maximum coverage of the United States is obtained, the radii are equal. The territories under the sweep of each of the circles drawn with the plant as center are taken as the areas to be served by the plant in the center of the circle, and the normative demand is ascertained on the basis of Chapter 9, Section 7.0.

5.3. Production Allocation Considerations: (2) Guesses by Order Processing Clerks

The second method is based on the existing allocation of production to the different plants. Customer orders originating in different States are allocated to different plants by the order processing department. This procedure does not take into account any of the advantages of specialization of effort by the plants, the respective inventory situations, or the sequence of decision processes whose physical correlates are the items produced. Again, the areas covered by the three plants are identified. The radius of the circle with plant C as center remains nearly the same as under the first method, the radius of plant A is much shorter and that of plant B much longer than under the first method. The actual volume of orders in dollars handled in the three areas is also ascertained.

5.4. Production Allocation Considerations: (3) Real Life Demand in Units and Dollars

The third method studies data of bookings for the first 20 weeks of the year by product and by plant. The assignment of the demand for products to plants A, B, and C is studied in terms of both the number of units and the dollar volume. The share of each plant of (1) the normative demand (quota) for products in product classes 01 and 02, *all products*, in dollars, (2) the actual demand (bookings) for products in product classes 01 and 02, *all products*, in dollars, (3) the actual demand (bookings) for products in product classes 01 and 02, *all products*, in units, and (4) the actual demand (bookings) for products in product classes 01 and 02, *ten products only*, are ascertained. The differences between the assignment under the existing freight map and the assignment under the equal radii freight map with respect to (1) and (2) are also investigated.

Table 12.6 presents the analysis of allocation of production among plants A, B, and C. It is seen that plant B is handling, by design or default, more than its due share under *both* the existing freight map and the equal radii map. This observation is true with respect to both the normative demand and the actual demand.

Table 12.6

Allocation of demand for production of product classes 01 and 02 among the three plants

	Plant A	Plant B	Plant C
Quota, all: 01 and 02 product classes;			
Existing map	35.48%	47.70%	16.82%
Equal radii map	44.76%	38.42%	16.82%
Bookings, all: 01 and 02 product classes;			
Existing map	33.04%	46.19%	20.77%
Equal radii map	41.69%	37.54%	20.77%
Bookings, all: 01 and 02 product classes; Quantity			
Existing map	36.00%	50.70%	13.30%
Bookings, 10 products 01 and 02 product classes; Quantity			
Existing map	39.36%	47.79%	12.85%

It is quite possible that the better capacity utilization at plant B, as indicated by the analysis in Table 12.6, in comparison with plants A and C, account largely for B's efficiency of production. In order to determine how many units of the ten products should be produced at A and how many at B, omitting C which is comparatively much smaller than both A and B, this qualitative feeling of efficiency of B has to be translated into comparable quantities.

The estimated *use of resources per unit* of each of the ten products provides this measure. It is seen from Table 12.7 that if 100 represents the "average" product, plant A's index of use of resources is estimated at 65.67 and plant B's index at 64.25, when product 011 is considered. Product 013 gives a resource-use index of 66.83 for B, 81.13 for A, and so on.

It is seen that in all the ten instances, B is found to be lower in resource-use index than A. Bearing in mind the possibility that this situation has been brought about by better capacity utilization, it may be inquired whether or not substantial gains could have been effected if B were to manufacture the entire supply offered by A and B together. This calculation is performed in terms of dollar-equivalents of the resource-use index.

In view of the lower costs of manufacture at plant B, made possible partly by the capacity utilization, if all the units of the 10 products now manufactured by plant A were manufactured by plant B, it would have resulted in an *additional gain* of $20 000 to the manufacturer in two product classes during the 20 weeks.

Table 12.7
Resource-use index of ten top sellers compared

Product	"Average"	Plant B	Plant A
011	100	64.25	65.67
021	100	53.21	60.60
022	100	51.70	55.92
023	100	51.44	54.35
012	100	62.57	64.62
024	100	61.90	67.60
013	100	66.83	81.13
014	100	59.84	65.28
015	100	58.82	69.00
016	100	56.20	57.64

6. APPLICATION 29: Isopieces Action Chart as a Decision Aid

To reduce the overtime encountered in plant A of 13.16 percent during the specimen week, it has been found necessary to allocate the customer dissatisfaction reflected in the loss of sales due to cancelled orders to two components: (1) delay component; and (2) defective component. Of the two, the former is more serious, 35 out of the 40 dissatisfied customers complaining about the delay in the shipment during the two week period when the probability sampling was conducted.

6.1. Translating the Loss in Sales to the Piece Production Level

It has been postulated in Section 3.1 that the interaction of decisions at the three management levels; risk management, process management, and process engineering, can be reflected in an exponential learning function. Applying the reasoning to the short period for which the data were analyzed, led to a rule of procedure: Raise the average number of pieces per job from 164.83 to 678.72, an increase by 311.77 percent. When this is accomplished, the problem of "special assignment" jobs leading to the overtime payments which caught the management attention in the first place will be solved.

Can the reasoning be extended to derive a rule of procedure in the day-to-day operations, so that corrective action can be undertaken long before significant overtime payments accumulate?

What is required is the association of the customer dissatisfaction with the company decisions. The customer dissatisfaction itself can be broken into the two components of delay and defect. Similarly, the company decisions can be broken down to risk management and nonrisk management (which may be a combination of a part of process management and a part of process engineering). The desired property of the rule of procedure would be to specifically relate the customer dissatisfaction to the *number of pieces per job*. The solution in Section 3.2 that the average number of pieces per job be raised from 164.83 to 678.72 is one instance of the application of such a rule of procedure.

6.2. Isopieces Action Chart

An illustrative relationship between the kind of customer dissatisfaction and the type of decision scores at the two levels is set forth in Table 12.8.

Table 12.8

Decision scores and customer dissatsfaction corresponding to pieces–production per worker–job

Percentage of customer Dissatisfaction		No. of Pieces Per Job Per Direct Operator Per Week	Decision Score	
Delay	Defect		Risk Management Level	Process Engineering Level
0%	0%	679	100	100
25%	25%	510	75	75
50%	50%	340	50	50
75%	75%	170	25	25
100%	100%	0	0	0

The risk management decision score is 75 when the percentage of customer dissatisfaction due to delays is 25 percent of all the complaints received during the time period selected. Giving equal weight to both risk management and process engineering level decisions, instead of 48.64 percent for risk management and 51.36 percent for process engineering as in Table 12.4, 25 percent customer dissatisfaction due to defect gives rise to a score of 75 at the process engineering level. This equality permits us to calculate more readily the changes in the number of pieces per job per direct operator per week. When there is no delay, and no defect, risk management attains a score of 100; so does process engineering. In the empirical example considered, 678.72 pieces per job per direct operator per week will correspond to these two perfect scores. When both the levels have half the score of 50 each, the number of pieces is half of 678.72, rounded off to 340.

The number of pieces can correspond to different combinations of scores on the risk management and process engineering levels. This is illustrated in Fig. 12.1. The diagonal line, through the second and fourth quadrants, represents the production of 340 pieces. This can arise when the risk management score is 50, and the process engineering score is 50. It can also arise when risk management score is 100 and process engineering score is 0, and so on.

Considering the 340 pieces as the average for the production and inventory process, we can indicate limits for corrective action, as shown in Figure 12.1. It is clear that when the risk management and process engineering scores are between 0 and 37.5 each, there is a desperate need for corrective action. In

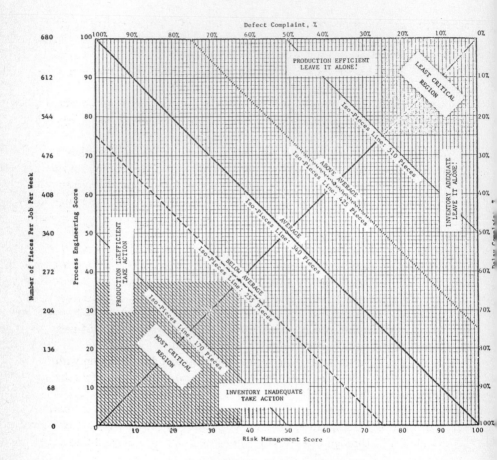

Figure 12.1. Isopieces action chart

the empirical example considered, the number of pieces produced per week
was 168.83. At least one of the two scores was below 37.5, which makes the
situation fall within the "most critical region", calling for desperate action.

A heuristic approach to the understanding and operational analysis of a production and inventory problem as one integrated problem has been attempted in this Chapter.

. The customers are serviced through units produced in the different plants. As a result, the customers are fully or partly satisfied. The dissatisfaction is classified into two, as arising from delay and from defect.

Delay is attributed to unsatisfactory inventory policies, and defect to unsatisfactory production practices. The former is treated as the responsibility of risk management, and the latter, that of process engineering.

The Isopieces Action Chart is developed as an analytical tool to indicate the need for, and the type of, decision process changes required to optimize decisions and output with respect to customer dissatisfaction, the delay component of which is associated with risk management level decisions pertaining to inventory maintenance and the defect component of which is associated with process engineering level decisions.

The empirical situation leading to the development of the Isopieces Action Chart is the significant overtime pay for special assignment jobs, coupled with customer dissatisfaction, experienced by a durable goods manufacturer. For OR/SA analysis, the data are reclassified in operational terms. Resource-use index of the three manufacturing plants is determined to allocate production to meet 1 000 customer orders a week. Seasonality analysis is made of past data, and three independent estimates of future demand.

An equation linear in logarithms connecting customer dissatisfaction with the different decisions is developed; also, an empirical learning function, the exponents of which are the loss in business due to delay and defect. The empirical results indicate the production *re*allocation of ten products to save $20 000 in 20 weeks, and the raising of the number of pieces per job from 164.83 to 678.72 through inventory maintenance in the light of careful forecasts.

PROBLEMS

The four chapters, 9, 10, 11 and 12, of part IV deal with the application of OR/SA Protocol to large, unstructured problems in the Private Sector. The two major problems vital to any manufacturing and sales operation are: (1) sales, and (2) production. This chapter deals with the problem of Production and Inventory, *leading to an action chart which indicates when to act. The purpose of the following questions is to develop an appreciation for the relationships between inventory, on the one hand, and resource allocation for production, on the other.*

A. *System Context*

1. How can you assess the evaluation of the performance by the outside world which passes judgment upon the production units?

2. What is the basic difference in the context of decision-making between production and sales?

3. Outline a method of weighting the different levels of production from the OVERVIEW context.

B. *System Cost*

4. How would you use customer dissatisfaction as a measure of cost?

5. What is the Opportunity Acquired by planning the use of the production resources?

C. *System Effectiveness – Absolute*

6. Contrast the effectiveness measures in production vs. sales.

7. How is the number of pieces produced a week used as a measure of effectiveness of the system?

8. What assumptions are needed to translate the customer dissatisfaction into the production pieces produced per week?

ANSWERS TO PROBLEMS

The intent of the Answers to Problems is not *to provide full-blown answers, but to indicate what appear to be the most important elements in discussing the problems. It is hoped that the user of the Answers will use them as helpful points of departure, and not as "the" Answers.*

CHAPTER 1

A. *The Discipline*

1. The year 1951 is the year that Arthur D. Little Co. in Cambridge, Massachusetts, claims to have pioneered industrial operations research in the United States. It was 1952 before Operations Research Society of America was founded. At the time of his writing, Bronowski did not have the benefit of knowledge of these important developments in identifying Operations Research as a discipline: the National Science Foundation currently lists Operations Research under both Mathematical Sciences (Specialty No. 082) and under Engineering (Specialty No. 477).

Reflecting as he did at the end of an exciting period of application of "the mathematics of differentials and of prediction" to survival problems in World War II, Bronowski could experience a let-down from the familiar past heights of mathematical application to the unfamiliar prospective depths of cost accounting, and time and motion study. If Operations Research were only the application of mathematics to problems, then there is no justification to name a new discipline: why not call it "applied mathematics"? Therefore, the issue is: what remains of Operations Research after all the applied mathematics is stripped away?

In a sense, Bronowski could be construed to be hinting at the answer when he says: "There is an extension of this to the *larger* economics of *whole industries and nations*." (italics supplied) "Whole Industries and Nations" are a large subject indeed. However, Bronowski considers the application of Operations Research to "Whole Industries and Nations" to be *un*challenging to "first-rate-scientists."

If larger issues of bigger problems could be handled by Operations Research, again, it has to be more than "applied economics" as suggested by Bronowski's reference to "the larger economics of whole industries and nations."

As a matter of fact, there was another important development in the threshold of which Bronowski was making his comments. In the 1950s the notion of the "weapon" had to be modified by the advent of technology to that of "weapon system." A rifle could be considered a weapon; its operation could be stated adequately in terms of the soldier, the rifle, the target, and the means to hit the target, viz., the bullet. However, when unmanned missiles emerged as a new operational concept in the '50s, it was inadequate to talk about the intercontinental ballistic missile as merely a weapon. The *analysis* of the weapon *systems* focuses attention upon larger problems of complex interacting parts and precision than in firing a simple weapon.

This shift from the smaller, "tactical" problems to the larger, "strategic" problems accented the establishment of the domain and contributions of Operations Research, apart from and beyond applied mathematics, applied economics, etc. The primary contribution is the OVERVIEW of the problem. Many disciplines may contribute to the emergence of the OVERVIEW, but something more than the sum of the parts has to emerge in the OVERVIEW. It is not unlike the medical doctor putting together symptoms, such as headache, shortness of breath, and radiating pain, and diagnosing a heart attack. Based on the strength of his diagnosis, he prescribes remedies.

The challenge of strategic problems facing industries and nations comes thoroughly disguised, offering hints of problems only through remote symptoms. What OVERVIEW would effectively diagnose the problem is the recurring challenge to the diagnostician; can the insights obtained from one large problem be effectively applied to another? Further, what is the prescription to solve the problem? The successful tackling of large problems such as lunar landing suggests the possibility that first-rate-scientists may find some challenge worthy of them. Problems even larger than lunar landing, such as the national delivery of health care, await them here on the earth. Diagnosis of the large problems, and prescriptions of their solutions, demand the transcending of the traditional boundaries of human knowledge, and demand the methodology of operations research/systems analysis.

2. Operations Research developments have been historically associated with *tactical* questions of World War II: in particular, the formation in August, 1940, of "Blackett's Circus" to find immediate answers to problems in the operational use of radar, upon which the defense of Great Britain depended; while the historical origins of Systems Analysis have been associated with *strategic* questions of post-World War II: in particular, Rand Corporation's assignment to recommend methods to select and evaluate weapon systems for development.

In Vol. I, the emphasis is upon large, *un*structured problems; in Vol. II, the emphasis is upon large, structured problems. The methods are largely statistical in Vol. I; they are largely mathematical in Vol. II.

The distinction that Systems Analysis deals with *un*structured problems, and Operations Research deals with structured problems, would have some validity in terms of their historic development. However, the analytic methodology refers to two aspects of the *same* problem, rather than two different problems, in practice. Therefore, concept and custom consider Operations Research/Systems Analysis as one and the same discipline.

B. *The Types of Problems*

3. See Chapter 1, Section 5.

4. See Chapter 1, Section 3.

C. *Types of Solutions*

5. The solutions to solution-oriented problems are specific value(s) of variables, which would fulfill the problem requirements and yield the maximum (minimum) value. For instance, how many units of which product(s) would yield the maximum profit, if the problem is correctly stated as a Linear Programming Problem?

The solutions to structure-oriented problems are value(s) of variables, which would maximize the understanding of the structure of the problem. For instance, what interactions can be included (ignored) in the successive decisions so that the effectiveness of decisions is maximized in planning the first lunar landing mission?

See Chapter 1, Section 6.2.

6. The principal test is whether or not the OR/SA study has identified a manageable number of variables and interactions as the most important. If it has so identified them, then the study has provided an OVERVIEW in the light of which the individual variables and interactions are implicitly ranked in order of importance to the problem as a whole. If the study merely says that there are a large number of variables and interactions, it has not contributed any *conceptual* understanding of the problem. Given the *initial* set of variables and interactions, what analytical approach is offered by the study: (1) to test if the identified set is in fact correct, or (2) to test how the identified set can be *operationally* manipulated? Has the study considered realistically the data problem? Has it specified what *action* would be taken if the initial guess is proven correct? Does it state explicitly the limitations of its approach and action recommendation?

CHAPTER 2

A. *Tactical Problems*

1. "Blackett's Circus" was fortunate in having its source of interest the highest in the land: "discussions that took place at the Prime Minister's fortnightly U-boat meetings." (Chapter 1, Section 1.3.)

2. See Chapter 1, Section 2, in particular Section 2.1.

3. See Chapter 1, Section 2, in particular Sections 2.2 and 2.3.

4. See Chapter 1, Section 1.3 for the Convoy Escort problem.

B. *Strategic Problems*

5. "The decision to concentrate a major part of the British War effort on the destruction of German housing." It could have been avoided if Blackett could have communicated with Churchill in terms that he could understand. There is more to communication than information; *what* is being said depends upon *who* says it and to *whom*.

6. In Chapter 1, Section 11, the difficulty of cost-effectiveness analysis is highlighted with respect to the Titan II force. We could simplify the cost effectiveness comparison between Titan II and Minuteman as follows:

$$\text{Cost Effectiveness (CE)} = \frac{\text{effectiveness (E)}}{\text{cost (C)}}$$

Schlesinger says that as a consequence of major deficiencies in information on the performance of the new missiles, "it was inevitable that only the *crudest* observations could be made regarding the *effectiveness component* of the decision-making scheme. *Cost considerations* therefore, became dominant." (italics supplied)

Cost itself comprises: (1) fixed cost (FC), and (2) variable cost (VC). Therefore, CE = E/(FC + VC). Because of unresolved technical problems, the VC part was "biased against Titan II because of the drastic underestimation of missile operations and maintenance costs."

Of the three elements, E was unavailable, VC was unreliable, leaving only FC as the determining component. Because of ignorance, E could be assumed to be the same for both Titan II and Minuteman. If the same E can be achieved at less cost, naturally that would be preferable. Of the cost components, VC is more intractable, because it relates to operating and maintaining a missile system which is not yet constructed. The FC part is closer in time, because it has to be incurred to produce the missile, before there can be any question of operating and maintaining it. For the same E, given equal VC, the choice would be the system with the lower FC. If, in addition, the VC was higher even on the basis of admittedly unreliable estimates, then that puts the other weapon system at an advantage from the CE point of view. According to Schlesinger Titan II VC was higher. Further, Minuteman FC was lower. Therefore, Minuteman with *lower* FC and *lower* VC won out.

The limitations of cost estimates, particularly of an entirely new weapon system, are quite apparent from the Titan II decision. In the absence of technical information on how the two weapon systems would perform, the decision essentially became one of cost estimates. In other words, he who had the best cost figures won the day.

C. *Mathematical Foundations*

7. Linear Programming, Theory of Games, and Dynamic Programming. Linear

Programming is best suited to handle large structured problems which can be
described by fixed technical coefficients of profits and production, and in
which interaction among the variables can be ignored. The solution is a fixed
set of numbers (e.g. units of Products X_1, X_2 ... which will maximize *total*
profit which set is found *iteratively*).

Theory of Games handles *inter*active decision problems, in which the outcome depends not only upon the moves of one party, but also the moves of
the other party. This interaction applies not only to the first move, but also
to the subsequent moves. Further, advantage can accrue to some participants
if they enter into cooperative arrangements among themselves against the
remaining participants.

Dynamic Programming can handle *un*structured problems in which, unlike
in Linear Programming, interactions cannot be ignored: in fact, interactions
are the most important elements. The emphasis is upon a decision-making
process in which insights obtained from decisions in one stage are applied to
the decisions in the next stage, the objective being to break up the problem
into so many stages (or so few stages) that can maximize the learning of the
interactions among the different variables.

8. Linear Programming, because of its emphasis upon known technical coefficients, and ignoring of interactions of variables, can provide an OVERVIEW
which is limited by the very requirement to ignore interactions. The OVER-
VIEW is derived from variables and their interactions, of which, Linear
Programming ignores the factor which is most important.

  Theory of Games recognizes interactions, because each move is contingent
upon other moves: one's own, and others'. Conceptually, each move has a
bearing on every other move: Computationally, however, a number of these
moves has to be ignored to arrive at a decision. One way of limiting the
computational considerations is to limit the choice of the participants to
strategies, which are a whole sequence of a number of moves. The advantage
of applying Game Theory accrues only if the players select strategies and stick
to them. The OVERVIEW depends upon the interaction of strategies.

Dynamic Programming treats interactions among variables as the central
element. The decision at each stage is based upon the OVERVIEW of the
problem as of that time. How much remains to be accomplished: and in how
many steps can it be accomplished are the principal criteria in decision-
making in Dynamic Programming. The OVERVIEW is thus part and parcel of

Dynamic Programming at each successive decision-making process, beginning with the first identification of the stages into which the problem can be meaningfully broken up.

D. *Professional Profile*

9. See Chapter 3. The essential elements of an OR/SA activity are: (1) diagnosis, and (2) prescription. The diagnosis must provide an OVERVIEW of the problem; and the prescription must be operational with respect to the OVERVIEW: given the OVERVIEW, what is to be done about it? In Chapter 3, Section 2, four major elements of OR/SA activity are identified to amplify the diagnosis and prescription functions.

10. According to Talcott Parsons, profession is:

> A category of occupational role which is organized about the mastery of and fiduciary responsibility for any important segment of society's cultured tradition including responsibility for its perpetuation *and* for its further development.[1]

The success of OR/SA as a profession, therefore, depends on its mastery of and fiduciary responsibility for an important segment of society's cultured tradition. Even as the preservation of human life is the "cultured tradition" of the medical profession, the twin functions of "diagnosis of and prescription for" decision-making in large, unstructured and large, structured problems are the "cultured tradition" of the OR/SA profession.

The profession has to identify a body of knowledge and processes which sets it apart from other professions. In addition to the body of knowledge, the profession must also establish standards of conduct worthy of the professional membership.

Before the standards can be enforced, there must be the substratum of organized and systematic approach to perception itself which is peculiar to the profession. In other words, for Operations Research/Systems Analysis to be a profession, it is necessary to have an organized and systematic approach which must be mastered to yield the perception that is peculiar to operations research. This body of organized knowledge must set itself apart from other

---

[1] Talcott Parsons, "Some Problems confronting Sociology as a Profession", *American Sociological Review*, Vol. 24, No. 4, August 1959, p. 547.

bodies of knowledge; otherwise, operations research would not merit separate status from say, applied Economics or applied Mathematics.

The growth and maturity of the organized knowledge peculiar to the profession depend upon the scholarly publications of both the theory and practice of the profession. The OR/SA as a profession has several scholarly journals: *Operations Research, Management Science*. The scholarly standards are high.

How many professionals, and would-be-professionals pay dues to belong to the ranks of the profession, because there is an organized body of knowledge and body of professionals with which it is worthwhile to be associated? What mechanism do the professionals have to exchange and express professional ideas? How wide is the scope in terms of the subject matter, the problems, and the national and international participation? See Chapter 1, Sections 15, 16 and 17.

CHAPTER 3

A. *System Context*

1. The context is that of the decision-maker; and the context of the decision-maker is his perception of the problem boundaries: (1) external boundaries of the problem, and (2) internal boundaries of the capabilities.

2. Three types of Context: (1) Uncertain, (2) Risky, and (3) Reduced Risk.

The external boundaries of the problem specify customer requirements; and the internal boundaries specify organismic capabilities to satisfy customer requirements. The three types of context characterize the perception of requirements and of capabilities. If what the customer wants is unknown (except in a vague sense), he cannot specify how the product and/or service should perform; in other words, he cannot specify the probability distribution of the performance characteristics: the context is UNCERTAIN. If the performance characteristics are known in general, the customer can specify the *form* of the probability distribution: the context is one of RISK. If, on the other hand, the customer knows exactly what he wants, he can specify the *form* and *parameters* of the probability distribution: the context is one of REDUCED RISK.

How long and how brightly should the light bulbs function can be stated in terms of both the probability distributions and their parameters, making the context one of reduced risk. However, if one is drilling for oil, the performance characteristics of the new well-to-be can be specified in general terms, using the experience of other similar wells, i.e. the *form* of the probability distribution of performance characteristics is known, but not its parameters, making the context one of risk. When the decision to land a man on the moon was made in 1961, the customer had no previous experience to specify even the form of the probability distribution of performance characteristics, making the context uncertain.

3. Even when the context is uncertain, the PDM can benefit from the System Context in identifying where his part of the operation should be going. He may be making just a small part, say the booster for the rocket which will launch the spacecraft; therefore, he cannot very well identify his booster's role in the total lunar mission. However, he can organize his world in terms of one decision-level above him; and one below him. He can evaluate his contribution to the level above him: how well does his booster function as part of the rocket? To him, the rocket is the System — the *organismic* level of decision-making. His own booster is at the *strategic* level of decision-making, being a component part of the organismic level. Suppliers of booster parts would be at the *tactical* level of decision-making.

The value of OR/SA effort is in identifying the operational measures of performance of the booster subsystem as part of rocket system; which, in turn, is a subsystem of propulsion. Propulsion, Guidance and Control comprise the Spacecraft subsystem, the Astronaut subsystem being the other major element in the Lunar Landing System. It would be desirable to indicate what part the booster itself contributes to the Lunar Landing System; but not necessary. Because of the distance from the highest decision-making levels, it is quite possible that the estimate of its own role in the total System by a sub-sub-sub-sub-subsystem may be slightly exaggerated. Nevertheless, the effort to place itself within the System context could be a useful exercise.

B. *System Cost*

4. (1) Cost of opportunity foregone. (2) Cost of opportunity acquired.

5. See Chapter 3, Section 6.1.

6. See Chapter 3, Sections 6, 7 and 8.

7. See Chapter 3, Sections 6, 7 and 8.

C. *System Effectiveness—Absolute*

8. Unless the System Objective is identified, the relative importance of each subsystem to the System cannot be explicated. To consider the contribution of all the major subsystems, the overall entity of which they are each an integral part has itself to be identified: and its objective specified.

9. How grave would be the consequences if a given objective is *not* fulfilled is easier to calibrate than the positive effects of fulfillment. For instance, 200 additional deaths attributable to atmospheric inversion are more readily understood as a grave consequence, than the greater fragrance of additional flowers in the park is appreciated as a desirable result. Further, appropriations can be urged to be made to avert 200 additional deaths more easily than to increase the fragrance in the park. Therefore, the importance of the contribution of a subsystem to a System is measured in terms of the negative consequences: how grave would be the consequences to the achievement of the System Objective if a subsystem objective is *not* fulfilled. Each non-fulfillment is expressed ordinally, as 'greater than' some other non-fulfillment; and then absolute numbers are used to reflect "by how much" is one non-fulfillment worse than another. The importance of the non-fulfillment at each level is expressed by the weight of each level in the System Hierarchy; and these weights modify each penalty score, so that each non-fulfillment can be compared horizontally with its peer non-fulfillments and vertically with its superior non-fulfillments.

10. The primary question of national security involves at least two parties, the hostile intentions of one at a future date are unknown at the time when future defenses are planned. Therefore, the assessment of the *interactive, potential, future* situation can, at best, be made in terms of comparison of situations: Situation Y in the future is more grave, less grave, just as grave as Situation X in the past. See Chapter 3, Section 7.2.1.

D. *System Effectiveness—Relative*

11. See Chapter 3, Section 8.

12. Insofar as the two subsystems are at the same horizontal level (e.g. Strategic, Tactical), they are equivalent in their importance. Therefore, the first basis for choice is the difference in the penalty for non-fulfillment of the two subsystems.

Next, the rate of change in the fulfillment of the System Objective corresponding to a small change in the two subsystem activities is compared. The subsystem which produces greater change per unit input of subsystem activity would be preferable.

If the two comparisons do not lead to the selection of the same subsystem, it may suggest that the subsystem with greater absolute impact (size) on the System Objective is relatively slower (speed) in its impact. The two elements, size and speed, may be given equal or unequal weights to choose between the two subsystems.

The foregoing selection procedure assumes that the subjective estimates of size are just as good or bad as the subjective estimates of speed. Because of the interactions in the *future* that enter into the estimates of speed, there are likely to be greater errors in speed than in size. If the nature and magnitude of the errors are the same, then the estimators must possess very special quirks in their prognostications.

It would be preferable to let the prognosticators identify their own degree of competence with respect to both size and speed estimating, so that by weighing the estimates with the respective indices of competence, the choice from among the two sets of action maybe made on a compatible basis.

CHAPTER 4

A. *Initial Problem Structure*

1. The "Do" Statement makes it mandatory that a specific policy action be taken as a result of the study. Lest the call to action be nothing more than

the projection of one's prejudices, the "Do" Statement requires that the intended consequences of the action be specifically recognized *prior* to taking the action.

The prescription is incorporated into the OR/SA sequence by Sequence 1: Initial Structure of the Problem. The "Do" Statement is an *initial* statement, which is intended to force into the open what the OR/SA study hopes to accomplish by way of impacting upon the decision-making process.

2. By evaluating the impact on the System Objective Fulfillment of the subsystem. See Answer to Chapter 3, Question 12.

B. *System Objective Accomplishment*

3. The effect of other subsystems upon the System Objective Accomplishment must be held constant in order to assess the role of a given subsystem. In other words, the "rate of change" in the accomplishment of System Objective is represented by the *partial* derivative of System Objective Accomplishment with respect to the given subsystem performance.

4. The principal assumption is that any change anywhere in the System will affect all other parts of the System. The available resources are limited; therefore, resources allocated to one subsystem have to be denied to all the others, making it imperative that the resource allocation be justified on the basis of its contribution to the System Objective Accomplishment.

C. *Cost Effectiveness Considerations*

5. See Chapter 3, Section 6, in particular Section 6.3.

6. The inherent error in estimating costs of products to be made in the future stems from the ingredient of time. A future product is by definition, one of which there is little experience; therefore, any estimates made are projections of experience elsewhere with products, or components of products, which may be considered applicable.

See Answer to Chapter 2, Question 6.

7. "Opportunity Acquired" is a *potential* capability. As a result of the new

product and/or services, is there any capability which has been realized for which there is no prior comparison?

The Ballistic Missile Early Warning System (BMEWS) was conceived to provide a capability for which there was no prior comparison. Missiles themselves were unknown theretofore; therefore, missile detection was unknown. The "Opportunity Acquired" could be calibrated on the basis of what would happen if there were no such Opportunity Acquired.

D. *Resource Allocation Subsystems*

8. See Chapter 4, Section 2.4.

9. The weighted penalty scores for non-fulfillment explicitly identify the precise contribution — in absolute and in relative terms. The allocation of resources to an activity based on its weighted penalty for non-fulfillment requires that if higher or lower allocation is made to that activity, appropriate adjustments have to be made in the allocation to every other activity in terms of its contribution to the System Objective Accomplishment.

CHAPTER 5

A. *Principal Decision-Maker (PDM) Roles*

1. At the highest level with respect to the organism, (the organismic level) the future is the prime concern of the PDM, while at the intermediate level with respect to the organism, (strategic level) the present is the prime concern of the SubPDM. There is thus an inherent conflict in terms of *time* between the two top-level decision-makers.

Both the SubPDM and Sub-subPDM are concerned primarily with the present. However, there is a difference between them: the SubPDM has a much broader *spatial* perspective than the Sub-subPDM: if, for instance, the former is entrusted with a number of products, the latter would be entrusted with say, a single product.

The PDM is also interested in the same product as the Sub-subPDM but from a different time and spatial point of view. The inherent conflict stems from the individual role orientation toward the System Objective Accomplishment, and is best viewed in terms of time and spatial dimensions.

2. (a) It is the user who has to evaluate how the PDM is able to satisfy the user demands. Therefore, the primary safeguard is to study the user requirements.

(b) To the extent that such requirements are not known, the PDM is obliged to employ his best guesses. In making those guesses, the PDM should identify the type of probabilities employed by him or in his behalf.

(c) The PDM responses should reflect a balancing of the two types of variables: (1) technological variables, and (2) environmental variables.

(d) The PDM should pre-specify the nature and magnitude of fulfillment of System Objective in terms of the technological variables that he can control, carefully indicating the limitations imposed upon the fulfillment by the environmental variables, which he cannot control.

B. *Defense and Non-Defense Objectives*

3. See Chapter 5, Section 6.

4. See Chapter 5, Sections 4.5–4.10 for non-defense sector and Section 5 for defense sector.

C. *Conflicting Information Demands*

5. See Chapter 5, Section 8.

6. See Chapter 5, Section 10.

CHAPTER 6

A. *System Context*

1. In a democracy, the Users are the people. Their Objectives are presumably

reflected in the votes of their Representatives in Congress. In Chapter 6, Section 4 two alternative objectives, viz., increasing the GNP, and survival, are briefly considered as User Objectives which the U.S. Budgetary Appropriations are designed to fulfill. Other objectives can well be proposed and defended. The criteria of choice between alternative objectives would be the relevance to the User Intentions, and the *operational* measures that can be associated with the particular objective.

2. To monitor the progress toward System Objective Accomplishment, the objective must be calibrated in operational terms. Further, how the measurement is to be carried out; and what it represents must be *pre*-specified. Otherwise, there can be serious disagreements on the measurement itself and the meaning of the measurement.

3. At least two competing choices at the *same* level must be considered in requesting appropriation for any activity. Further, it is desirable to relate to two successive levels of *higher* hierarchy than the level at which the two choices are compared. See Chapter 6, Section 7.

4. See Chapter 6, Sections 8.4 and 8.1−8.3.

B. *System Cost*

5. The improvement in the quality of life as a result of ecological improvement is an Opportunity Acquired, in the sense that survival up to age say, 95, by large part of the population is unknown heretofore.

   With the improvement in the *quality* of life, there can also be an associated improvement in the *quantity* of life. An Opportunity Acquired is the specifiable increase in the number of people living *longer* and *better*. This increase maybe a liability or an asset, depending upon how the increased total years of life are able to produce more than, or less than, what is required to maintain life.

6. The Administrative Division of the Department of the Interior has to identify its mission in terms of the System Objective Accomplishment. It should also identify at least one other means of fulfillment of the particular objective, say, via another Administrative Division.

Within the framework of the competition with other Divisions, the alternatives open to the particular Division have to be weighed in terms of their (potential) contributions to the System Objective Accomplishment. The dollars and cents of each alternative must reflect the total cost of making that alternative operational. The percentage that the particular alternative represents in the total allocation of the Division should be compared with the percentage that the alternative would contribute toward the total System Objective Accomplishment.

7. See Chapter 6, Sections 7.3.3 and 7.1–7.3.

C. *System Effectiveness–Absolute*

8. The ecological investment is designed to avert ecological disaster while the national defense investment is designed to avert national annihilation. The ecological disaster can affect both the nation and its would be adversaries. Therefore, it may be argued that the averting of the ecological disaster is more important than the averting of national annihilation.

9. The penalty scores are ordinal, in the sense that they permit the specification of the relationship "greater than". An ordinal preference can*not* indicate "by how much" A is greater than B, but simply that A is greater – by 1 point, 2 points, 239 points or 1 000 001 points. However, to make the allocation it is necessary to know by how much A is preferred to, or is greater than B, so that the allocation of resources may be made according to their relative importance. For this, the ordinal scale must be converted into *cardinal*: there must be a zero point, and a scale which specifies the distance between zero and unity (0 and 1).

The principal limitation comes from the devising of a scale. The scale has necessarily to be subjective. Further, not one, but *several scales* would be involved at the different levels of the hierarchy. The validity of the scales would vary depending upon the level of the decision-maker in the hierarchy, and the relevance of his experience in constructing the scale.

D. *System Effectiveness–Relative*

10. Consider the tactical choice: Improve Fire Prevention/Fighting Tech-

niques, in Chapter 6, Section 7.3.1. It is one of the four tactical choices designed to achieve the strategic level objective: Prevent Further Loss of Trees, as shown in Fig. 6.2. The prevention of further loss of trees is one of three ways of achieving the organismic objective: Preserve Oxygen Source.

Any subsystem performance at the tactical level should be compared with its peer group(s) to determine its impact at least two levels above, i.e., organismic level.

The System Objective in ecological investment is *not*: Preserve Oxygen Source. It is the organismic objective in *one round*. At least another round upward is necessary to reach the System Objective. In the *second round*, the organismic objective: Preserve Oxygen Source becomes the tactical objective for the next round. It is one of the five means of achieving the next higher level objective, i.e., strategic objective: Avert National Ecological Disaster. The National Disaster can refer to Nation 1, Nation 2, ..., Nation n. The organismic objective is: Avert *International* Ecological Disaster as shown in Fig. 6.1.

The subsystem performance is identified as: Improve Fire Prevention/ Fighting Techniques. What is its contribution to the change in the rate of achievement of the System Objective: Avert International Ecological Disaster? Will a 100% increase in the investment in the program to improve fire prevention/fighting techniques lead to a 100% increase in the averting of international ecological disaster; or 50%, or 25%, or 5%? The answer will depend upon the *horizontal* and the *vertical* comparisons and interrelationships. In the absence of direct experience in the averting of international ecological disaster directly attributable to improved fire preventing/fighting techniques, the answer has to depend upon the logical relationships that can be established with peer choices at the tactical level, and superior choices at the strategic and organismic levels.

11. See Answer to Question 9. In Chapter 6, Section 6.2, *illustrative* scores of 100 and 80 were given respectively to averting ecological disaster and to improving the environment. In Section 6.3.2, a consistent set of scores was devised for the second highest level of objective; and in Section 7.3.1, the scores for several tactical choices were assigned. Further, in Section 7.3.1, penalty levels were associated with each hierarchical level. The principal limitation is in the repeatability of the various scales of penalties for non-fulfillment.

CHAPTER 7

A. *System Context*

1. The principal distinction between the User Objectives of health care and ecological investment is that the former is *personal*, while the latter is *societal*.

The individual nature of health makes the operational measurement of *national* delivery of health care harder to achieve than the measurement of averting ecological disaster. The percentage of the people *un*able to pursue their choices because of lack of health would be an operational measure of the national delivery of health care. The number of occasions on which "episodes" have been averted would be a positive operational measure of the User Objective with respect to ecological investment; and, the number of episodes similar to the atmospheric inversion experienced by New York City on Thanksgiving Day, 1966 would be a negative operational measure.

Health can be monitored on a day-to-day basis via individual records, while ecological imbalance makes its undeniable impact on an entire area. Individual unhealth can be detected and prevented, or minimized in its impact; however ecological imbalance can at best be anticipated in time to institute defensive measures, such as evacuating a whole town before a hurricane, but hardly prevented.

2. The System Objective of the private sector is *profit*; while the System Objective of the public sector is *service*. If the two sectors are to work together, the accomplishment of the service function satisfactorily to the public sector must be stimulated by the accrual of profit to the private sector.

During the '50s and '60s the Government felt that it needed the assistance of the private sector in the form of "Think Tanks". The "profit" stimulus to the private sector took the form of significantly higher salaries to the staff members of the Think Tanks than what they could be paid under Government Pay Scales. The Think Tanks themselves were "not for profit". However, the principle of *profit,* i.e., monetary stimulus to those performing a *Service* in behalf of national security was observed.

3. See Chapter 7, Table 7.2, and Section 4.2.

B. *System Cost*

4. Principally, the opportunity to earn income which is foregone entirely during the period of illness, and partially during the post-illness period. The deficiency in the actual production of goods and services is real; however, it will not be reflected in the earnings of the individual who is paid at the same rate of compensation when ill or well. The impairment to productivity is what should be reflected in the cost of opportunity foregone due to illness.

5. The cost of Opportunity Acquired is the cost attributable to the *increase* in the *quality* and *quantity* of life brought about by the national delivery of health care. As a result of the virtual eradication of malaria, plague and tuberculosis in India, the *quantity* of life, as reflected in the number of years lived by the population, significantly increased. The *quality* of life, as reflected in the amount of work that could be done by the population, now greatly relieved from the ravages of the major killer diseases, also increased significantly in the post-War period. The computation of the benefits of the Opportunity Acquired can be done in terms of the Life Table Population discussed in Chapter 5, Section 4.8.1. It should be noted that the *increase* in the Life Table Population earnings, arrived at by "after" and "before" comparisons is what should be credited to the Opportunity Acquired.

The Opportunity Acquired brings not only benefits, but also costs. To the costs of *acquiring* the new opportunity (such as the expenses for controlling the three diseases), must be added the new costs of *maintaining* the increased quantity and quality of life. Whenever the additional earnings from the Opportunity Acquired do *not* offset the expenses to maintain them, that is an added cost of Opportunity Acquired.

Further, the benefits and costs are to be considered both in time and space: in time, as reflected in the number of women surviving through the child-bearing period, giving birth to *additional* children, who in turn, will contribute to larger numbers; in space, as reflected in intra- and international migrations.

C. *System Effectiveness—Absolute*

6. See Chapter 7, Section 5.

7. See the answer to Question 1. The principal difficulty is the difference between the clinical definition of capability to work, and the personal disposition to work i.e., the objective and the subjective measures; while in the case of ecological investment, the measure can be largely objective, such as the absence of episodes.

A related difficulty is the aggregation of individual preferences which are subjective. To avoid ecological disaster, there are different available paths. Should more trees be grown for enjoyment; or should the use of the environmental resources be regulated more strictly: enjoyment or enforcement? Personal preferences vary; but they have to be equitably incorporated in the actual implementation of ecological investment. There is a similar question of preferences in the delivery of health care to all the people in the country, each of whom has personal preferences, which again, have to be incorporated equitably in the actual implementation of the national delivery of health care. Nobel Laureate Kenneth Arrow has demonstrated the logical incompatibility between individual values and social choice: which is the inherent difficulty in devising an operational measure of social service, such as health care delivery.

D. *System Effectiveness–Relative*

8. The research results may relate to the modification of a current procedure, or a protocol; or they may relate to an innovation. Depending upon the entrenchment of the procedure or protocol, its modification would be easy or difficult. With respect to an innovation, such as the Salk Vaccine for Polio, the urgent need to prevent Polio would be heavily circumscribed by the caution in risking untried methods.

The principal elements in the implementation of research results with respect to both modification and innovation must be *operationally* identified while contemplating investment in research. Just as the prospects of a research breakthrough have to be evaluated before the investment is made, so also the prospects of research implementation must be evaluated concurrently, so that the investment in research may be made with full cognizance of the rate of change of implementation and the rate of change of breakthroughs.

9. The investment in basic data on individual health should depend upon the

use made of such data for diagnosis and prescription. In Chapter 7, Section 6, the elements of health data for individualized care and cure are discussed; and in Section 7, the allocation mechanism of aggregate resources for individualized health care and cure is developed.

10. See Chapter 7, Section 7.

CHAPTER 8

A. *System Context*

1. The principal distinction between the User objective of air pollution reduction and health care is that the former is *societal*, while the latter is *personal*.

Air pollution reduction tends to make an enabling contribution to the community as a whole, while the health care delivery presents a personal contribution. While the smog can be seriously irritating, it does not prevent a person from attending to his work. Therefore, the reduction in air pollution will be perceived very gradually: "Ah, I can breathe easier, or I can see better, or my eyes do not water as they used to". However, if someone were sick in bed, his relief in being able to work again would be felt immediately: "I can work today, which I could not do yesterday".

2. The primary purpose of an index of air pollution control is to assess the improvement in reducing air pollution. Therefore, the principal pollutants must be included in the index.

More than an absolute measure, the index should indicate the *relative* change in the air pollution.

Since all the pollutants cannot be reduced at the same rate, and since the cost of reducing the different pollutants will be different, it is essential that the pollutants be weighted in the index. The primary weighting should be in terms of the impact of the pollutant upon the quality of life.

Secondary weighting of the pollutants should incorporate physical properties of the pollutant: tonnage, pervasiveness, toxicity, corrosiveness, and soiling. See Chapter 8, Section 2.

3. The relaxing of sulphur content standards of coal used in the generation of power during the energy crisis showed the priority of objectives: energy before environment. This incident underscores the necessity to consider air pollution as part of the problem of pollution itself; and pollution itself as a problem accompanying the use of power. Even if all uses of power (energy) were to come to an immediate stop, the problem of pollution will still remain (in the form of organic pollution). There is pollution in the very generation of power, to the extent that the entire matter is not converted into energy. Then there is the pollution from unused energy as in the case of unburned gases in the automobile. The two types of pollution must be considered as part and parcel of the same problem. In Chapter 8, the Air Quality Act implementation provides the organismic perspective. Of course, air pollution is a subset of pollution; which is a subset of the Power-and-Pollution.

B. *System Cost*

4. In Chapter 8, Section 3, the added cost of living in a dirty environment is estimated in terms of: inside maintenance, outside maintenance, laundry and cleaning, hair and facial care. (See Table 8.4).

Each of the foregoing elements is a cost of opportunity foregone by the individual. In addition, the impairment to the capability to do work (including the option to enjoy refraining from work) must be included as a cost of opportunity foregone. Just as the money spent on inside maintenance, outside maintenance, laundry and cleaning, and hair and facial care cannot be used for other purposes, so also the work that could not be performed (or the leisure that could not be enjoyed) because the air pollution significantly affected the earning of income from work imposes cost of foregone opportunity.

In addition to the absence of earnings, there is also the cost of impaired effectiveness in performing work.

In general, the $120 billion is simply the *governmental* expenditure on air pollution reduction; to which must be added significant *personal* expenditures to live with air pollution.

5. Any significant reduction of air pollution would contribute a number of elements of opportunity acquired: (1) the apprecitation in land values, (2) the reduction in the impairment to work, (3) the reduction in the cost of

upkeep, (4) the improvement in the outlook of individuals in the community, and the consequent preparedness to pursue activities of one's choice.

There is likely to be a decided advantage to the younger generation which will grow up enjoying much better health. The additional work days gained by air pollution reduction will extend beyond the present generation, and go into the future.

These elements of productivity, both in the present and in the future, can be assigned $-value in terms of the output generated by increased man hours. These values, directly attributable to opportunities acquired by air pollution reduction, must be weighed against the $120 billion and other personal costs. The $120 billion investment may be found to be inordinately high if only the *present* costs are considered. However, when the opportunity acquired in the *future* generations is considered in addition, the investment may be found well worth while.

6. The system cost aspects must include both the Power and the Pollution factors. True, if there were no production in the private sector, there would be little pollution; but by the same token, there would be little income. When a chemical plant of Union Carbide was forced to be closed down in the interest of preventing pollution, it also closed out the jobs of those employed at the plant.

Even when the plant is not shut down, the cost of reducing pollution can be sizeable. The added cost, of course, will be passed on to the customers. The installation of air pollution reduction equipment in automobiles is a visible increase in cost in the interest of air pollution reduction. The cost of electricity produced from better quality coal would, again be, passed on to the customer directly. In a study by the Environmental Protection Agency, the cost of pollution reduction measures was assessed at a 2—3 percent reduction in the growth of Gross National Product: which means ($1\,000 \times 0.03 =$) $30 billion. Evenly distributed among the 100 million workers of America, it means ($30 \times 10^9/100 \times 10^6 =$) $300 *less* earnings a year. At the poverty level of $3,000 a year, the reduction amounts to *10 percent*. This reduction in personal income must be offset by the *de*crease in inside and outside maintenance, laundry and cleaning, and hair and facial care, and the *in*crease in opportunity acquired (which generates additional working days, and therefore additional income).

The Environmental Impact Statements which are required to be filed with the Federal Government when new activities are undertaken (e.g., new plants, new business) is a clear recognition of the public responsibility of private undertakings. The implementation of the principle depends upon the careful compromises between the quantity and quality of life.

C. *System Effectiveness—Absolute*

7. See Chapter 8, Section 3.

8. The principal argument would be that air pollution reduction is *prevention*, while health care delivery is *cure*. In particular, the cost of respiratory diseases which are aggravated by air pollution, can be compared with the effectiveness of air pollution reduction in ameliorating the same diseases, in arguing for prevention instead of cure.

D. *System Effectiveness—Relative*

9. See Chapter 4, Section 2.1 for the discussion of air stagnation as a contributory cause to some 200 excess deaths. That air pollution is associated with the occurrence and worsening of many serious respiratory diseases appears to be established. To relate the investment in automobile reduction to potential decrease in deaths, it is necessary to identify by how much the decrease is related to the reduction in air pollution. It would require precise knowledge of the etiology of the different diseases; and what is more, the precise measurements of the changes in air pollution and the changes in the excess deaths.

10. See Chapter 8, Section 1.2.

The added political consideration would be that the drivers of 100 million automobiles on the road are interested in the improved operation of their vehicle; in particular, if the air pollution reduction is likely to improve the mileage per gallon obtained through better burning of gasoline. Because of the universal interest, the Federal Government will be interested in the investment in research to control automobile emission; which means that it would be politically fashionable at the Federal level, the State level, and even the County level.

CHAPTER 9

A. *System Context*

1. The single measure of performance would be the rates of change in sales and profits by industry. The figures are based on income tax forms filed quarterly by the corporations. The *Quaterly Financial Report for Manufacturing Corporations* publishes 10 tables (discussed in Chapter 9, Section 4.7) which provide a number of competitive measures of performance for the private company.

2. The profitability of each product would vary, some being more profitable than others. From the company's point of view, profits are most important; but the number of units of sales of products does not directly indicate profitability.

It may well be that, for the company's growth, the number of units of some products should be *reduced*, instead of increased. To judge a company's performance by the *volume* of sales would not reflect the *value* of sales. How many dollars are brought in is more important to the company than how many units were sold.

3. See Chapter 9, Section 3.

B. *System Cost*

4. See Chapter 9, Section 5.

5. Depends upon the specific data that the "key plants" data bank offers, and the use they can be put to to increase profits. Alternatively, how much would it cost you to collect the same data? Further, how much significant error would enter your decisions if you did not have the "key plants" data?

6. The allocation would depend upon which of the two provides closer prediction of your own sales potentials — trading center area figures or standard metropolitan area center figures.

Answers to problems of Chapter 10

CHAPTER 10

A. *System Effectiveness—Absolute*

1. Bookings are orders placed with the company for its products, converted into dollars and cents. The hundreds of products of a company can all be expressed in terms of dollars and cents, making the bookings a yardstick applicable to company performance of different *divisions*, as well as in different *time periods*.

2. See Chapter 10, Sections 2 and 3.

3. See Chapter 10, Sections 2 and 3.

B. *System Effectiveness—Relative*

4. The principal assumption is that the effect of all other subsystems upon the System Performance is held constant, so that the performance of the particular subsystem alone is associated with the System Performance.

Usually, the effect of the various subsystems is considered to be additive; the effect of rain is added to the effect of sunshine, both of which are added to the effect of the fertilizer upon the System Performance of the crop in the field. The *partial* correlation coefficient of say, fertilizer, would be determined by separating the crop into two parts: (1) the crop attributable to fertilizer, and (2) the crop attributable to all other subsystems, such as rain and sunshine.

5. Linearity; additivity of effects. See Chapter 10, Sections 1 and 6.

6. The closeness of the prediction for the group of observations. See Chapter 10, Section 6.

CHAPTER 11

A. *Empirical Measures of Effectiveness—Absolute*

1. It is extremely difficult to guard against the tendency to equate sales with salesmanship. The problem is aggravated when the same salesman is handling different products for which different managers are responsible.

The subjective scale is necessarily ordinal, it being easier to say that A is a better salesman than B, without saying by how much. When different sales managers evaluate the same salesman, there would tend to be a fair agreement on who is the best and who is the worst, the disagreement being greater with respect to those in the middle.

There would be considerable differences among the sales managers in comparing one salesman with another, particularly when it comes to quantifying the "salesmanship" on a numerical scale. The "10" on a scale of 0—10, as well as the "0" would tend to be the same on the scale of each sales managers. However, the in-between scores are likely to be highly variable in terms of their significance. Therefore, the weight associated with each of the numerical scores must be carefully assigned before deriving an aggregate score out of the individual scores.

2. The simplest assumption is the linear assumption, the sales being assumed to be a linear function of the external potentials and the internal potentials, as in Section 2. For the limitation of the hypothesis of linear relationship, see Chapter 10, Section 1.

B. *Empirical Measures of Effectiveness—Relative*

3. See Chapter 11, Section 2 and Section 5.

4. See Chapter 11, Section 3.

C. *Empirical Measures of Subsystem Performance*

5. See Chapter 11, Section 4.

6. See Chapter 11, Sections 5 and 6.

CHAPTER 12

A. *System Context*

1. By the orders placed for the products and/or services; and by the cancellations of those orders.

2. See Chapter 12, Section 1.

3. See Chapter 12, Section 2.

B. *System Cost*

4. See Chapter 12, Section 3.

5. Improved effectiveness in the use of resources. See Section 5.

C. *System Effectiveness–Absolute*

6. The production effectiveness is measured *internally*: the units of outputs per unit of input (manpower-machine unit), while the sales effectiveness is measured *externally*: the profit contribution per unit of salesman effort (manpower-unit).

7. See Chapter 12, Section 6.

8. See Chapter 12, Section 6.1.

NAME INDEX

Ackoff, Russel L., 70n
Adam, 294
Anderson, Odin W., 215n, 216, 216n, 240, 241n
Antosiewicz, H.A., 51n
Arnoff, E. Leonard, 70n
Arrow, Kenneth, 456
Ascombe, F.J., 346n
Ash, Roy L., 158, 159n

Bartlett, John, 46n
Bellman, Richard, 23, 51, 52, 52n, 53, 53n, 54
Beveridge, William, 230, 230n
Birnkrant, Harry, 185
Blackett, P.M.S., 27, 27n, 28, 28n, 29, 29n, 30, 30n, 31, 31n, 32, 32n, 33, 33n, 34n, 35, 35n, 36, 36n, 39, 39n, 41, 41n, 43, 43n, 44, 54, 57, 76, 78, 440
Blomquist, E.T., 261, 271, 271n
Boucher, W.I., 56n, 58, 60n, 61n, 65n, 70n, 103
Bowditch, 348
Broder, David S., 159n
Bronowski, J., 20, 21, 21n, 38, 38n, 45, 45n, 46, 437, 438
Buck, 343, 344, 344n, 347n

Cartright, J., 270n
Chacko, George K., 69n, 73n, 131n, 151n, 152n, 185, 193n, 212n, 213n, 243n, 258n, 349n, 353n, 356n, 388n, 401n, 402n
Chacko, Rajah Y., 89n
Charnes, A., 51

Chartrand, Robert L., 256n
Chevalier, Maurice, 89n
Chouikha, Abdelhai, 185
Churchill, Winston S., 25, 27n, 29, 29n, 30, 30n, 31, 31n, 35, 41, 42, 42n, 44, 46, 440
Churchman, C. West, 70n
Cobb, C.W., 390n
Cooper, W.W., 47n, 51
Coull, J., 270n
Crownover, James E., 185

Daddario, Emilio Q., 257
Dallavalle, J.M., 270n
Dantzig, George B., 23, 47, 47n, 48, 49, 50, 50n, 51, 53, 54n, 55, 70
Delly, J.G., 270n
DeTocqueville, Alexis, 5, 5n
Dodge, Harold F., 401, 401n, 402, 404n
Douglas, Paul H., 390, 390n
Draftz, R.C., 270n
Dresher, Melvin, 56n
Dreyfus, Stuart E., 52n, 53n, 54
Dror, Yehezkel, 68, 68n
Duke of Wellington, 89
Durand, D., 386n
Durant, Will, 232, 233n

Eisenhower, 64, 65

Fankhauser, Robert K., 128n
Fensterstock, Jack C., 128n
Fischer, R.A., 381, 381n, 386, 386n
Fisher, Gene, 102, 105
Francis, Bert R., 185
Freeman, J., 228n

465

SUBJECT INDEX

133, 134, 135, 136, 141, 143, 145,
146, 147, 148, 155, 163, 164, 168,
172, 173, 175, 181, 183, 184, 186,
188, 189, 195, 196, 199, 205, 206,
214, 223, 226, 226n, 227, 228, 232,
252, 254, 255, 258, 261, 279, 280,
296, 297, 371, 416, 431, 448, 449,
456, 464
  allocation, 12, 13, 16, 81, 136, 155,
  157, 204, 208, 211, 228, 241, 243,
  254, 256
  human, 147, 148, 157
  natural, 148
  private, 225
  public, 225
  use, 12, 14
Resources Use Index, 409, 428, 431, 435
risk(y), 12, 81, 90, 91, 93, 95, 100, 108,
  109, 134, 137, 142, 428, 444
  management, 419–421, 423, 432,
  433, 435
roll on/roll off (RO–RO) ships, 24, 64,
  66

sales, xi, 12, 14, 15, 17, 85, 286, 287,
  288, 289, 290, 291, 292, 293, 294,
  295, 296, 297, 298, 314, 323, 330,
  331, 332, 333, 333n, 334, 335, 340,
  341, 342, 354, 361, 362, 363, 364,
sequential analysis, 54
shipment, 329, 330, 331
Simplex, Simplex method, xi, 13, 50, 70
Skybolt, 24, 64, 65
  365, 366, 367, 368, 370, 372, 374,
  376, 378, 379, 380, 383, 389, 391,
  401, 406, 408, 409, 410, 421, 422,
  423, 426, 428, 432, 435, 436, 461,
  463, 464
  organization, 289
  potentials, 286, 287
  retail (see U.S. Retail Sales Volume)
  volume, 334, 339, 341, 342, 348,
  350, 352, 356–358, 362, 364, 368–
  371, 378, 393

salesman, 12, 14, 285, 291, 292, 293,
  295, 297, 331, 332, 340, 354, 362,
  363, 364, 365, 366, 368, 369, 370,
  371, 375, 376, 377, 378, 379, 380,
  381, 382, 383, 384, 385, 387, 388,
  389, 390, 391, 392, 393, 394, 395,
  396, 398, 399, 400, 401, 402, 405,
  406, 407, 410, 411, 463, 464
Sales Management, 286, 316, 333, 334,
  339, 393n, 400
Sales Manager, 288, 290, 291, 292, 293,
  295, 298, 340, 366, 372, 382, 389,
  405
samples, sampling, 316, 323, 387, 401,
  401n, 402, 404n, 405, 422
  plan, 402, 405, 406
Saudi Arabia, 90
scale, returns to, 363, 390, 391, 398–
  400
  constant, 391
  decreasing, 391
  increasing, 391, 398–400
scientific method, 24, 72, 73, 193
sealift, 63, 66, 67
Secretary of Defense, 24, 61, 61n, 62n,
  64n, 138, 139, 140, 142, 163, 169,
  170, 290
Secretary of State, 143
sensitivity, 82, 83, 89, 108, 115, 117,
  120, 126, 131, 132, 134, 135
Society for the Advancement of Management, 84, 85n
solution(s), ix, x, xi, 3, 17, 19, 20, 21,
  25, 26, 34, 35, 49, 50, 53, 76, 77,
  84, 90, 100, 123, 212, 236, 243,
  343, 387, 439
solution-oriented, 21, 439
space, space mission, 4, 6, 52, 53, 72,
  139, 140, 155, 163, 167, 171, 183,
  214, 221, 299
  spacecraft, 10, 52, 445
  technology, 139, 167
stage(s), 4, 19, 52, 53, 61, 65, 101, 442,
  443